ry

MICROCOMPUTER GRAPHICS

MICROCOMPUTER GRAPHICS
Techniques and Applications

Donald Hearn

M. Pauline Baker

Computer Science Division
Western Illinois University

Prentice-Hall, Inc.
Englewood Cliffs, New Jersey 07632

Library of Congress Cataloging in Publication Data

HEARN, DONALD.
    Microcomputer graphics.

    Bibliography: p.
    Includes index.
    1. Computer graphics.   2. Microcomputers—Programming.
I. Baker, M. Pauline.   II. Title.
T385.H4 1983   001.64'43   82-23097
    ISBN 0-13-580670-4
    ISBN 0-13-580662-3 (pbk.)

Editorial/production supervision
  and interior design by Kathryn Gollin Marshak
Page layout by Bruce Kenselaar
Cover design by Jeannette Jacobs
Manufacturing buyer: Gordon Osbourne

Printed in the United States of America

10 9 8 7 6 5 4

ISBN 0-13-580670-4
ISBN 0-13-580662-3 {PBK}

Prentice-Hall International, Inc., *London*
Prentice-Hall of Australia Pty. Limited, *Sydney*
Editora Prentice-Hall do Brasil, Ltda., *Rio de Janeiro*
Prentice-Hall Canada, Inc., *Toronto*
Prentice-Hall of India Private Limited, *New Delhi*
Prentice-Hall of Japan, Inc., *Tokyo*
Prentice-Hall of Southeast Asia Pte. Ltd., *Singapore*
Whitehall Books Limited, *Wellington, New Zealand*.

Contents

List of Programming Examples

List of Color Photographs

Figure A Three-dimensional displays can be used for preliminary inspection of the appearance of a design. (Courtesy Lexidata Corp.)

Figure B CAD methods are used in the design of electronic components, such as this computer board. (Courtesy Lexidata Corp.)

Figure C Artists design animated cartoons and movies using computer graphics systems. (Courtesy Chromatics, Inc.)

Figure D Abstract designs can be created in many forms on a video graphics monitor. (Courtesy Los Alamos National Laboratory)

Figure E Artists use computer graphics to design oriental rug patterns. (Courtesy Lexidata Corp.)

Figure F A computer workstation for commercial artists producing advertising layouts with image processing techniques. (Courtesy COMTAL Corp.)

Figure G Image processing methods are used in medical applications to view the functioning of physiological systems. (Courtesy Lexidata Corp.)

Figure H A computer plot, color coded to show relative brightness, of 16 million density points observed for the Whirlpool nebula by astronomers reveals two galaxies. (Courtesy Los Alamos National Laboratory)

Figure I Computer model of a test surface used in studying atomic and nuclear collisions. (Courtesy Los Alamos National Laboratory)

Figure J Three-dimensional pressure chart. (Reprinted with permission from ISSCO, San Diego, CA)

Figure K   Three-dimensional graphs can illustrate several relationships within one graph. (Reprinted with permission from ISSCO, San Diego, CA)

Figure L   Color-coded diagram to explain the operation of a nuclear reactor. (Courtesy Los Alamos National Laboratory)

Figure M   Computer-generated view of a runway used in flight simulators for pilot training. (Courtesy Evans and Sutherland)

Figure N   Combining graphs is an effective way to convey several kinds of information with one display. (Reprinted with permission from ISSCO, San Diego, CA)

Figures O and P   Three-dimensional graphs can be constructed in a variety of forms. (Reprinted with permission from ISSCO, San Diego, CA)

Preface

This book presents an introduction to computer graphics with special emphasis on techniques for microcomputers. Low-cost microcomputers have made graphics a generally available resource, and we explore here the many capabilities of these small systems for a variety of uses, including animation and the generation of two- and three-dimensional pictures and graphs.

We have organized the book into five parts. In Part I, we survey some of the ways computer graphics is used in areas of design, image processing, business, art, education, research, and the home. The general hardware and software characteristics of graphics systems are discussed, and a review is given of the capabilities of specific microcomputers.

Starting with graphics fundamentals in Part II, we introduce methods for producing displays with both characters and pixels. Picture-drawing and graph-plotting techniques, including considerations for shading and color, are treated in some detail.

Special effects and manipulations are taken up in Part III. Here we look at display transformations, animation, and spotlighting and clipping methods.

In Part IV, we explore three-dimensional graphics. We examine methods for erasing hidden lines, for generating perspective views, and for transforming three-dimensional displays. Techniques are discussed for both pictures and graphs.

Use of computer graphics methods in business applications, education, and the home is considered in Part V. This final part deals with program design, special graphing techniques, simulations, computer-assisted instruction, household budget and nutrition charts, and game playing.

The graphics methods discussed throughout this book are illustrated with programs written in BASIC, the standard language available on most microcomputers. All programs were developed and tested on microcomputer systems.

These examples are meant to clarify implementation details for graphics routines. Many statements in the examples could be restructured or eliminated to produce more efficient coding, but they have been intentionally written in their present form to provide clearer explanations of the processing steps. Program variable names have been limited to a length of two characters in most cases, since some microcomputers have this restriction. We have used longer variable names in those few situations where we felt that clarity of program documentation was an overriding factor. Since there exists no single set of graphics statements that applies to all systems, our programming examples use a hybrid set of graphics commands adapted from those available on the various microcomputers. This hypothetical set of graphics statements is related to corresponding actual statements on specific microcomputers in Appendix A.

Donald Hearn
M. Pauline Baker

Part I

INTRODUCTION

(What Is
Microcomputer Graphics?)

The value of a picture as a means for communicating information quickly and accurately has long been recognized. Throughout history we have developed various printing, photographic, and reproduction methods for creating visual displays. Now, the modern digital computer has taken us into the era of computer graphics. As an introduction to this field, we will look at some of the many applications possibilities. We will see how different people are using computer graphics, and what equipment and methods they are using. Then we will survey the capabilities of microcomputers for graphics applications.

Chapter 1

Graphics
and Computers

1-1 WHO USES COMPUTER GRAPHICS?

One of the first uses of computer graphics was as an aid to design. Computer-aided design (CAD) and computer-aided manufacturing (CAM) remain major graphics applications areas. Here, computer displays provide a means for automating engineering drawings, architectural plans, commercial art layouts, or manufacturing processes. Drafting plans using CAD methods can produce an outline or rendering of a machine part from any viewing angle by specifying the dimensions of the part to the computer graphics system. Using similar graphics methods, the manufacturing layouts for a part are drawn and displayed. These layouts can be used to show the path to be taken by machine tools over the part surfaces during the manufacturing of the part. Numerically controlled machine tools are then set up to produce parts according to the layout patterns.

Automobile, aircraft, and aerospace design engineers use CAD techniques to help in designing surface contours. Wire frame drawings can be displayed on a video screen to test the appearance of body shapes for automobiles, airplanes, or spacecraft. These drawings can be created to display the entire surface outline or individual sections, such as a car fender or an airplane wing. More detail can be added to the computer-generated displays at each stage of the design process. A final, realistic rendering of the object allows the designer to see what the finished product will look like. (See the color insert for examples of this and other applications.)

Electrical and electronic circuits are designed with CAD methods. Starting with pictorial symbols that represent the different components, an electronics designer can build up a circuit on the screen by adding components one at a time. With a video display of a building layout, an electrical designer can try out different arrangements for electrical outlets or fire warning systems.

Architects, too, use building layouts produced by CAD methods as design aids. These layouts are displayed in many forms. Floor plans are useful for

3

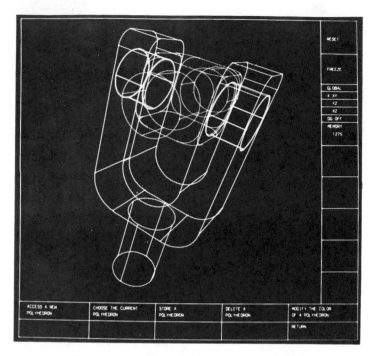

Figure 1–1 Drafting layouts are a common application of computer-aided design (CAD) techniques. (Courtesy Evans and Sutherland)

Figure 1–2 Wire frame sketches produced by CAD methods can be used for the initial design of car, plane, or spacecraft bodies. (Courtesy Evans and Sutherland)

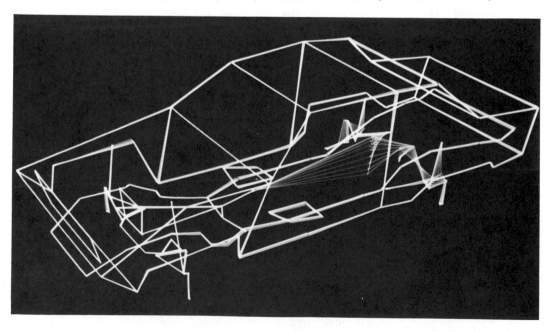

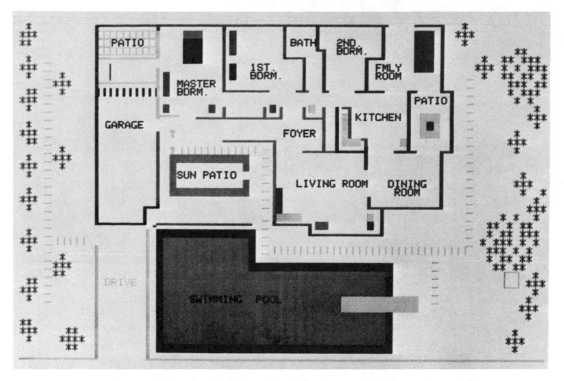

Figure 1–3 Video displays of building layouts are useful in architectural design. (Courtesy Intelligent Systems Corp.)

designing room arrangement, door and window placement, or the location of various facilities. Three-dimensional displays are used to view the appearance of a single building design or to test the appearance of a complex arrangement of buildings (a mall, university campus, or a medical complex).

Computer graphics techniques are used by artists. Animated cartoons and movies are produced with the aid of graphics displays. Abstract and geometric patterns are generated by graphics systems for use in creative design. Computer-generated patterns are used in many commercial applications, including the design of textiles. Commercial artists also make use of image-processing methods for applications involving retouching and rearranging photographs or other artwork.

Image processing is a graphics technique that produces visual displays from photographs or TV scans. Although this technique uses computers to generate graphics displays, it differs from conventional computer graphics methods. In computer graphics, a visual display is "created" by the graphics system for the application specified. In image processing, a visual display is produced by digitizing the shading and color patterns of a photograph or TV scan and "transferring" this information to the screen. Techniques are then used to rearrange the picture parts and to enhance color separations or shading for picture improvement. Medical researchers utilize image-processing methods with X-ray photography to view the functioning of internal physiological systems. The same

5

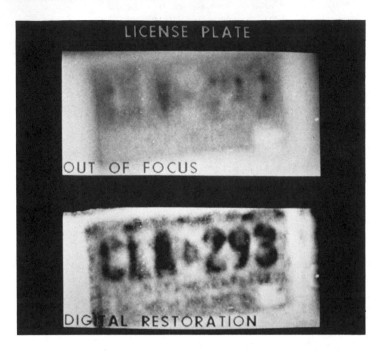

LICENSE PLATE

OUT OF FOCUS

DIGITAL RESTORATION

Figure 1-4 Image processing methods can make a blurred photograph of a license plate legible. (Courtesy Los Alamos National Laboratory)

methods are useful for viewing any system or object that we cannot see directly, like TV scans from spacecraft or views from the eye of an industrial robot.

Researchers in many areas rely on computer graphics as an important tool in studying the characteristics of systems. Astronomers, collecting data on stars and galaxies, make graphical models that help to explain the structure and behavior of celestial objects. Without the aid of these plots, data tables containing millions of values would be difficult to interpret. Biological, physical, and chemical systems are graphically modeled as a means of gaining a better understanding of the system structure. In addition to models, computer-generated graphs and charts are used to interpret mathematical relationships or to study trends in the behavior of systems.

Data plotted on graphs or charts can take a variety of forms. Two-dimensional weather maps, for example, can be constructed by graphics systems from data supplied by observation stations. Pressure or temperature variations over geographical areas can be compared in three-dimensional plots.

Similar techniques are used in many business and government applications. This applications area represents one of the largest groups of computer graphics users. Various types of line graphs and bar charts are used for summarizing financial and statistical data. Three-dimensional pictures and graphs are used to show multiple relationships. Geographical plots are used for displaying many types of regional or global statistics. These computer displays are often generated for managerial reports, for consumer information bulletins, or for visual aids to be used during presentations.

Educational and training applications utilize computer graphics. Pictures and graphs are used to explain the operation of various systems. Realistic visual simulations are used in the training of airplane pilots and ship captains. Classroom

Figure 1–5 Computer graphics weather map. (Courtesy Genisco Computers Corp.)

Figure 1–6 Financial bar chart. (Courtesy Precision Visuals, Inc., Boulder, CO)

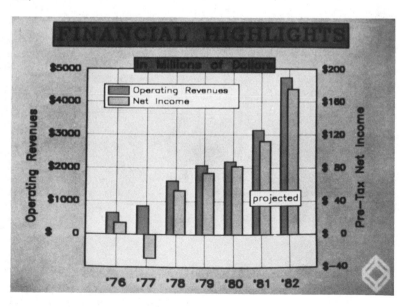

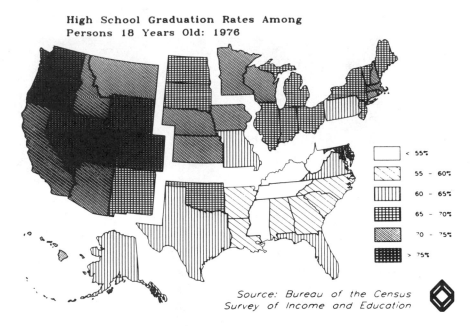

	< 55%
	55 - 60%
	60 - 65%
	65 - 70%
	70 - 75%
	> 75%

Source: Bureau of the Census
Survey of Income and Education

Figure 1–7 Computer-generated geographical plot. (Courtesy Precision Visuals, Inc., Boulder, CO)

Figure 1–8 Graph useful for classroom demonstration of the behavior of undamped and damped harmonic motion systems. (Reprinted with permission from ISSCO, San Diego, CA)

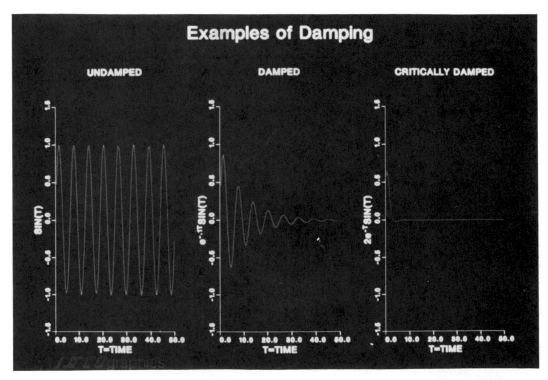

Figure 1–9 Graphics designs can be produced on a printer for a variety of home uses.

demonstrations, computer-generated exams, and self-study programs all employ graphics displays.

We can apply computer graphics methods for our own personal use. Printed pictures can be used on personalized stationery, on home-designed greeting cards, or as wall decorations. Pictures displayed on a video screen can be used in computer games or in educational programs. We can use computer-designed graphs and charts to monitor our diets, budgets, or financial investments.

1–2 HOW COMPUTER PICTURES ARE DESIGNED AND DISPLAYED

A computer graphics system can be set up in a number of ways, depending on the applications area. Highly specialized systems, such as those used in flight simulators for pilot training, are designed to perform a specific function (displaying aerial views of airports or aircraft carrier decks). General-purpose systems allow us to create many different kinds of pictures and graphs.

COMPUTER GRAPHICS SYSTEMS

The typical components of a general-purpose computer graphics system are a video display screen, typewriter-like keyboard, the graphics programs, and, of course, the processing and memory units of a computer. Additional input and output devices, other than the keyboard and video screen, can be attached to most graphics systems.

Figures 1–10 and 1–11 show examples of commercial computer graphics workstations. In these illustrations, a design "drawn" on the graphics tablet is displayed on a video screen. When the design is completed, it can be saved on a magnetic disk and reproduced on paper using a plotter. Graphics displays are

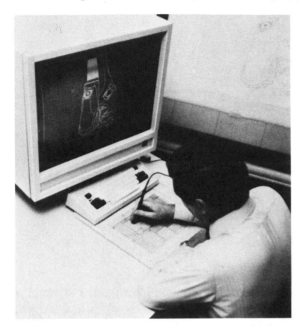

Figure 1–10 A designer at a CAD-CAM workstation views a layout, produced with a graphics tablet. (Courtesy Applicon)

Figure 1–11 A graphics workstation showing (left to right) a large digitizing board, desk, graphics tablet, video display and keyboard, and a plotter. The desk contains a computer processor, main memory, disk unit, and magnetic tape cartridge unit. (Courtesy Vector Automation, Inc.)

often reproduced on 35-mm slides or on transparencies for use with overhead projectors. Several displays can be combined into a filmstrip for use as a motion picture sequence. The digitizing board in Fig. 1–11 is used to transfer (digitize) existing paper layouts into computer storage. A graphics tablet is a smaller version of the digitizing board and can be used for the same purpose. Stored digitized layouts are then available for screen display, where they can be modified or combined with other drawings to form composite layouts.

VIDEO DISPLAYS

Most computer graphics display devices are some type of **cathode ray tube** (CRT). Figure 1–12 illustrates the basic operation of a CRT. A beam of electrons (cathode rays), emitted from an electron gun, passes through a focusing and deflection system and strikes a phosphor-coated screen. Voltages applied to the electron gun determine the number of electrons emitted. The focusing and deflection system, also controlled by voltages, produces electric and magnetic fields to focus the beam onto a particular spot on the screen. When the electron beam strikes the phosphor coating, the screen lights up at that spot. The intensity of a light spot depends on the number of electrons in the beam. By directing the beam to various points on the screen, we are able to display a picture.

The light emitted by the phosphor coating on a display screen lasts only a small fraction of a second. Therefore, we need some method for maintaining the screen picture so that we can see it. There are two fundamental approaches to maintaining a display on a CRT.

One method for keeping the phosphor glowing on a video screen is to repeatedly pass the electron beam over the same screen points. This type of display is called a **refresh CRT**. It turns out that we need to refresh a screen

Figure 1–12   Basic operation of a CRT.

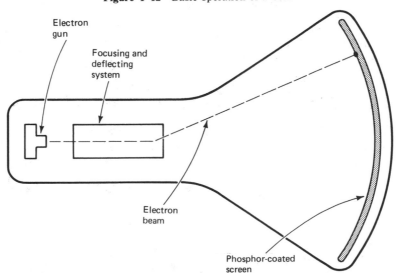

Electron gun

Focusing and deflecting system

Electron beam

Phosphor-coated screen

picture about 30 times each second; otherwise, it flickers. Typical refresh CRTs are designed to redraw the picture between 30 and 60 times per second.

Another method for maintaining the screen image is to use an additional electron gun (the flood gun) and a special wire screen (collector grid) that stores the screen picture pattern as an electric charge distribution (Fig. 1–13). This type of display is called a **direct-view storage tube**, or DVST. The electron gun sweeps over the screen once and, in the process, stores a charge pattern on the collector grid that corresponds to the screen picture. The flood gun, emitting a continuous flood of low-speed electrons, activates the screen phosphor according to the charge pattern on the collector grid and thus keeps the phosphor glowing at the correct locations on the screen.

Video displays designed as refresh CRTs can be organized to operate as random-scan or raster-scan devices. **Random-scan** display units operate by directing the electron beam only to those parts of the screen where the picture is to be drawn. **Raster-scan** displays pass the electron beam over all parts of the screen, turning the beam intensity on and off to coincide with the picture definition. A home TV display is an example of a raster-scan CRT. The electron beam in a raster-scan system is made to sweep across each horizontal line of the picture tube from top to bottom. Usually, the refresh cycle is set up so that the electron beam sweeps across every other line on one pass from top to bottom, then returns to sweep across the remaining lines on the next pass. This interlacing of the scan lines helps to reduce flicker, since we essentially see the entire screen display in one-half the time it would have taken to sweep across all the lines from top to bottom.

Color is produced in a video display by using more than one type of phosphor coating on the screen. Different phosphors emit different–colored light, and combinations of light from two or more phosphors can produce a range of colors.

Figure 1–13   Basic operation of a DVST.

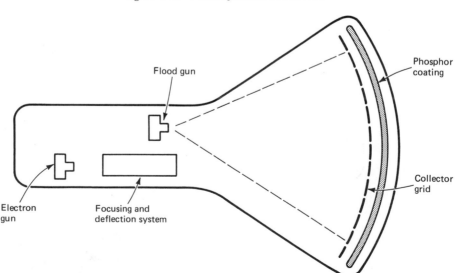

Many computer graphics displays use a shadow-mask CRT to produce color. This is the type of CRT used in color TV sets. A shadow-mask CRT has the screen coated with tiny triangular patterns, each containing three different phosphor dots. One phosphor dot of the triangle emits red light, another emits green light, and the third emits blue light. This type of CRT has three electron guns, one for each color, and a shadow-mask grid just behind the phosphor-coated screen. The purpose of the shadow mask is to focus the electrons from each gun so as to strike only the correct color dot in any triangle. Setting intensity levels for the three electron guns sets the color combination for each triangle of phosphor dots. Each triangular pattern is so small that it appears as one color point on the screen.

Some graphics displays use a beam-penetration method for obtaining color. In this case, the screen is completely coated with two phosphor layers, usually red and green. A beam of slower electrons will excite only the outer, or red, layer. A beam of faster electrons will penetrate the red phosphor into the green layer, producing light with some combination of red and green. The speed of the electrons, and hence the screen color at any point, is set by the beam acceleration voltage.

Techniques other than the basic CRT design have been used for constructing video displays. These devices include plasma panel displays, laser scan displays, light-emitting diodes (LEDs), and liquid-crystal (LCD) systems.

Figure 1–14   Graphics display terminal. (Courtesy Digital Engineering, Inc.)

Display devices for graphics applications are available as separate terminals or as part of stand-alone computer systems. Graphics terminals ordinarily have little or no processing capability and must be connected to an external computer, which may be a large facility or a small-scale system. Some graphics displays have built-in computer processor units and can operate on their own without being connected to an external computer. Both terminals and complete graphics systems are available in a wide range of screen sizes and capabilities.

GRAPHICS PROGRAMMING

The voltage levels applied to a display device to produce particular patterns and colors on the screen result from graphics commands within a display program. These display programs are often written in FORTRAN, Pascal, BASIC, or assembly language, using special graphics statements. Custom-made graphics languages have also been developed for some applications.

Graphics statements are translated by the computer processor into voltage levels that must be applied to the video unit in order to obtain the screen display defined by these statements. Display programs for graphics applications can create static pictures or graphs, modify and rearrange views, or produce animated scenes.

Figure 1–15 Three-dimensional rotations of a displayed object are accomplished with graphics statements in the display program. (Courtesy Selanar Corp.)

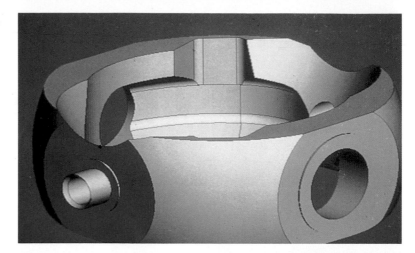

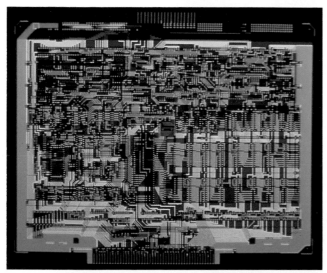

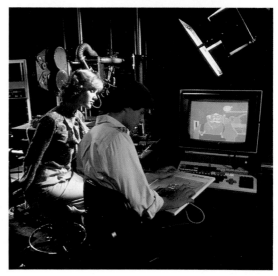

Figure C

Figure D

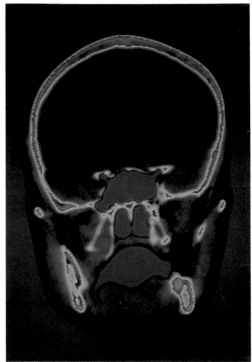

Figure E

Figure G

Figure F

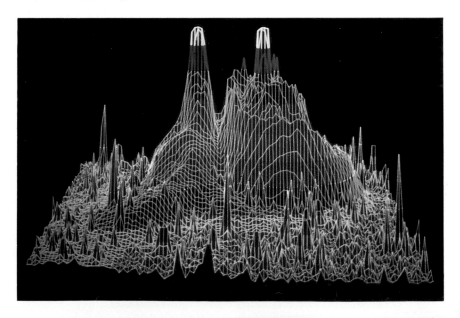

Figure H

Figure I

Figure J

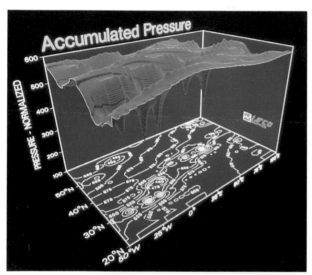

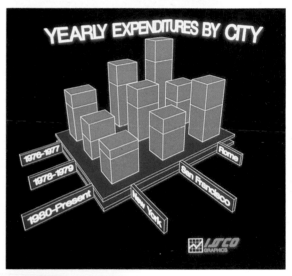

Figure K

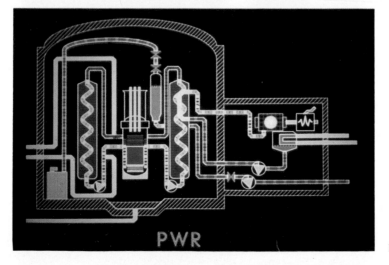

Figure L

Figure M

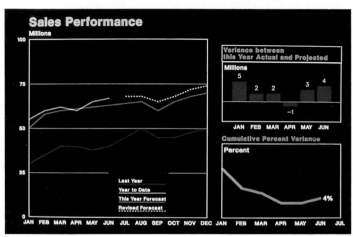

Figure N

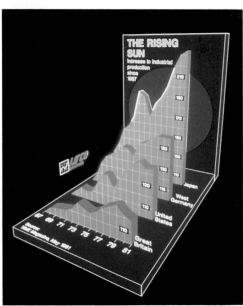

Figure O

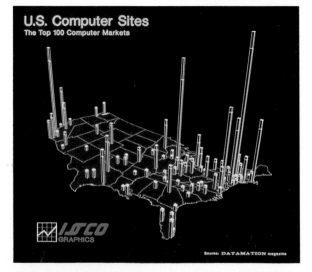

Figure P

Chapter 2

Microcomputers and Their Graphics Capabilities

Development of microprocessor technology has led to the design of small-scale computer systems with a broad range of graphics capabilities. These desk-top computers are configured for graphics uses in the office, in research and design, in schools, and as personal computers. Their low cost, compact size, and versatility make them highly suitable for a wide variety of graphics applications.

Some microcomputers are designed to operate with a built-in video display, while others must be attached to a separate terminal or TV set. Many of the systems with graphics capabilities can produce both color and black-and-white displays. Graphics systems are often characterized by the number of available colors and by the number of points—referred to as the resolution—that can be plotted on the screen. Resolution for graphics systems is given in terms of the number of horizontal and vertical display points available. These numbers are set by the graphics computer system, but are also dependent on the type of video display device used. Systems using a standard TV monitor have an upper limit of about 512 points horizontally and 256 points vertically. Special graphics terminals and monitors are capable of much higher resolution.

Tape casettes, floppy disks, and hard disk units are typical storage devices used with microcomputers. Printers, plotters, graphics tablets, and light pens are also available for many systems. A small computer system can be set up as a stand-alone graphics workstation, or it can be connected to a larger computer facility. When tied into a large computer, microcomputers operate as intelligent terminals. In this capacity, a network of microcomputers is sometimes put together so as to have time-sharing access to data bases and to high-quality printers or plotters.

BASIC is the higher-level programming language commonly used with microcomputers. Other languages available on some systems include Pascal, FORTRAN, COBOL, APL, PL/1, FORTH, and specialized graphics packages.

The graphics capabilities within these languages vary from simple character printing statements to advanced picture drawing and manipulation commands.

In the following sections we take a look at some specific microcomputer graphics systems. A few of these systems are designed mainly for graphics, but most are general-purpose computers that can be used for many applications besides graphics.

APPLE COMPUTERS

Both 8-bit and 16-bit Apple computers are available. The 8-bit Apple II and Apple III series of microcomputers are based on the 6502 microprocessor. These computers are designed to be used with an external video monitor or color television set. Several resolution levels are available in various graphics modes. Maximum resolution is 280 by 192 on the Apple II and 560 by 192 on the Apple III. Extensive graphics capabilities are provided, and most graphics modes allow 16 colors.

Figure 2–1 Apple II microcomputer system with video monitor, disk, and printer. (Courtesy Apple Computer, Inc.)

RADIO SHACK COMPUTERS

A Z80 microprocessor is used in the 8-bit TRS–80 computers, except for the Color Computer, which has a 6809 CPU. The MC68000 is the basis for the 16-bit TRS–80 systems. Most Radio Shack systems have a built-in display device, but the TRS–80 Color Computer can be used with a TV or external video monitor. The Model II Graphics Option provides several black-and-white graphics commands with a resolution of 640 by 240. The TRS–80 Color Computer systems allow eight colors and a resolution of 256 by 192, with the Extended Color BASIC Option.

Figure 2–2 Radio Shack Color Computer with color monitor, disk, and printer. (Courtesy Radio Shack, a division of Tandy Corp.)

IBM PERSONAL COMPUTERS

This 16-bit computer has an Intel 8088 microprocessor. It is designed to be used with an external video monitor or TV. With the Color/Graphics Monitor Adapter Option, two resolution modes are available: 320 by 200 and 640 by 200. Sixteen colors can be used in a two-palette arrangement at the lower resolution level. The IBM PC provides extensive graphics capabilities at both resolutions.

Figure 2–3 IBM Personal Computer system with monochrome monitor and printer. (Courtesy IBM Corp.)

ATARI COMPUTERS

The Atari 400 and 800 series microcomputers are built around the 6502 microprocessor. A TV or external video monitor must be connected to these units. Resolution levels available in graphics modes 3 through 8 on the Atari computers range from 40 by 20 to 320 by 192. The different graphics modes support picture-drawing commands and allow various combinations of the 16 available colors to be used for the border, background, and foreground of a display.

COMMODORE COMPUTERS

An extensive line of microcomputers featuring special keyboard graphics characters is available from Commodore Computer Systems. These systems include the PET and CBM series, and most are equipped with a built-in video display. The VIC–20 (based on a 6502 microprocessor), the Commodore–64, and the PET II are designed to be attached to an external color monitor or TV. Add-on modules, such as the Super Expander for the VIC–20, provide extended graphics capability in the form of special graphics commands.

Figure 2–4 Atari 800 microcomputer system with video monitor, disks, cassette, and printer. (Courtesy Atari Inc.)

Figure 2–5 Commodore CBM microcomputer system with disks and printer. (Courtesy Commodore Business Machines, Inc.)

HEWLETT-PACKARD COMPUTERS

These computers include a range of graphics systems, from the Series 80 Personal Computers (HP–85, HP–86, and HP–87) to the professional systems like the HP–9845 (System 45) and the Engineering Graphics System (EGS)/45. Graphics terminals, such as the HP–2623, connect to external computer systems. Most HP graphics computers have built-in video displays (the HP–86 has a detached monitor) and special graphics commands. The HP–85 has a resolution of 192 by 256, and the HP–87 has an upper resolution of 544 by 240. The professional systems include higher resolutions, color, and specialized graphics packages.

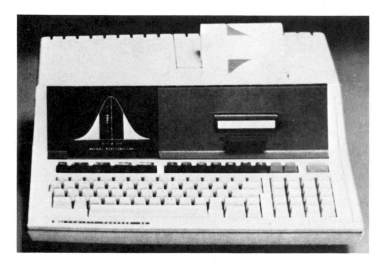

Figure 2–6 Hewlett-Packard HP–85 microcomputer system. (Courtesy Hewlett-Packard)

TEKTRONIX COMPUTERS

The 4050 series of professional microcomputer systems from Tektronix offers advanced graphics capabilities. These systems feature the direct-view storage CRT. Resolution on the 4051 and the 4052 is 1024 by 780, while resolution on the 4054 is 4096 by 3125. A line of graphics terminals, some featuring color, is also available from Tektronix. Highly sophisticated graphics commands are included in the graphics systems as built-in functions.

INTELLIGENT SYSTEMS COMPUTERS

Formerly called Intecolor computers, these color graphics systems include the 8000 series and 3650/9650 series of microcomputers. An 8080A microprocessor is the basis for these systems. All have built-in video displays with eight color choices for foreground and eight for background. Standard resolution is 160 by 192, but a resolution of 384 by 480 is available on some systems. Built-in functions provide an extensive set of graphics commands.

Figure 2–7 Tektronix 4052 microcomputer system. (Courtesy Tektronix, Inc.)

Figure 2–8 Intecolor microcomputer system. (Courtesy Intelligent Systems Corp.)

CHROMATICS COMPUTERS

Color Graphics (CG) systems from Chromatics include both 8-bit (Z80) and 16-bit (MC68000) microcomputers. These professional systems have built-in video displays that allow up to 256 simultaneous color combinations. Screen resolution varies from 512 by 512 to 1024 by 768. An extensive set of color graphics commands are provided with these systems.

CROMEMCO COMPUTERS

A Z80A microprocessor-based graphics system is available from Cromemco Inc. This system features a built-in video display, offering a menu of over 4000 colors. Resolution is 754 by 482. The system includes an extensive set of special graphics commands.

Graphics microcomputer systems and video terminals are available from many other sources. The small Sinclair ZX Spectrum is a Z80A-based system that is designed to be attached to an external video monitor or TV. This system features eight colors, a resolution of 256 by 192, and special graphics commands. BMC offers a Z80 color graphics system featuring 64 colors and hues on a built-in video display with a resolution of 640 by 200. NEC has an eight-color, Z80 based graphics system with a 160 by 100 built-in video display. The Genisco intelligent graphics terminals feature a range of colors and resolutions (such as 1392 by 1024 in the G–6100). Vector Automation's GRAPHICUS–80 intelligent graphics terminal includes an extensive set of graphics commands and a resolution of 4096 by 4096.

Part II

BASIC GRAPHICS

(Getting Started)

We begin with basic graphics concepts and methods for constructing displays. A simple method for creating computer-generated pictures and graphs is through the use of standard output statements provided in a programming language. In BASIC, we can use the PRINT statement to assemble letters, numbers, and other symbols into graphics patterns. More powerful graphics techniques are available on many microcomputer systems in the form of special graphics commands. Using these commands, we can "draw" displays with points and lines. We consider fundamental methods using both the PRINT statement and special graphics statements.

Chapter 3

Simple Pictures

Pictures can be constructed by arranging characters to form the shapes required in the display. Figure 3–1 illustrates a simple picture outlined with unconnected characters. Such pictures are usually easy to construct with the BASIC language PRINT statement and are useful for some applications. Figure 3–2 shows the same picture formed with continuous lines, using special graphics commands. In this chapter we take a look at the capabilities of the PRINT statement to produce graphical output, then introduce the graphics commands that are typical of many microcomputer systems.

Figure 3–1 Graphics output formed with characters, using the PRINT statement.

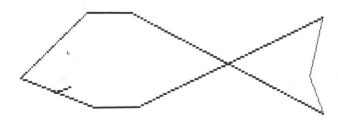

Figure 3–2 Graphics output formed with continuous lines, using special graphics statements.

3–1 PRINT STATEMENT GRAPHICS

Characters can be displayed along the print lines of a video screen or printer with the PRINT statement. We can display any of the letters, digits, punctuation marks, and other symbols that make up the BASIC language character set. For example, the program statement

```
10 PRINT   "* * * *"
```

will display the pattern of four asterisks at the beginning of a print line. We can display a box outline with

```
10 PRINT   "* * * * * * * * * * * * * *"
20 PRINT   "*                         *"
30 PRINT   "*                         *"
40 PRINT   "* * * * * * * * * * * * * *"
```

or oversize letters with statements such as

```
10 PRINT   "GGGGG  RRRR    AAA   PPPP   H   H  I  CCCCC  SSSSS"
20 PRINT   "G    G R   R  A   A  P   P  H   H  I  C      S    "
30 PRINT   "G      R   R  A   A  P   P  H   H  I  C      SSS  "
40 PRINT   "G   GG RRRR   AAAAA  PPPP   HHHHH  I  C        SSS "
50 PRINT   "G    G R   R  A   A  P      H   H  I  C          S"
60 PRINT   "GGGGG  R   R  A   A  P      H   H  I  CCCCC  SSSSS"
```

Similarly, Prog. 3–1 will produce the fish of Fig. 3–1.

Program 3–1   Figure outline (fish) using the PRINT statement.

```
10 'PROGRAM 3-1. FISH USING PRINT STATEMENTS
20  PRINT "              ****"
30  PRINT "          **      ***                    *"
40  PRINT "      ***            **              ** *"
50  PRINT "     *                  **         **   *"
60  PRINT "  *   **                *        **     *"
70  PRINT "*                          *  ***       *"
80  PRINT " *                        ****        *"
90  PRINT "   **                 ***     ***     *"
100 PRINT "     ****      *******          ***   *"
110 PRINT "        *******                  **   *"
120 PRINT "                                    ***"
130 END
```

We can position pictures on the pages of a printer or along any of the available print lines of a video screen. The number of print lines available for displaying pictures on a screen depends on the microcomputer system we are using. Screen size varies from about 16 to 48 lines, with 23 to 80 or more characters allowed per line. If we wanted to center the word GRAPHICS on a 40-

character by 16-line screen, we would position the word to start at location 17 on line 8. One way this could be accomplished is with a series of PRINT statements to skip seven lines, followed by the statement, PRINT TAB(17); "GRAPHICS".

Complex pictures can be set up for display by first drawing the picture outline on graph paper. We can then determine the character print positions for display of the picture outline or silhouette from the graph. Each horizontal line of characters on the graph paper becomes one print line. Graph paper is usually

Figure 3–3   A figure outlined on customized graph paper (formed by printing a page of plus signs) is used to determine the character print positions for Prog. 3–2.

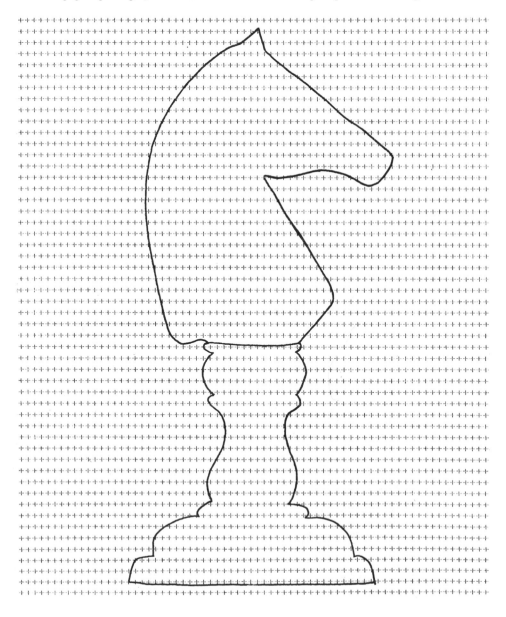

divided into squares, but the area occupied by a character on the screen is a rectangle—often a little higher than it is wide. If we use square graph paper to determine print positions, the displayed picture will be distorted. We can make customized graph paper for any system by printing a page filled with plus (+) signs, as shown in Fig. 3–3. Program 3–2 outputs a silhouette of the picture outlined in this figure.

Program 3–2   Figure silhouette (chess piece) using the PRINT statement.

```
10 'PROGRAM 3-2. CHESSPIECE SILHOUETTE USING PRINT STATEMENTS.
20   PRINT TAB(10);"                     #"
30   PRINT TAB(10);"                   #####"
40   PRINT TAB(10);"                  ########"
50   PRINT TAB(10);"                #############"
60   PRINT TAB(10);"               ################"
70   PRINT TAB(10);"              ####################"
80   PRINT TAB(10);"             #######################"
90   PRINT TAB(10);"            ##########################"
100  PRINT TAB(10);"           ##############################"
110  PRINT TAB(10);"          ################################"
120  PRINT TAB(10);"         ###################################"
130  PRINT TAB(10);"         ####################################"
140  PRINT TAB(10);"        ######################################"
150  PRINT TAB(10);"        #######################################"
160  PRINT TAB(10);"        ####################          ###"
170  PRINT TAB(10);"        #####################"
180  PRINT TAB(10);"        #####################"
190  PRINT TAB(10);"        #####################"
200  PRINT TAB(10);"        #######################"
210  PRINT TAB(10);"        #######################"
220  PRINT TAB(10);"       #########################"
230  PRINT TAB(10);"        #########################"
240  PRINT TAB(10);"        #########################"
250  PRINT TAB(10);"        ###########################"
260  PRINT TAB(10);"        ###########################"
270  PRINT TAB(10);"          ###########################"
280  PRINT TAB(10);"          ##########################"
290  PRINT TAB(10);"          #########################"
300  PRINT TAB(10);"          ########################"
310  PRINT TAB(10);"            ####################"
320  PRINT TAB(10);"              ###############"
330  PRINT TAB(10);"            #################"
340  PRINT TAB(10);"             ################"
350  PRINT TAB(10);"             ###############"
360  PRINT TAB(10);"              #############"
370  PRINT TAB(10);"               ###########"
380  PRINT TAB(10);"               ###########"
390  PRINT TAB(10);"               ###########"
400  PRINT TAB(10);"               ###########"
410  PRINT TAB(10);"               ###########"
420  PRINT TAB(10);"               ###########"
430  PRINT TAB(10);"              ###############"
440  PRINT TAB(10);"              ###############"
450  PRINT TAB(10);"              ###############"
460  PRINT TAB(10);"             ###############"
470  PRINT TAB(10);"           #######################"
480  PRINT TAB(10);"         ##############################"
490  PRINT TAB(10);"         ###############################"
500  PRINT TAB(10);"        ################################"
510  PRINT TAB(10);"#######################################"
520  PRINT TAB(10);"########################################"
530  PRINT TAB(10);"########################################"
540 END
```

Since lines 370 through 420 in Prog. 3–2 are identical, we could use a loop containing a single PRINT statement instead of these six lines. For any picture containing repeated or symmetric patterns, we can devise loops to construct the pattern. The pyramid of Fig. 3–4, for example, can be displayed with Prog. 3–3.

```
                A
               AAA
              AAAAA
             AAAAAAA
            AAAAAAAAA
           AAAAAAAAAAA
          AAAAAAAAAAAAA
         AAAAAAAAAAAAAAA
        AAAAAAAAAAAAAAAAA
       AAAAAAAAAAAAAAAAAAA
      AAAAAAAAAAAAAAAAAAAAA
     AAAAAAAAAAAAAAAAAAAAAAA
    AAAAAAAAAAAAAAAAAAAAAAAAA
   AAAAAAAAAAAAAAAAAAAAAAAAAAA
  AAAAAAAAAAAAAAAAAAAAAAAAAAAAA
```

Figure 3–4 Symmetrical patterns, such as this pyramid output of Prog. 3–3, can be produced with loops that minimize the number of PRINT statements.

```
10  'PROGRAM 3-3. PROGRAM TO DRAW PYRAMID
20  K=30
30  FOR N = 1 TO 29 STEP 2
40      PRINT TAB(K);
50      FOR J = 1 TO N
60          PRINT "A";
70      NEXT J
80      PRINT
90      K = K - 1
100 NEXT N
110 END
```

Program 3–3 Symmetrical pattern (pyramid) using the PRINT statement and program loops.

The number of PRINT statements needed for a display could also be reduced if the positions to be printed are encoded in the DATA statements. This encoded data can then be read from the DATA statements, decoded, and printed. There are many ways we can encode the print lines. As an example, each line in a picture can be stored as a pair of numbers. The first number gives the starting print position and the second number states how many characters are to be printed on that line. Program 3–4 produces the silhouette of Fig. 3–3 using this encoding scheme.

Shading in pictures can be accomplished with the PRINT statement by varying the type of characters used in the display. Asterisks, ampersands, and other such symbols will produce darker areas than O's or I's. It's possible on some printers to get darker shading with overprinting, that is, placing two or more characters in the same print position.

The special graphics characters available on a particular microcomputer provide another method for varying the texture of pictures. These characters come in a variety of shapes and patterns depending on the system. They may appear on the keyboard and can be included in a PRINT statement like any other

Program 3-4   Chess piece silhouette using the PRINT statement and encoded data.

```
10 'PROGRAM 3-4. CHESSPIECE SILHOUETTE WITH ENCODED DATA.
20      'EACH PRINT LINE IS STORED AS A PAIR OF NUMBERS.
30      'FIRST NUMBER IS POSITION TO START PRINTING,
40      'SECOND NUMBER IS HOW MANY CHARACTERS TO PRINT.
50      'INPUT IS TERMINATED BY READING 0,0.
60      'CHARACTER TO PRINT CAN BE CHANGED IN LINE 110.
70 READ P, N
80  IF P = 0 AND N = 0 THEN 200
90  PRINT TAB(P);
100 FOR K = 1 TO N
110     PRINT "#";
120 NEXT K
130 GOTO 70
140 DATA 28,1,25,5,22,9,20,13,19,16,17,20,16,23,15,26,14,29,14
150 DATA 32,13,35,13,36,12,37,12,36,12,19,44,3,12,20,12,21,12,22
160 DATA 12,23,12,24,12,25,13,25,13,26,13,27,14,27,14,26,15,24,15
170 DATA 23,17,19,22,13,20,17,20,17,21,15,22,13,23,11,23,11,23,11
180 DATA 23,11,23,11,23,11,21,15,21,15,21,15,21,15,17,23,13,31,13
190 DATA 31,13,31,10,37,10,37,10,37,0,0
200 END
```

character. On other systems, we can display special characters with the statement PRINT CHR$(A), where A is the ASCII code of a desired character. Figure 3–5 displays a picture produced with graphics characters.

Figure 3-5   A picture formed with special graphics characters.

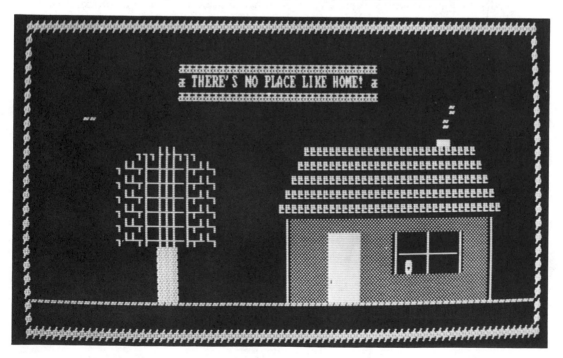

3–2 PIXEL GRAPHICS CONCEPTS

Each character printed on a video screen occupies a small rectangle. This area is subdivided on many microcomputers into a grid of even smaller rectangles. These smaller rectangles are called **picture elements** or **pixels**, or simply **points**. The number of pixels occupied by a single character depends on the system. From 2 to 8 points might be included horizontally, and from 3 to 12 vertically. Figure 3–6 illustrates a 2 by 4 **pixel grid** corresponding to the area occupied by a character. A video screen used with this system will thus contain twice as many points as characters across the screen and four times as many points vertically. If this system has 48 print lines with 80 characters per line, we could plot a point in any one of 160 positions horizontally across the screen and in any one of 192 vertical positions.

Pixels are directly accessible for use when in the **graphics mode**. To enter the graphics mode, some systems require that we type in a special initialization command, such as GR or SCREEN. Other systems automatically enter the graphics mode when we give any of the special graphics commands, such as to plot a point or draw a line.

Plotting a point on a video screen means that we instruct the computer to "turn on" the small rectangle of light at the required pixel position. Individual pixel positions are referenced by **coordinates**. That is, we must specify the location of a pixel as a pair of integers (X,Y). The first integer, X, gives the horizontal distance across the screen, and the second integer, Y, gives the vertical distance. Many microcomputers require that these distances be measured from left to right and top to bottom. This means that the screen is referenced with the **origin** of the coordinate system at the upper left corner, as shown in Fig. 3–7. The X, or horizontal coordinate, can range from left to right through integer values 0, 1, 2, . . ., up to some maximum XM. The Y, or vertical coordinate, can range from top

Figure 3–6 The area occupied by a character is divided into a grid of smaller rectangular pixels.

Character area

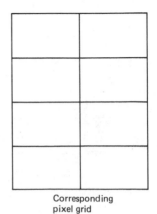

Corresponding
pixel grid

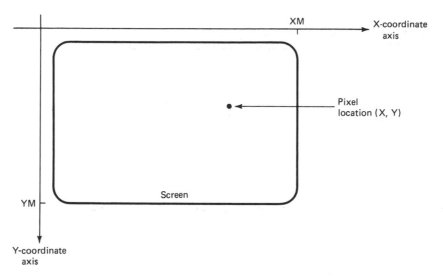

Figure 3–7 The coordinate system used by many microcomputers places the origin at the upper left corner of the screen.

to bottom through the integer values 0, 1, 2, . . ., YM. For this coordinate reference, the position of the pixel at the upper left corner of the screen is specified as (0,0). Pixel coordinates for the point at the lower right corner are (XM,YM). The Apple, TRS–80, IBM, and ATARI microcomputers use this coordinate reference. All of our graphics discussions will be based on this coordinate system.

Some microcomputers use the more conventional reference with the origin at the lower left corner of the screen. For these systems, the pixel at the lower left corner has position (0,0) and the pixel at the upper right (XM,YM). Hewlett-Packard, Tektronix, and Intecolor are examples of systems that place the coordinate origin at the lower left corner of the screen. Our programming examples can be converted to this coordinate system by replacing any Y value of a plotted point with the value YM−Y.

Values for maximum screen width and height, XM and YM, vary from about 40 to several hundred, although much higher values are available. Larger values for XM and YM allow us to draw smoother-looking lines since each point occupies a smaller area on the screen. The number of pixels along a line is referred to as the resolution of the system. Figure 3–8 shows the effects of higher resolution and lower resolution on the appearance of straight lines. Horizontal and vertical lines will appear smooth regardless of the resolution. For diagonal lines, the lower the **resolution**, the greater the "stair step" appearance of the lines.

Resolution is stated more precisely in terms of the number of pixels that can be plotted per centimeter (cm). Thus a larger screen plotting the same number of pixels across its width as a smaller screen will have lower resolution (fewer points per centimeter). With most microcomputers, video screens of different physical dimensions can be used. But changing the screen size does not change the number of pixels provided by the computer. This number is fixed by the graphics

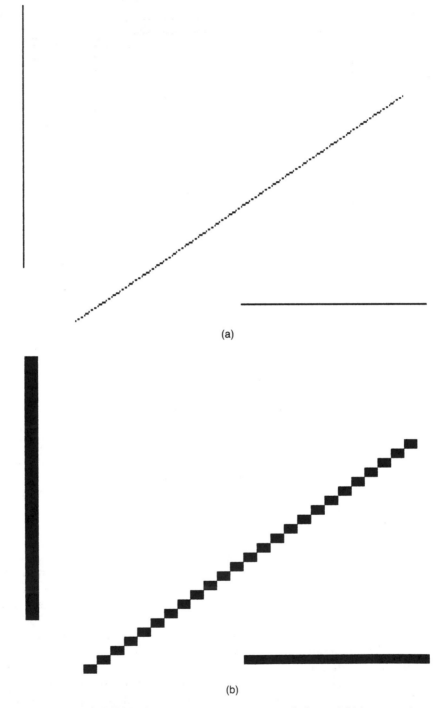

(a)

(b)

Figure 3–8 Straight lines drawn with (a) higher resolution and (b) lower resolution.

capabilities designed for the particular system. Some systems will allow us to choose between various **resolution modes**. These modes are usually referred to as **low resolution** (providing fewer points), **medium resolution** (providing more points), and **high resolution** (providing the most points).

3–3 PLOTTING POINTS

In order to plot a point on a video screen, we must state the appropriate graphics commands. Unlike the PRINT statement, graphics commands are not standardized. Different microcomputer systems use different commands to accomplish the same operation. Since the basic operations in graphics (entering a particular resolution mode, plotting points, and so forth) are the same, we can discuss these operations in terms of a hypothetical set of graphics commands. This set of hypothetical commands will be used in all subsequent discussions. The correspondence between these commands and the actual statements for a particular system are given in Appendix A.

For some systems we must enter the graphics mode and state the resolution required. Our hypothetical set of commands will assume only one resolution mode, with the command to accomplish graphics initialization defined as:

GRAPHICS — Enters the graphics mode.

Once in the graphics mode, we may plot a point by stating the command:

POINTPLOT X,Y — Places a pixel on the screen at coordinates X,Y. X and Y may be numeric constants or expressions. If noninteger, they will be rounded.

Point plotting commands on some systems may truncate numbers to integers, rather than rounding. An example of the use of GRAPHICS and POINTPLOT is given in Prog. 3–5. This program plots a point at the location specified in the input statement.

We should not try to plot a point beyond the screen limits. This could either produce an error in program execution or a distortion in the point position due to **wraparound** effects. Wraparound occurs when a point, plotted beyond the limits on one side of the screen, "wraps around" and appears on the other side of the

Program 3–5 Plotting a point.

```
10 'PROGRAM 3-5. PLOTS A SINGLE POINT
20  PRINT "INPUT PIXEL COORDINATES AS AN INTEGER PAIR"
30  INPUT X, Y
40  GRAPHICS
50  POINTPLOT X,Y
60  END
```

screen. To avoid these problems, neither the horizontal nor the vertical coordinate should ever become negative or exceed the maximum screen locations. We can ensure that we do not attempt plotting beyond the screen boundaries by including the tests of (3–1) in our programs.

$$0 <= X <= XM$$
$$0 <= Y <= YM$$

(3–1)

In these tests, XM is the maximum horizontal pixel location allowed, and YM is the maximum vertical pixel location. Program 3–6 shows the use of these tests for a screen size of 280 by 160 pixels.

```
10 'PROGRAM 3-6. TEST FOR SCREEN LIMITS AND PLOT
20   PRINT "INPUT PIXEL COORDINATES AS AN INTEGER PAIR"
30   INPUT X, Y
40   IF X < 0 OR X > 279 OR Y < 0 OR Y > 159 THEN 80
50   GRAPHICS
60   POINTPLOT X,Y
70   GOTO 90
80   PRINT "ATTEMPT TO PLOT OFF SCREEN"
90   END
```

Program 3–6　Point plotting and off-screen tests.

For many applications it is convenient to be able to "erase" a point that we previously plotted. We introduce the following command to accomplish this:

POINTOFF X,Y — Erases the pixel previously plotted at position X,Y.
　　　　　　　X and Y may be numeric expressions or constants. If noninteger,
　　　　　　　they will be rounded.

If the pixel at location X,Y is not turned on, POINTOFF will have no visible effect. Program 3–7 shows how this command can be used to turn off a pixel after a delay time of about 2 seconds.

Program 3–7　Point plotting and erasing.

```
10 'PROGRAM 3-7. TURN POINT ON AND OFF
20   PRINT "ENTER MAXIMUM HORIZONTAL AND VERTICAL"
30   PRINT "VALUES FOR THIS RESOLUTION MODE"
40   INPUT XM, YM
50   PRINT "ENTER X AND Y FOR POINT TO BE PLOTTED"
60   INPUT X, Y
70   IF X < 0 OR X > XM OR Y < 0 OR Y > YM THEN 130
80   GRAPHICS
90   POINTPLOT X,Y
100 FOR J = 1 TO 1000: NEXT J
110 POINTOFF X,Y
120 GOTO 140
130 PRINT "ATTEMPT TO PLOT OFF SCREEN"
140 END
```

Delay loops, as in statement 80 of Prog. 3–7, can be inserted into graphics programs to make points blink. They can also be used to hold a picture for viewing before the next picture is created. These loops will provide a delay time of about 1 second for every 500 iterations of the loop, depending on the processing speed of a particular system.

We often want to erase the entire screen before creating a display or listing a program. For this purpose, we define:

CLEARSCREEN — Erases the screen and returns the cursor to the
    top left corner of the screen.

This statement may be used with or without the GRAPHICS mode. Use of CLEARSCREEN is illustrated in Prog. 3–8, which plots a random pattern of points. The RND function used in this program takes different forms in different versions of BASIC.

Program 3–8 Plotting a pattern of random points.

```
10  'PROGRAM 3-8. PLOTTING RANDOM POINTS
20  PRINT "ENTER MAXIMUM HORIZONTAL AND VERTICAL"
30  PRINT "VALUES FOR THIS RESOLUTION MODE"
40  INPUT XM, YM
50  PRINT "ENTER NUMBER OF POINTS TO BE PLOTTED"
60  INPUT P
70  CLEARSCREEN
80  GRAPHICS
90  FOR K = 1 TO P
100     X = XM * RND(0)
110     Y = YM * RND(0)
120     POINTPLOT X,Y
130 NEXT K
140 END
```

3–4 DRAWING LINES

POINTPLOT can be used to draw lines. To create a straight line, we plot all the available pixels along a straight path between the two endpoints of the line. These pixels are 1 unit apart, so that POINTPLOT will draw a vertical line, for example, when the Y coordinate is repeatedly increased by 1 and the X coordinate is held constant. Programs 3–9 and 3–10 provide examples of drawing vertical and horizontal lines. These programs produce continuous lines since each pixel plotted is a small rectangle adjoined to the previously plotted pixel.

Drawing diagonal lines is less straightforward. In order to draw a diagonal line using POINTPLOT, we must calculate coordinate values along the path of the line. To do this we use the calculation in (3–2), which relates X and Y values for a straight line.

$$Y = M*X + B \qquad (3–2)$$

Program 3–9 Drawing a vertical line by plotting points.

```
10 'PROGRAM 3-9. PROGRAM TO DRAW VERTICAL LINE
20  CLEARSCREEN
30  PRINT "INPUT MAXIMUM HORIZONTAL AND VERTICAL"
40  PRINT "VALUES FOR THIS RESOLUTION MODE"
50  INPUT XM, YM
60  PRINT "INPUT THE X COORDINATE FOR THE VERTICAL LINE"
70  INPUT X
80  IF X >= 0 AND X <= XM THEN 110
90  PRINT "X COORDINATE BEYOND SCREEN LIMITS. TRY AGAIN."
100 GOTO 60
110 PRINT "INPUT THE Y END POINTS"
120 INPUT Y1, Y2
130 IF Y1 >= 0 AND Y1 <= YM  AND Y2 >= 0 AND Y2 <= YM THEN 160
140 PRINT "Y COORDINATE BEYOND SCREEN LIMITS. TRY AGAIN."
150 GOTO 110
160 CLEARSCREEN
170 GRAPHICS
180 FOR Y = Y1 TO Y2
190     POINTPLOT X,Y
200 NEXT Y
210 END
```

Program 3–10 Drawing a horizontal line by plotting points.

```
10 'PROGRAM 3-10. PROGRAM TO DRAW HORIZONTAL LINE
20  CLEARSCREEN
30  PRINT "INPUT MAXIMUM HORIZONTAL AND VERTICAL"
40  PRINT "VALUES FOR THIS RESOLUTION MODE"
50  INPUT XM, YM
60  PRINT "INPUT THE Y COORDINATE FOR THE HORIZONTAL LINE"
70  INPUT Y
80  IF Y >= 0 AND Y <= YM THEN 110
90  PRINT "Y COORDINATE BEYOND SCREEN LIMITS. TRY AGAIN."
100 GOTO 60
110 PRINT "INPUT THE X END POINTS"
120 INPUT X1, X2
130 IF X1 >= 0 AND X1 <= XM  AND X2 >= 0 AND X2 <= XM THEN 160
140 PRINT "X COORDINATE BEYOND SCREEN LIMITS. TRY AGAIN."
150 GOTO 110
160 CLEARSCREEN
170 GRAPHICS
180 FOR X = X1 TO X2
190     POINTPLOT X,Y
200 NEXT X
210 END
```

In this equation, M is the **slope** of the line, which may be positive, negative, or zero. When M is zero, we have a horizontal line. For very large magnitudes of M, we have nearly vertical lines. The **Y-intercept**, B, is the value that Y would have if the line were projected to intercept the Y axis (where X is 0). If B is zero, we have a line that projects right through the coordinate origin.

We can program a general line-drawing algorithm using POINTPLOT and the equation of (3–2). Program 3–11 illustrates line drawing with values for M and B entered as input. This program first determines whether the specified line can be drawn on the screen. If no part of the line can be plotted within the coordinate boundaries of the screen, the program simply prints that message. If some part of the line can be drawn, Prog. 3–11 plots the visible part of the line from one screen boundary to another. Figure 3–9 shows the output of Prog. 3–11 for the case M = 1. The line shown appears opposite from what we would expect when graphed in a conventional coordinate system, where a line with positive slope slants up from left to right. This occurs because our point (0,0) is at the upper left corner of the screen. We can modify this program to produce conventionally oriented lines by multiplying each input value of the slope by –1 and by changing each input B value to YM—B.

Program 3–11 will not produce continuous lines when the magnitude of the slope is greater than 1. In this case, we will have gaps between the plotted pixels. This can be corrected by incrementing the Y coordinate by 1 unit instead of the X coordinate when ABS(M) > 1. We could also modify the program to position the

Program 3–11 General line drawing using the line equation and point plotting.

```
10 'PROGRAM 3-11. GENERAL LINE DRAWING USING POINTPLOT
20  CLEARSCREEN
30  PRINT "ENTER MAXIMUM HORIZONTAL AND VERTICAL"
40  PRINT "VALUES FOR THIS RESOLUTION MODE"
50  INPUT XM, YM
60  PRINT "ENTER THE SLOPE AND Y-INTERCEPT"
70  INPUT M, B
80              'IF SLOPE IS NEGATIVE AND LINE INTERCEPTS Y AT A
90              'VALUE LESS THAN 0, LINE IS BEYOND SCREEN COORDINATES.
100 IF M < 0 AND B < 0 THEN PRINT "LINE OFF SCREEN": GOTO 430
110             'IF SLOPE IS POSITIVE BUT LINE INTERCEPTS Y AT A VALUE
120             'GREATER THAN YM, LINE IS BEYOND SCREEN COORDINATES.
130 IF M > 0 AND B > YM THEN PRINT "LINE OFF SCREEN": GOTO 430
140             'OTHERWISE, FIND LEFTMOST POINT OF LINE.
150             'IF Y-INTERCEPT IS BETWEEN 0 AND YM THEN LEFTMOST
160             'POINT IS AT LEFT EDGE OF SCREEN.
170 X1 = 0
180             'IF SLOPE IS NEGATIVE AND LINE INTERCEPTS Y AT A VALUE
190             'GREATER THAN YM, LEFTMOST POINT IS ALONG BOTTOM EDGE OF
200             'SCREEN (WHERE Y = YM) SO X1 = (YM - B) / M.
210 IF M < 0 AND B > YM THEN X1 = (YM - B) / M
220             'IF THIS LEFTMOST POINT IS BEYOND XM, LINE IS OFF SCREEN.
230 IF X1 > XM THEN PRINT "LINE OFF SCREEN": GOTO 430
240             'IF SLOPE IS POSITIVE AND LINE INTERCEPTS Y AT A POINT LESS
250             'THAN 0, LEFTMOST POINT IS ALONG TOP EDGE OF SCREEN
260             '(WHERE Y = 0) SO X1 = (0 - B) / M OR X1 = -B / M.
270 IF M > 0 AND B < 0 THEN X1 = -B / M
280             'IF THIS POINT IS BEYOND XM, LINE IS OFF SCREEN.
290 IF X1 > XM THEN PRINT "LINE OFF SCREEN": GOTO 430
300             'OTHERWISE, LINE IS AT LEAST PARTIALLY ON SCREEN.  START AT
310             'LEFTMOST POINT OF LINE (X1).  USING INCREASING VALUES OF
320             'X, CALCULATE NEW Y VALUES AND PLOT X,Y.  CONTINUE UNTIL
330             '1.  X > XM (LINE GOES TO RIGHT EDGE OF SCREEN)
340             '2.  Y < 0  (LINE GOES OFF TOP EDGE OF SCREEN) OR
350             '3.  Y > YM (LINE GOES OFF BOTTOM EDGE OF SCREEN)
360 CLEARSCREEN
370 GRAPHICS
380 FOR X = X1 TO XM
390     Y = M * X + B
400     IF Y < 0 OR Y > YM THEN 430
410     POINTPLOT X,Y
420 NEXT X
430 END
```

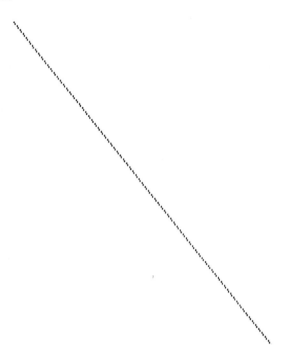

Figure 3–9 Straight line with a slope of 1 and Y-intercept of 0, drawn by Prog. 3–11.

line so that it is drawn in the center of the screen. Methods for accomplishing this are discussed in Chapter 4 when we consider graphs.

If we want to plot a line between certain endpoint coordinates, we need to determine the slope and Y-intercept in order to calculate points along the line. Specifying the line endpoints as (X1,Y1) and (X2,Y2), we can calculate M and B from the relations

$$M = (Y2 - Y1) / (X2 - X1)$$
$$B = Y1 - M * X1$$

(3–3)

A program for line drawing based on the equations in (3–3) would accept the coordinates of the endpoints as input, calculate M and B, and plot coordinates along the line between the stated endpoints.

Many microcomputer systems provide a graphics command that will automatically draw a line between two given endpoints. We define the following function to accomplish this task.

DRAWLINE X1,Y1 TO X2,Y2 — Draws a straight line from position X1,Y1 to position X2,Y2. X1, Y1, X2, Y2 may be numeric constants or expressions. If noninteger, they will be rounded.

Program 3–12 uses the DRAWLINE command to draw a line between any two specified endpoints.

Program 3–12   Drawing a line with the line-drawing statement.

```
10  'PROGRAM 3-12. GENERAL LINE DRAWING USING DRAWLINE
20  CLEARSCREEN
30  PRINT "ENTER MAXIMUM HORIZONTAL AND VERTICAL"
40  PRINT "VALUES FOR THIS RESOLUTION MODE"
50  INPUT XM, YM
60  PRINT "INPUT COORDINATES FOR FIRST POINT"
70  INPUT X1, Y1
80  IF X1 >= 0 AND X1 <= XM THEN 110
90  PRINT "X COORDINATE BEYOND LIMITS. DO OVER"
100 GOTO 60
110 IF Y1 >= 0 AND Y1 <= YM THEN 140
120 PRINT "Y COORDINATE BEYOND LIMITS. DO OVER"
130 GOTO 60
140 PRINT "INPUT COORDINATES FOR NEXT POINT"
150 INPUT X2, Y2
160 IF X2 >= 0 AND X2 <= XM THEN 190
170 PRINT "X COORDINATE BEYOND LIMITS. DO OVER"
180 GOTO 140
190 IF Y2 >= 0 AND Y2 <= YM THEN 220
200 PRINT "Y COORDINATE BEYOND LIMITS. DO OVER"
210 GOTO 140
220 CLEARSCREEN
230 GRAPHICS
240 DRAWLINE X1,Y1 TO X2,Y2
250 END
```

3–5 PICTURE DRAWING AND COLOR

Point-plotting and line-drawing commands provide the basic tools for producing graphics displays. With these commands, we can construct figure outlines, silhouettes, three-dimensional shapes, and complex scenes. In addition, with many graphics systems, we can enhance our pictures with color.

COLOR

The ability to add color to graphics displays can be a valuable asset. We can use color to make a display easier to understand. Complex displays can be clarified by using colors to distinguish different objects or areas. Color can be used to accent or highlight important parts of a display or to add realism. We can also use color simply to produce a more attractive display. In some applications, such as textile design, color may be essential.

We add the following hypothetical statement to our set of special graphics commands:

COLOR F,B — Sets the color of pixels displayed by subsequent commands to color F (foreground) on a screen of color B (background). F and B may be numeric constants or expressions. If noninteger, they will be rounded.

Color codes for F and B:

0—black	4—green
1—white	5—yellow
2—blue	6—light blue
3—red	7—orange

Several COLOR statements may be used in a program. For example, the following sequence of statements will set the screen background to light blue, then display patterns in colors of red, green, and yellow.

COLOR 3,6

.

.

.

COLOR 4,6

.

.

COLOR 5,6

Setting foreground and background to the same color (F = B) makes subsequent displays invisible. Setting F equal to B and then replotting a line visible on the screen "erases" the line. If no color command is stated in a program, we will assume that the system has a standard default, such as white on a black background.

Appendix A lists the correspondence of the COLOR F,B command to the color specification format required with different systems. The number of colors available on different microcomputers can vary from 2 (black and white) to about 20. Some systems have more color options, and others restrict colors to fixed combinations. Sometimes the color option can be used outside the graphics mode for setting character color.

Choice of color combinations for a particular display should be carefully considered. A random selection can produce a glaring, unpleasant effect. Using fewer colors in a display is usually best. A background chosen as the "complement" of one of the foreground colors can be attractive. Complement color combinations include red and blue-green, blue and orange, yellow and purple-blue, and green and magenta (red-purple). A light background (say, blue) can be used to good effect with darker colors. If many colors are to be used in a display, a gray or neutral background is best. Black borders around different color areas can help to reduce clashes when many colors are used.

PICTURE DRAWING

Examples of the use of POINTPLOT, DRAWLINE, and COLOR in creating pictures are given in the following programs. In Prog. 3–13 we draw a triangle,

Program 3–13   General polygon drawing and color.

```
10 'PROGRAM 3-13. GENERAL POLYGON DRAWING PROGRAM
20      'PROGRAM TO DRAW POLYGON OF UP TO TEN SIDES.  POINTS ARE
30      'INPUT IN THE ORDER IN WHICH THEY SHOULD BE CONNECTED.
40      'POLYGON IS DISPLAYED IN FOREGROUND AND BACKGROUND COLOR
50      'COMBINATIONS, WITH A TIME DELAY BETWEEN EACH SUCCESSIVE
60      'DISPLAY.
70      '**************************************************************
80 CLEARSCREEN
90 DIM X(10), Y(10)
100 PRINT "ENTER MAXIMUM HORIZONTAL AND VERTICAL COORDINATES"
110 INPUT XM, YM
120 PRINT "HOW MANY POINTS ARE THERE IN YOUR POLYGON?"
130 INPUT N
140 PRINT "INPUT POINTS IN THE ORDER THEY SHOULD BE CONNECTED"
150 FOR K = 1 TO N
160      INPUT X(K), Y(K)
170      IF X(K) >= O AND X(K) <= XM THEN 200
180      PRINT "X COORDINATE OUT OF RANGE. TRY AGAIN."
190      GOTO 160
200      IF Y(K) >= O AND Y(K) <= YM THEN 230
210      PRINT "Y COORDINATE OUT OF RANGE. TRY AGAIN."
220      GOTO 160
230 NEXT K
240 GRAPHICS
250 FOR F = 0 TO 7
260      FOR B = 0 TO 7
270           COLOR F,B
280           CLEARSCREEN
290           FOR K = 1 TO N-1
300                DRAWLINE X(K),Y(K) TO X(K+1),Y(K+1)
310           NEXT K
320           'CONNECT LAST POINT TO THE FIRST
330           DRAWLINE X(N),Y(N) TO X(1),Y(1)
340           PRINT "HIT ANY KEY FOR NEXT COLOR COMBINATION"
350           IF INKEY$="" THEN 350
360      NEXT B
370 NEXT F
380 END
```

rectangle, or general polygon of any number of sides in various color combinations. Coordinates for the vertices of the figure are input in the order they are to be connected and stored in arrays X and Y. The polygon is then displayed by drawing a line from point X(1),Y(1) to point X(2),Y(2), then to point X(3),Y(3), and so on.

Program 3–13 also illustrates another form of time delay. In this case, execution stops indefinitely at line 350. The program will resume interaction with us when we hit any key on the keyboard. The function INKEY$, available in some versions of BASIC, is initialized by the system to the null string. When executed, it assumes the value of the key currently being pressed on the keyboard, if any. This type of time delay is particularly useful if the program is producing a series of displays that are being used in conjunction with a report or presentation. It is often helpful to include a "prompt" with the time delay, particularly if we are writing a program to be used by other people. We included the message HIT ANY KEY FOR NEXT COLOR COMBINATION before line 350 in Prog. 3–13 to indicate that the program is in a time delay. In order not to print the message over our picture, we might simply print these instructions once at the beginning of the program execution. Then the program could clear the screen, draw the picture, and wait for the required action.

A technique for producing solid color areas is illustrated with Prog. 3–14. Some systems have additional graphics options to achieve this, but line-drawing routines allow us to create special effects as we "paint." In this program, any rectangular area on the screen is chosen by specifying the opposite corners of the rectangle.

Solid color areas can be produced by drawing horizontal, vertical, or diagonal lines. We can vary the order of drawing lines and the choice of color to produce special effects. For example, we could fill in a rectangular area with randomly colored horizontal lines, drawn alternately from the top and bottom and meeting in the middle.

Shading in our pictures can be obtained by partially filling in areas, such as with every other line, or every third line. We could also draw lines in both directions, spaced to obtain a crosshatched shading. Another possibility is to vary the spacing between the shading lines to produce a gradual dark to light (or light to dark) shading. The spacing between lines could be increased slowly by 1 or 2 units, or we could increase spacing more rapidly by doubling the previous spacing to get the next spacing length. Figure 3–10 shows some shading patterns possible with points and lines.

We would expect programs such as 3–14 to show a square on the screen if we filled an area with an equal number of pixels in the horizontal and vertical

Program 3–14   Painting solid color rectangles.

```
 10  'PROGRAM 3-14. PRODUCES SOLID COLOR RECTANGLE
 20  CLEARSCREEN
 30  PRINT "ENTER MAXIMUM HORIZONTAL AND VERTICAL"
 40  PRINT "COORDINATES FOR THIS RESOLUTION MODE"
 50  INPUT XM, YM
 60  PRINT "INPUT TOP LEFT CORNER COORDINATES"
 70  INPUT X1, Y1
 80  IF X1 >= 0 AND X1 <= XM AND Y1 >= 0 AND Y1 <= YM THEN 110
 90  PRINT "COORDINATE OUT OF RANGE. DO OVER"
100  GOTO 60
110  PRINT "INPUT BOTTOM RIGHT CORNER COORDINATES"
120  INPUT X2, Y2
130  IF X2 >= 0 AND X2 <= XM AND Y2 >= 0 AND Y2 <= YM THEN 160
140  PRINT "COORDINATE OUT OF RANGE. DO OVER"
150  GOTO 110
160  PRINT "INPUT COLOR FOREGROUND AND BACKGROUND CODES"
170  INPUT  F, B
180  IF F >= 0 AND F <= 7 AND B >= 0 AND B <= 7 THEN 210
190  PRINT "COLOR CODE OUT OF RANGE"
200  GOTO 160
210  CLEARSCREEN
220  GRAPHICS
230  COLOR F,B
240  FOR Y = Y1 TO Y2
250      DRAWLINE X1,Y TO X2,Y
260  NEXT Y
270  END
```

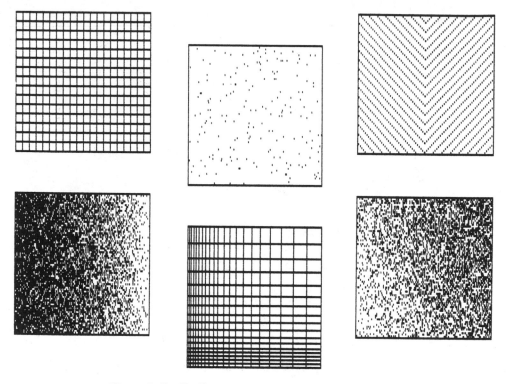

Figure 3–10 Shading patterns possible with pixel graphics.

directions. This will not be the case for systems in which the resolution in the X direction is significantly different from that in the Y direction. For example, we might have a system in which a 100-pixel horizontal line on the screen measures 6 cm long, but a 100-pixel vertical line measures 8 cm. The X resolution is then 100/6, while the Y resolution is 100/8. A 100 x 100 pixel box drawn on the screen will appear as a rectangle, somewhat taller than it is wide. To make the box into a square, we could either plot more points in the X direction or fewer points in the Y direction. Suppose that we want to modify the number of pixels in the Y direction. We can determine the number of pixels needed in the Y direction to make a square by multiplying the original vertical length (100) by the ratio of Y resolution to X resolution (100/8 divided by 100/6, or 3/4). The result is 75, so we need to plot 75 points in the Y direction to make a square.

To determine the **resolution ratio** (sometimes called the aspect ratio) for any system, we can draw a 50-pixel or 100-pixel line on the screen in each direction and measure line lengths. The ratio of the X length to the Y length would be used to adjust the number of pixels needed in the Y direction. The ratio of Y length to X length would be used to adjust the number of pixels in the X direction. Adjusting one of these directions for all points of a display allows us to draw figures in proper proportions. Program 3–15 demonstrates resolution correction, as well as the use of shading and color in creating a picture (Fig. 3–11).

Program 3–15 Sailboat drawn with shading and resolution correction.

```
10  'PROGRAM 3-15. PROGRAM DRAWS SAILBOAT FROM GRAPH PAPER LAYOUT
20      '(CORRECTED FOR DIFFERENT X AND Y RESOLUTIONS).   ALSO FILLS
30      'IN AND SHADES IRREGULARLY SHAPED AREAS. POINTS TAKEN FROM
40      'GRAPH PAPER ARE READ FROM DATA STATEMENTS.   Y VALUES ARE
50      'ADJUSTED BASED ON RESOLUTION RATIO, BY MULTIPLYING BY R.
60  CLEARSCREEN
70  R = 5 / 6
80  PRINT "ENTER MAXIMUM HORIZONTAL AND VERTICAL"
90  PRINT "VALUES FOR THIS RESOLUTION MODE"
100 INPUT XM, YM
110 CLEARSCREEN
120 GRAPHICS
130     'DRAW BOAT MAST
140 COLOR 2,6           'DRAW BLUE MAST ON LIGHT BLUE BACKGROUND
150 READ XT, YT, XB, YB
160 YT = YT * R          'ADJUST FOR RESOLUTION DIFFERENCES
170 YB = YB * R
180 IF YT < 0 OR YT > YM OR YB < 0 OR YB > YM THEN 960
190     'MAKE THE MAST 5 LINES THICK
200 FOR K = 0 TO 4
210     DRAWLINE XT+K,YT TO XB+K,YB
220 NEXT K
230     'READ COORDINATES FOR LEFT SIDE
240     'MAKE FILLED IN BOAT BOTTOM
250 COLOR 3,6
260 READ XL1, YL1, XL2, YL2
270     'ADJUST Y COORDINATES FOR RESOLUTION DIFFERENCE
280 YL1 = YL1 * R
290 YL2 = YL2 * R
300 IF YL1 < 0 OR YL1 > YM OR YL2 < 0 OR YL2 > YM THEN 960
310     'FIND SLOPE & Y-INTERCEPT FOR LEFT SIDE
320 ML = (YL2 - YL1) / (XL2 - XL1)
330 BL = YL1 - ML * XL1
340     'READ COORDINATES FOR RIGHT SIDE
350 READ XR1, YR1, XR2, YR2
360     'ADJUST Y COORDINATES FOR RESOLUTION DIFFERENCE
370 YR1 = YR1 * R
380 YR2 = YR2 * R
390 IF YR1 < 0 OR YR1 > YM OR YR2 < 0 OR YR2 > YM THEN 960
400     'FIND SLOPE AND Y-INTERCEPT FOR RIGHT SIDE
410 MR = (YR2 - YR1) / (XR2 - XR1)
420 BR = YR1 - MR * XR1
430     'USING APPROPRIATE SLOPES AND Y-INTERCEPTS, CALCULATE
440     'LEFT & RIGHT X VALUES AND DRAW LINE TO FILL IN AREA
450 FOR Y = YL1 TO YL2
460     XL = (Y - BL) / ML
470     XR = (Y - BR) / MR
480     DRAWLINE XL,Y TO XR,Y
490 NEXT Y
500     'MAKE SOLID BIG SAIL
510 COLOR 0,6
520 READ X1, Y1, X2, Y2
530     'ADJUST Y COORDINATES FOR RESOLUTION DIFFERENCE
540 Y1 = Y1 * R
550 Y2 = Y2 * R
560 IF Y1 < 0 OR Y1 > YM OR Y2 < 0 OR Y2 > YM THEN 960
570 DRAWLINE X1,Y1 TO X2,Y2
580 DRAWLINE X2,Y2 TO X1,Y2
590 M = (Y2 - Y1) / (X2 - X1)    'FIND M & B OF DIAGONAL SIDE
600 B = Y1 - M * X1
610     'CALCULATE POINTS ALONG TOP EDGE OF SAIL
620 FOR X = X1 TO X2 STEP -1
```

Program 3–15 (cont.)

```
630      Y = M * X + B
640      DRAWLINE X,Y TO X,Y2
650 NEXT X
660      'DRAW LITTLE FLAG
670 COLOR 3,6
680 READ X1, Y1, X2, Y2
690      'ADJUST Y COORDINATES FOR RESOLUTION DIFFERENCE
700 Y1 = Y1 * R
710 Y2 = Y2 * R
720 IF Y1 < 0 OR Y1 > YM OR Y2 < 0 OR Y2 > YM THEN 960
730 FOR Y = Y1 TO Y2 STEP 2
740      DRAWLINE X2,Y2 TO X1,Y
750 NEXT Y
760      'MAKE SHADED SMALL SAIL
770 C = 5
780 READ X1, Y1, X2, Y2
790      'ADJUST Y COORDINATES FOR RESOLUTION DIFFERENCE
800 Y1 = Y1 * R
810 Y2 = Y2 * R
820 IF Y1 < 0 OR Y1 > YM OR Y2 < 0 OR Y2 > YM THEN 960
830 DRAWLINE X1,Y1 TO X2,Y2
840 DRAWLINE X1,Y2 TO X2,Y2
850 M = (Y2 - Y1) / (X2 - X1)     'FIND M & B OF DIAGONAL SIDE
860 B = Y1 - M * X1
870 X = X1 + C
880      'CALCULATE POINTS ALONG TOP EDGE OF SAIL
890 Y = M * X + B
900 DRAWLINE X,Y TO X,Y2
910 C = C - C * .1
920 X = X + C
930      'HAVE WE REACHED THE RIGHT EDGE OF THE SAIL? IF SO, STOP
940 IF X <= X2 THEN 890
950 GOTO 1020
960 PRINT "Y COORDINATE OFF SCREEN AFTER RESOLUTION CORRECTION"
970 DATA 140,10,140,110
980 DATA 95,110,105,125,190,110,180,125
990 DATA 140,25,80,105
1000 DATA 140,10,125,20
1010 DATA 145,20,185,100
1020 END
```

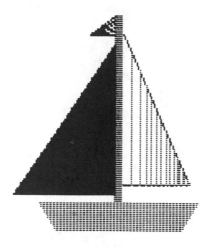

Figure 3–11 Picture output of Prog. 3–15, with shading and resolution correction.

With Prog. 3–16, we create a color pattern on the screen. The output of this program is given in Fig. 3–12. By combining line drawing, color, and the random number generator, we could produce a variety of color patterns.

Program 3–16   Random color patterns.

```
10 'PROGRAM 3-16.  COLOR PATTERNS.
20  CLEARSCREEN
30  PRINT "ENTER MAXIMUM HORIZONTAL AND VERTICAL"
40  PRINT "VALUES FOR THIS RESOLUTION MODE"
50  INPUT XM, YM
60  XC = XM / 2
70  YC = YM / 2
80  CLEARSCREEN
90  GRAPHICS
100 FOR X = 0 TO XM
110     C = INT((RND(1) * 8)
120     COLOR C,0
130     DRAWLINE XC,YC TO X,0
140 NEXT X
150 FOR Y = 0 TO YM
160     C = INT((RND(1) * 8)
170     COLOR C,0
180     DRAWLINE XC,YC TO XM,Y
190 NEXT Y
200 FOR X = XM TO 0 STEP -1
210     C = INT((RND(1) * 8)
220     COLOR C,0
230     DRAWLINE XC,YC TO X,YM
240 NEXT X
250 FOR Y = YM TO 0 STEP -1
260     C = INT((RND(1) * 8)
270     COLOR C,0
280     DRAWLINE XC,YC TO 0,Y
290 NEXT Y
300 END
```

Figure 3–12   Graphics pattern produced by Prog. 3–16.

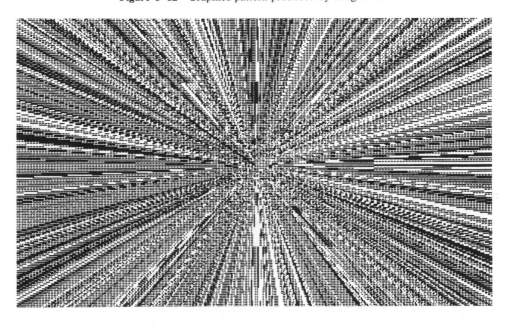

Pictures can also be constructed interactively. We could use the keyboard to interact with a program to sketch a picture as in Prog. 3–17. This program plots points in a direction specified by the keyboard input. Other input devices, such as a light pen, digitizing tablet, or paddles, could be used for interactive picture construction. These devices are discussed in more detail in Chapter 11. An interactive method for constructing a picture with straight line segments is illustrated with Prog. 3–18.

Program 3–17   Interactive sketching.

```
10 'PROGRAM 3-17. INTERACTIVELY SKETCHES PICTURES.
20  CLEARSCREEN
30  PRINT
40  PRINT "THIS PROGRAM LETS YOU SKETCH PICTURES INTERACTIVELY, USING"
50  PRINT "THE KEYBOARD TO CONSTRUCT YOUR DISPLAY.  THE PROGRAM"
60  PRINT "CONTINUOUSLY MONITORS THE KEYBOARD WAITING FOR SOME INPUT"
70  PRINT "SIGNAL.  IT DETERMINES WHAT KEY HAS BEEN PRESSED AND THEN"
80  PRINT "ADJUSTS THE X OR Y VALUE ACCORDINGLY."
90  PRINT
100 PRINT "HIT THE D KEY TO EXTEND YOUR LINE DOWNWARD"
110 PRINT "HIT THE U KEY TO EXTEND YOUR LINE UPWARD"
120 PRINT "HIT THE R KEY TO EXTEND YOUR LINE TO THE RIGHT"
130 PRINT "HIT THE L KEY TO EXTEND YOUR LINE TO THE LEFT"
140 PRINT "HIT THE S KEY TO STOP"
150 PRINT
160 PRINT "ENTER MAXIMUM HORIZONTAL AND VERTICAL"
170 PRINT "VALUES FOR THIS RESOLUTION MODE"
180 INPUT XM, YM
190 PRINT
200 PRINT "INPUT STARTING COORDINATES"
210 INPUT X, Y
220 CLEARSCREEN
230 GRAPHICS
240 IF X < 0 OR X > XM OR Y < 0 OR Y > YM THEN 330
250 POINTPLOT X,Y
260 A$ = INKEY$: IF A$ = "" THEN 260
270 IF A$ = "D" THEN Y = Y + 1: GOTO 240
280 IF A$ = "U" THEN Y = Y - 1: GOTO 240
290 IF A$ = "R" THEN X = X + 1: GOTO 240
300 IF A$ = "L" THEN X = X - 1: GOTO 240
310 IF A$ = "S" THEN 340
320 GOTO 240
330 PRINT "COORDINATE OUT OF RANGE"
340 END
```

Program 3–18   Interactive picture design using lines.

```
10 'PROGRAM 3-18.  INTERACTIVE PICTURE CONSTRUCTION.
20     'INTERACTIVELY DRAWS LINES. ALLOWS USER TO
30     'INPUT STARTING AND ENDING COORDINATES OF
40     'EACH LINE AS WELL AS DESIRED COLOR FOR THE
50     'LINE. DRAWS PICTURE AND THEN ALLOWS USER
60     'TO KEEP OR ERASE EACH LINE.
70     '********************************************
80  DIM X1(20), Y1(20), X2(20), Y2(20), C(20)
90  CLEARSCREEN
```

Program 3–18 (cont.)

```
100 PRINT "ENTER MAXIMUM HORIZONTAL AND VERTICAL"
110 PRINT "VALUES FOR THIS RESOLUTION MODE"
120 INPUT XM, YM
130 T = 1            'T IS NUMBER OF LINES
140 CLEARSCREEN
150 GRAPHICS
160 PRINT "(ENTER -1, -1 TO QUIT)"
170      'INPUT COORDINATES FOR EACH LINE
180 PRINT "ENTER FIRST POINT OF LINE";
190 INPUT X, Y
200 IF X = -1 AND Y = -1 THEN 650
210 IF X >= 0 AND X <= XM AND Y >= 0 AND Y <= YM THEN 240
220 PRINT "FIRST COORDINATE OUT OF RANGE.   TRY AGAIN."
230 GOTO 180
240 X1(T) = X
250 Y1(T) = Y
260 PRINT "ENTER SECOND POINT OF LINE";
270 INPUT X, Y
280 IF X = -1 AND Y = -1 THEN 650
290 IF X >= 0 AND X <= XM AND Y >= 0 AND Y <= YM THEN 320
300 PRINT "SECOND COORDINATE OUT OF RANGE. TRY AGAIN."
310 GOTO 260
320 X2(T) = X
330 Y2(T) = Y
340      'CHOOSE COLOR OF LINE
350 PRINT "ENTER COLOR OF LINE";
360 INPUT S
370 IF S >= 0 AND S <= 15 THEN 400
380 PRINT "COLOR CODE MUST BE IN THE RANGE 0 - 15"
390 GOTO 350
400 C(T) = S
410 GOSUB 570             'DRAW PICTURE
420      'SHOULD LINE BE KEPT OR DISCARDED?
430 PRINT "KEEP OR ERASE LAST LINE (TYPE K OR E)";
440 INPUT A$
450 IF A$ = "K" OR A$ = "E" THEN 480
460 PRINT "ENTER K OR E ONLY"
470 GOTO 430
480 IF A$ <> "K" THEN 530
490      'KEEP LINE
500 T = T + 1            'GET READY FOR NEXT LINE
510 GOTO 160
520      'DISCARD LINE
530 T = T - 1
540 GOSUB 570            'DRAW PICTURE WITHOUT LAST LINE
550 T = T + 1            'GET READY FOR NEXT LINE
560 GOTO 160
570      'DRAWS PICTURE
580 CLEARSCREEN
590 FOR K = 1 TO T
600     COLOR C(K),0    'SET FOREGROUND TO DESIRED COLOR
610     DRAWLINE X1(K),Y1(K) TO X2(K),Y2(K)
620 NEXT K
630 COLOR 1,0           'SET FOREGROUND,BACKGROUND TO WHITE ON BLACK
640 RETURN
650 GOSUB 570
660 END
```

PROGRAMMING PROJECTS

3–1. Using the PRINT statement, write a program that will clear the screen and display the word "HELLO" (or any other word you choose) in large letters at the center of the screen.

3–2. Display the following patterns, using loops and the PRINT statement.

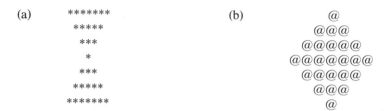

```
(a)     *******          (b)           @
         *****                        @@@
          ***                        @@@@@
           *                        @@@@@@@
          ***                        @@@@@
         *****                        @@@
        *******                        @
```

3–3. Sketch the outline of some figure or scene on graph paper. Fill in the outline with some character and display the silhouette on the screen using the PRINT statement.

3–4. Produce the silhouette for Prob. 3–3 by encoding the data, as in Prog. 3–4.

3–5. Write a program to produce the scene of Fig. 3–5, using special characters and the PRINT statement.

3–6. Draw a picture with the PRINT statement from encoded data in a DATA statement that will allow several different characters per line. Data for each print line are to include the following information: (1) the ASCII code for each character on the line, (2) the starting position of the character on each print line, and (3) the number of consecutive positions occupied by each character. The ASCII code will be used in the CHR$ function to print out that character.

3–7. Using pixel graphics, write a program that clears the screen and draws a word in the center of the screen in large letters.

3–8. Modify Prog. 3–11 so that a solid line is drawn for all values of the slope of the line.

3–9. Modify Prog. 3–11 to draw a line with given slope and Y-intercept from any specified point on the screen to the edge of the screen.

3–10. Write a program, using a point-plotting routine and the equations of (3–3), that will draw a line between two given endpoints.

3–11. Using a line-drawing routine, write a program to display a rectangle from input data that specifies the rectangle center (XC,YC) and the width (W) and height (H). The rectangle is to be drawn with sides parallel to the coordinate axes.

3–12. Modify the program of Prob. 3–11 to paint the rectangle in a specified color and to display any number of overlapping, colored rectangles.

3–13. Modify the program of Prob. 3–11 to fill in the rectangle with dots, where the spacing between dots is specified by input. Also display any specified number of overlapping, shaded rectangles.

3–14. Write a program to display the shading patterns shown in Fig. 3–10.

3–15. Lay out a figure or scene on graph paper and write a program to display the layout, using a line-drawing command and shading patterns.

3–16. Modify Prog. 3–17 to allow lines to be interactively drawn along diagonals, as well as horizontally and vertically.

3–17. Modify Prog. 3–17 to interactively draw lines with specified lengths.

Chapter 4

Simple Graphs

Data listed in tables are usually harder to interpret than when presented in graph form. Graphs allow us to grasp the information content of a set of numbers more quickly. They can clearly show the various data relationships that are often difficult to pick out in a simple listing of the numbers. We can construct graphs using either the PRINT statement or the special graphics commands introduced in Chapter 3. The PRINT statement method can be useful for some applications, but the graphics commands allow us to create more detailed and informative graphs.

4–1 FUNDAMENTALS: DATA TREND GRAPHS

An elementary type of graph is one that shows the general trend or ''shape'' of the data, with little or no explicit labeling. A trend graph for the data listed in Fig. 4–1 would provide an overall picture of sales fluctuations during the year. We could orient this graph so that sales magnitudes are represented either horizontally or vertically. Figure 4–2 shows these two graph orientations. In Fig. 4–2(a), months would be counted down from the top of the screen, and sales magnitudes would be scaled to fit across the screen, from left to right. Figure 4–2(b) illustrates the case in which months would be counted across from the left of the screen and magnitude scaled vertically.

Figure 4–1 Sample sales data table.

Month	Number of items sold	Month	Number of items sold
Jan	210	Jul	410
Feb	150	Aug	390
Mar	99	Sep	300
Apr	250	Oct	651
May	183	Nov	724
Jun	352	Dec	516

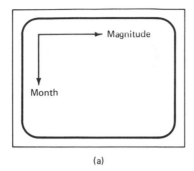
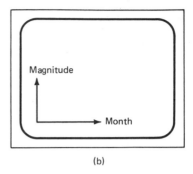

(a)   (b)

Figure 4–2 The sample sales data magnitudes of Fig. 4–1 can be graphed (a) horizontally or (b) vertically.

PRINT STATEMENT METHOD

We can construct a trend graph for the data in Fig. 4–1 by printing characters in screen positions that correspond to relative sales magnitudes. Suppose that we want the data magnitudes represented horizontally on a video screen that has 25 lines and 80 characters per line. Character positions along each print line are numbered from 1 to 80, left to right; and print lines are counted 1 to 25 from the top down. Let us represent months along every other print line from the top of the screen and use the character positions 25 through 75 along each print line to represent the sales magnitudes. The maximum sales data value will then correspond to position 75 on the twenty-first line from the top of the screen (for November), and the minimum sales data value will correspond to position 25 on line 5 (for March).

Scaling each of the data values to be in the interval 25 to 75 is accomplished with the following calculation:

$$\text{Print position along a line} = (\text{data value} - \text{minimum data value})$$

$$* \frac{\text{print position range}}{\text{data range}} \qquad (4\text{–}1)$$

$$+ \text{ minimum print position}$$

For our sample data, the data range is 724 minus 99, or 625. The print position range is 75 minus 25, or 50, and we have chosen 25 as our minimum print position. Horizontal print position for each of the data values is then found as

$$\text{Print position} = (\text{data value} - 99) * \frac{50}{625} + 25$$

or

$$P = (\text{data} - 99) * .08 + 25$$

Program 4–1 uses this equation to produce the data trend graph of Fig. 4–3. Each print position is calculated and rounded to the nearest whole number using the INT function. The program can be generalized for any set of data and display size by using calculation (4–1) with the maximum and minimum data values and print positions as input.

To produce graphs that have magnitudes represented vertically [Fig. 4–2(b)], we make two changes to Prog. 4–1. First, for each data item, we need to determine the proper print line that will correspond to the magnitude of the data

Program 4–1   Horizontal data trend graph using the PRINT statement.

```
10 'PROGRAM 4-1.  HORIZONTAL DATA TREND USING PRINT STATEMENTS
20      'SALES VALUES ARE SCALED TO LIE BETWEEN COLUMNS 25 - 75.
30      'MONTHS ARE COUNTED DOWN FROM THE TOP, USING EVERY OTHER LINE.
40   CLEARSCREEN
50   R = (75 - 25) / (724 - 99)           'R IS RATIO TO USE IN SCALING
60   FOR K = 1 TO 12
70      READ S
80      P = INT((S - 99) * R + 25 + .5)
90      PRINT TAB(P); "*"
100     PRINT
110 NEXT K
120 DATA 210,150,99,250,183,352,410,390,300,651,724,516
130 END
```

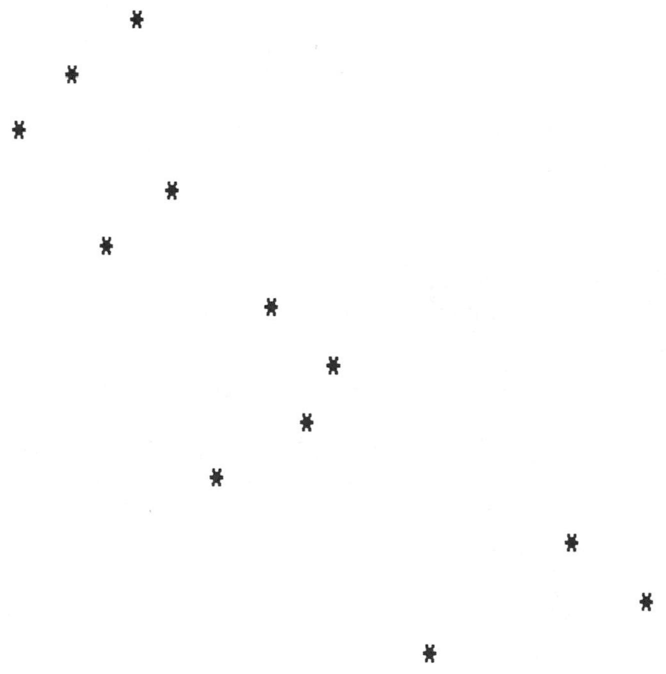

Figure 4–3   Data trend graph produced by Prog. 4–1, with the sales magnitudes of Fig. 4–1 represented horizontally.

value. Second, we select a position along this line based on which month corresponds to the data item. Each data value is represented by printing a character at this row and column position.

Special BASIC commands can be used to select line and column positions. These commands are different on different computer systems. We define the following hypothetical statement that will select line and column positions for us:

POSITION R,C — Positions the screen cursor at column C of print line (row) R. R and C may be constants or expressions. If noninteger, they are rounded.

The POSITION statement will be used to select the character position for the next PRINT statement encountered in a program. Print lines are numbered from 1 at the top of the screen to the maximum number at the bottom of the screen. Correspondence of this statement to those used with various microcomputers is listed in Appendix A.

For the data of Fig. 4–1 and a 40–column screen with 24 lines, let us now represent months in every third column starting at 3 and continuing through 36. We will plot sales magnitudes using the top 20 lines of the screen. Then the largest magnitude (724) is plotted at location 33 (for November) on the print line at the top of the screen (print line 1). Position along each print line is determined by $3*M$, where M is the number of the month (January = 1, February = 2, and so on). To scale the sales magnitudes onto the 20 print lines, we use the general rule:

$$\text{Print line number} = (\text{maximum data value} - \text{data value}) * \frac{\text{print line range}}{\text{data range}} + \text{minimum print line number} \quad (4\text{--}2)$$

In this example, we have chosen a print line range of 19 (or $20 - 1$), and a minimum print line number of 1. Figure 4–4 shows the vertical graph produced by Prog. 4–2.

Program 4–2 Vertical data trend graph using the PRINT statement.

```
10 'PROGRAM 4-2.  VERTICAL DATA TREND USING PRINT STATEMENTS
20      'SALES VALUES ARE SCALED TO PRINT BETWEEN LINES 1 - 20.
30      'MONTHS USE EVERY 3RD COLUMN STARTING AT 3 AND CONTINUING
40      'ACROSS TO 36.
50   CLEARSCREEN
60   T = (20 - 1) / (724 - 99)
70   FOR M = 1 TO 12
80      READ S
90      RO = INT((724 - S) * T + 1 + .5)
100     CO = M * 3
110     POSITION RO,CO
120     PRINT "*";
130  NEXT M
140  DATA 210,150,99,250,183,352,410,390,300,651,724,516
150  END
```

Figure 4–4 Data trend graph produced by Prog. 4–2, with the sales magnitudes of Fig. 4–1 represented vertically.

Program 4–2 can be generalized to allow a variable graph position. The desired number of lines and column positions along each line are then entered as input. Data range and the maximum data value would be determined by the program as the data are entered.

PIXEL GRAPHICS METHOD

Using special graphics commands to form data graphs means that we now think of the screen in terms of coordinates instead of print lines and character positions. Let us replot the graph produced by Prog. 4–2 using the POINTPLOT command. Suppose that we have a resolution of 128 pixels in the horizontal direction and 48 pixels vertically. We can position the graph so that we use the pixel rows from 0 to 40 and the pixel columns from 10 to 120. Months will be plotted across the screen at every tenth pixel, starting with location 10. Data magnitudes will be scaled between the vertical pixels 0 and 40, using the following calculation:

$$Y \text{ coordinate} = (\text{maximum data value} - \text{data value}) * \frac{\text{vertical pixel range}}{\text{data range}} + \text{minimum } Y \text{ coordinate} \qquad (4\text{–}3)$$

Program 4–3 produces the resulting vertical data trend graph using pixels. Plotting the data so that magnitudes are represented horizontally is a matter of interchanging the role of the X and Y coordinates, taking screen dimensions into account.

Program 4–3   Vertical data trend graph using point plotting.

```
10 'PROGRAM 4-3. VERTICAL DATA TREND USING POINTPLOT.
20      'SALES VALUES ARE SCALED TO PIXELS 0 - 40.   MONTHS
30      'USE EVERY 10TH PIXEL STARTING AT 10 AND CONTINUING
40      'ACROSS TO 120.
50  CLEARSCREEN
60  GRAPHICS
70  R = (40 - 0) / (724 - 99)     'R IS RATIO TO USE IN SCALING
80  X = 10
90  FOR K = 1 TO 12
100     READ S
110     Y = INT((724 - S) * R + .5)
120     POINTPLOT X,Y
130     X = X + 10
140 NEXT K
150 DATA 210,150,99,250,183,352,410,390,300,651,724,516
160 END
```

Line segments connecting the data points can be included when we plot graphs with pixels. Program 4–4 produces the line graph shown in Fig. 4–5.

Program 4–4   Vertical data trend graph using line drawing.

```
10 'PROGRAM 4-4. VERTICAL DATA TREND WITH CONNECTED LINES.
20      'SALES VALUES ARE SCALED TO PIXELS 0 - 40.   MONTHS
30      'USE EVERY 10TH PIXEL STARTING AT 10 AND CONTINUING
40      'ACROSS TO 120. VALUES OF CONSECUTIVE MONTHS ARE CONNECTED.
50  CLEARSCREEN
60  DIM X(12), Y(12)
70  R = (40 - 0) / (724 - 99)             'R IS RATIO TO USE IN SCALING
80  X1 = 10
90  FOR M = 1 TO 12
100     READ S
110     Y(K) = INT((724 - S) * R + .5)
120     X(K) = X1
130     X1 = X1 + 10
140 NEXT M
150 GRAPHICS
160 FOR K = 1 TO 11
170     DRAWLINE X(K),Y(K) TO X(K+1),Y(K+1)
180 NEXT K
190 DATA 210,150,99,250,183,352,410,390,300,651,724,516
200 END
```

Figure 4–5   Data trend graph produced by Prog. 4–4, with the sales magnitudes of Fig. 4–1 plotted vertically and joined with straight lines.

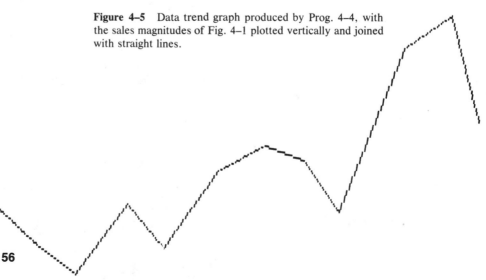

4-2 LABELED GRAPHS

The fundamental techniques of the preceding section are useful for quickly plotting simple graphs and displaying data trends. But data trend graphs convey very little quantitative information. Usually, we are interested in determining more precise information from graphs. Labeling of the data point coordinates along the coordinate axes allows us to determine more exact relationships and to interpolate between the data points.

Labeled graphs require some modification to the data scaling equations (4-1), (4-2), and (4-3). The data range in these equations now corresponds to the labeled graph range. If we plot a data set with a range from -96 to 89 in a graph labeled from -100 to 100, the data range to be used is 200 (the range of the graph). Similarly, the minimum data value would be -100, and the maximum data value would be 100.

Coordinate axes for the X and Y directions can be constructed with a series of printed plus signs or dashes, using the PRINT statement. Such a labeled graph is produced by Prog. 4-5 and is displayed in Fig. 4-6.

Program 4-5 Labeled data graph using the PRINT statement.

```
10 'PROGRAM 4-5. LABELED DATA GRAPH USING PRINT STATEMENTS.
20      'SALES VALUES ARE SCALED TO COLUMNS 12 - 76.   MONTHS USE
30      'EVERY PRINT LINE, STARTING FROM THE TOP.
40   CLEARSCREEN
50   PRINT TAB(28); "ANNUAL SALES TREND"
60   PRINT
70   PRINT TAB(12); "        1        2        3        4        5        6        7
     8"
80   PRINT TAB(12); "        O        O        O        O        O        O        O
     O"
90   PRINT TAB(12); "O        O        O        O        O        O        O        O
     O"
100 PRINT TAB(12); "+--------+--------+--------+--------+--------+--------+--------+---
    ----+"
110 R = (76 - 12) / (800 - 0)
120 LO = 10000
130 HI = 0
140 T = 0        'T IS TOTAL OF ALL DATA VALUES
150 FOR K = 1 TO 12
160     READ M$, S
170     IF S < LO THEN LO = S
180     IF S > HI THEN HI = S
190     T = T + S
200     P = INT((S-0) * R + 12 + .5)
210     PRINT M$; TAB(12); "!"; TAB(P); "*"; TAB(76); "!"
220 NEXT K
230 PRINT TAB(12); "+--------+--------+--------+--------+--------+--------+--------+---
    ----+"
240 PRINT
250 PRINT TAB(25); "MINIMUM SALES -- "; USING "###"; LO
260 PRINT TAB(25); "MAXIMUM SALES -- "; USING "###"; HI
270 PRINT
280 PRINT TAB(25); "AVERAGE SALES -- "; USING "###.#"; T/12
290 DATA "JANUARY",210,"FEBRUARY",150,"MARCH",99
300 DATA "APRIL",250,"MAY",183,"JUNE",352
310 DATA "JULY",410,"AUGUST",390,"SEPTEMBER",300
320 DATA "OCTOBER",651,"NOVEMBER",724,"DECEMBER",516
330 END
```

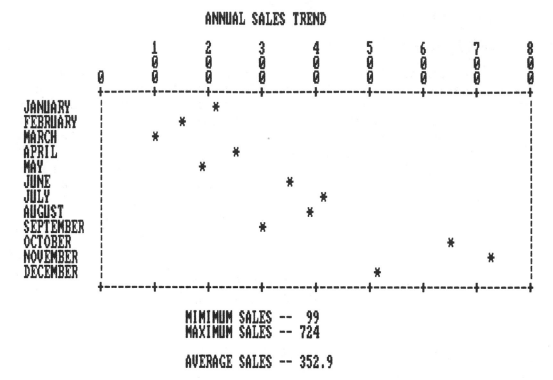

Figure 4–6 Labeled graph with coordinate axes. Output by Prog. 4–5, using the PRINT statement.

Pixel graphics offers a more flexible method for constructing coordinate axes by drawing lines. A labeled graph is produced with this method by Prog. 4–6. The resulting output is shown in Fig. 4–7.

Program 4–6 Labeled graph using line drawing.

```
10 'PROGRAM 4-6. LABELED DATA CHART WITH CONNECTING LINES USING PIXELS.
20      'ASSUME A SCREEN SIZE OF 640 x 200 PIXELS, WITH 25 PRINT
30      'LINES AND 80 CHARACTERS PER LINE. SALES VALUES
40      '(in the range of 0 - 800) ARE SCALED TO PIXELS 27-155.
50      'MONTHS USE EVERY 40 PIXELS, STARTING AT 148.
60 DIM X(12), Y(12)
70 CLEARSCREEN
80 GRAPHICS
90 PRINT
100 PRINT TAB(31); "ANNUAL SALES FIGURES"
110 DRAWLINE 128,27 TO 128,155
120 DRAWLINE 608,155 TO 608,27
130      'MAKE NOTCHES FOR SALES MAGNITUDES & CHART LINES
140 FOR Y = 27 TO 155 STEP 16
150      DRAWLINE 125,Y TO 608,Y
160 NEXT Y
170      'LABEL THE NOTCHES
180 RO = 20      'START AT ROW 20
190 FOR S = 0 TO 800 STEP 100
200      POSITION RO,13
210      PRINT USING "###"; S
```

58

Program 4-6 (cont.)

```
220     RO = RO - 2
230 NEXT S
240     'MAKE NOTCHES FOR MONTHS
250 FOR CO = 19 TO 74 STEP 5
260     POSITION 20,CO
270     PRINT "+";
280 NEXT CO
290 PRINT TAB(19);"J    F    M    A    M    J    J    A    S    O    N    D"
300 PRINT TAB(19);"A    E    A    P    A    U    U    U    E    C    O    E"
310 PRINT TAB(19);"N    B    R    R    Y    N    L    G    P    T    V    C"
320 POSITION 11,3
330 PRINT "MONTHLY"
340 POSITION 13,3
350 PRINT " SALES"
360     'DRAW CHART LINES
370 T = (155 - 27) / (800 - 0)
380 X1 = 148
390 FOR K = 1 TO 12
400     X(K) = X1
410     X1 = X1 + 40
420     READ S
430     Y(K) = INT((800 - S) * T + 27 + .5)
440 NEXT K
450 FOR K = 1 TO 11
460     DRAWLINE X(K),Y(K) TO X(K+1),Y(K+1)
470     'MAKE LINE DOUBLE THICKNESS
480     DRAWLINE X(K),Y(K)-1 TO X(K+1),Y(K+1)-1
490 NEXT K
500 DATA 210,150,99,250,183,352,410,390,300,651,724,516
510 END
```

Figure 4–7 Labeled graph with coordinate axes. Output by Prog. 4–6, using pixel graphics methods.

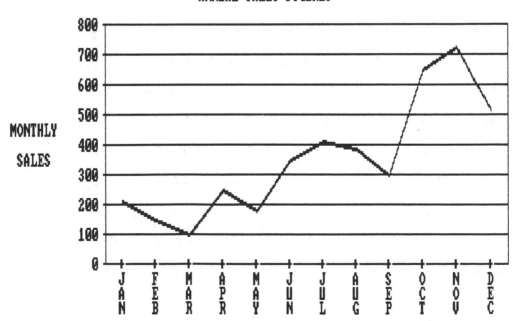

In constructing labeled graphs, we should observe the following guidelines. Labeling should be simple and to the point. Too much labeling can clutter the graph and detract from its effectiveness to convey information. For clear labeling, larger letters and numbers are more effective than small print. If possible, identifying labels should be placed on the lines or in the areas they are meant to identify instead of placing them in separate tables or legends. Divisions for the coordinate axis referencing magnitudes should be chosen in easily comprehended steps, such as multiples of 10 rather than multiples of 8. Including a zero point aids in interpretation. The divisions should be spaced and labeled with tic marks to make interpolation between data points easy. We should also construct data lines to be thicker or more intense than the coordinate axes and grid lines. These ideas were taken into consideration in the construction of the graph in Fig. 4–7.

4–3 BAR GRAPHS—COLOR AND SHADING

A useful technique for making data graphs more easily interpreted is the plotting of data magnitudes as "bars" instead of points. This technique is illustrated in Prog. 4–7, using PRINT statement methods. Figure 4–8 shows the resulting bar graph.

Program 4–7   Labeled bar graph using the PRINT statement.

```
10  'PROGRAM 4-7. LABELED BAR CHART (HORIZONTAL) USING PRINT STATEMENTS.
20      'SALES VALUES ARE SCALED TO COLUMNS 12 - 76.   MONTHS USE
30      'EVERY PRINT LINE, STARTING FROM THE TOP.
40  CLEARSCREEN
50  PRINT TAB(34); "ANNUAL SALES"
60  PRINT
70  PRINT TAB(12); "         1        2        3        4        5        6        7
    8"
80  PRINT TAB(12); "         O        O        O        O        O        O        O
    O"
90  PRINT TAB(12); "O        O        O        O        O        O        O        O
    O"
100 PRINT TAB(12); "+--------+--------+--------+--------+--------+--------+--------+---
    ----+"
110 R = (76 - 12) / (800 - 0)
120 FOR K = 1 TO 12
130     READ M$, S
140     P = INT((S - 0) * R + 12 + .5)
150     PRINT M$; TAB(12); "!";
160     FOR C = 13 TO P
170         PRINT "*";
180     NEXT C
190     PRINT TAB(76); "!"
200 NEXT K
210 PRINT TAB(12); "+--------+--------+--------+--------+--------+--------+--------+---
    ----+"
220 DATA "JANUARY",210,"FEBRUARY",150,"MARCH",99
230 DATA "APRIL",250,"MAY",183,"JUNE",352
240 DATA "JULY",410,"AUGUST",390,"SEPTEMBER",300
250 DATA "OCTOBER",651,"NOVEMBER",724,"DECEMBER",516
260 END
```

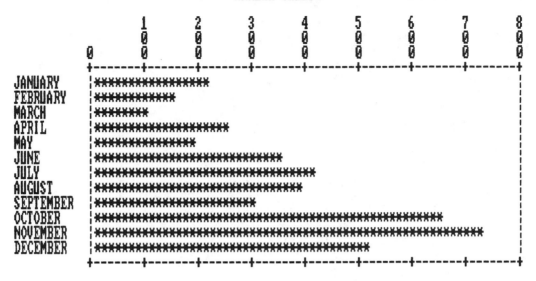

Figure 4–8 Labeled bar graph produced by Prog. 4–7, using the PRINT statement.

An example of the use of pixel graphics in the construction of bar graphs is given in Prog. 4–8. This pixel bar graph is plotted in Fig. 4–9. We have made the width of the bars in this graph greater than the spacing between the bars. This is a good practice, as narrower bars are usually less effective.

Program 4–8 Labeled bar graph using line drawing.

```
10 'PROGRAM 4-8. LABELED VERTICAL BAR CHART USING PIXEL GRAPHICS.
20      'ASSUME A SCREEN SIZE OF 640 x 200 PIXELS, WITH 25 PRINT
30      'LINES AND 80 CHARACTERS PER LINE.
40      'SALES VALUES (in the range of 0 - 800) ARE SCALED TO PIXELS
50      '27 - 155.   MONTHS USE EVERY 40 PIXELS, STARTING AT 136.
60 DIM X(12), Y(12)
70 CLEARSCREEN
80 GRAPHICS
90 PRINT
100 PRINT TAB(31); "ANNUAL SALES FIGURES"
110 DRAWLINE 128,24 TO 128,163
120 DRAWLINE 128,163 TO 608,163
130 DRAWLINE 608,163 TO 608,24
140 DRAWLINE 608,24 TO 128,24
150     'MAKE NOTCHES FOR SALES MAGNITUDES
160 FOR Y = 27 TO 155 STEP 8
170     DRAWLINE 125,Y TO 131,Y
180 NEXT Y
190     'LABEL THE NOTCHES
200 RO = 20      'START AT ROW 20
210 FOR S = 0 TO 800 STEP 100
220     POSITION RO,13
230     PRINT USING "###"; S
240     RO = RO - 2
250 NEXT S
260     'MAKE NOTCHES FOR MONTHS
270 FOR CO = 19 TO 74 STEP 5      'START AT COLUMN 19
```

Program 4-8 (cont.)

```
280      POSITION 21,CO
290      PRINT "+";
300 NEXT CO
310 PRINT TAB(19);"J    F    M    A    M    J    J    A    S    O    N    D"
320 PRINT TAB(19);"A    E    A    P    A    U    U    U    E    C    O    E"
330 PRINT TAB(19);"N    B    R    R    Y    N    L    G    P    T    V    C"
340 POSITION 11,3
350 PRINT "MONTHLY"
360 POSITION 13,3
370 PRINT " SALES"
380      'DRAW CHART BARS
390 T = (155 - 27) / (800 - 0)
400 X1 = 136      'FIRST BAR STARTS AT 136
410 FOR K = 1 TO 12
420      READ S
430      Y = INT((800 - S) * T + 27 + .5)
440      FOR X = X1 TO X1+24
450          DRAWLINE X,Y TO X,155
460      NEXT X
470      X1 = X1 + 40
480 NEXT K
490 DATA 210,150,99,250,183,352,410,390,300,651,724,516
500 END
```

Figure 4–9   Labeled bar graph produced by Prog. 4–8, using pixel graphics.

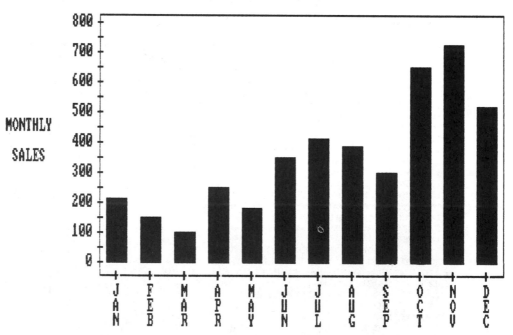

Color in bar graphs can be used to provide greater clarity or to improve the appearance of the graph. The choice of color combinations should be carefully considered, as discussed in Section 3–5. Inclusion of too many colors or clashing colors can actually decrease the effectiveness of the graph.

Various shading patterns can be used with color or black-and-white graphs. As with colors, we should select shading patterns that do not detract from the graph's effectiveness. Bizarre or clashing patterns should be avoided. If adjacent areas are to be shaded, graduating the shading used from darkest to lightest is most effective. Program 4–9 produces a graph shaded according to this scheme, as shown in Fig. 4–10.

Graphs can be constructed with the interactive methods discussed for pictures. We can sketch a graph from keyboard input, or we can trace a graph onto the screen using a light pen or digitizing tablet. Once on the screen, we can add axes and labeling to the graph and store it for future use in reports or presentations. We could also enlarge or reduce the graph, or transform it in any of the ways discussed in Part III.

Program 4–9   Shaded bar graph using pixel graphics.

```
10  'PROGRAM 4-9. SHADED BAR CHART USING PIXEL GRAPHICS.
20      'ASSUME A SCREEN SIZE OF 640 x 200 PIXELS, WITH 25
30      'PRINT LINES AND 80 CHARACTERS PER LINE. SALES
40      'VALUES (in the range of 0 - 800) ARE SCALED TO
50      'PIXELS 36 - 156.  EACH QUARTER USES 64 PIXELS
60      'ACROSS, STARTING AT 160
70      '***********************************************************
80   CLEARSCREEN
90   GRAPHICS
100  PRINT
110  PRINT TAB(28); "QUARTERLY SALES BY REGION"
120      'MAKE BOX FOR CHART
130  DRAWLINE 128,24 TO 128,162
140  DRAWLINE 128,162 TO 608,162
150  DRAWLINE 608,162 TO 608,24
160  DRAWLINE 608,24 TO 128,24
170      'MAKE NOTCHES FOR SALES MAGNITUDES
180  FOR Y = 36 TO 156 STEP 8
190      DRAWLINE 125,Y TO 131,Y
200  NEXT Y
210      'LABEL NOTCHES
220  RO = 20
230  FOR S = 0 TO 30 STEP 10
240      POSITION RO,13
250      PRINT USING "##"; S
260      RO = RO - 5
270  NEXT S
280      'LABEL QUARTERS
290  POSITION 23,1
300  PRINT TAB(22); " FIRST      SECOND      THIRD      FOURTH"
310  PRINT TAB(22); "QUARTER     QUARTER     QUARTER    QUARTER"
320  POSITION 12,3
330  PRINT "SALES"
```

Program 4-9 (cont.)

```
340 POSITION 14,2
350 PRINT "(millions)"
360      'LABEL REGIONS
370 POSITION 8,67: PRINT "WEST"
380 POSITION 13,67: PRINT "SOUTH"
390 POSITION 18,67: PRINT "MIDWEST"
400      '********* CONSTRUCT BARS, ONE FOR EACH QUARTER ***********
410 T = (156 - 36) / (30 - 0)
420 XL = 160      'FIRST QUARTER'S BAR STARTS AT 160
430 XR = XL + 64
440 FOR Q = 1 TO 4        'THERE ARE FOUR QUARTERS
450      YB = 156
460      'A IS USED TO ADJUST THE VALUE YT (THE SCALED SALES MAGNITUDE)
470      'FOR EACH REGION.  ADJUSTMENT IS NECESSARY SINCE THE SHADED
480      'AREAS REPRESENTING QUARTERLY SALES FOR EACH REGION ARE STACKED
490      'ON TOP OF EACH OTHER.
500      A = 0
510      FOR D = 1 TO 3    'FOR EACH QUARTER, THERE'S DATA FOR 3 DISTRICTS
520         READ S
530         'CONVERT TO MILLIONS
540         S = S / 10 ^ 6
550         YT = INT((30 - S) * T + 36 + .5)
560         'ADJUST YT BY THE AMOUNT A. A IS THE AREA THAT HAS ALREADY
570         'BEEN TAKEN UP BY PREVIOUS REGIONS SALES MAGNITUDES.
580         YT = YT - A
590         DRAWLINE XL,YT TO XL,YB       'DRAW BOUNDARY FOR THIS PART
600         DRAWLINE XR,YT TO XR,YB
610         DRAWLINE XL,YT TO XR,YT
620         'FILL IN UPPER RIGHT TRIANGLE OF THIS PART
630         FOR X1 = XR TO XL STEP -D * 3
640            X = X1
650            Y = YT
660            POINTPLOT X,Y
670            Y = Y + 1
680            X = X - 1
690            IF Y <= YB AND X > XL THEN 660
700         NEXT X1
710         'FILL IN LOWER LEFT TRIANGLE OF THIS PART
720         FOR Y1 = YT TO YB STEP D * 3
730            Y = Y1
740            X = XR
750            POINTPLOT X,Y
760            Y = Y + 1
770            X = X - 1
780            IF Y < = YB AND X > XL THEN 750
790         NEXT Y1
800         'FIND ADJUSTMENT THAT WILL BE NEEDED FOR NEXT DISTRICT
810         A = 156 - YT
820         YB = YT - 1
830      NEXT D
840      'ADVANCE ACROSS TO NEXT QUARTER'S COLUMN
850      XL = XL + 96
860      XR = XL + 64
870 NEXT Q
880 DATA 7000000,11000000,4000000
890 DATA 8800000,10500000,7000000
900 DATA 4000000,12000000,8500000
910 DATA 7000000,11333000,10500000
920 END
```

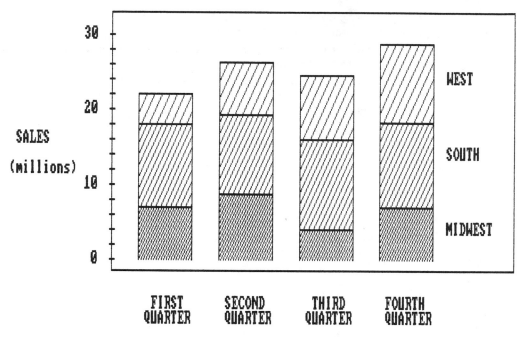

Figure 4–10 Bar graph with shading, output by Prog. 4–9.

PROGRAMMING PROJECTS

4–1. Write a program to display a trend graph with data magnitudes plotted horizontally. Use the PRINT statement and the relationship in (4–1) to position the graph on the screen. Input to the program will include the minimum and maximum print positions and the minimum and maximum data values. Data range, print position range, and print position for each data point will then be calculated. Allow for any number of data points.

4–2. Write a program to display a trend graph with data magnitudes plotted vertically, using the PRINT statement. Include a routine to determine the minimum and maximum data values from the input data set, containing an arbitrary number of data points. Input the minimum and maximum print line numbers and calculate print line range and data range. Position each data point according to the relationship (4–2).

4–3. Modify Prog. 4–7 to produce a vertical bar chart using the PRINT statement.

4–4. Write a program to plot a pixel data trend graph horizontally. Input will include minimum and maximum pixel positions. The minimum and maximum data values will be determined from the input data set. Calculations will include the data range, horizontal pixel range, and X coordinate for each data value.

4–5. Modify the program of Prob. 4–4 to join the plotted data values with straight lines to produce a "curve" plot.

4–6. Modify the program of Prob. 4–4 to include straight line segments (joining the data points) and coordinate axes with labeling.

4–7. Modify Prog. 4–9 to produce a horizontal bar graph. Allow colors and shading patterns to be selected as input.

4–8. Write a program to interactively create a graph as the data are input. That is, the points or bars will be displayed as each data point is entered. Minimum and maximum data values can be entered first, together with the pixel range.

Chapter 5

Curved Lines

Curved lines can be incorporated into our pictures and graphs using basic methods introduced in the preceding chapters. A PRINT statement approximation of the shape of a curved line is shown in Fig. 5–1. We determine character print positions along the curve path from the equation for the curve or from a plot of the curve on graph paper. Since the PRINT statement method has limited effectiveness for displaying curves, we will concentrate our discussion on pixel graphics methods.

Figure 5–1 Printed characters can be used to approximate the general shape of a curve.

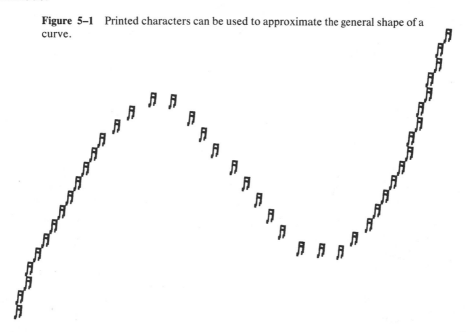

Pixel graphics provides a means for more accurate representation of curves. We can approximate a curve shape with straight line segments or closely spaced points. The higher the resolution of the system used, the better the approximation we can attain. Figure 5–2 shows the effect of varying the line-segment length on the appearance of a curve. As the number of line segments included between the arc endpoints, (X1,Y1) and (X2,Y2), is increased, the curve appears smoother. However, the more line segments we use, the more time the system will take to create the display. In some applications, such as animation, we want the display to be produced rapidly. So we might accept fewer points and line segments in the approximation of a curve in order to attain greater speed in the execution of the program.

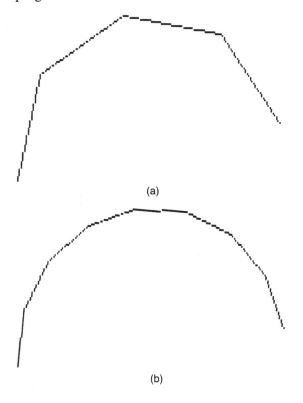

(a)

Figure 5–2 Approximating a curve: (a) with 4 straight line segments, and (b) with 8 straight line segments.

(b)

5–1 CIRCLES

The most commonly encountered curve is the circle. This curve is useful as a fundamental component in building pictures and in displaying pie charts (Section 5–4).

To plot a circle on a video screen, we need to specify its position and size (Fig. 5–3). Position is specified as the coordinates (XC,YC) of the center of the circle. Size is given by the radius R. We also need the rule or equation for determining the pixel coordinates along the required circular path. The equation of a circle may be stated in several forms. A convenient form is to determine successive coordinate positions (X,Y) along the circle boundary from the value of the angle measured clockwise from a horizontal line (Fig. 5–4). Using this method, we can calculate X and Y values from XC, YC, R, and A as

$$X = XC + R*COS(A)$$
$$Y = YC + R*SIN(A) \qquad\qquad (5\text{--}1)$$

Angle A is measured in **radians**. Radian angles vary from a value of 0 at the horizontal to 6.283185 (2 * PI) after one complete revolution back to the horizontal. These radian values correspond to the degree range 0 to 360.

Figure 5–3   Circle with radius R and center coordinates (XC,YC).

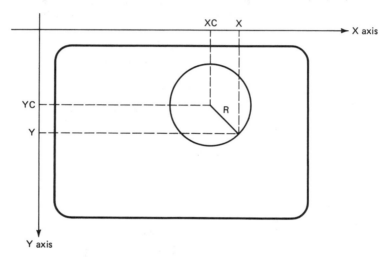

Figure 5–4   Coordinate positions (X,Y) along a circular path are determined from the radius R and values of the angle A, measured clockwise from the horizontal.

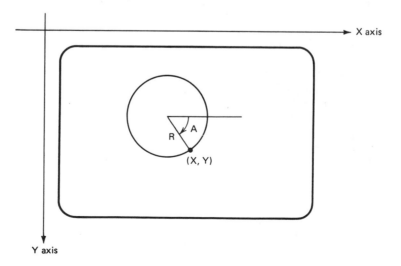

LINE-DRAWING ALGORITHM

We can devise a circle generating program, using the calculations in (5–1), to display a circle approximated with straight line segments. Program 5–1 accepts the parameters XC, YC, R, and the number of points to be plotted as input and produces output as illustrated in Fig. 5–5.

Including fewer line segments along the boundary will speed up the drawing of circles. The individual line segments may then become more noticeable, and we may have a polygon appearance instead of a circle [Fig. 5–5(a)].

We may find our circle plotted as an ellipse on systems with different resolutions in the X and Y directions. As discussed in Section 3–5, we can compensate for resolution differences by adjusting Y values. To modify our circle program for resolution differences, we multiply the term $R * SIN(A)$ by the ratio of Y resolution to X resolution.

Program 5–1   Circle generator using line drawing and angular increments.

```
10  'PROGRAM 5-1. CIRCLE GENERATOR USING LINE DRAWING
20  CLEARSCREEN
30  PRINT "ENTER MAXIMUM HORIZONTAL AND VERTICAL"
40  PRINT "VALUES FOR THIS RESOLUTION MODE"
50  INPUT XM, YM
60  PRINT
70  PRINT "ENTER COORDINATES FOR CENTER OF CIRCLE"
80  INPUT XC, YC
90  IF XC < 0 OR XC > XM OR YC < 0 OR YC > YM THEN 350
100 PRINT
110 PRINT "ENTER RADIUS OF CIRCLE"
120 INPUT R
130 IF R < 0 THEN 350
140 IF XC + R > XM OR XC - R < 0 OR YC + R > YM OR YC - R < 0 THEN 350
150 PRINT
160 PRINT "ENTER NUMBER OF POINTS TO BE PLOTTED"
170 INPUT N
180     'RE = RADIAN EQUIVALENT OF 360 DEGREES
190 RE = 360 * 3.141593 / 180
200 DA = RE / N           'DIVIDE CIRCLE INTO N PARTS
210 CLEARSCREEN
220 GRAPHICS
230 X1 = XC + R
240 Y1 = YC
250 FOR A = DA TO RE STEP DA
260     X2 = XC + R * COS(A)
270     Y2 = YC + R * SIN(A)
280     DRAWLINE X1,Y1 TO X2,Y2
290     'SAVE THE NEW ENDPOINT
300     X1 = X2
310     Y1 = Y2
320 NEXT A
330 DRAWLINE X1,Y1 TO XC+R,YC
340 GOTO 390
350 PRINT "COORDINATE OUT OF RANGE.  ENTER S TO EXIT OR R TO REPEAT."
360 INPUT C$
370 IF C$ = "S" THEN 390
380 IF C$ = "R" THEN 70
390 END
```

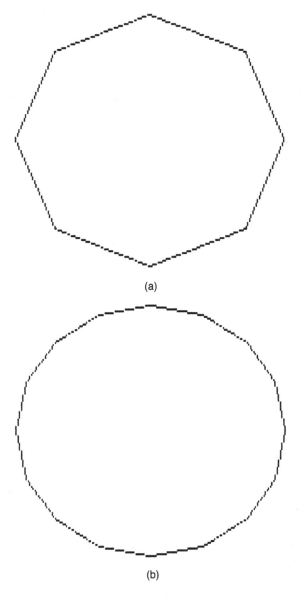

(a)

(b)

Figure 5-5 Circle approximated with (a) 8 straight line segments and (b) 16 line segments, by Prog. 5-1.

POINT–PLOTTING ALGORITHMS

Plotting pixels along the circumference and omitting the connecting line segments will also speed up circle drawing. This saves the time of drawing the line segments, and the eye tends to fill in the curved path between pixels (Fig. 5–6) if the pixels are not plotted too far apart. The more pixels we include, the better the approximation. We obtain the best possible approximation to a circle when the pixels are as close as we can plot them. In this case the pixels are plotted at the adjacent grid points closest to the desired circular path. The distance between

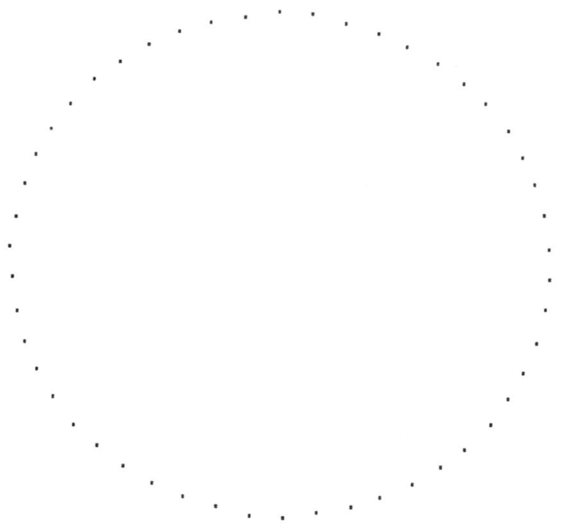

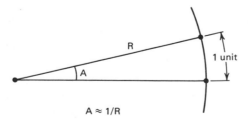

Figure 5-6 Circle plotted with pixels.

adjacent grid points is one unit in the horizontal and vertical directions. Therefore, the angular separation (in radians) of two grid points on a circle can be approximated as the inverse of the radius of the circle, as shown in Fig. 5-7. This approximation works well for most cases. A smaller angular step size will ensure that the circle contains no gaps, but then we duplicate the calculation and plotting of some of the points.

Another time-saver we can employ is to take the symmetry of the circle into account. We do not have to individually calculate every point on the curve. The top half has the same shape as the bottom half; the left half has the same shape as the right. This means that each X value on the circle corresponds to two Y values, and each Y value corresponds to two X values, as illustrated in Fig. 5-8. Taking this idea a step further, we can get four more points on the circle by interchanging all the X and Y coordinates. That is, if (X,Y) is a point on the circle, (Y,X) is also on the circle. This means that we only have to calculate the points along one-eighth of the circular path (a 45-degree segment). All of the remaining points on the full circle can be obtained from these points. Figure 5-9 shows the eight points that can be plotted on a circle by calculating only the position of the one point at coordinates (9, 2). The circle in this figure is centered at the origin of a coordinate system. For a circle centered at position (XC,YC), we add XC to all X-coordinate values, and we add YC to all Y-coordinate values. This moves the circle from the origin to the desired position. In Chapter 6 we discuss the movement of displayed objects from one location to another in greater detail.

Figure 5-7 Relation between angular separation A (in radians) of two points plotted one unit apart and the radius R of a circle passing through the two points.

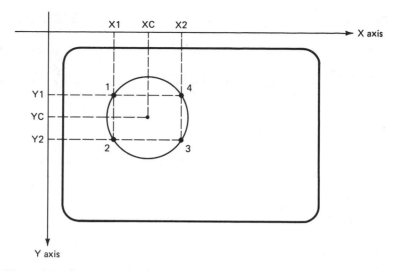

Figure 5–8 Symmetry of a circle. Points 1 and 2 have the same X value; points 1 and 4 have the same Y value.

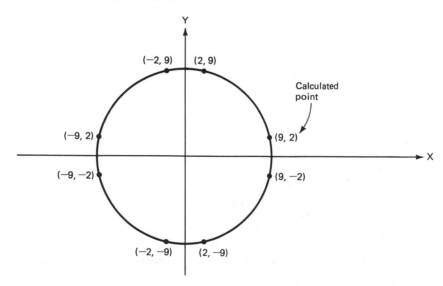

Figure 5–9 If the pixel at location (9,2) is calculated to be on a circle, then all eight points shown can be plotted.

Program 5–2 illustrates the plotting method for circle generation that calculates only the points in the interval from 0 to 45 degrees. The remaining points are obtained by symmetry. We could eliminate the four point-plotting statements at the beginning of Prog. 5–2 by starting the loop with the value A=0. This would result in fewer program statements, but each of the four initial points would then be plotted twice. Some other points may be plotted twice in any case. This occurs for larger values of R and is the result of the rounding process in the POINTPLOT command. Also, this program will leave some small gaps in those

Program 5-2   Circle generator using point plotting and angular increments.

```
10 'PROGRAM 5-2. CIRCLE GENERATOR USING POINT PLOTTING.
20      'CALCULATES POINTS ON THE CIRCLE FROM 0 TO 45 DEGREES
30      'AND PLOTS ALL SYMMETRIC POINTS.
40  CLEARSCREEN
50  PRINT "ENTER MAXIMUM HORIZONTAL AND VERTICAL"
60  PRINT "VALUES FOR THIS RESOLUTION MODE"
70  INPUT XM, YM
80  PRINT
90  PRINT "ENTER COORDINATES FOR CENTER OF CIRCLE"
100 INPUT XC, YC
110 IF XC < 0 OR XC > XM OR YC < 0 OR YC > YM THEN 440
120 PRINT
130 PRINT "ENTER RADIUS OF CIRCLE"
140 INPUT R
150 IF R < 0 THEN 440
160 IF XC + R > XM OR XC - R < 0 OR YC + R > YM OR YC - R < 0 THEN 440
170 CLEARSCREEN
180 GRAPHICS
190     'RA = RESOLUTION ADJUSTMENT
200 RA = 5/6
210 POINTPLOT XC+R,YC
220 POINTPLOT XC-R,YC
230 POINTPLOT XC,YC+R*RA
240 POINTPLOT XC,YC-R*RA
250 DA = 1 / R
260     'RE = RADIAN EQUIVALENT OF 45 DEGREES
270 RE = 45 * 3.141593 / 180
280 FOR A = DA TO RE STEP DA
290     DX = R * COS(A)
300     DY = R * SIN(A)
310     GOSUB 340
320 NEXT A
330 GOTO 480
340     'PLOT ALL SYMMETRIC POINTS
350 POINTPLOT XC+DX,YC+DY*RA
360 POINTPLOT XC-DX,YC+DY*RA
370 POINTPLOT XC+DX,YC-DY*RA
380 POINTPLOT XC-DX,YC-DY*RA
390 POINTPLOT XC+DY,YC+DX*RA
400 POINTPLOT XC-DY,YC+DX*RA
410 POINTPLOT XC+DY,YC-DX*RA
420 POINTPLOT XC-DY,YC-DX*RA
430 RETURN
440 PRINT "COORDINATE OUT OF RANGE.  ENTER S TO STOP OR R TO REPEAT."
450 INPUT C$
460 IF C$ = "S" THEN 480
470 IF C$ = "R" THEN 90
480 END
```

circles with small values of R. This is again due to the rounding of the coordinate values to be plotted.

We can make an additional improvement in the speed of the circle-drawing programs by calculating coordinates of the points to be plotted in a form that does not use the sine (SIN) and cosine (COS) functions. A method for accomplishing this is to calculate the position of pixels on the circle from the coordinates of the previously obtained pixels. If the coordinates (X1,Y1) have been calculated to be on the circle, we can obtain the next point (X2,Y2) on the circle as

$$X2 = XC + (X1 - XC) * CA + (Y1 - YC) * SA$$
$$Y2 = YC + (Y1 - YC) * CA - (X1 - XC) * SA \qquad (5\text{--}2)$$

In these equations, CA and SA are constants calculated from the fixed angular step size DA as

$$CA = COS(DA) \qquad SA = SIN(DA) \qquad (5\text{--}3)$$

The calculations in (5–2) can be used in Prog. 5–1 or Prog. 5–2 to determine pixel coordinates for points along the circle without requiring calculation of the SIN and COS functions at each step. The starting point for circle generation using (5–2) has coordinates X1 = XC, Y1 = YC + R. Calculations are terminated when X2–XC > = Y2–YC. With this method, we can plot eight points on the circle for each point calculated with the equations in (5–2). Compensation for resolution differences is accomplished here by multiplying the (Y1−YC) term in the X2 calculation by the ratio of X resolution to Y resolution and multiplying the (X1−XC) term in the Y2 calculation by the ratio of Y resolution to X resolution.

Finally, we can eliminate the roundoff necessary in the POINTPLOT operation. This is accomplished by taking unit steps in one of the coordinate directions instead of using the angular calculations. In this case we use calculations that do not involve angles and that require no rounding. These methods are more complicated to devise. They are based on the idea that we move along the X axis (or Y axis) one unit at a time, finding the nearest grid point to the desired circle. Program 5–3 is an example of this approach. We start with the pixel coordinates (XC,YC+R). At each succeeding step, one unit is added to the X coordinate. The corresponding Y coordinate for the nearest grid point to the circle is then determined. This Y value will either be the current Y coordinate or have a value one less than the current Y value. We determine which of these two points to plot by examining the value of a parameter P. This parameter gives an estimate of which point is closest to the path of the circle. When P >= 0, we subtract one from the current Y value; otherwise, we keep the current Y value. The speed of execution of Prog. 5–3 can be increased somewhat by carrying out all calcuations in integer arithmetic, if this is an option on the system. We can adjust for resolution differences by multiplying calculated values of Y in Prog. 5–3 by the ratio of Y resolution to X resolution before we enter the subroutine to plot the points.

A special circle-drawing graphics command is available with some micro-computer systems. We introduce the following into our hypothetical set of graphics commands:

CIRCLEPLOT XC,YC,R — Plots a circle of pixels with center (XC,YC)
and radius R. XC, YC, and R may be numeric constants or
expressions. If noninteger, they are rounded.

This command will be used in all subsequent programs involving circles, and we will assume that CIRCLEPLOT performs circle generation according to the method of Prog. 5–3. Correspondence of this command with the actual statements that are available on particular systems is given in Appendix A. For those systems with no circle-drawing statement, Prog. 5–3 can be implemented as a BASIC subroutine.

Program 5–3 Circle generator using point plotting and unit X increments.

```
10  'PROGRAM 5-3. CIRCLE PLOTTING USING UNIT INCREMENTS
20      'ALONG THE X AXIS AND CALCULATING THE CORRESPONDING
30      'Y VALUE.
40  CLEARSCREEN
50  PRINT "ENTER MAXIMUM HORIZONTAL AND VERTICAL"
60  PRINT "VALUES FOR THIS RESOLUTION MODE"
70  INPUT XM, YM
80  PRINT
90  PRINT "ENTER COORDINATES FOR CENTER OF CIRCLE"
100 INPUT XC, YC
110 IF XC < O OR XC > XM OR YC < O OR YC > YM THEN 530
120 PRINT
130 PRINT "ENTER RADIUS OF CIRCLE"
140 INPUT R
150 IF R < O THEN 530
160 IF XC + R > XM OR XC - R < O OR YC + R > YM OR YC - R < O THEN 530
170 CLEARSCREEN
180 GRPHICS
190     'RA = RESOLUTION ADJUSTMENT
200 RA = 5/6
210 X = O
220 Y = R
230     'VALUE OF P INDICATES WHICH
240     'VALUE OF Y IS CLOSEST TO CIRCLE
250 P = 3 - 2 * R
260 GOSUB 370
270 IF P >= O THEN 300
280 P = P + 4 * X + 6
290 GOTO 320
300 P = P + 4 * (X - Y) + 10
310 Y = Y - 1
320 X = X + 1
330 GOSUB 430
340 IF X < Y THEN 260
350 IF X = Y THEN GOSUB 370
360 GOTO 570
370     'PLOT 4 POINTS
380 POINTPLOT XC+X,YC+Y*RA
390 POINTPLOT XC-X,YC-Y*RA
400 POINTPLOT XC+Y,YC-X*RA
410 POINTPLOT XC-Y,YC+X*RA
420 RETURN
430     'PLOT ALL SYMMETRIC POINTS
440 POINTPLOT XC+X,YC+Y*RA
450 POINTPLOT XC-X,YC+Y*RA
460 POINTPLOT XC+X,YC-Y*RA
470 POINTPLOT XC-X,YC-Y*RA
480 POINTPLOT XC+Y,YC+X*RA
490 POINTPLOT XC+Y,YC-X*RA
500 POINTPLOT XC-Y,YC+X*RA
510 POINTPLOT XC-Y,YC-X*RA
520 RETURN
530 PRINT "COORDINATE OUT OF RANGE.  ENTER S TO STOP OR R TO REPEAT."
540 INPUT C$
550 IF C$ = "S" THEN 570
560 IF C$ = "R" THEN 90
570 END
```

5–2 OTHER CURVES

Although the circle is the curve most commonly encountered, various other curves have frequent applications in graphics. We can display these other curves with methods similar to those employed for circles. Pixels on the curve (or the character print positions) can be calculated from the equations for the curve and adjusted for the resolution difference, if necessary. We can then plot the pixels at convenient locations on the screen and join these pixels with line segments. For some curves, we may be able to take symmetry or other considerations into account to reduce computation.

The curves discussed in this section can be used to graphically model the applications areas cited or, in some cases, to provide a curve fit to data tables. Curve-fitting methods (such as the least-squares method) allow a smooth curve representation to be plotted for a set of tabular data points.

ELLIPTICAL CURVES

An elliptical curve may be thought of as a variation of the circle, although in the strict sense the circle is a special case of an ellipse. If we stretch a circle in one direction (say, the X direction), we have an ellipse. Equations for the ellipse can be written in the form

$$X = XC + RX * COS(A)$$
$$Y = YC + RY * SIN(A) \tag{5–4}$$

In these equations, A is the angle measured in radians from the horizontal in a clockwise direction (Fig. 5–10). If RX > RY, the ellipse is longer in the X direction. If RY > RX, the ellipse is longer in the Y direction. We have a circle for the case RX = RY.

Figure 5–10 An ellipse plotted from equations (5–4) with RX > RY and center at coordinates (XC,YC).

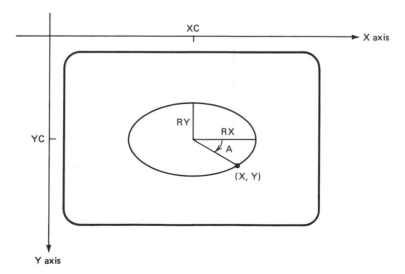

Elliptical curves are useful in many areas of graphics modeling. The orbits of satellites are elliptical. Some machine and equipment parts have elliptical shapes. A three-dimensional view of a cylinder will show the ends of the cylinder as ellipses when viewed at an angle. Having the capability to readily display ellipses increases our flexibility to produce a broad range of graphics applications displays.

The programs to generate circles in Section 5–1 can be modified to produce either circles or ellipses. We can accomplish this by replacing the equations in (5–1) with the more general equations in (5–4). Some microcomputers offer the ellipse option with the circle-generating command.

SINE CURVES

We can write the general equation for a sine curve as

$$Y = H * SIN(W * X + D) \tag{5-5}$$

Figure 5–11 shows a plot of the sine curve drawn on a conventional coordinate reference system. The frequency W specifies the number of oscillations (or cycles) of the curve for a given range of X. The parameter D specifies the displacement (shift) of the curve to the right or left. When D is set to a value of zero, we have the standard sine curve, and D = PI / 2 produces the standard cosine curve. Figure 5–12 plots three cycles of the sine curve for parameter values H = 50, W = 2 * PI / 50, D = 0 over the range X = 0 to X = 150. This curve is produced by Prog. 5–4.

Output from Prog. 5–4 is obtained by taking unit steps in the X direction, calculating the Y values, and joining the resulting points with line segments. This

Figure 5–11   Standard sine curve of equation (5–5). One cycle of the curve is plotted between X values of − D/W and (2 * PI − D)/W, while the Y coordinate oscillates between a maximum value of H and a minimum value of − H.

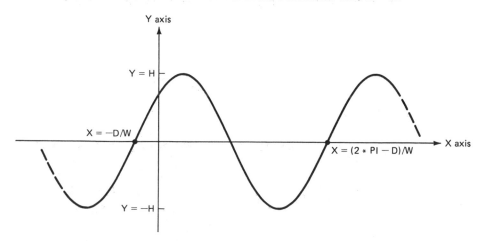

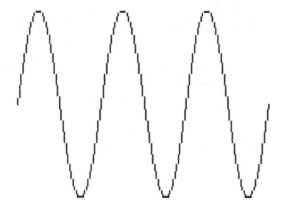

Figure 5–12 Three cycles of a sine curve plotted by Prog. 5–4.

```
10 'PROGRAM 5-4. SINE CURVES.
20   CLEARSCREEN
30   PRINT "PROGRAM GENERATES SINE CURVES USING"
40   PRINT
50   PRINT "       Y = H * SIN (W * X + D)          "
60   PRINT
70   PRINT "ENTER MAXIMUM VERTICAL VALUE FOR THIS RESOLUTION MODE"
80   INPUT YM
90   M = YM / 2
100 PRINT "ENTER HEIGHT OF THE CURVE (H), FREQUENCY (W),"
110 PRINT "DISPLACEMENT (D).   H CAN BE NO GREATER THAN ONE-HALF"
120 PRINT "THE HEIGHT OF THE SCREEN (THE VALUE OF YM)"
130 INPUT H, W, D
140 IF H > M THEN 100
150 PRINT "ENTER MINIMUM AND MAXIMUM VALUES OF X"
160 INPUT XL, XR
170 CLEARSCREEN
180 GRAPHICS
190 Y1 = H * SIN(W * XL + D)
200 IF Y1 >= 0 THEN Y1 = M - Y1
210 IF Y1 < 0 THEN Y1 = M + ABS(Y1)
220 X1 = XL
230 FOR X2 = XL TO XR
240     Y2 = H * SIN(W * X2 + D)
250     IF Y2 >= 0 THEN Y2 = M - Y2
260     IF Y2 < 0 THEN Y2 = M + ABS(Y2)
270     DRAWLINE X1,Y1 TO X2,Y2
280     'SAVE NEW POINT
290     X1 = X2
300     Y1 = Y2
310 NEXT X2
320 END
```

Program 5–4 Sine curve plotting.

program does not consider the symmetry of the function. However, every one-quarter cycle of a sine curve can be repeated from the points between X = −D / W and X = (PI / 2 − D) / W: the "first quadrant." That is, if we know that (X,Y) is a point on the sine curve in the first quadrant, then the following points are also on the curve for the first complete cycle: (PI − X,Y), (3 ∗ PI / 2 − X,−Y), (2 ∗ PI − X,−Y). These symmetry points can be plotted repeatedly through as many cycles as we wish to display without having to recompute values from equation (5–5).

Sine curves are useful in graphics applications involving repeated motion. These applications include simulating voice patterns, music, the vibrations of a spring, the bouncing of a ball, or the swing of a pendulum. In the case of a spring or ball we also have to account for friction. The amplitude of the motion decreases with each cycle. We can model this decrease in amplitude by multiplying the sine function in (5–5) by the exponential function $EXP(-K*X)$. The constant K determines the rate at which the amplitude decreases. A value of 0.1 for K will decrease the amplitude by a factor of approximately $\frac{1}{2}$ after one cycle. Both the SIN and EXP functions are available in all versions of BASIC.

POLYNOMIAL CURVES

This class of curves contains an essentially endless list of equations. These equations all have the same basic structure and include the straight line and parabola. The straight line equation can be written as

$$Y = C1*X + C2 \qquad (5-6)$$

where the constants C1 and C2 are fixed numbers that specify the slope and Y-intercept of the line. These numbers are called the coefficients of the equation. The straight line is classified as a polynomial of degree 1. Adding terms to this equation that contain higher integer powers of X produces polynomials of higher degree. A polynomial of degree 2 (a parabola) is written as

$$Y = C1*X^2 + C2*X + C3 \qquad (5-7)$$

Parabolas may be used to approximate the shape of data tables (for data trends or interpolative information) or to model the motions of objects. The path (trajectory) of a ball thrown across some distance describes a parabola. The ball rises to some maximum height, then drops back to the ground. Height is measured by the Y coordinate; horizontal distance is measured by the X coordinate. Maximum height for the ball will occur when the X coordinate has the value

$$X = -C2 / (2*C1) \qquad (5-8)$$

Figure 5–13 plots the parabolic trajectory for a set of coefficients input to Prog. 5–5. This curve is symmetric about the X value given in (5–8), so that Prog. 5–5 calculates points for only one-half the X range.

Program 5–5 outputs any given parabola, specified by coefficients C1, C2, and C3. Depending on the value of the coefficient C1, a parabola will either increase to a maximum Y value or decrease to a minimum Y value at the midpoint X value (5–8). The Y value at the midpoint will be a maximum if C1 < 0, or a minimum if C1 > 0. This program plots the parabola so that the midpoint of the curve is plotted at the middle of the top of the screen (for C1 < 0), or at the middle of the bottom of the screen (for C1 > 0).

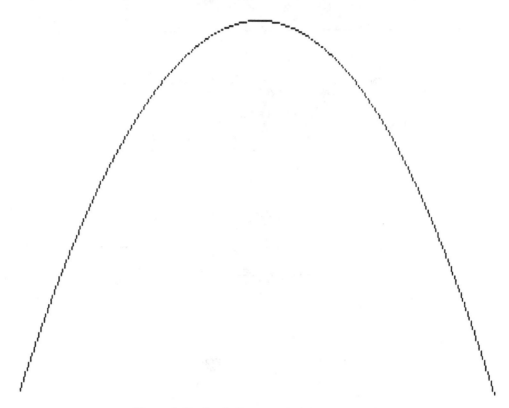

Figure 5–13 Parabolic curve plotted by Prog. 5–5.

Program 5–5 Plotting a parabola.

```
10 'PROGRAM 5-5. PARABOLIC CURVES FROM POLYNOMIAL EQUATIONS.
20      'PLOTS THE CENTER SECTION OF A PARABOLA (i.e., where the curve
30      'turns around). THE VERTEX IS CALCULATED, ADJUSTED TO LIE AT
40      'A Y VALUE OF 0 OR AT THE SCREEN MAXIMUM (DEPENDING ON THE
50      'PARTICULAR CURVE), AND PLOTTED MIDWAY ALONG THE X AXIS.
60      'Y VALUES ALONG THE LEFT HALF OF THE CURVE ARE CALCULATED (USING
70      'DECREASING VALUES OF X) AND PLOTTED, ALONG WITH THE SYMMETRIC
80      'POINT ON THE RIGHT HALF OF THE CURVE. LINES ARE DRAWN BETWEEN
90      'ADJACENT POINTS TO GIVE A CONTINUOUS CURVE.
100     '*******************************************************************
110 CLEARSCREEN
120 PRINT "THIS PROGRAM PLOTS A PARABOLIC CURVE FROM THE EQUATION"
130 PRINT
140 PRINT "    Y = C1 * X ^ 2 + C2 * X + C3"
150 PRINT
160 PRINT "IF C1 IS LESS THAN 0, THE CURVE WILL GO UP TO SOME MAXIMUM"
170 PRINT "POINT AND THEN COME DOWN. IF C IS GREATER THAN 0, THE CURVE"
180 PRINT "WILL GO DOWN TO SOME MINIMUM POINT AND THEN COME BACK UP."
190 PRINT
200 PRINT "ENTER VALUES FOR C1, C2, C3. (C1 may not be zero)"
210 INPUT C(1), C(2), C(3)
220 IF C(1) = 0 PRINT "0 entered for C1": GOTO 200
230 PRINT
240 PRINT "ENTER MAXIMUM HORIZONTAL AND VERTICAL VALUES"
250 PRINT "FOR THIS RESOLUTION MODE"
260 INPUT XM, YM
```

Program 5-5 (cont.)

```
270 XC = INT(XM / 2)              'XC IS MIDWAY ACROSS SCREEN
280    'FIND X VALUE OF VERTEX
290 X = -C(2) / (2 * C(1))
300    'FIND Y VALUE OF VERTEX
310 YV = C(1) * X * X + C(2) * X + C(3)
320    'IS VERTEX THE MINIMUM OR MAXIMUM VALUE FOR THIS CURVE?
330    'IF MINIMUM, Y1 = YM. IF MAXIMUM, Y1 = O.
340 IF C(1) < 0 THEN Y1 = O
350 IF C(1) > 0 THEN Y1 = YM
360 XL1 = XC
370 XR1 = XC
380 XL2 = XC
390 XR2 = XC
400 CLEARSCREEN
410 GRAPHICS
420    'CALCULATE POINTS TO THE LEFT OF THE VERTEX
430 X = X  - 1
440    'WITH THIS NEW X VALUE, SOLVE THE POLYNOMIAL EQUATION FOR Y.
450    'EVALUATE THE POLYNOMIAL USING THE FOLLOWING LOOP. CAN BE USED
460    'TO SOLVE POLYNOMIALS OF ANY DEGREE.
470 N = 3
480 Y = C(1)
490 FOR K = 2 TO N
500    Y = Y * X + C(K)
510 NEXT K
520    'ADJUST THE VALUE OF Y BEFORE PLOTTING ON SCREEN
530 IF C(1) < 0 THEN Y2 = YV - Y
540 IF C(1) > 0 THEN Y2 = YM - (Y - YV)
550 XL2 = XL2 - 1
560 XR2 = XR2 + 1
570    'ARE ALL POINTS STILL ON THE SCREEN?
580 IF Y2 < 0 OR Y2 > YM OR XL2 < 0 OR XL2 > XM THEN 650
590 DRAWLINE XL1,Y1 TO XL2,Y2
600 DRAWLINE XR1,Y1 TO XR2,Y2
610 Y1 = Y2
620 XL1 = XL2
630 XR1 = XR2
640 GOTO 430
650 END
```

Higher-order polynomial curves can be plotted by expanding Prog. 5–5 to accept the degree and coefficients required for these equations:

$$Y = C(1)*X^N + C(2)*X^{(N-1)} + \ldots + C(N-1)*X + C(N) \quad (5-9)$$

Polynomial equations of various degree N can be useful for data fitting. For a table of data points, we may be able to draw a smooth curve through the data with, say, a third- or fourth-degree polynomial. Plotting a polynomial may require some experimenting with the data range. We might first list the points on the curve for the X range of interest, then determine an appropriate scaling to produce the curve in a certain area of the screen.

NORMAL CURVES

The normal, or Gaussian, curve (sometimes called the bell curve) has the equation

$$Y = EXP(-0.5*(X - M)^\wedge 2 / S^\wedge 2) / (S*SQR(2*PI))\qquad(5\text{--}10)$$

where Y is the probability of having a particular X value in a data set. M is the average (or mean) for all the X values, and S is the standard deviation.

Equation (5–10) is an example of a probability distribution. There are many other probability distribution curves, but the normal curve is of primary importance because many commonly occurring phenomena approximately follow this probability distribution. The probability that an employee in a large organization will have a specified salary X can be estimated as Y in this equation. The value X = M is the mean salary of all the employees, and the value of S provides a measure of the spread of salaries above and below this mean. Approximately 68 percent of the employees will have salaries within 1 standard deviation of the mean (M − S to M + S), and approximately 99 percent will have salaries within the range of 3 standard deviations of the mean (M − 3*S to M + 3*S). Other applications of the normal curve include displaying the probability distribution of the lifetimes of electrical or mechanical parts, variations in sizes of manufactured items, height of U.S. women in a given age range, rate of return on stocks, or daily temperature variations in some city.

Figure 5–14 illustrates the shape of the normal probability curve. This figure was obtained from Prog. 5–6, which accepts a data set as input, calculates M and S, and plots the normal curve. Values for M and S are calculated by standard equations. Normal curves are symmetrical about the mean (X = M), so that Prog. 5–6 need only compute points over one-half of the curve. The curve is centered on the screen with Y values scaled between 50 and 150 over 4 standard deviations.

Figure 5–14   Normal probability curve plotted with M = 51.8 and S = 29.2 by Prog. 5–6.

Program 5-6 Plotting the normal curve.

```
10  'PROGRAM 5-6. PLOTS NORMAL CURVE DERIVED FROM SAMPLE DATA (UP TO
20     '500 VALUES). CURVE IS CENTERED ACROSS X AXIS, AND SCALED TO
30     'LIE BETWEEN Y VALUES OF 50 AND 150. POINTS ALONG LEFT SIDE
40     'OF CURVE ARE CALCULATED AND PLOTTED. SYMMETRIC POINTS ARE
50     'PLOTTED ON RIGHT SIDE OF CURVE.
60     '**********************************************************
70  CLEARSCREEN
80  DIM D(500)
90  PI = 3.14159
100 PRINT "ENTER MAXIMUM HORIZONTAL VALUE FOR THIS RESOLUTION MODE"
110 INPUT XM
120 XC = XM / 2        'XC IS CENTER OF X-AXIS
130 PRINT "ENTER THE NUMBER OF SAMPLE VALUES"
140 INPUT N
150     'FIND THE AVERAGE
160 PRINT "ENTER THE VALUES ONE AT A TIME"
170 T = 0
180 FOR K = 1 TO N
190     INPUT D(K)
200     T = T + D(K)
210 NEXT K
220 M = T / N             'M IS THE MEAN OF DATA VALUES
230     'CALCULATE THE STANDARD DEVIATION
240 T = 0
250 FOR K = 1 TO N
260     T = T + (D(K) - M) ^ 2
270 NEXT K
280 V = T / N              'V IS VARIANCE
290 SD = V ^ .5           'SD IS STANDARD DEVIATION
300     'FIND CENTER POINT (MAXIMUM) OF CURVE
310     'Y IS AT ITS MAXIMUM WHEN X = M. ARGUMENT
320     'FOR EXP IS 0 AND EXP(0) = 1
330 X = M
340 YV = 1 / (SD * SQR(2 * PI))
350     'THE RANGE OF CURVE POINTS (0 - YV) IS SCALED TO
360     '50 - 150 ALONG THE Y-AXIS
370 YS = (150 - 50) / (YV - 0)
380     'AND SCALED TO 0 - XM ALONG THE X AXIS
390 XS = (XM - 0) / (8 * SD)
400 XL1 = XC
410 XR1 = XC
420 Y1 = 50
430 CP = SD * SQR(2 * PI)        'CALCULATE CONSTANT PART OF EQUATION
440     'CALCULATE POINTS ALONG LEFT SIDE OF CURVE. PLOT BOTH SIDES.
450 CLEARSCREEN
460 GRAPHICS
470 FOR X = M-1 TO M-4*SD STEP -1
480     Y = EXP(-.5 * (X - M) ^ 2 / V) / CP
490     'ADJUST Y TO LIE BETWEEN 50 - 150
500     Y2 = (YV - Y) * YS + 50
510     'ADJUST X TO LIE BETWEEN 0 - XM
520     XL2 = XC - ((M - X) * XS)
530     XR2 = XC + ((M - X) * XS)
540     DRAWLINE XL1,Y1 TO XL2,Y2
550     DRAWLINE XR1,Y1 TO XR2,Y2
560     'SAVE THESE POINTS
570     XL1 = XL2
580     XR1 = XR2
590     Y1 = Y2
600 NEXT X
610 END
```

We have surveyed, in this section, the curves most widely used. There are many other curves that can be useful in a particular graphics application. Bezier and B-spline curves are useful in displaying three-dimensional surfaces, as for automobile and aircraft body design. Legendre and Bessel functions can be used in modeling physical systems, such as atomic and molecular structure, temperature distributions, or gravitational fields. The Poisson and hypergeometric probability distributions are useful for modeling statistical applications. These models include the simulation of customer lines with different numbers of tellers at a bank, or graphing various alternative selections of project teams from a group of employees.

5–3 PICTURES WITH CURVES

Programs in this section provide picture-drawing examples using curves. With Prog. 5–7, we produce the picture of Fig. 5–15, drawn with short straight-line segments from a graph paper layout. Figure 5–16 shows a fire truck containing circles, a spiral, and a normal curve, drawn by Prog. 5–8. Program 5–9 outputs graphics "art" using curves. This program demonstrates some of the many possibilities using trigonometric functions. The resulting patterns are shown in Fig. 5–17.

Program 5–7   Dinosaur drawn with curves approximated by short line segments.

```
10  'PROGRAM 5-7. DINOSAUR USING SHORT LINE SEGMENTS TO GIVE CURVES.
20      'POINTS WERE DERIVED FROM GRAPH PAPER DRAWING. ASSUME SCREEN
30      'SIZE OF 640 x 200 PIXELS.
40  CLEARSCREEN
50  GRAPHICS
60  R = 5/6
70      'DRAW ONE PART OF THE PICTURE AT A TIME
80  READ N       'READ HOW MANY POINTS IN THIS PART
90  IF N = 0 THEN 420
100 READ X1, Y1
110 Y1 = Y1 * R              'ADJUST Y VALUES FOR RESOLUTION
120 FOR P = 2 TO N
130     READ X2,Y2
140     Y2 = Y2 * R
150     DRAWLINE X1,Y1 TO X2,Y2
160     X1 = X2
170     Y1 = Y2
180 NEXT P
190 GOTO 80
200     'data for main part of body
210 DATA 38,223,60,180,71,173,65,174,63,179,64,180,62,185,62,187,60
220 DATA 192,60,194,57,200,57,202,55,183,55,182,59,172,58
230 DATA 171,62,165,57,170,50,220,31,233,31,245,40,260,60,290,67,315,72
240 DATA 345,80,360,87,380,105,400,127,425,145,452,155,502,164,450,164
250 DATA 434,162,415,158,395,153,362,138,323,132,283,125
260     'data for large leg
270 DATA 16,289,92,250,120,250,135,260,157,233,163,247,163,240,165
280 DATA 257,164,256,166,272,159,270,153,278,140,280,120,285,120
290 DATA 310,120,330,112
300     'data for small leg
```

Program 5-7 (cont.)

```
310 DATA 11,295,127,303,158,278,162,288,162,282,163
320 DATA 291,164,283,165,315,162,315,157,325,137,323,132
330     'data for arm
340 DATA 11,238,77,220,87,192,99,192,102,195,100
350 DATA 198,102,200,100,203,102,205,98,218,96,255,83
360     'data to fill in body
370 DATA 3,258,114,245,105,228,93
380 DATA 3,222,86,215,77,210,65
390     'data for eye
400 DATA 4,220,42,210,45,215,40,220,42
410 DATA 0
420 END
```

Figure 5-15 Picture drawn from a graph paper layout by Prog. 5-7, using straight line segments to approximate curves.

Program 5-8 Fire truck drawn with curve equations.

```
10 'PROGRAM 5-8. FIRE TRUCK WITH STRAIGHT LINES,
20    'CIRCLES, ARCS, BELL CURVE, AND SPIRAL.
30    '*********************** DRAW OUTLINE ********************
40  CLEARSCREEN
50  GRAPHICS
60  READ X1, Y1
70  FOR K = 1 TO 8
80      READ X2, Y2
90      DRAWLINE X1,Y1 TO X2,Y2
100     X1 = X2
110     Y1 = Y2
120 NEXT K
130     'DOOR AND WINDOW
140 FOR M = 1 TO 2
150     READ N
160     READ X1, Y1
170     FOR K = 1 TO N
180         READ X2, Y2
190         DRAWLINE X1,Y1 TO X2,Y2
200         X1 = X2
210         Y1 = Y2
220     NEXT K
230 NEXT M
240     '*********** FINISH BODY, LADDER, BELL STAND ***********
250 FOR L = 1 TO 13
```

Program 5-8 (cont.)

```
260     'READ COORDINATES, THICKNESS, DIRECTION OF THICKNESS
270     READ X1, Y1, X2, Y2, T, D$
280     IF D$ = "X" THEN 350
290     'MAKE THICK IN Y DIRECTION
300     FOR K = 0 TO T - 1
310         DRAWLINE X1,Y1+K TO X2,Y2+K
320     NEXT K
330     GOTO 390
340     'MAKE THICK IN X DIRECTION
350     FOR K = 0 TO T - 1
360         DRAWLINE X1+K,Y1 TO X2+K,Y2
370     NEXT K
380     Y1 = Y2
390 NEXT L
400     '*********************** MAKE WHEELWELLS ******************
410 FOR K = 1 TO 2
420     READ XC, YC, R
430     FOR A = 3.14159 TO 6.28318 STEP 1/R
440         XW = XC + R * COS(A)
450         YW = YC + R * SIN(A)
460         POINTPLOT XW,YW
470     NEXT A
480     COLOR 0,0
490     DRAWLINE XC-R+1,YC TO XC+R-1,YC           'ERASE BODY LINE
500     COLOR 1,0
510 NEXT K
520     '****************** MAKE TIRES AND HUBCAPS ***************
530 FOR K = 1 TO 4
540     READ X,Y,R
550     CIRCLEPLOT X,Y,R
560 NEXT K
570     '************************* MAKE HOSE *********************
580 R = 1
590 A = .01
600 READ XC, YC
610 X1 = XC + R * COS(-A) * 1.4          'STRETCH SPIRAL IN X DIRECTION
620 Y1 = YC + R * SIN(-A)
630 A = A + .1
640 R = R + .13
650 X2 = XC + R * COS(-A) * 1.4
660 Y2 = YC + R * SIN(-A)
670 DRAWLINE X1,Y1 TO X2,Y2
680 X1 = X2      'SAVE CURRENT POINTS
690 Y1 = Y2
700 IF R < 22 THEN 630
710     '********************** LABELS **********************
720 POSITION 15,33
730 PRINT "NO. 9"
740 POSITION 19,27
750 PRINT "BMFD"
760     '********************** MAKE BELL ********************
770 READ M, SD
780 CP = SD * SQR(6.28318)
790 YV = 1 / CP
800 RY = (90-60) / YV
810 RX = (186-159) / (3.4*SD)
820 XL1 = 166
830 XR1 = 166
840 Y1 = 60
850 FOR X = M-1 TO M-1.7*SD STEP -1
860     Y = EXP(-.5 * (X - M) ^ 2 / (SD * SD)) / CP
```

Program 5-8 (cont.)

```
870      Y2 = (YV - Y) * RY + 60
880      XL2 = 166 - ((M - X) * RX)
890      XR2 = 166 + (M - X) * RX
900      DRAWLINE XL1,Y1 TO XL2,Y2
910      DRAWLINE XR1,Y1 TO XR2,Y2
920      XL1 = XL2
930      XR1 = XR2
940      Y1 = Y2
950 NEXT X
960 DRAWLINE XL1,Y1 TO XR1,Y1
970 CIRCLEPLOT 166,Y1+2,3        'BELL CLAPPER
980      '***************************************************************
990 DATA 12,164,313,164,295,100,251,100,237,60,194,60,194,92,27,92,27,164
1000 DATA 5,201,68,201,156,245,156,245,100,233,68,201,68
1010 DATA 4,205,73,205,100,240,100,230,73,204,73
1020 DATA 194,60,194,164,1,X,34,100,187,100,3,Y,34,124,187,124,3,Y
1030 DATA 55,103,55,124,3,X,76,103,76,124,3,X,98,103,98,124,3,X
1040 DATA 120,103,120,124,3,X,142,103,142,124,3,X,163,103,163,124,3,X
1050 DATA 187,92,187,68,2,X,187,68,165,52,2,Y,165,52,165,60,2,X
1060 DATA 125,153,126,159,3,X
1070 DATA 66,164,27,276,164,25,66,164,22,276,164,22,66,164,8,276,164,8
1080 DATA 147,147
1090 DATA 1,7
1100 END
```

Figure 5–16   Picture drawn by Prog. 5–8, using curve equations.

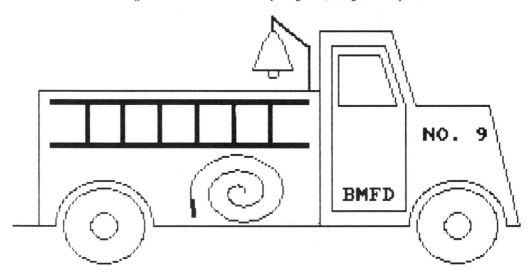

Program 5–9   Art patterns with curves.

```
10 'PROGRAM 5-9. CURVE PATTERNS
20    CLEARSCREEN
30    XM = 319
40    YM = 199
50    GRAPHICS
60      '********************** CLOVER *********************************
70    XC = 160      'CENTER ON SCREEN
80    YC = 100
90    FOR R = 20 TO 50 STEP 15
```

Program 5-9 (cont.)

```
100      X1 = XC
110      Y1 = YC
120      FOR A = 0 TO 6.28318 STEP 1/R
130          R1 = R * SIN(2 * A)
140          X2 = XC + R1 * COS(A)
150          Y2 = YC + R1 * SIN(A)
160          DRAWLINE X1,Y1 TO X2,Y2
170          X1 = X2        'SAVE CURRENT POINTS
180          Y1 = Y2
190      NEXT A
200 NEXT R
210      '
220      '**************** SIDE FIGURES  (CARDIOIDS) ******************
230 XL = 60        'CENTER POINT OF LEFT FIGURE IS XL,YC
240 YC = 100
250 XR = 260      'CENTER POINT OF RIGHT FIGURE IS XR,YC
260 FOR R = 15 TO 25 STEP 10
270      XL1 = XL
280      XR1 = XR
290      YL1 = YC
300      YL3 = YC
310      YR1 = YC
320      YR3 = YC
330      FOR A = 0 TO 3.14159 STEP 1/R
340          R1 = R * SIN(A / 2)
350          DX = R1 * COS(A)
360          DY = R1 * SIN(A)
370          XL2 = XL + DX
380          YL2 = YC + DY
390          YL4 = YC - DY
400          DRAWLINE XL1,YL1 TO XL2,YL2
410          DRAWLINE XL1,YL3 TO XL2,YL4
420          XR2 = XR - DX
430          YR2 = YC + DY
440          YR4 = YC - DY
450          DRAWLINE XR1,YR1 TO XR2,YR2
460          DRAWLINE XR1,YR3 TO XR2,YR4
470          XL1 = XL2
480          YL1 = YL2
490          YL3 = YL4
500          XR1 = XR2
510          YR1 = YR2
520          YR3 = YR4
530      NEXT A
540 NEXT R
550      '
560      '********************** FLOWER PATTERNS *********************
570 READ XC,YC,R,P       'CENTER, RADIUS, NUMBER OF PETALS
580 IF XC = 0 THEN 820
590 GOSUB 620
600 GOTO 570
610 GOTO 820
620 '######################### MAKE FLOWER PATTERNS ##################
630      X1 = XC + R
640      Y1 = YC
650      FOR A = 0 TO 6.28318 STEP 1/R
660          R1 = R * COS(P * A)
670          X2 = XC + R1 * COS(A)
680          Y2 = YC + R1 * SIN(A)
690          DRAWLINE X1,Y1 TO X2,Y2
700          X1 = X2
710          Y1 = Y2
```

Program 5-9 (cont.)

```
720      NEXT A
730 RETURN
740 '###############################################################
750 DATA 200,30,15,7
760 DATA 100,170,15,6
770 DATA 60,25,15,8
780 DATA 40,150,14,5
790 DATA 230,169,20,8
800 DATA 230,169,30,4
810 DATA 0,0,0,0,0,0,0
820 END
```

Figure 5–17   Graphics art patterns produced by Prog. 5–9.

5–4 GRAPHS AND PIE CHARTS

Curves are useful for many types of graphs and charts. The programs in this section illustrate graphing techniques using curves.

GRAPHS

We can display graphs using the points given in data tables or using points calculated from equations. To graph a table of data values, we can plot the points and connect them with straight line segments or we could use a curve-fitting method. Curves can be drawn to fit a data set with an analytic technique (such as the least-squares method). We could use an interactive method that sketches a curve from keyboard instructions or light-pen input. To graph an equation, we calculate coordinates from the equation and either plot closely spaced points or straight line segments connecting the points.

    An example of plotting any specified curve equation is given by Prog. 5–10. Graph dimensions for the selected curve are input to the program. Figure 5–18 plots the output of Prog. 5–10 for a third-degree polynomial.

Program 5–10 General graph plotting using any input equation.

```
10 'PROGRAM 5-10. PLOTS ANY EQUATION.
20     'ALLOWS USER TO TYPE IN EQUATION AT LINE 450 AND TO ENTER
30     'MINIMUM AND MAXIMUM X AND Y VALUES FOR WHICH THE EQUATION
40     'IS TO BE PLOTTED. PROGRAM DRAWS A GRID USING PIXELS 74-574
50     'ON THE X-AXIS AND 12-188 ON THE Y-AXIS.
60     '**************************************************************
70 CLEARSCREEN
80 PRINT "DO YOU WANT INSTRUCTIONS? (TYPE Y OR N)"
90 INPUT I$
100 IF I$ = "N" THEN 220
110 PRINT "THIS PROGRAM DISPLAYS THE GRAPH OF ANY EQUATION"
120 PRINT "DRAWN ON A GRID ON THE SCREEN. THE EQUATION"
130 PRINT "MUST BE ENTERED AT LINE 450. YOUR EQUATION MUST"
140 PRINT "USE VARIABLE Y AS THE DEPENDENT VARIABLE AND X AS"
150 PRINT "THE INDEPENDENT VARIABLE (E.G., Y = 6 * X + 20)."
160 PRINT "ONCE YOUR EQUATION HAS BEEN ENTERED AND YOU TYPE"
170 PRINT "RUN, YOU WILL BE ASKED TO SPECIFY THE MINIMUM AND"
180 PRINT "MAXIMUM X COORDINATES FOR WHICH YOU WANT THE"
190 PRINT "EQUATION PLOTTED, AS WELL AS THE MINIMUM AND"
200 PRINT "MAXIMUM Y VALUES THAT SHOULD APPEAR ON THE GRID."
210 PRINT
220 PRINT "DOES LINE 450 CONTAIN YOUR EQUATION? (TYPE Y OR N)"
230 INPUT E$
240 IF E$ = "Y" THEN 300
250 IF I$ = "N" THEN 780
260 PRINT
270 PRINT "TYPE LINE NUMBER 450 FOLLOWED BY YOUR EQUATION."
280 PRINT "HIT RETURN AND TYPE RUN."
290 GOTO 780
300     'GRAPHS EQUATION ON A GRID
310 PRINT
320 PRINT "ENTER MINIMUM AND MAXIMUM X VALUES FOR WHICH"
330 PRINT "THE EQUATION SHOULD BE PLOTTED."
340 INPUT XL, XR
350 PRINT
360 PRINT "ENTER THE MINIMUM AND MAXIMUM Y VALUES THAT SHOULD"
370 PRINT "APPEAR ON THE GRID."
380 INPUT YB, YT
390 GOSUB 520        'DRAW GRID
400     'DRAW EQUATION
410 XA = (564 - 84) / XD
420 YA = (180 - 20) / YD
430 FOR XG = 84 TO 564
440     X = XL + (XG - 84) / 484 * XD
450     Y = X ^ 3 - 27 * X
460     YG = 180 - (Y - YB) * YA
470     IF YG < 20 OR YG > 180 THEN 490
480     POINTPLOT XG,YG
490 NEXT XG
500 POSITION 1,1
```

Program 5-10 (cont.)

```
510 GOTO 780
520       'DRAWS GRID WITH LABELS
530 CLEARSCREEN
540 GRAPHICS
550 FOR Y = 20 TO 180 STEP 32
560       DRAWLINE 74,Y TO 574,Y
570 NEXT Y
580 FOR X = 84 TO 564 STEP 96
590       DRAWLINE X,12 TO X,188
600 NEXT X
610 XD = XR - XL
620 YD = YT - YB
630 R = 23
640 FOR K = 0 TO 5
650       POSITION R,1
660       S = YB + YD * K / 5
670       PRINT USING "####.##";S
680       R = R - 4
690 NEXT K
700 C = 7
710 FOR K = 0 TO 5
720       POSITION 25,C
730       S = XL + XD * K / 5
740       PRINT USING "####.##";S;
750       C = C + 12
760 NEXT K
770 RETURN
780 END
```

Figure 5-18   Graph of the function $X \wedge 3 - 27 * X$, output by Prog. 5–10.

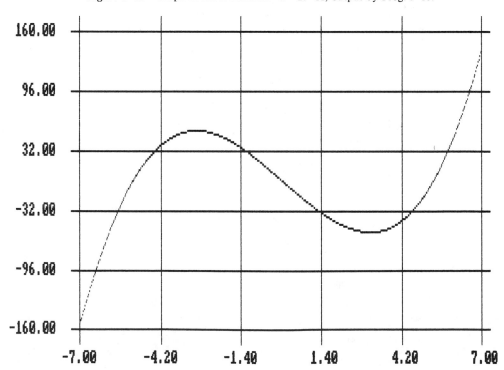

PIE CHARTS

A circle-drawing algorithm is the main ingredient in a program to make pie charts. Program 5–11 illustrates this application. Input to the program includes the name and relative size (data value) for each division of the chart. Positioning of a division name on the chart is accomplished by locating the angle corresponding to the centerline for the appropriate sector. If the sector is on the right side of the pie chart, the name starts on this bisecting line 4 units beyond the circumference. If the sector is on the left, the name ends on the bisecting line. We locate the label starting positions by converting pixel coordinates to character print positions. This is done by dividing the X coordinate by the number of horizontal pixels in a character and by dividing the Y coordinate by the number of vertical characters in a pixel. Figure 5–19 shows a pie chart produced by Prog. 5–11.

To be effective, pie charts should be drawn with no more than five or six slices. Shading and color selections for pie charts are similar to those for bar graphs. Shading patterns should be simple and graduated from dark to light around the chart. Labels should be on or close to the areas they are meant to identify.

The kind of graph or chart we choose for displaying data information can have a great influence on the effectiveness of the presentation. Pie charts are best used to convey information about percentages. We could also use a bar chart for percentages, with each bar divided into percentage sections. Line graphs and bar charts are good choices for conveying information about data quantities, such as sales amounts. We can graph sales amounts over time or relative to some other parameter, such as sales region. In general, either the horizontal or vertical axis could be chosen for sales regions, but time is usually best represented on the horizontal axis. More complex data relationships may be graphed by including more than one curve in a graph, overlapping the bars of a bar graph, or using a three-dimensional graph.

Program 5–11 Pie chart.

```
10 'PROGRAM 5-11. LABELED PIE CHART.
20  CLEARSCREEN
30  DIM N$(8), V(8)
40  PRINT "ENTER MAXIMUM HORIZONTAL AND VERTICAL"
50  PRINT "VALUES FOR THIS RESOLUTION MODE"
60  INPUT XM, YM
70  PRINT "ENTER NUMBER OF CHARACTERS THAT CAN BE"
80  PRINT "PRINTED ACROSS SCREEN IN THIS
90  PRINT "RESOLUTION MODE"
100 INPUT C1
110 PC = XM / C1        'PC IS PIXELS PER CHARACTER HORIZONTALLY
120 PRINT "ENTER NUMBER OF PRINT LINES AVAILABLE"
130 PRINT "IN THIS RESOLUTION MODE"
140 INPUT R1
150 PR = YM / R1        'PR IS PIXELS PER CHARACTER VERTICALLY
160 PRINT
170 PRINT "ENTER CENTER COORDINATES FOR PIE CHART"
180 INPUT XC, YC
190 PRINT "ENTER RADIUS"
```

```
200 INPUT R
210 IF XC+R > XM OR XC-R < 0 OR YC+R > YM OR YC-R < 0 THEN 830
220 PRINT
230 PRINT "ENTER NUMBER OF DIVISIONS (UP TO 8)"
240 INPUT N
250 PRINT "ENTER TITLE OF CHART"
260 INPUT T$
270 PRINT "ENTER NAME AND VALUE FOR EACH DIVISION"
280 T = 0
290      'INPUT DATA. FIND TOTAL (T) OF ALL VALUES.
300 FOR K = 1 TO N
310      INPUT N$(K), V(K)
320      T = T + V(K)
330 NEXT K
340 CLEARSCREEN
350 GRAPHICS
360 POSITION 1,INT(C1 / 2 - .5 * LEN(T$))        'CENTER THE TITLE
370 PRINT T$
380 CIRCLEPLOT XC,YC,R
390 YA = 5 / 6         'YA IS RESOLUTION ADJUSTMENT
400 B = 0                 'B IS ANGLE THAT DETERMINED PRECEDING LINE
410 S = 0
420 RE = 360 * 3.14159 / 180     'RE IS RADIAN EQUIVALENT OF 360
430 FOR K = 1 TO N
440         'LINE TO PLOT IS BASED ON THE VALUE OF THIS
450         'DIVISION PLUS PRECEDING DIVISIONS
460      S = S + V(K)
470         'ANGLE TO USE IS THE PERCENTAGE OF THE
480         'CIRCLE EQUAL TO S / T
490      A = RE * S / T
500      XP = XC + R * COS(A)
510      YP = YC + R * SIN(A) * YA
520      DRAWLINE XC,YC TO XP,YP
530      'PUT LABEL ON DIVISION
540         'FIND A POINT 4 UNITS OUTWARD FROM THE CENTER
550         'POINT OF THE ARC BELONGING TO THE DIVISION
560      AC = B + (A - B) / 2     'AC IS THE ANGLE FROM HORIZONTAL OF THE LINE
570      XL = XC + (R + 4) * COS(AC)      'THAT WOULD HALVE THIS DIVISION
580      YL = YC + (R + 4) * SIN(AC) * YA
590         '(XL,YL) IS THE POINT USED TO ANCHOR LABEL
600         'USE THE POINT AS START OF LABEL IF IT'S ON RIGHT
610         'SIDE OF CIRCLE, AS END OF LABEL IF IT'S ON LEFT,
620         'AS MIDPOINT IF IT'S ON TOP OR BOTTOM OF CIRCLE
630      'POINT IS START OF LABEL
640      IF XL > XC + 10 THEN 740
650      'POINT IS END OF LABEL
660      IF XL < XC - 10 THEN 710
670         'OTHERWISE POINT IS MIDPOINT OF LABEL. ADJUST XL BY
680         'ONE-HALF THE NUMBER OF PIXELS NEEDED FOR LABEL
690      XL = XL - LEN(N$(K)) / 2 * PC
700      GOTO 740
710         'POINT IS END OF LABEL. MOVE BACK BY THE NUMBER
720         'OF PIXELS REQUIRED FOR LABEL
730      XL = XL - LEN(N$(K)) * PC
740         'CONVERT THE PIXEL LOCATION (XL,YL) TO THE CLOSEST
750         'CORRESPONDING PRINT POSITION
760      RO = INT(YL / PR + .5) + 1
770      CO = INT(XL / PC + .5) + 1
780      POSITION RO,CO
790      PRINT N$(K);
800      B = A
810 NEXT K
820 GOTO 840
830 PRINT "COORDINATE OUT OF RANGE"
840 END
```

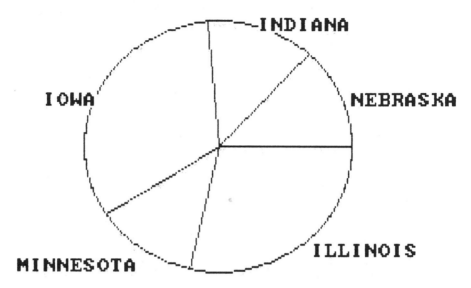

Figure 5–19 Pie chart output of Prog. 5–11.

PROGRAMMING PROJECTS

5–1. Modify Prog. 5–1 to input the angular step size for plotting a circle, instead of the number of points. The program will then display a triangle for an input angular step size of 120 degrees and a square for an input of 90 degrees.

5–2. Devise a program to display a circular arc, for given radius and center coordinates. The arc can be specified by input values for the coordinate endpoints or for the beginning and ending angles.

5–3. Devise a program to display a crescent (or moon shape) using two circular arcs with different radii.

5–4. Write a program to produce a solid-color circle. Paint the interior with any chosen color by drawing diameter lines across the circle in that color. Using equations (5–1), the endpoints of any diameter line are 180 degrees apart. Special effects can be obtained by varying the color as each diameter is drawn.

5–5. The interior of a circle can be filled with dots of variable spacing by plotting points from the center out to the circumference. Write a program to paint a circle in this way using equations in (5–1) and varying the radius from zero to R.

5–6. Write a program to paint the interior of a circle using horizontal lines. For a circle with center point (XC,YC), the X coordinates of the endpoints of a horizontal line across the circle are

$$XC - SQR(R \char`^ 2 - (Y - YC) \char`^ 2) \quad \text{and} \quad XC + SQR(R \char`^ 2 - (Y - YC) \char`^ 2)$$

The Y coordinates are varied from YC − R to YC + R. Varying the spacing between the lines and plotting points instead of solid lines produces different shading patterns. (Painting with vertical lines is accomplished by interchanging values for X and Y and for XC and YC in the calculations.)

5–7. Write a program to display an elliptical curve, painted by any of the methods of Prob. 5–4, 5–5, or 5–6.

5–8. Modify Prog. 5–4 to produce a sine-curve graph with labeled axes. Reduce the amount of computation by taking advantage of the symmetry of the sine function. The program should use equation (5–5), with any values for H, W, and D as input. Scale and plot three cycles of the curve from X = −D / W to X = (6 ∗ PI − D) / W.

5–9. The program outlined in Prob. 5–8 can be modified to display a damped sine function by multiplying the sine function by EXP(-K ∗ X) for each value of X. Plot the resulting curve for X = 0 to X = (10 ∗ PI − D) / W for any positive input value of K.

5–10. Write a program to display a set of data points as small circles, with each circle centered on the coordinates of a data point. Include labeled coordinate axes in the display.

5–11. Write a program to interactively draw a curve to fit a set of plotted data points. The program should allow the curve to be sketched around the data points through keyboard input, or with other interactive devices.

5–12. Write a program to display a set of data points and the parabolic curve that most closely fits the data set. For a set of N input data points, (X(1),Y(1)), (X(2),Y(2)), . . ., (X(N),Y(N)), the coefficients of the parabola [C1, C2, C3 in equation (5–7)] can be determined using the least-squares method. The following set of equations are to be solved simultaneously for C1, C2, and C3:

$$\Sigma \, Y(I) = C1 * \Sigma \, X(I) \,^\wedge 2 + C2 * \Sigma \, X(I) + C3 * N$$
$$\Sigma \, X(I) * Y(I) = C1 * \Sigma \, X(I) \,^\wedge 3 + C2 * \Sigma \, X(I) \,^\wedge 2 + C3 * \Sigma \, X(I)$$
$$\Sigma \, (X(I) \,^\wedge 2) * Y(I) = C1 * \Sigma \, X(I) \,^\wedge 4 + C2 * \Sigma \, X(I) \,^\wedge 3 + C3 * \Sigma \, X(I) \,^\wedge 2$$

where the symbol Σ (sigma) means sum over all values of I from 1 to N.

5–13. Lay out a figure or scene on graph paper and write a program to display the layout, using appropriate curve functions to approximate the outline. Fill in the display with color or shading patterns.

Part III

INTERMEDIATE GRAPHICS

(What More Can We Do?)

So far we have focused on fundamental computer graphics techniques for constructing simple displays. We have seen how to create graphs and pictures of various kinds. Now we will consider ways to manipulate these displays. We will see how we can modify parts of displays and how we can produce animation.

Chapter 6

Transforming Displays

The transformation methods discussed in this chapter provide the basic tools for manipulating displays. Understanding the principles necessary for modifying or transforming a developed display will greatly increase our ability to produce effective computer graphics. Specific uses of these transformation methods include moving pictures and graphs from one screen location to another, developing a composite picture from simpler parts, creating inserts for a developed display, enlarging the size of a picture or graph for clarity or insertion of more detail, reducing the size of a display in order to be able to add explanatory information such as notes or another picture, and animating displays.

These alterations to simple pictures and graphs are brought about through the application of the three basic transformations: (1) movement of a displayed object from one screen location to another (translation), (2) enlargement or reduction in the size of a displayed picture or graph (scaling), and (3) changes in the direction of orientation of a graphics representation (rotation).

6–1 CHANGING POSITIONS (TRANSLATION)

Techniques for changing screen position allow us to construct a picture or graph in any part of the screen and then move it to any other screen location. We may want only to rearrange the display or we may want to build up a display a piece at a time from a set of component parts.

TRANSLATING A POINT

Relocating a displayed point merely requires that we change the screen coordinates of the point to correspond to the new screen position. To move a point horizontally to the right by 15 locations, we add 15 to the present X coordinate. If we also want to move the point up the screen by 40 locations, we need to subtract 40 from the present Y coordinate. We can state the general rule for moving a point about the screen from location (X,Y) to a new location (XT,YT) in terms of **translation distances** H and V:

$$XT = X + H$$
$$YT = Y + V$$

(6–1)

A positive value for H indicates displacement of the point horizontally to the right, while a positive value for V indicates displacement vertically toward the bottom of the screen. Negative values for H or V will translate the point to the left or up, respectively.

   In translating a displayed point, we should use values for H and V that keep the point within the screen boundary. Very small values for H and V should also be avoided. If values for H and V are both less than 0.5, the original point will simply be replotted. This can amount to a significant slowing down of the program for many repeated replots in a picture.

TRANSLATING A PICTURE

Moving a picture from one screen location to another means that we translate all points of the picture and then redraw all the lines connecting the translated points. To avoid changing the shape of an object, we must displace all points by the same distance. That is, calculations (6–1) are applied with the same H value for all horizontal coordinates and the same V value for all vertical coordinates of the picture. Using a different H or a different V for different points in the picture will distort the original display. We usually want to translate objects without distortion, but producing such distortions can be the basis for experimenting with design shapes or for game playing.

   Coordinate endpoints for each line in a picture can be conveniently stored in an array. For a simple picture, we can store the points in a one-dimensional array in the order that we want them connected. But if we have a more complicated figure, a point may connect to several lines or we may have parts in the picture that are not connected by lines to other parts, as in Fig. 6–1. We could then store coordinate values in two-dimensional arrays. One subscript of the array identifies the picture part, the other subscript tells us which point of that part. Thus, (X(2,1),Y(2,1)) could be used to store the coordinates for the first point of part 2 of the picture (such as the boy in Fig. 6–1). Two-dimensional arrays are used in Prog. 6–1 to store coordinates defining the details of Fig. 6–1. This program lets us translate the picture components to any screen position, as many times as we wish.

   Program 6–1 stores the translated coordinates in the original arrays X and Y. If we wanted to save the original position, we could store translated coordinates in different arrays, such as XT and YT. Saving the original position is desirable if we just want to test new positions for visual effect or if we want to display the object in both positions. If there is no reason to save the original position of the picture, we save storage space by recalculating coordinates in the original arrays X and Y.

For objects with symmetry or with boundaries calculated from equations, we do not have to add translation distances to each point of the object to relocate it. To move a circle or ellipse, for instance, we only need to translate the figure center and calculate the new points along the boundary using routines discussed in Chapter 5. To relocate a rectangle, we could translate one corner and redraw the rectangle using values for the width and height.

Program 6–1   Translating pictures (boy, dog, and hydrant).

```
10 'PROGRAM 6-1. TRANSLATION OF PICTURE PARTS.
20       'DRAWS PICTURE AND ALLOWS USER TO TRANSLATE PARTS OF
30       'THE DISPLAY TO OTHER LOCATIONS. PICTURE PARTS ARE
40       'STORED IN ARRAYS X AND Y. TRANSLATED POINTS REPLACE
50       'THE ORIGINAL POINTS IN X AND Y.
60  CLEARSCREEN
70  DIM X(5,50), Y(5,50), N(5)
80  XM = 319      'XM,YM ARE MAXIMUM PIXEL VALUES FOR THIS SYSTEM
90  YM = 199
100      '************* READ PICTURE PARTS AND DRAW **************
110 PN = 1      'PN IS PART NUMBER
120 E = 0
130 READ XD, YD
140 IF XD >= 0 THEN 200
150      'STORE # OF ELEMENTS IN PN IN N(PN)
160 N(PN) = E
170 IF XD = -100 THEN 240
180 PN = PN + 1
190 GOTO 120
200 E = E + 1
210 X(PN,E) = XD
220 Y(PN,E) = YD
230 GOTO 130
240 GRAPHICS
250 GOSUB 510      'DRAW PICTURE
260      '
270      '********* PRINT INSTRUCTIONS FOR TRANSLATING **********
280 POSITION 22,1
290 PRINT "      1-BOY  2-DOG  3-HYDRANT"
300 PRINT "    PICTURE PART TO MOVE (0 TO END)";
310 INPUT P
320 POSITION 22,1
330 PRINT "                                        "
340 PRINT "                                        ";
350 IF P = 0 THEN 730
360 POSITION 23,1
370 PRINT "  H AND V AMOUNT TO MOVE";
380 INPUT H, V
390      '
400      '****************** RECALCULATE POINTS ******************
410 FOR J = 1 TO N(P)
420     X(P,J) = X(P,J) + H
430     Y(P,J) = Y(P,J) + V
440     IF X(P,J)>=0 AND X(P,J)<=XM AND Y(P,J)>=0 AND Y(P,J)<=YM THEN 470
450     PRINT "COORDINATE OUT OF RANGE"
460     GOTO 730
470 NEXT J
480 GOSUB 510
```

Program 6-1 (cont.)

```
490 GOTO 280
500 '
510 '######################## DRAW ROUTINE ###############################
520 CLEARSCREEN
530 FOR K = 1 TO PN
540     FOR J = 1 TO N(K)-1
550         DRAWLINE X(K,J), Y(K,J) TO X(K,J+1), Y(K,J+1)
560     NEXT J
570 NEXT K
580 RETURN
590 '##################################################################
600 DATA 85,70,90,75,105,60,105,80,85,110,95,110,110,85
610 DATA 125,110,135,110,115,80,115,60,130,75,135,70,115,45
620 DATA 115,40,125,30,125,15,110,10,95,15,95,30,105,40,105,45,85,70
630 DATA -1,-1
640 DATA 50,90,62,110,58,110,50,90,42,110,38,110,50,90
650 DATA 45,100,20,100,10,90,22,110,18,110,10,90,3,110
660 DATA 0,110,10,90,0,80,10,90,50,90,40,80,50,70,55,75,60,78,60,82,50,90
670 DATA -1,-1
680 DATA 290,110,290,98,288,98,288,92,286,92,286,88
690 DATA 286,88,288,88,288,82,290,82,290,73,287,73,287,70,290,70,290,65
700 DATA 295,60,305,60,310,65,310,70,313,70,313,73,310,73,310,110,290,110
710 DATA -100,-100
720 '##################################################################
730 END
```

Figure 6–1 Translation of a picture component from the original position (a) to position (b), then to position (c) by Prog. 6–1.

1-BOY   2-DOG   3-HYDRANT
PICTURE PART TO MOVE (0 TO END)? ■

(a)

Figure 6-1 (cont.)

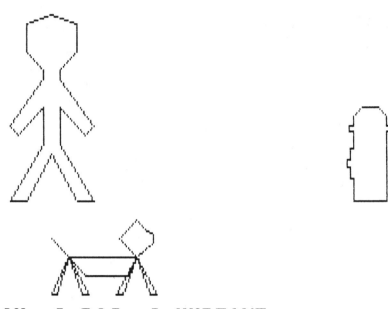

1-BOY   2-DOG   3-HYDRANT
PICTURE PART TO MOVE (0 TO END)?

(b)

(c)

TRANSLATING A GRAPH

The methods and considerations discussed for translating pictures also apply to graphs—all points of the graph are reassigned new values (within the screen limits) and all lines are redrawn at the new location. Labeling could then be added at appropriate places within the new graph, or we could translate the label positions together with the other pixel coordinates of the display.

To translate character labels, we need to express translation distances H and V in terms of character position changes. We get the horizontal shift of a label by dividing H by the number of horizontal points in the character pixel grid. We get the vertical shift by dividing V by the number of vertical points in the character pixel grid. For an 8 by 12 pixel grid, the line number of a label would be displaced by a distance of V/12 and the horizontal position of a label would be shifted by a distance of H/8. If labels are to be translated, we should choose H and V to be multiples of the character grid dimensions. This will keep the labels in the same relative graph positions after translation.

A method for moving a labeled bar graph is given in Prog. 6–2. We use an 8 by 12 pixel grid for translating labels. The LEN function is used to get the length of each string label in checking for possible translation off screen.

Program 6–2   Translating a graph.

```
10 'PROGRAM 6-2. TRANSLATING A LABELED HORIZONTAL BAR GRAPH.
20      'ASSUME A SCREEN SIZE OF 280 x 160 PIXELS WITH 35 CHARACTERS
30      'PER LINE AND 15 PRINT LINES (EACH CHARACTER OCCUPIES AN
40      '8 x 12 PIXEL AREA). A VARIABLE NUMBER (UP TO 8) OF LABELS
50      'AND MAGNITUDES AND A GRAPH TITLE ARE READ FROM DATA
60      'STATEMENTS. LABELS ARE STORED IN THE ARRAY L$. PRINT
70      'POSITION OF EACH LABEL IS STORED IN ARRAYS R AND C. LABELS
80      'MAY BE UP TO 8 CHARACTERS IN LENGTH AND OCCUPY THE FIRST 8
90      'COLUMNS OF A PRINT LINE. MAGNITUDES ARE SCALED TO USE PIXELS
100     '64 - 160. ENDPOINTS OF THE BAR FOR EACH GRAPH DIVISION ARE
110     'STORED IN ARRAYS X AND Y. ONCE THE GRAPH IS CREATED, IT MAY
120     'BE TRANSLATED TO SOME OTHER LOCATION ON THE SCREEN. TRANSLATED
130     'POINTS ARE STORED IN NEW ARRAYS.
140 '**************************************************************
150 CLEARSCREEN
160 DIM X(8,2), Y(8,2), L$(9), R(9), C(9)
170 DIM XT(8,2), YT(8,2), LT$(9), RT(9), CT(9)
180      '
190      '************** READ DATA FOR GRAPH AND DRAW **************
200 READ MI, MA     'READ MINIMUM AND MAXIMUM VALUES TO USE FOR DATA RANGE
210 RM = (160 - 64) / (MA - MI)
220     'READ DATA FOR GRAPH
230 READ N          'READ NUMBER OF DIVISIONS
240 FOR K = 1 TO N
250     READ L$(K),M
260     R(K) = K+2     'SAVE FIRST 2 ROWS FOR TITLE AND SPACE
270     C(K) = 1
280     X(K,1) = 64
290     X(K,2) = INT((M - MI) * RM + 64 + .5)
```

Program 6-2 (cont.)

```
300     Y(K,1) = (K + 1) * 8 + 1        'TOP OF BAR
310     Y(K,2) = Y(K,1) + 4             'BOTTOM OF BAR
320 NEXT K
330 READ L$(N+1)      'READ TITLE
340 R(N+1) = 1
350 C(N+1) = 10 - LEN(L$(N+1)) / 2           'CENTER AROUND COLUMN 10
360         'COPY ORIGINAL VALUES TO ARRAYS USED TO HOLD TRANSLATED
370         'POINTS SINCE THESE ARE USED TO DRAW GRAPH
380 FOR K = 1 TO N
390     RT(K) = R(K)
400     CT(K) = C(K)
410     FOR J = 1 TO 2
420         XT(K,J) = X(K,J)
430         YT(K,J) = Y(K,J)
440     NEXT J
450 NEXT K
460 RT(N+1) = R(N+1)
470 CT(N+1) = C(N+1)
480 GRAPHICS
490 GOSUB 830                 'DRAW GRAPH
500     '
510     '*********** PRINT INSTRUCTIONS FOR TRANSLATING **********
520 POSITION 20,1
530 PRINT " H AND V AMOUNTS TO MOVE FROM";
540 PRINT " ORIGINAL. ENTER 0,0 TO SEE";
550 PRINT " ORIGINAL, -999,-999 TO END";
560 INPUT H, V
570         'ERASE INSTRUCTIONS
580 POSITION 20,1
590 PRINT "                              ";
600 PRINT "                              ";
610 PRINT "                              ";
620 PRINT "                              ";
630 IF H = -999 THEN 1080
640     '
650     '**************** RECALCULATE POINTS ********************
660 FOR K = 1 TO N
670     RT(K) = R(K) + INT(V / 12)
680     IF RT(K) < 1 OR RT(K) > 15 THEN 980
690     CT(K) = C(K) + INT(H / 8)
700     IF CT(K) < 0 OR CT(K) + LEN(L$(K)) > 35 THEN 980
710     FOR J = 1 TO 2
720         XT(K,J) = X(K,J) + H
730         IF XT(K,J) < 0 OR XT(K,J) > 279 THEN 1000
740         YT(K,J) = Y(K,J) + V
750         IF YT(K,J) < 0 OR YT(K,J) > 159 THEN 1000
760     NEXT J
770 NEXT K
780 RT(N+1) = R(K) + INT(V / 12)
790 CT(N+1) = C(K) + INT(H / 8)
800 GOSUB 830
810 GOTO 520
820 '
830 '####################### DRAW ROUTINE ###################################
840 CLEARSCREEN
850 POSITION RT(N+1),CT(N+1)
860 PRINT L$(N+1)
870 PRINT
880 FOR K = 1 TO N
890     POSITION RT(K),CT(K)
900     PRINT L$(K);
```

```
910      'DRAW BAR FOR THIS DIVISION
920      FOR YT = YT(K,1) TO YT(K,2)
930          DRAWLINE XT(K,1),YT TO XT(K,2),YT
940      NEXT YT
950 NEXT K
960 RETURN
970 '#######################################################################
980 PRINT "LABEL OFF SCREEN"
990 GOTO 1080
1000 PRINT "GRAPH POINT OFF SCREEN"
1010 GOTO 1080
1020 '#########################
1030 DATA 0,800
1040 DATA 4
1050 DATA FIRST,600,SECOND,500,THIRD,800,FOURTH,400
1060 DATA "QUARTERLY SALES"
1070 '#########################
1080 END
```

6–2 CHANGING SIZES (SCALING)

Having created a display, we may decide to change its size in order to clarify the information presented or to fit this display into a larger graphics picture. The size of a picture or graph is changed by multiplying all distances between points by the amount that we wish to enlarge or reduce the display. If we want to double the size of a rectangle, all line lengths are multiplied by 2; if the size is to be cut in half, all lengths are multiplied by $\frac{1}{2}$.

Scaling an object requires that we also specify the location of the object after enlargement or reduction. We may scale an object with respect to some central point of the object, a point on its boundary, or any point outside the figure. For example, we may decide to enlarge a rectangle keeping the lower left corner at the same position after enlargement, or we might enlarge the rectangle about its center point (Fig. 6–2).

Figure 6–2   (a) Rectangle with center at (XB,YB) and lower left corner at (X,Y);
(b) scaling with (X,Y) fixed enlarges the box toward the upper right of the screen;
(c) scaling with (XB,YB) fixed enlarges the box out from the center point.

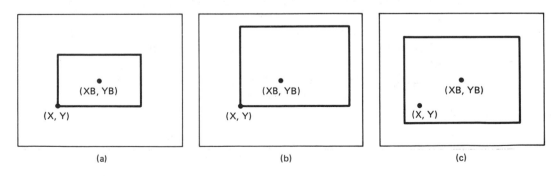

(a)   (b)   (c)

SCALING A LINE

A horizontal line with left X coordinate X(1) and right X coordinate X(2) has length

$$L = X(2) - X(1) \qquad (6\text{–}2)$$

Changing the length of the line means that we multiply L by a **horizontal scaling factor**, say HS, to produce the new length:

$$\begin{aligned} LS &= L*HS \\ &= X(2)*HS - X(1)*HS \qquad (6\text{–}3) \\ &= XS(2) - XS(1) \end{aligned}$$

where the array XS stores the scaled coordinates and HS must be a positive number (HS > 0). The scaling factor HS will produce a longer line if HS > 1. A shorter line will result if HS < 1. If HS = 1, there is no change in the length of the line.

Since scaling a line affects the value of the coordinate endpoints, we need to specify where the line is to be redrawn. For the horizontal line we might keep the left end fixed, or the right end fixed, or the midpoint of the line fixed, or we might move the scaled line to an altogether new position. Suppose that we want to keep the left end of the line where it is. The new coordinates of the line after scaling are then

$$\begin{aligned} XS(1) &= X(1) \\ XS(2) &= X(1) + (X(2) - X(1))*HS \end{aligned} \qquad (6\text{–}4)$$

If we want the right end to remain where it is, the new coordinates of the line are

$$\begin{aligned} XS(1) &= X(2) - (X(2) - X(1))*HS \\ XS(2) &= X(2) \end{aligned} \qquad (6\text{–}5)$$

Keeping the middle of the line nailed down, we have

$$\begin{aligned} XS(1) &= XM - ((X(2) - X(1)) / 2)*HS \\ XS(2) &= XM + ((X(2) - X(1)) / 2)*HS \end{aligned} \qquad (6\text{–}6)$$

where XM is the line midpoint (Fig. 6–3), which we can calculate as XM = (X(1) + X(2)) / 2.

If we want to move a scaled line to a new screen position, we could first translate the line to that new position and then scale it about one of the endpoints or the midpoint. A general approach is to pick a reference point that we consider fixed, such as XF in Fig. 6–3. We then get the new endpoints by scaling the distances between each original endpoint and XF by our scaling factor HS. The new endpoints, after scaling, can then be calculated as

$$\begin{aligned} XS(1) &= (X(1) - XF)*HS + XF \\ XS(2) &= (X(2) - XF)*HS + XF \end{aligned} \qquad (6\text{–}7)$$

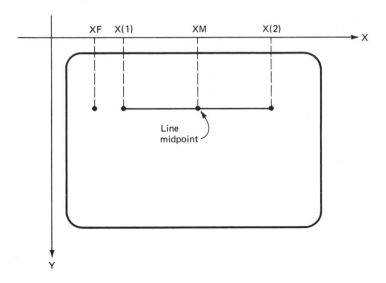

Figure 6–3   A horizontal line with endpoints at X(1) and X(2) has length X(2) − X(1) and a midpoint at position XM = X(1) + (X(2) − X(1)) / 2.

Any point on or off the screen can be chosen for XF. If XF is chosen to be X(1) or X(2) or XM, we have the results given in relations (6–4), (6–5), or (6–6).

Considerations for scaling a vertical line are similar to those for scaling a horizontal line. The length of a vertical line with endpoints Y(1) and Y(2) is

$$L = Y(2) - Y(1) \tag{6–8}$$

Scaling this line by a **vertical scaling factor** VS will produce a line of new length:

$$
\begin{aligned}
LS &= L * VS \\
&= Y(2) * VS - Y(1) * VS \\
&= YS(2) - YS(1)
\end{aligned}
\tag{6–9}
$$

where the array YS is used to store the new endpoints. The scaling factor VS must be positive and the line may be redrawn about any specified fixed point, such as Y(1) or Y(2) or the line midpoint. Specifying a vertical fixed point as YF, we can calculate the scaled coordinates of the line as

$$
\begin{aligned}
YS(1) &= (Y(1) - YF) * VS + YF \\
YS(2) &= (Y(2) - YF) * VS + YF
\end{aligned}
\tag{6–10}
$$

Lines displayed at any arbitrary angle (Fig. 6–4) can be enlarged or reduced by scaling both the horizontal length component X(2) − X(1) and the vertical length component Y(2) − Y(1) relative to a **fixed coordinate position** (XF,YF). We can write relations (6–7) and (6–10) in the following factored form:

$$XS(1) = X(1) * HS + XF * (1 - HS)$$
$$YS(1) = Y(1) * VS + YF * (1 - VS)$$
$$XS(2) = X(2) * HS + XF * (1 - HS) \qquad (6-11)$$
$$YS(2) = Y(2) * VS + YF * (1 - VS)$$

The expressions $XF * (1 - HS)$ and $YF * (1 - VS)$ are each constant, so we only have to evaluate them once for all coordinates. To enlarge or reduce a diagonal line without changing the slope, we must set $HS = VS$.

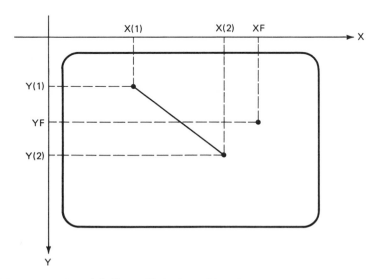

Figure 6-4   A straight line, with horizontal length component $X(2) - X(1)$ and vertical length component $Y(2) - Y(1)$, can be scaled relative to any fixed point (XF, YF).

SCALING A DISPLAY

Scaled pictures and graphs are uniformly enlarged or reduced by setting HS and VS to the same value, S. Relations (6-11) are then be used to calculate new coordinates for all the points of the scaled display. The enlarged or reduced picture is displayed by drawing the connecting lines for these new points. For figures with curved lines it may not be necessary to apply (6–11) to every point of the picture. To scale a circle with radius R, we only need to compute the new coordinates for the center of the circle, using (6–11), and calculate the new radius as $R * S$. The routines of Section 5–1 can then be used to display the scaled circle.

In some cases we may want to stretch a display in one direction (say, the vertical direction) and maintain the original size in the other direction (horizontal). To turn a square into a rectangle, we could double the height only. This is accomplished by setting the vertical scaling factor VS to 2 for the calculations involving vertical coordinates and by setting the horizontal scaling factor HS to 1 for the calculations involving the horizontal coordinates. This technique can be useful in experimenting with or adjusting the proportions of picture components. We can also use nonuniform scaling to build composite pictures from a set of standard shapes, such as a square which we can scale to any size rectangle.

Program 6–3 gives an example of picture scaling. Input to the program is composed of the picture definition and scaling factors HS and VS. The program scales the total picture or any selected component of the picture. A sample output is shown in Fig. 6–5.

Program 6–3 Scaling picture parts (car).

```
10  'PROGRAM 6-3. SCALING ALL OR PART OF A PICTURE.
20     'DRAWS CAR AND ALLOWS USER TO SCALE PART OR ALL OF
30     'CAR. IF SCALING PART, PROGRAM SETS A POINT TO BE
40     'FIXED. IF SCALING ALL, USER CAN INPUT POINT TO
50     'BE FIXED. SCALED POINTS REPLACE ORIGINAL VALUES
60     'IN ARRAYS X AND Y.
70  CLEARSCREEN
80  DIM X(5,100), Y(5,100), N(5)
90  PRINT "ENTER MAXIMUM HORIZONTAL AND VERTICAL"
100 PRINT "VALUES FOR THIS RESOLUTION MODE"
110 INPUT XM, YM
120     '
130     '************* READ PICTURE PARTS AND DRAW ***************
140 PN = 1          'PN IS PART NUMBER
150 E = 0           'E IS AN ELEMENT OF THE PART
160 READ XD, YD
170 IF XD >= 0 THEN 240     'IS THIS A NEW DATA POINT?
180     'OTHERWISE, IT'S END OF PART. STORE CURRENT COUNT OF E IN N(PN)
190 N(PN) = E
200 IF XD = -100 THEN 280    'IF END OF DATA, DRAW PICTURE
210     'OTHERWISE, NEW PART. READ ELEMENTS FOR THAT PART.
220 PN = PN + 1
230 GOTO 150
240 E = E + 1
250 X(PN,E) = XD
260 Y(PN,E) = YD * 5/6      'ADJUST Y POINTS FOR RESOLUTION DIFFERENCE
270 GOTO 160
280 GRAPHICS
290 GOSUB 770
300     '
310     '****************** PRINT INSTRUCTIONS ********************
320 POSITION 21,1
330 PRINT "1-FRONT 2-BODY 3-REAR 4-ALL 0-STOP";
340 POSITION 22,1
350 PRINT "PICTURE PART TO SCALE";
360 INPUT P
370 POSITION 21,1
380 PRINT "                                    ";
390 PRINT "                                    ";
400 IF P = 0 THEN 1100
410 POSITION 21,1
420 PRINT "H AND V AMOUNTS TO SCALE";
430 INPUT HS, VS
440 POSITION 21,1
450 PRINT "                                    ";
460     '
470     '******** RECALCULATE POINTS FOR APPROPRIATE PICTURE PART ********
480     'WHEN SCALING PARTS OF THE PICTURE, SCALING IS RELATIVE
490     'TO CENTER POINT OF CAR. WHEN SCALING WHOLE CAR, USER
500     'MUST INPUT POINT THAT IS TO REMAIN FIXED.
```

Program 6-3 (cont.)

```
510 IF P = 4 THEN 670          'SCALE ALL PARTS
520      'JUST SCALE ONE PART
530 IF P = 1 THEN 560
540 IF P = 2 THEN 590
550 IF P = 3 THEN 620
560 XF = X(1,2)
570 YF = Y(1,2)
580 GOTO 640
590 XF = X(2,2)
600 YF = Y(2,2)
610 GOTO 640
620 XF = X(3,2)
630 YF = Y(3,2)
640 GOSUB 870        'DO SCALING
650 GOSUB 770        'DRAW
660 GOTO 320
670 POSITION 21,1        'SCALING WHOLE CAR
680 PRINT "SCALE AROUND WHAT POINT";
690 INPUT XF, YF
700 FOR P = 1 TO PN          'SCALE EACH PART
710     GOSUB 870
720 NEXT P
730 GOSUB 770               'DRAW
740 GOTO 320
750 '
760 '####################### DRAW ROUTINE ##############################
770     'DRAWS PICTURE
780 CLEARSCREEN
790 FOR K = 1 TO PN
800     FOR J = 1 TO N(K)-1
810         IF X(K,J)<0 OR X(K,J)>XM OR Y(K,J)<0 OR Y(K,J)>YM THEN 1090
820         DRAWLINE X(K,J), Y(K,J) TO X(K,J+1), Y(K,J+1)
830     NEXT J
840 NEXT K
850 RETURN
860 '####################### SCALING ROUTINE ##########################
870     'SCALES PICTURE PART
880 FOR J = 1 TO N(P)
890     X(P,J) = X(P,J) * HS + XF * (1 - HS)
900     Y(P,J) = Y(P,J) * VS + YF * (1 - VS)
910 NEXT J
920 RETURN
930 '####################################################################
940     'FRONT OF CAR
950 DATA 220,90,210,90,210,60,250,65,260,90,250,90
960 DATA 250,100,240,110,230,110,220,100,220,90
970 DATA 230,80,240,80,250,90
980 DATA -1,-1
990     'MIDBODY
1000 DATA 210,90,160,90,160,60,205,60,187,35,160,35
1010 DATA 160,30,190,30,210,60
1020 DATA -1,-1
1030     'BACK OF CAR
1040 DATA 120,90,160,90,160,60,120,60,135,35,160,35
1050 DATA 160,30,130,30,115,60,80,60,75,90,90,90
1060 DATA 90,100,100,110,110,110,120,100,120,90,110,80,100,80,90,90,90,100
1070 DATA -100,-100
1080 '####################################################################
1090 PRINT "COORDINATE OUT OF RANGE"
1100 END
```

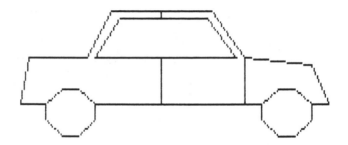

1-FRONT 2-BODY 3-REAR 4-ALL 0-STOP
PICTURE PART TO SCALE? ■

(a)

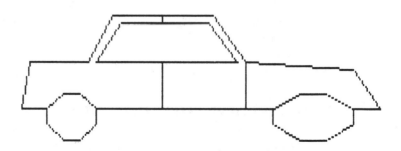

1-FRONT 2-BODY 3-REAR 4-ALL 0-STOP
PICTURE PART TO SCALE? ■

(b)

Figure 6-5 Scaling picture components from the original (a), with an enlargement of the front section (b), and an overall reduction (c), by Prog. 6-3.

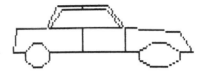

```
1-FRONT 2-BODY 3-REAR 4-ALL 0-STOP
PICTURE PART TO SCALE? ■
```

(c)

Figure 6-5 (cont.)

Graphs are scaled with the same methods illustrated in Prog. 6–3. Since labeling cannot be scaled (the size of a character is fixed), we need to consider the placement of labels after scaling the pixel lengths. We can do this manually by examining the graph after scaling, or we can calculate new starting positions for the strings relative to some point on the graph. As an alternative, we could create labels with pixels. Then the labels could be scaled together with all other parts of the graph.

6–3 CHANGING ORIENTATIONS (ROTATION)

In many applications, we would like to be able to change the orientation of a display. We may decide to change a bar graph so that the bars are drawn horizontally instead of vertically. Rotating the display by 90 degrees can be a convenient technique for accomplishing this without having to reconstruct the graph. In simulation and game-playing applications we often want to display rotating objects.

ROTATING A POINT

Figure 6–6 illustrates rotation of a point. The **rotation path** is along a circular arc from position (X,Y) to position (XR,YR) about a **pivot point** (XO,YO). Angle A in this figure specifies the amount of rotation from (X,Y) to (XR,YR). The rotated coordinates (XR,YR) are calculated from the values of A, (XO,YO), and (X,Y) as

$$XR = XO + ((X - XO) * COS(A)) + ((Y - YO) * SIN(A))$$
$$YR = YO + ((Y - YO) * COS(A)) - ((X - XO) * SIN(A))$$

(6–12)

Coordinate values for the pivot point (XO,YO) can be chosen to be at any convenient location—either on the screen or beyond the screen boundaries in any direction. This point is not plotted and is only chosen as a reference to determine the circular path of rotation, as shown in Fig. 6–7.

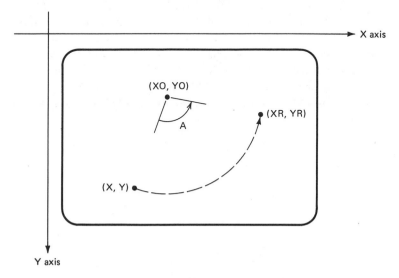

Figure 6–6 Rotating a point at position (X,Y) to position (XR,YR) about the point (XO,YO). The point rotates through an angle A along a circular path.

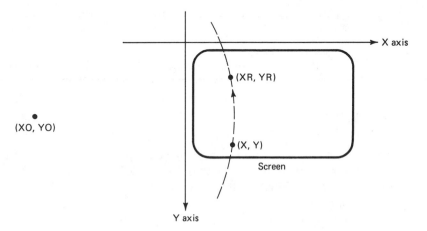

Figure 6–7 Values for the coordinates of the pivot point (XO,YO) can be chosen to be off screen, as well as within the screen coordinate boundaries.

Rotation angle A is measured in a counterclockwise direction from the starting position (X,Y) of the point. This is assuming that the origin of our coordinate system is at the upper left corner of the screen. For computer systems referencing the coordinate origin at the lower left, angle A will be measured in a clockwise direction. This angle will usually be given a value between zero radians and $2*PI$ (6.283185) radians. Other angles may be specified, but they simply repeat the rotations in this range.

The distance that the point moves along the circle path for a specified angle A depends on the distance of (X,Y) from the pivot point (XO,YO). The farther (XO,YO) is from (X,Y), the greater the distance traveled from (X,Y) to (XR,YR). Figure 6–8 shows the relationship between the pivot distance R, the angle A, and the displacement D from (X,Y) to (XR,YR). For small rotation angles, D is approximately equal to the product $R*A$. If R is 50, a point could be rotated a distance of about 1 unit (to a neighboring pixel location) with an angle A of 0.02 radian.

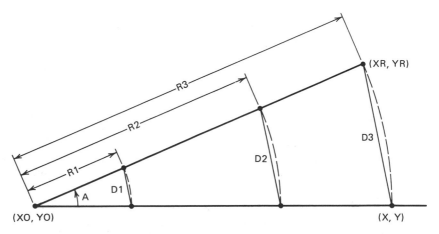

Figure 6–8 For small values of the rotation angle A, the distance D, from (X,Y) to (XR,YR), is approximately equal to the pivot distance R times rotation angle A. As R gets larger, D gets larger, for the same rotation angle A.

ROTATING A DISPLAY

To change the orientation of a displayed object, we first select the pivot point. Then the rotated coordinate positions of all points in the object are calculated with relations (6–12). Finally, the screen is cleared and the object lines are redrawn using the rotated coordinates.

Program 6–4 rotates a picture about any selected pivot point (XO,YO) through any specified rotation angle A, provided that the rotated position is on the screen. Output of the program for rotation angles of 90 degrees and 180 degrees are shown in Fig. 6–9. The pivot point for rotation in this example is chosen at the center of the figure.

Program 6–4 Rotating pictures (clown).

```
10  'PROGRAM 6-4. ROTATING A PICTURE.
20      'DRAWS PICTURE AND ALLOWS USER TO INPUT THE ANGLE OF
30      'DESIRED ROTATION. ROTATED POINTS ARE STORED IN XR AND YR.
40  CLEARSCREEN
50  DIM X(7,100), Y(7,100), N(7)
60  DIM XR(7,100), YR(7,100)
70  PRINT "ENTER MAXIMUM HORIZONTAL AND VERTICAL"
80  PRINT "VALUES FOR THIS RESOLUTION MODE"
90  INPUT XM, YM
100     '
110     '************* READ PICTURE PARTS AND DRAW ******************
120 PN = 1           'PN IS PART NUMBER
130 E = 0            'E IS AN ELEMENT OF THE PART
140 READ XD, YD
150 IF XD >= 0 THEN 220     'IS THIS A NEW DATA POINT?
160     'OTHERWISE, IT'S END OF PART. STORE CURRENT COUNT OF E IN N(PN)
170 N(PN) = E
180 IF XD = -100 THEN 260    'IF END OF DATA, DRAW PICTURE
190     'OTHERWISE, NEW PART. READ ELEMENTS FOR THAT PART.
200 PN = PN + 1
210 GOTO 130
220 E = E + 1
230 X(PN,E) = XD
240 Y(PN,E) = YD * 5/6      'ADJUST Y POINTS FOR RESOLUTION DIFFERENCE
250 GOTO 140
260     'COPY ORIGINAL VALUES TO ARRAYS USED TO HOLD ROTATED
270     'POINTS, SINCE DRAW ROUTINE USES THESE ARRAYS
280 FOR P = 1 TO PN
290     FOR E = 1 TO N(P)
300         XR(P,E) = X(P,E)
310         YR(P,E) = Y(P,E)
320     NEXT E
330 NEXT P
340 GRAPHICS
350 GOSUB 590     'DRAW PICTURE
360     '
370     '****************** PRINT INSTRUCTIONS *********************
380 POSITION 22,1
390 PRINT "ANGLE TO ROTATE FROM ORIGINAL POSITION";
400 POSITION 23,1
410 PRINT "(0-360, OR -1 TO END)";
420 INPUT A
430 POSITION 22,1
440 PRINT "                                        ";
450 PRINT "                                        ";
460 IF A < 0 THEN 900
470 A = A * 3.14159 / 180     'CHANGE DEGREES TO RADIANS
480 POSITION 22,1
490 PRINT "ABOUT WHAT POINT";
500 INPUT XO, YO
510     '
520     '**************** RECALCULATE POINTS ***********************
530 FOR P = 1 TO PN          'ROTATE EACH PART
540     GOSUB 680
550 NEXT P
560 GOSUB 590                'DRAW
570 GOTO 370
580 '
590 '######################### DRAW ROUTINE ############################
600 CLEARSCREEN
610 FOR P = 1 TO PN
620     FOR E = 1 TO N(P)-1
```

Program 6-4 (cont.)

```
630        IF XR(P,E)<0 OR XR(P,E)>XM OR YR(P,E)<0 OR YR(P,E)>YM THEN 890
640        DRAWLINE XR(P,E), YR(P,E) TO XR(P,E+1), YR(P,E+1)
650     NEXT E
660 NEXT P
670 RETURN
680 '######################### ROTATE ROUTINE #############################
690 FOR E = 1 TO N(P)
700     XR(P,E) = XO + (X(P,E)-XO) * COS(A) + (Y(P,E)-YO) * SIN(A) * 6/5
710     YR(P,E) = YO + (Y(P,E)-YO) * COS(A) - (X(P,E)-XO) * SIN(A) * 5/6
720 NEXT E
730 RETURN
740 '####################################################################
750 DATA 160,60,170,50,170,40,160,30,150,30,140,40,140,50
760 DATA 150,60,178,60,165,63,173,70,160,67,155,78,150,67
770 DATA 140,72,145,65,130,65,150,60,100,70,90,70,90,80,100
780 DATA 80,110,90,130,80,120,140,120,150,130,160,120,170,125
790 DATA 175,140,170,140,160,150,150,155,110,170,150,180,160,180
800 DATA 170,200,170,200,165,190,160,195,150,195,140,175,80,200
810 DATA 30,190,20,190,10,180,10,180,20,170,60
820 DATA -1,-1
830 DATA 147,42,153,42,-1,-1
840 DATA 150,38,150,45,-1,-1
850 DATA 157,42,163,42,-1,-1
860 DATA 160,38,160,45
870 DATA -100,-100
880 '####################################################################
890 PRINT "COORDINATE OUT OF RANGE"
900 END
```

Figure 6–9 Rotating a picture from the original position (a), through 90 degrees (b), and through 180 degrees (c), by Prog. 6–4.

**ANGLE TO ROTATE FROM ORIGINAL POSITION
(0-360, OR -1 TO END)?** ■

(a)

Figure 6-9 (cont.)

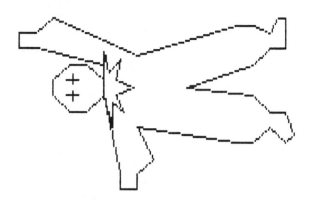

ANGLE TO ROTATE FROM ORIGINAL POSITION
(0-360, OR -1 TO END)? ■

(b)

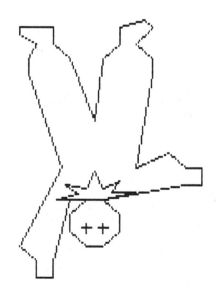

ANGLE TO ROTATE FROM ORIGINAL POSITION
(0-360, OR -1 TO END)? ■

(c)

Rotating a display can cause the picture or graph to be distorted if the X resolution of the system is different from the Y resolution. We adjust for resolution differences in Prog. 6–4 by multiplying the term $(Y - YO) * SIN(A)$ on line 700 by the ratio of X resolution to Y resolution and multiplying the term $(X - XO) * SIN(A)$ on line 710 by the ratio of Y resolution to X resolution. This is equivalent to rotating the display along an elliptical path, which looks circular on the screen.

6–4 COMBINED TRANSFORMATIONS

A general transformation program for combining translation, scaling, and rotation is given in Prog. 6–5. The program illustrates a procedure for constructing bar graphs using transformations. We plot the data in the upper left screen corner, then repeatedly select transformations or the termination code. This lets us try out positions and scalings until we are satisfied with the final display. Figure 6–10 shows the original graph and its final position on the screen.

Program 6–5 Combined transformations on graphs.

```
10 'PROGRAM 6-5. TRANSFORMING A BAR GRAPH.
20      'ASSUME A SCREEN SIZE OF 280 x 160 PIXELS. A VARIABLE
30      'NUMBER OF DATA VALUES (UP TO 8) ARE READ FROM DATA
40      'STATEMENTS. AN AXIS IS DRAWN AND DATA VALUES ARE
50      'SCALED TO USE PIXELS 10 - 110 ALONG THE X AXIS.
60      'CORNERS OF THE BAR FOR EACH GRAPH ARE STORED IN
70      'ARRAYS X AND Y. ONCE THE GRAPH IS CREATED ANY COMBINATION
80      'OF TRANSLATION, SCALING, AND ROTATION TRANSFORMATIONS MAY
90      'BE APPLIED. TRANSFORMED POINTS REPLACE THE ORIGINAL VALUES
100     'STORED IN ARRAYS X AND Y.
110 CLEARSCREEN
120 DIM X(8,4), Y(8,4), N(8)
130     '
140     '**************** READ DATA FOR GRAPH ********************
150 READ MI, MA     'READ MINIMUM AND MAXIMUM VALUES TO USE FOR DATA RANGE
160 RM = (110 - 10) / (MA - MI)
170 READ D          'D IS NUMBER OF DIVISIONS
180 IF D <= 8 THEN 210
190 PRINT "ONLY 8 DIVISIONS ARE ALLOWED"
200 GOTO 980
210 FOR K = 1 TO D
220     READ M
230     N(K) = 4
240     X(K,1) = 10
250     Y(K,1) = 15 + (K-1) * 10     'SUCCESSIVE BARS GO DOWN THE SCREEN
260     X(K,2) = INT((M - MI) * RM + 10 + .5)
270     Y(K,2) = Y(K,1)
280     X(K,3) = X(K,2)
290     Y(K,3) = Y(K,1) + 6
300     X(K,4) = 10
310     Y(K,4) = Y(K,3)
320 NEXT K
330     'STORE POINTS FOR GRAPH AXES
340 K = D + 1
350 N(K) = 3
360 X(K,1) = 110
```

```
370 Y(K,1) = 10
380 X(K,2) = 10
390 Y(K,2) = 10
400 X(K,3) = 10
410 Y(K,3) = 15 + 10 * D
420 GRAPHICS
430 GOSUB 610              'DRAW GRAPH
440      '
450      '**************** PRINT INSTRUCTIONS *******************
460 POSITION 22,1
470 PRINT "1-TRANSLATE  2-SCALE  3-ROTATE  4-STOP";
480 POSITION 23,1
490 PRINT "WHAT TRANSACTION";
500 INPUT T
510 POSITION 22,1
520 PRINT "                                       "
530 PRINT "                                       ";
540      'GO TO ROUTINE FOR SPECIFIC TRANSFORMATION
550 IF T = 1 THEN GOSUB 710
560 IF T = 2 THEN GOSUB 820
570 IF T = 3 THEN GOSUB 1010
580 IF T = 4 THEN 1220
590 GOSUB 610              'DRAW
600 GOTO 450
610 '######################## DRAW ROUTINE ########################
620 CLEARSCREEN
630 FOR K = 1 TO D+1
640      FOR J = 1 TO N(K)-1
650          IF X(K,J)<0 OR X(K,J)>279 OR X(K,J+1)<0 OR X(K,J+1)>279 THEN 1200
660          IF Y(K,J)<0 OR Y(K,J)>159 OR Y(K,J+1)<0 OR Y(K,J+1)>159 THEN 1200
670          DRAWLINE X(K,J),Y(K,J) TO X(K,J+1),Y(K,J+1)
680      NEXT J
690 NEXT K
700 RETURN
710 '######################## TRANSLATION ROUTINE ########################
720 POSITION 22,1
730 PRINT "H AND V AMOUNTS TO TRANSLATE";
740 INPUT H, V
750 FOR K = 1 TO D+1
760      FOR J = 1 TO N(K)
770          X(K,J) = X(K,J) + H
780          Y(K,J) = Y(K,J) + V
790      NEXT J
800 NEXT K
810 RETURN
820 '######################## SCALING ROUTINE ########################
830 POSITION 22,1
840 PRINT "H AND V AMOUNTS TO SCALE":
850 INPUT HS, VS
860 POSITION 22,1
870 PRINT "                                       "
880 POSITION 22,1
890 PRINT "FIXED POINT";
900 INPUT XF, YF
910      'CALCULATE CONSTANT PART OF EQUATIONS
920 XC = XF * (1 - HS)
930 YC = YF * (1 - VS)
940 FOR K = 1 TO D+1
950      FOR J = 1 TO N(K)
960          X(K,J) = X(K,J) * HS + XC
970          Y(K,J) = Y(K,J) * VS + YC
980      NEXT J
```

Program 6-5 (cont.)

```
990 NEXT K
1000 RETURN
1010 '######################### ROTATION ROUTINE #########################
1020 POSITION 22,1
1030 PRINT "ANGLE TO ROTATE";
1040 INPUT A
1050 A = A * 3.14159 / 180        'CONVERT TO RADIANS
1060 POSITION 22,1
1070 PRINT "                                        "
1080 POSITION 22,1
1090 PRINT "ABOUT WHAT POINT";
1100 INPUT XO, YO
1110 FOR K = 1 TO D+1
1120     FOR J = 1 TO N(K)
1130         XH(K,J) = X(K,J)     'HOLD X(K,J) FOR USE IN Y CALCULATION
1140         X(K,J) = XO + (X(K,J)-XO) * COS(A) + (Y(K,J)-YO) * SIN(A) * 6/5
1150         Y(K,J) = YO + (Y(K,J)-YO) * COS(A) - (XH(K,J)-XO) * SIN(A) * 5/6
1160     NEXT J
1170 NEXT K
1180 RETURN
1190 '####################################################################
1200 PRINT "COORDINATE OUT OF RANGE"
1210 DATA 0,700,5,400,700,300,500,600
1220 END
```

Figure 6-10   A graph, originally displayed as shown in (a), is positioned on the screen as in (b) with Prog. 6-5, through combined translation, scaling, and rotation transformations.

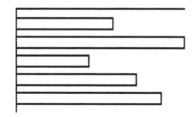

1-TRANSLATE   2-SCALE   3-ROTATE   4-STOP
WHAT TRANSACTION? ■

(a)

Figure 6-10 (cont.)

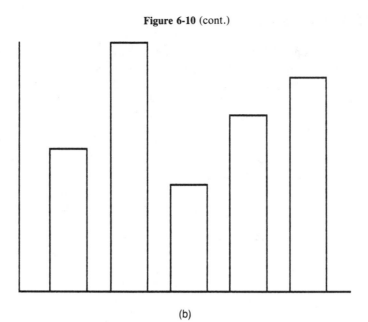

(b)

The order in which we perform translation and rotation can affect the final displayed position of an object. As shown in Fig. 6–11, when we rotate an object about a point external to the object, the final transformed position will depend on whether we translate before or after we rotate.

Figure 6–11   Final position of an object after translation and rotation (about a point external to the object) depends on the order of these transformations. In (a), translation is performed first; in (b), translation is performed last.

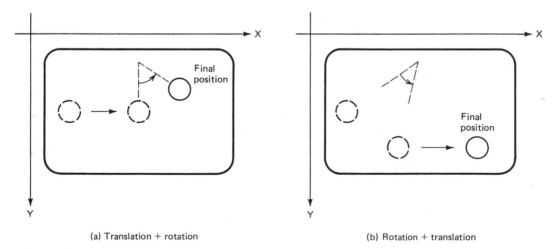

(a) Translation + rotation   (b) Rotation + translation

PROGRAMMING PROJECTS

6–1. Write a program to translate a circle to any input screen location by translating the circle center and redrawing the circle at the new position.

6–2. Modify the program of Prob. 6–1 to scale the circle (relative to its center) and paint the interior after it is translated. Parameters for translating, scaling, and coloring the circle are to be set by input.

6–3. Write a program to translate any character string from one screen location to another, based on the method discussed with Prog. 6–2. Allow both the pixel grid size for characters and translation distances to be specified as input. No part of the character string should be translated off screen.

6–4. Write a program that will scale and display any input polygon, taking the polygon center (the centroid) as a fixed point. The centroid X coordinate is calculated as the average value of the X coordinates of the vertices. The centroid Y coordinate is calculated as the average value of the Y coordinates of the vertices.

6–5. Write a program to scale an input figure with respect to any specified direction. The direction is to be specified by an angle A, measured from the horizontal, as shown in Fig. 6–12. This scaling can be accomplished by rotating the object counterclockwise through the angle A, applying the scaling transformations with HS = S1 and VS = S2, then rotating the object back (through a rotation angle of −A) to its original position. The parameters A, S1, and S2 are to be determined as input.

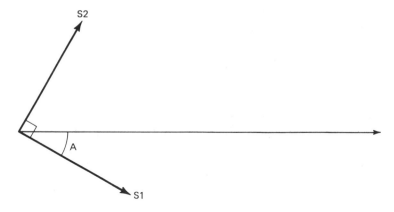

Figure 6–12   Scaling directions specified by an angle A for scaling factors S1 and S2.

6–6. Modify Prog. 6–5 so that string labels can be automatically repositioned on scaled graphs. Determine the new starting position of a label by scaling the distance from the fixed point to the original starting position.

6–7. Write a program that will perform any transformation (translation, scaling, rotation) on a word drawn with pixels in large letters. Stretching the letters along a diagonal (as outlined in Prob. 6–5) slants the letters.

6–8. Write a general transformation program that will translate, scale, or rotate any figure or scene. The figure or scene can be stored in two-dimensional arrays from a graph paper layout. Input parameters will determine the type of transformation to be applied.

Chapter 7

Animation

We can apply basic transformation methods (translation, scaling, rotation) to animate displays. The technique used here is to display an object, erase it, apply transformations, and display the transformed object. When this procedure is repeated several times, we have motion. This is the way animated cartoons are produced. The artist draws each filmstrip frame for the cartoon with slight changes in positions and sizes of objects. Viewing the frames rapidly, one after the other, produces movement.

7–1 POINTS AND CIRCLES

Programs to produce a moving pixel on the screen are adaptations of the translation programs discussed in Chapter 6. Instead of moving the point once, we keep moving it. We can cause the point to move in a straight line or along a curved path.

STRAIGHT–LINE PATH

As a simple example of straight-line animation, let us consider moving a pixel horizontally across the screen. If we want to move the pixel from left to right, we can start the pixel at some location, say (X1,Y), and stop it at some position (X2,Y), where X2 > X1. The animation process then consists of a series of translations from X1 to X2, one unit at a time. At each step, we erase the previously plotted point (X,Y) and plot the next point (X+1,Y). Motion to the left is accomplished by decreasing the X coordinate by one unit at each step. Combining these two motions, we can "bounce" the point back and forth between X1 and X2. In Prog. 7–1 we illustrate this motion. The pixel initially moves to the right with a positive unit increment (DX = 1). When it reaches the point (X2,Y), we reverse the increment (DX = −DX) to make it negative and to move the pixel to the left. At (X1,Y), we reverse the increment again. The program repeats this motion indefinitely.

Program 7–1 can be expanded to draw in the vertical boundaries at X1 and X2, so that the point appears to bounce off these walls. But then we have to change the turnaround point so that we do not erase any of the wall as the point bounces off. We do this by turning the point around 1 unit before it gets to the wall.

Moving a point back and forth along a straight path in the Y direction means that we set up vertical boundaries (Y1 and Y2) and animate the point with a fixed X coordinate. To get motion in any other direction, we increment both the X coordinate and Y coordinate. This process is similar to drawing a straight line, except that we now erase each plotted point before we plot the next one. We can specify the path of motion in various ways. We could choose endpoints for the path, we could use the equation for the line (slope and Y-intercept), or we could select any X and Y increments (DX,DY). In the first two cases, we need to set values for DX and DY so that the ratio DY/DX is equal to the slope of the line.

An example of diagonal straight-line motion is given in Prog. 7–2. Here we bounce a point around inside a box. We select a box size and begin by moving the point diagonally down the screen to the right, with increments of 1 unit for both coordinates. When the point encounters a side of the box it changes direction, as shown in Fig. 7–1. If the point bounces off a vertical side, the X increment changes sign (DX = −DX). If the point bounces off a horizontal side, the Y increment changes sign (DY = −DY). Both increments change sign at a corner.

We can speed up the bouncing pixel in Prog. 7–2 by selecting larger values for DX and DY. Choosing these increments equal to 5 moves the pixel around five

Program 7–1 Bouncing a point horizontally.

```
10 'PROGRAM 7-1. BOUNCING A POINT BETWEEN VERTICAL WALLS.
20  CLEARSCREEN
30  PRINT "ENTER MAXIMUM HORIZONTAL AND VERTICAL"
40  PRINT "VALUES FOR THIS RESOLUTION MODE"
50  INPUT XM, YM
60  PRINT "ENTER X VALUES FOR LEFT WALL AND RIGHT WALL"
70  INPUT XL, XR
80  IF XL >= XR OR XL < 0 OR XR > XM THEN 210
90  DX = 1
100 X = XL + INT((XR-XL) / 2)     'START POINT MIDWAY BETWEEN WALLS
110 Y = INT(YM / 2)
120 CLEARSCREEN
130 GRAPHICS
140      '*********************************************
150 POINTPLOT X,Y
160 IF X > XL AND X < XR THEN 180     'IF STILL WITHIN WALLS, CONTINUE
170 DX = -DX                          'ELSE, TURN AROUND
180 POINTOFF X,Y
190 X = X + DX                        'MOVE POINT
200 GOTO 150
210 END
```

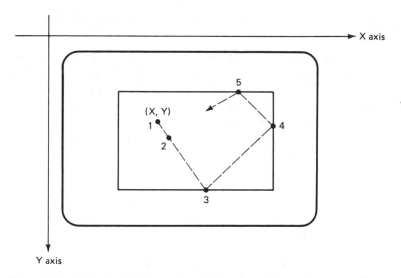

Figure 7–1 Path of a bouncing pixel inside a box. Starting from coordinates (X,Y) at position 1, the pixel will have coordinates (X + DX,Y + DY) at position 2. At position 3, the direction of travel changes by setting DY = − DY. The direction of motion is changed again at position 4 with DX = − DX, and at position 5 with DY = − DY.

Program 7–2 Bouncing a point inside a box using unit increments.

```
10 'PROGRAM 7-2. BOUNCING A POINT WITHIN A BOX.
20      'DX = DY = 1.
30   CLEARSCREEN
40   PRINT "ENTER MAXIMUM HORIZONTAL AND VERTICAL"
50   PRINT "VALUES FOR THIS RESOLUTION MODE"
60   INPUT XM, YM
70   PRINT "ENTER X VALUES FOR LEFT AND RIGHT WALL"
80   INPUT XL, XR
90   IF XL >= XR OR XL < 0 OR XR > XM THEN 330
100  PRINT "ENTER Y VALUES FOR TOP AND BOTTOM OF BOX"
110  INPUT YT, YB
120  IF YT >= YB OR YT < 0 OR YB > YM THEN 330
130  DX = 1
140  DY = 1
150  X = XL + INT((XR-XL) / 2)
160  Y = YT + INT((YB-YT) / 2)          'START THE POINT IN MIDDLE OF BOX
170  CLEARSCREEN
180  GRAPHICS
190      '********************* DRAW BOX *************************
200  DRAWLINE XL,YT TO XR,YT
210  DRAWLINE XR,YT TO XR,YB
220  DRAWLINE XR,YB TO XL,YB
230  DRAWLINE XL,YB TO XL,YT
240      '******************* BOUNCE POINT *********************
250  POINTPLOT X,Y
260  IF X = XL+1 OR X = XR-1 THEN DX = -DX      'IF WE'RE ONE UNIT AWAY FROM
270  IF Y = YT+1 OR Y = YB-1 THEN DY = -DY      'BOX SIDE, REVERSE DIRECTION
280  POINTOFF X,Y            'ERASE CURRENT POINT
290  X = X + DX              'CALCULATE NEW POINT
300  Y = Y + DY
310  GOTO 250
320      '***********************************************************
330  PRINT "ERROR IN CHOICE OF BOX WALLS"
340  END
```

times faster. Choosing one increment larger than the other (such as DX > DY) moves the pixel faster in the direction with the larger increment. We can, as an alternative, slow the pixel motion in one direction by giving the increment for that direction a value less than one (say, 0.5). Changing the magnitude of the increments during program execution can speed up and slow down the motion as the pixel bounces around. If only one increment magnitude is changed as the pixel rebounds from a wall, we get a skidding effect.

Program 7–2 can be modified to work with any values for either increment, DX or DY, by changing the rebound test. The direction of motion of the pixel must be reversed whenever either the X coordinate or Y coordinate would be incremented through a wall of the box. We can make this change in Prog. 7–2 by replacing lines 260 through 270 with the following:

```
260 IF DX > 0 THEN 268     'GOING TOWARD RIGHT
262     'OTHERWIDE, GOING LEFT AND DX IS NEGATIVE
264 IF X + DX <= XL THEN DX = -DX
266 GOTO 269
268 IF X + DX >= XR THEN DX = -DX
269     'TEST FOR Y
270 IF DY > 0 THEN 278     'GOING DOWN
272     'OTHERWISE, GOING UP AND DY IS NEGATIVE
274 IF Y + DY <= YT THEN DY = -DY
276 GOTO 280
278 IF Y + DY >= YB THEN DY = -DY
```

The program segment above has the effect of rebounding the pixel before it gets to the walls of the box when either DX or DY is greater than 1. To get a more realistic bounce, we can plot the pixel near the wall before reversing its direction of motion. We could do this by always choosing the increments and box size so that the distance across the box in either direction is an integral multiple of the increment for that direction. This is probably a little too restrictive for many applications. A more general solution to this problem is to project the path of the pixel to the wall and determine the intersection point. Then we can produce a display that rebounds the pixel at the walls for any increment chosen.

Figure 7–2 depicts the path of pixel motion toward a vertical boundary of a box. Starting from position (X,Y), the intersection point (XI,YI) on this boundary is determined from the equation for the straight line path:

$$YI = M*XI + (Y - M*X) \qquad (7-1)$$

with XI = XR at the right boundary and XI = XL at the left boundary. The slope, M, of the line is calculated from the coordinate increments as

$$M = DY / DX \qquad (7-2)$$

Equations (7–1) and (7–2) can be used to determine intersection positions for any boundary and any of the possible directions of travel. For intersection with the top or bottom of the box, XI is calculated from (7–1) as XI = X + (YI − Y) / M, where

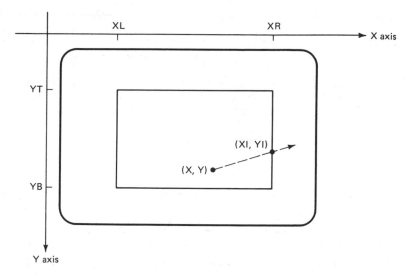

Figure 7–2 A pixel at position (X,Y), traveling along the diagonal path indicated inside a box, will intersect the right boundary at position (XI,YI).

YI = YT or YI = YB (Fig. 7–2). At each of these rebound positions, we plot the pixel 1 unit inside the boundary and reverse the direction of motion. An application of this method for a bouncing ball is given in Prog. 7–3.

A moving circle provides the basis for many animation applications involving a bouncing ball. The methods discussed for points can be used to bounce a circle around as if it were a big point. We move the circle center and test for intersection of the circle boundary with the turnaround positions. A bouncing ball inside a box is displayed by Prog. 7–3, using the techniques discussed for rebounding points. The ball is rebounded from a wall by finding the intersection of the ball's path with the wall and turning the ball around at a point 1 unit inside the wall.

Program 7–3 Bouncing a ball inside a box.

```
10 'PROGRAM 7-3. BOUNCING BALL WITHIN A BOX.
20     'DX = DY = 5. IF BALL IS GOING TO GO BEYOND A BOUNDARY,
30     'FIND INTERSECTION OF BALL & BOUNDARY THEN DRAW BALL.
40     'REVERSE BALL'S DIRECTION, AND CONTINUE.
50     '*********************************************************
60 CLEARSCREEN
70 PRINT "ENTER MAXIMUM HORIZONTAL AND VERTICAL"
80 PRINT "VALUES FOR THIS RESOLUTION MODE"
90 INPUT XM, YM
100 PRINT "ENTER X VALUES FOR LEFT AND RIGHT WALL"
110 INPUT XL, XR
120 IF XL >= XR OR XL < 0 OR XR > XM THEN 940
130 PRINT "ENTER Y VALUES FOR TOP AND BOTTOM OF BOX"
140 INPUT YT, YB
150 IF YT >= YB OR YT < 0 OR YB > YM THEN 940
160 DX = 5        'BALL TRAVELS 5 UNITS IN EACH STEP
170 DY = 5
180 R = 3        'R IS RADIUS OF BALL
190 XN = XL + INT((XR-XL) / 2)    'START BALL IN MIDDLE OF BOX
200 YN = YT + INT((YB-YT) / 2)
210 CLEARSCREEN
```

Program 7-3 (cont.)

```
220 GRAPHICS
230     '********************** DRAW BOX **************************
240 DRAWLINE XL,YT TO XR,YT
250 DRAWLINE XR,YT TO XR,YB
260 DRAWLINE XR,YB TO XL,YB
270 DRAWLINE XL,YB TO XL,YT
280     '********************* BOUNCE BALL *********************
290 COLOR 0,0
300 CIRCLEPLOT X,Y,R                'ERASE CURRENT BALL POSITION
310 COLOR 1,0
320 CIRCLEPLOT XN,YN,R              'DRAW NEW POSITION
330 X = XN                         'SAVE CURRENT POSITION IN X AND Y
340 Y = YN
350 BX = 0                         'BX AND BY ARE SWITCHES TO INDICATE
360 BY = 0                         'WHICH WALL WE'RE GOING TO HIT
370 M = DY / DX                    'M IS SLOPE OF BALL'S PATH
380     '
390     '*************************************************************
400     'WILL WE HIT A VERTICAL WALL?
410 IF DX > 0 THEN 480             'WE'RE GOING TO THE RIGHT
420     'OTHERWISE WE'RE GOING TO THE LEFT (DX IS NEGATIVE)
430 IF X + DX - R > XL THEN 530         'WE'RE STILL WITHIN THE BOX
440 BX = 1                         'GOING OUT OF BOX AT AN X WALL
450 XN = XL + R + 1                'NEW X IS JUST INSIDE LEFT WALL
460 GOTO 530
470     '^^^^^^^^^^^^^^^^^^^^^^^^^^^^^^^^^^^^^^^^^^^^^^^^^^^^^^^^^^^
480     'GOING RIGHT
490 IF X + DX + R < XR THEN 530         'WE'RE STILL WITHIN THE BOX
500 BX = 1                         'GOING OUT OF BOX AT AN X WALL
510 XN = XR - R - 1                'NEW X IS JUST INSIDE RIGHT WALL
520     '*************************************************************
530     'WILL WE HIT A HORIZONTAL WALL?
540 IF DY > 0 THEN 610             'WE'RE GOING DOWN
550     'OTHERWISE WE'RE GOING UP (DY IS NEGATIVE)
560 IF Y + DY - R > YT THEN 670         'WE'RE STILL WITHIN THE BOX
570 BY = 1                         'GOING OUT OF BOX AT A Y WALL
580 YN = YT + R + 1                'NEW Y IS JUST INSIDE OF TOP
590 GOTO 670
600     '^^^^^^^^^^^^^^^^^^^^^^^^^^^^^^^^^^^^^^^^^^^^^^^^^^^^^^^^^^^
610     'GOING DOWN
620 IF Y + DY + R < YB THEN 670         'WE'RE STILL WITHIN THE BOX
630 BY = 1                         'GOING OUT OF BOX AT A Y WALL
640 YN = YB - R - 1                'NEW Y IS JUST INSIDE OF BOTTOM
650     '
660     '*************************************************************
670     'ARE WE BOUNCING OFF NO WALLS, AN X WALL, A Y WALL, OR BOTH WALLS?
680 IF BX = 0 AND BY = 0 THEN 730       'NOT BOUNCING
690 IF BX = 0 AND BY = 1 THEN 770       'BOUNCING OFF Y
700 IF BX = 1 AND BY = 0 THEN 810       'BOUNCING OFF X
710 IF BX = 1 AND BY = 1 THEN 850       'BOUNCING OFF BOTH (IN A CORNER)
720 '
730 '####################### NOT BOUNCING ########################
740 XN = X + DX
750 YN = Y + DY
760 GOTO 290
770 '####################### BOUNCE OFF Y WALL ###################
780 XN = (YN - Y) / M + X
790 DY = - DY
800 GOTO 290
810 '####################### BOUNCE OFF X WALL ###################
820 YN = (XN - X) * M + Y
```

```
830 DX = -DX
840 GOTO 290
850 '##################### GOING INTO A CORNER #####################
860     'WHICH WALL WOULD IT HIT FIRST?
870 IF ABS(XN - X) < ABS(YN - Y) THEN 810        'BOUNCE OFF X
880 IF ABS(YN - Y) < ABS(XN - X) THEN 770        'BOUNCE OFF Y
890     'BALL IS EQUAL DISTANCE FROM X AND Y WALLS ON EACH SIDE OF CORNER
900 DX = -DX
910 DY = -DY
920 GOTO 290
930 '####################################################################
940 PRINT "ERROR IN CHOICE OF BOX WALLS"
950 END
```

We could draw a more realistic ball in Prog. 7–3 by filling in the interior of the circle with a foreground color. The program could also be modified to accept the box boundaries, the ball size, and the ball's starting position as input.

CURVED PATHS

Animating a pixel or circle along a specified curved path is accomplished by determining positions from the path equation. The motion is begun at a specified starting postion and terminated at a specified stopping point. We can move a pixel along a circular or elliptical path with the circle-drawing techniques discussed in Section 5–1, or with the rotation methods of Section 6–3. To get smooth motion around a circle, we want the pixel positions spaced evenly along the path. This means that we would use trigonometric equations for calculating coordinate positions, with an equal angular distance between positions. Large angular increments between points (say, 30 degrees) are used to produce faster motion. Varying the radius of a circle results in a spiraling motion. Rotations along circular paths provide a basis for modeling satellite orbits, the solar system, or machine parts.

A pixel moving along a parabola simulates the path of motion of an object tossed into the air. The distance that the object travels is determined by how fast it is initially projected into the air and the angle of this projection, measured from the horizontal, as shown in Fig. 7–3. From the values of the projection speed S and projection angle A, we can calculate the range R and maximum height HT as

$$R = S*S*SIN(2*A) / G$$

$$HT = ((S*SIN(A))^2) / (2*G)$$

(7–3)

where G is the acceleration due to gravity (980 cm/sec $*$ sec). For a fixed value of S, we get maximum range at an angle of 45 degrees. Height, HT, is largest when we throw the object straight up (A = 90 degrees). Pixel positions along this curve are obtained by varying X from 0 to R and calculating the corresponding Y values from the equation

$$Y = C1*X^2 + C2*X + YO$$

(7–4)

where YO is any starting value we choose on the screen, and the constants C1 and C2 are determined as

$$C1 = G / (2 * (S * COS(A))^2)$$

$$C2 = -TAN(A)$$

(7–5)

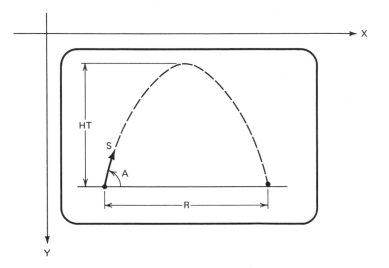

Figure 7–3 An object tossed into the air with initial speed S at an angle A will rise to height HT and land a distance R away from the starting point. Both the height HT and range R can be calculated from values for the projection speed S and projection angle A.

Program 7–4 animates a point along a parabolic path. Coordinates for the starting position (XO,YO) are specified as input. The projection angle A and initial speed S are also determined as input. Angle A is limited to values between 0 and 90 degrees, so that the motion is to the right (Fig. 7–3). Values for S in the range 200 to 600 provide curves with maximum height HT and range R at about 200. Other ranges for S can be chosen by changing the value of G. We can vary the initial and final positions of the pixel in this program to simulate other similar types of motion. Tossing an object from the top of a building or hill means that we start and stop the motion at different Y values. To simulate the path of an object dropped from a moving airplane, the object begins at maximum height, HT, and falls to the ground.

Simulation of a bouncing ball is displayed by Prog. 7–5. The ball is dropped from some height H and bounces across the screen. Each bounce is decreased a little in height as the ball travels across the screen (Fig. 7–4). A SIN function is used to obtain an oscillating motion, and the EXP function is used to decrease the amplitude. Since we want the motion to begin at coordinates (0,H), we set D = PI/2 in the SIN function. Next we choose a distance of 40 between bounces, so that several bounces can be displayed across the screen. We do this by setting W = PI/40. Finally, we want to display the ball exactly when it hits the ground at

Program 7-4 Animating a point along a parabolic path.

```
10  'PROGRAM 7-4. MOVING ALONG A PARABOLIC CURVE
20  CLEARSCREEN
30  PRINT "ENTER MAXIMUM HORIZONTAL AND VERTICAL"
40  PRINT "FOR THIS RESOLUTION MODE"
50  INPUT XM, YM
60  PRINT "ENTER COORDINATES OF START POSITION"
70  INPUT XO, YO
80  IF XO >= O AND XO <= XM AND YO >= O AND YO <= YM THEN 110
90  PRINT "RE-ENTER START POSITION"
100 GOTO 60
110 PRINT "ENTER ANGLE (0 - 90)"
120 INPUT A
130 A = A * 3.14159 / 180        'CONVERT A TO RADIANS
140 PRINT "ENTER SPEED (100 - 600)"
150 INPUT S
160 G = 980                'G IS GRAVITY
170 R = S * S * SIN(2 * A) / G          'R IS RANGE OF TRAVEL ACROSS X AXIS
180 IF XO + R <= XM THEN 210            'WILL WHOLE CURVE FIT ON SCREEN?
190 PRINT "RE-ENTER ANGLE AND SPEED"    'IF NOT, ENTER NEW VALUES
200 GOTO 110
210 HT = ((S * SIN(A)) ^ 2) / (2 * G)         'HT IS HEIGHT OF CURVE
220 IF HT > O AND HT <= YM THEN 260     'WILL WHOLE CURVE FIT ON SCREEN?
230 PRINT "RE-ENTER ANGLE AND SPEED"
240 GOTO 110
250     'CALCULATE COEFFICIENTS OF EQUATION
260 C1 = G / (2 * (S * COS(A)) ^ 2)
270 C2 = - TAN(A)
280 CLEARSCREEN
290 GRAPHICS
300     '****************** MOVE POINT ALONG CURVE *********************
310 FOR X = O TO R
320     Y = C1 * X * X + C2 * X + YO
330     POINTPLOT X+XO,Y
340     POINTOFF X+XO,Y
350 NEXT X
360 END
```

Program 7-5 Bouncing motion of a dropped ball.

```
10  'PROGRAM 7-5. BOUNCING BALL DROPPED FROM SOME HEIGHT.
20      'PROGRAM SIMULATES BOUNCING OF A DROPPED BALL.
30  CLEARSCREEN
40  PRINT "ENTER MAXIMUM HORIZONTAL AND VERTICAL"
50  PRINT "VALUES FOR THIS RESOLUTION MODE"
60  INPUT XM, YM
70  PRINT "BALL IS DROPPED FROM WHAT HEIGHT";
80  INPUT H
90  W = 3.14159 / 40           'DISTANCE FROM BOUNCE TO BOUNCE IS 40
100 D = 90 * 3.14159 / 180     'DISPLACE BY 90 DEGREES (EXPRESSED AS RADIANS)
110 K = .01                    'K IS DAMPING FACTOR
120 CLEARSCREEN
130 GRAPHICS
140 DRAWLINE O,YM TO XM,YM            'DRAW GROUND
150     '
160     '****************** DROP BALL AND BOUNCE *******************
170 FOR XN = O TO XM-10 STEP 4        '4 EVENLY DIVIDES INTO 40
180     YN = H * SIN(W * XN + D) * EXP(-K * XN)
190     YN = YM - ABS(YN) - 3
200     COLOR O,O
210     CIRCLEPLOT X,Y,2            'ERASE CURRENT POSITION
220     COLOR 1,O
230     CIRCLEPLOT XN+10,YN,2          'DRAW NEW POSITION
240     X = XN + 10       'STORE CURRENT POSITION IN X AND Y
250     Y = YN
260 NEXT XN
270 END
```

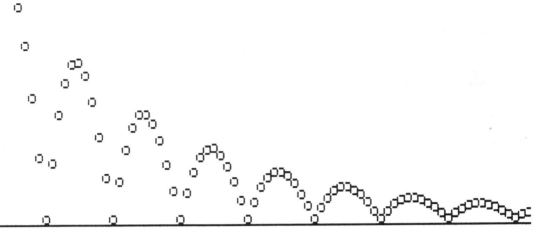

Figure 7–4 The motion of a ball bouncing from left to right, displayed by Prog. 7–5.

each bounce. This means that the increment for X must be chosen so that it divides evenly into 40. For this example, the X increment is set to 4, and the ball is displayed each time it bounces at X = 20, 60, 100, and so on. The final display is offset 10 pixels to the right so that motion does not begin at the edge of the screen.

Circles can be utilized in animated displays in a variety of ways. Moving wheels can be simulated by translating the circle center and rotating the spokes of the wheel. By scaling circles, we can simulate motion toward or away from us. Interactive input can be used to produce motion along an arbitrary path. Using the keyboard, paddles, or light pen, we could direct objects in any direction with any specified speed.

7–2 LINES AND POLYGONS

Simple motion of a line or polygon on a video screen is accomplished with the same basic techniques used to move a point or circle. We display all the lines of the object, erase the object, and redraw all the lines in a new position. Repeating this sequence over and over again produces object motion. Animating an object involves additional considerations when we want to rotate or scale the object or when we want to move different parts of the object differently.

LINES

A line drawn between points (X,Y1) and (X,Y2) is moved vertically by incrementing only the Y coordinate. Program 7–6 bounces a vertical line up and down between two fixed boundaries. The motion of this pogo stick is speeded up or slowed down with choices for DY in the range 1 to 20. This program never lets the line reach or overshoot the boundaries set at the top (YT) and at the bottom (YB).

We can animate the vertical line horizontally by incrementing the X coordinate instead of the Y coordinate. In this case, we might bounce it off

132

Program 7-6   Bouncing a line vertically.

```
10  'PROGRAM 7-6. MOVING VERTICAL LINE UP AND DOWN.
20  CLEARSCREEN
30  PRINT "ENTER MAXIMUM HORIZONTAL AND VERTICAL"
40  PRINT "VALUES FOR THIS RESOLUTION MODE"
50  INPUT XM, YM
60  PRINT "ENTER Y VALUES FOR TOP AND BOTTOM BOUNDARIES OF BOUNCE"
70  INPUT YT, YB
80  IF YT < YB AND YT >= 0 AND YB <= YM THEN 110
90  PRINT "BAD BOUNDARIES. CHOOSE YT < YB AND BOTH BETWEEN 0 AND";YM
100 GOTO 60
110 PRINT "ENTER AMOUNT FOR CHANGING Y VALUES OF LINE"
120 INPUT DY
130 X = INT(XM / 2)             'CENTER LINE ACROSS SCREEN
140 Y1 = YT + INT((YB - YT) / 2) - 20          'ENDPOINTS ARE 20 UNITS UP AND
150 Y2 = YT + INT((YB - YT) / 2) + 20          'DOWN FROM CENTER OF BOUNDARIES
160 CLEARSCREEN
170 GRAPHICS
180     '*************************************************************
190 COLOR 1,0
200 DRAWLINE X,Y1 TO X,Y2
210 IF DY > 0 THEN 250          'LINE IS GOING DOWN
220     'OTHERWISE LINE IS GOING UP (DY IS NEGATIVE)
230 IF Y1 + DY <= YT THEN DY = -DY          'REVERSE DIRECTION
240 GOTO 270
250     'LINE IS GOING DOWN
260 IF Y2 + DY >= YB THEN DY = -DY          'REVERSE DIRECTION
270     'ERASE CURRENT LINE, CALCULATE NEW POSITION, GOTO DRAW
280 COLOR 0,0
290 DRAWLINE X,Y1 TO X,Y2
300 Y1 = Y1 + DY
310 Y2 = Y2 + DY
320 GOTO 180
330 END
```

vertical walls positioned at XL and XR. Incrementing both coordinates moves the line diagonally. We could then bounce the line around on straight paths much as we did with a single pixel. Horizontal lines, or lines drawn at any angle, are moved about with similar methods. We move both endpoints of the line with the same increments, DX and DY. The line moves faster for larger increment values and changes direction whenever we change the sign of one or both increments.

Lines can be moved along curved paths by varying the magnitude of DX and DY as the lines move. To move a line along a particular curved path, we keep some point of the line on the curve as it moves. For example, Prog. 7-7 moves one end of a horizontal line in a circle. The line moves back and forth and up and down, simulating motion of a horizontal bar attached to a rotor (Fig. 7-5).

In some cases we would like to have a line turn as it moves along a curved path. Figure 7-6 shows positions and orientations of a line (with an arrow tip) whose left endpoint traverses a parabolic path as the line turns to stay tangent to the curve at each step. This motion could simulate the appearance of an arrow shot into the air. To get this motion, we need to change the slope of the line as it moves. For the parabola equation (7-4), the slope of a line tangent to the curve is calculated from the value of the X position:

$$M = 2*C1*X + C2 \qquad\qquad (7-6)$$

Program 7–7 Moving a line in a circle.

```
10 'PROGRAM 7-7. CIRCULAR MOVEMENT OF A HORIZONTAL LINE.
20  CLEARSCREEN
30  PRINT "ENTER MAXIMUM HORIZONTAL AND VERTICAL"
40  PRINT "VALUES FOR THIS RESOLUTION MODE"
50  INPUT XM, YM
60  XC = INT(XM / 2) - 40        'XC AND YC WILL BE CIRCLE CENTER
70  YC = INT(YM / 2)
80  R = 50                'R IS RADIUS
90  YA = 5/6              'YA IS RESOLUTION ADJUSTMENT
100     'CALCULATE X1 POINTS AT EVERY 15 DEGREES ALONG THE CIRCLE
110 RE = 360 * 3.14159 / 180        'CONVERT 360 TO RADIANS
120 DA =  15 * 3.14159 / 180        'CONVERT 15 TO RADIANS
130 CLEARSCREEN
140 GRAPHICS
150     '***********************************************************
160 FOR A = DA TO RE STEP DA
170     COLOR 0,0
180     DRAWLINE X,Y TO X + 80,Y         'ERASE CURRENT LINE
190     X = XC + R * COS(A)
200     Y = YC + R * SIN(A) * YA
210     COLOR 1,0
220     DRAWLINE X,Y TO X + 80,Y         'LINE IS 80 UNITS LONG
230 NEXT A
240 GOTO 160
250 END
```

Figure 7–5 Positions of a line with left endpoint moving in a circle, as output by Prog. 7–7. The horizontal line starts at the right, moves down and to the left, and moves around the circular path back to the starting position.

The coordinates (X1,Y1) of the other end of the line can be determined from this slope and the line length L, as indicated in Fig. 7–7. From this diagram we obtain the relationships for the sides of the triangle with hypotenuse L as

$$X1 - X = L * COS(AS)$$
$$Y1 - Y = L * SIN(AS)$$

$$(7–7)$$

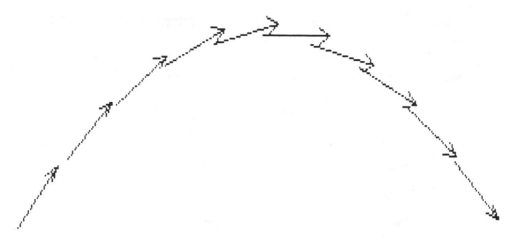

Figure 7–6 Appearance of a line whose left endpoint moves along a parabola, with the line remaining tangent to the path as it travels left to right. Displayed by Prog. 7–8.

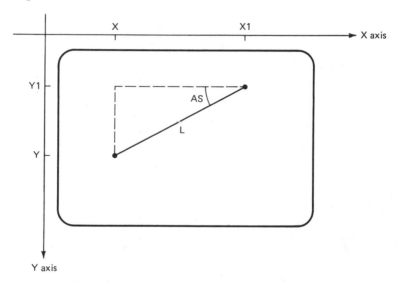

Figure 7–7 Coordinate values (X1,Y1) for one end of a line can be calculated from the values for the line length L, the slope angle AS, and the coordinate values (X,Y) of the other end of the line. The slope angle AS is determined from the value for the slope M as AS = ATN(M).

The angle AS is the angle that the line makes with the horizontal. This angle is calculated from the slope M:

$$AS = ATN(M) \tag{7–8}$$

The motion of the arrow in Fig. 7–6 along a parabola is produced by Prog. 7–8, using equations (7–7) and (7–8). We draw in the tip of the arrow at each position with short lines attached to the point (X1,Y1). These short lines have slopes that are only slightly different from the slope M for the arrow shaft. In this

Program 7-8   Motion of an arrow along a parabolic path.

```
10  'PROGRAM 7-8. ARROW SHOT ALONG A PARABOLIC PATH.
20      'REPEATEDLY DRAWS AND ERASES AN ARROW WHOSE TAIL
30      'IS A POINT ON A PARABOLA. REMAINDER OF THE ARROW
40      'IS FOUND USING THIS TAIL POINT, THE SLOPE OF THE
50      'LINE TANGENT TO THE CURVE AT THIS POINT, AND THE
60      'LENGTH OF THE ARROW
70  '*****************************************************************
80  CLEARSCREEN
90  PRINT "ENTER MAXIMUM HORIZONTAL AND VERTICAL"
100 PRINT "VALUES FOR THIS RESOLUTION MODE"
110 INPUT XM, YM
120 PRINT "ENTER COORDINATES OF START POSITION"
130 INPUT XO, YO
140 IF XO>=0 AND XO<=XM AND YO>=0 AND YM<=YM THEN 170
150 PRINT "START POSITION OFF SCREEN"
160 GOTO 120
170 PRINT "ENTER ANGLE (0 - 90)";
180 INPUT A
190 A = A * 3.14159 / 180        'EXPRESS A AS RADIANS
200 PRINT "ENTER SPEED (100 - 600)";
210 INPUT S
220 G = 980              'G IS FORCE OF GRAVITY
230 LA = 40              'LA IS LENGTH OF ARROW
240 LT = 8               'LT IS LENGTH OF TIP OF ARROW
250     'FIND RANGE AND HEIGHT OF ARROW'S FLIGHT
260 R = S * S * SIN(2 * A) / G       'R IS RANGE (ON X AXIS) OF ARROW FLIGHT
270 IF XO + R <= XM THEN 300       'WILL ARROW'S ENDPOINTS FIT ON SCREEN?
280 PRINT "RE-ENTER ANGLE AND SPEED"
290 GOTO 170
300 HT = ((S * SIN(A)) ^ 2) / (2 * G)    'HT IS HEIGHT OF ARROW
310 IF HT > 0 AND HT <= YM THEN 340      'WILL ARROW PATH FIT ON SCREEN?
320 PRINT "RE-ENTER ANGLE AND SPEED"
330 GOTO 170
340     'DETERMINE COEFFICIENTS FOR PARABOLA'S EQUATION
350 C1 = G / (2 * (S * COS(A)) ^ 2)
360 C2 = - TAN(A)
370 CLEARSCREEN
380 GRAPHICS
390     '******************** MOVE ARROW ************************
400     'FIND ARROW TAIL POINTS ALONG THE PARABOLA AND DRAW ARROW
410 FOR X = 0 TO R STEP R/10     'PLACE ARROW AT SUCCESSIVE TENTHS OF R
420     Y = C1 * X * X + C2 * X + YO
430     'X AND Y ARE THE TAILPOINTS ON THE PARABOLA
440     'FIND OTHER ENDPOINT OF ARROW
450     M = 2 * C1 * X + C2      'M IS SLOPE OF THE ARROW
460     A1 = ATN(M)             'INVERSE TANGENT OF M GIVES ANGLE A1
470     Y1 = Y + LA * SIN(A1)
480     X1 = X + LA * COS(A1)
490     IF X1 > XM OR Y1 > YM THEN 800           'IS OTHER ENDPOINT ON SCREEN?
500     GOSUB 730       'ERASE ARROW
510     'CALCULATE ARROW TIP
520     M2 = M + .75            'SLOPE OF ONE TIP
530     A2 = ATN(M2)
540     X2 = X1 - LT * COS(A2)
550     Y2 = Y1 - LT * SIN(A2)
560     M3 = M - .75            'SLOPE OF SECOND TIP
570     A3 = ATN(M3)
580     X3 = X1 - LT * COS(A3)
590     Y3 = Y1 - LT * SIN(A3)
600     GOSUB 670        'DRAW ARROW
610     XS = X               'SAVE CURRENT POSITION IN XS, YS, X1S, Y1S
620     YS = Y
630     X1S = X1
```

Program 7-8 (cont.)

```
640       Y1S = Y1
650 NEXT X
660 GOTO 800
670 '####################### DRAW ARROW #########################
680 COLOR 1,0
690 DRAWLINE X,Y TO X1,Y1
700 DRAWLINE X1,Y1 TO X2,Y2
710 DRAWLINE X1,Y1 TO X3,Y3
720 RETURN
730 '####################### ERASE ARROW #########################
740 COLOR 0,0
750 DRAWLINE XS,YS TO X1S,Y1S
760 DRAWLINE X1S,Y1S TO X2,Y2
770 DRAWLINE X1S,Y1S TO X3,Y3
780 RETURN
790 '#############################################################
800 END
```

program, we choose one of these slopes to be 0.75 greater than M and the other to be 0.75 less than M. The length of each short line is chosen to be 8 and the arrow shaft length is set to 40.

Motion of a line tangent to any curve can be produced by the methods of Prog. 7–8. We move one end of the line along the curve, compute the slope at each position, determine the slope angle, and calculate the coordinates for the other end of the line using equation (7–7). The slope of a line tangent to a curve at any point is determined from the equation for that curve. As an example, a third-degree polynomial equation written as

$$Y = C1*X^3 + C2*X^2 + C3*X + C4 \qquad (7\text{–}9)$$

has a slope at position X of

$$M = 3*C1*X^2 + 2*C2*X + C3 \qquad (7\text{–}10)$$

The general sine curve

$$Y = H*SIN(W*X + D) \qquad (7\text{–}11)$$

has a slope at position X calculated from the COS function:

$$M = H*W*COS(W*X + D) \qquad (7\text{–}12)$$

Moving a line tangent to a circle or ellipse can be accomplished with the rotation transformations.

We can spin a line about any fixed point by performing repeated rotations. Program 7–9 outputs a line rotating about its midpoint. This type of motion could be used to represent the spokes of a rotating wheel. The rotation equations used in this program have been factored and rewritten in a form that reduces computation time.

Moving lines can be used to animate displays in several ways. We can use a moving line in a game application to represent a paddle or racquet and hit bouncing balls. We can also move the component lines of a picture in different ways to represent more complex motion, as in the simulation of a walking figure.

Program 7–9   Motion of a spinning line.

```
10 'PROGRAM 7-9. ROTATING LINE AROUND ITS MIDPOINT.
20  CLEARSCREEN
30  PRINT "ENTER MAXIMUM HORIZONTAL AND VERTICAL"
40  PRINT "VALUES FOR THIS RESOLUTION MODE"
50  INPUT XM, YM
60  XC = INT(XM / 2)              'CENTER AND ROTATE LINE ABOUT SCREEN MIDPOINT
70  YC = INT(YM / 2)
80  X1 = XC - 10                  'LINE IS 20 UNITS LONG, CENTERED ON MIDPOINT
90  X2 = XC + 10
100 Y1 = YC
110 Y2 = YC
120 YA = 5/6                      'YA IS RESOLUTION ADJUSTMENT FOR Y VALUES
130 XA = 6/5                      'XA IS RESOLUTION ADJUSTMENT FOR X VALUES
140 A = 15 * 3.14159 / 180        'EXPRESS 15 DEGREES AS RADIANS
150     'CALCULATE CONSTANT PARTS OF ROTATION EQUATIONS
160 CA = COS(A)
170 SX = SIN(A) * XA
180 SY = SIN(A) * YA
190 XE = XC - XC * CA - YC * SX           'FIND CONSTANT PART OF
200 YE = YC - YC * CA + XC * SY           'ROTATION EQUATIONS
210 CLEARSCREEN
220 GRAPHICS
230     '**************** ROTATE ENDPOINTS & DRAW ****************
240 X1R = XE + X1 * CA + Y1 * SX
250 Y1R = YE + Y1 * CA - X1 * SY
260 X2R = XE + X2 * CA + Y2 * SX
270 Y2R = YE + Y2 * CA - X2 * SY
280     'ERASE OLD LINE
290 COLOR 0,0
300 DRAWLINE X1,Y1 TO X2,Y2
310     'DRAW NEW LINE
320 COLOR 1,0
330 DRAWLINE X1R,Y1R TO X2R,Y2R
340     'SAVE CURRENT POINTS FOR LATER ERASING
350 X1 = X1R
360 Y1 = Y1R
370 X2 = X2R
380 Y2 = Y2R
390 GOTO 230
400 END
```

POLYGONS

A polygon is specified by the coordinates for its vertices, which can be stored in the order they are to be connected. Moving the polygon means moving all vertex points and redrawing the polygon. Program 7–10 moves a truck outline from left to right across a screen, as illustrated in Fig. 7–8. The program will move any object defined in the DATA statements; but the more lines in the object, the slower the animation. We can generalize this motion to any direction by using increments for both the horizontal and vertical directions, as in previous examples.

Scaling a polygon simulates motion toward or away from us. A boat sails into the sunset in Fig. 7–9, as produced by Prog. 7–11. The boat is repeatedly scaled relative to a point on the horizon, causing it to recede into the distance.

Program 7–10   Motion of a truck along a straight line.

```
10 'PROGRAM 7-10. TRUCK MOVING ACROSS SCREEN.
20  CLEARSCREEN
30  DIM X(20), Y(20), XT(20)
40  XM = 300     'XM IS MAXIMUM X VALUE FOR THIS SYSTEM
50  READ N       'N IS NUMBER OF POINTS IN PICTURE
60  FOR K = 1 TO N
70      READ X(K), Y(K)
80      'STORE X IN ALTERNATE ARRAY SINCE IT IS USED TO DRAW
90      XT(K) = X(K)
100 NEXT K
110 H = 15
120 GRAPHICS
130 GOSUB 260            'DRAW
140     '***************** TRANSLATE, ERASE, DRAW **************
150 FOR K = 1 TO N
160     XT(K) = X(K) + H          'NO NEED TO TRANSLATE Y
170 NEXT K
180 GOSUB 320            'ERASE PICTURE IN OLD POSITION
190 GOSUB 260            'DRAW PICUTRE IN NEW POSITION
200 IF XT(14) + H > XM THEN 430          'IF MOVING RIGHTMOST POINT TAKES US
210                                      'OFF SCREEN, STOP. ELSE, CONTINUE.
220 FOR K = 1 TO N
230     X(K) = XT(K)                'SAVE CURRENT POSITION IN X
240 NEXT K
250 GOTO 140
260 '######################### DRAW ROUTINE #########################
270 COLOR 1,0
280 FOR K = 1 TO N-1
290     DRAWLINE XT(K),Y(K) TO XT(K+1),Y(K+1)
300 NEXT K
310 RETURN
320 '######################### ERASE ROUTINE #########################
330 COLOR 0,0
340 FOR K = 1 TO N-1
350     DRAWLINE X(K),Y(K) TO X(K+1),Y(K+1)
360 NEXT K
370 RETURN
380 '################################################################
390 DATA 19
400 DATA 10,90,20,90,20,93,22,97,30,97,32,93,32,90
410 DATA 78,90,78,93,82,97,88,97,90,93,90,90,100,90
420 DATA 100,70,80,70,75,55,10,55,10,90
430 END
```

Figure 7–8   Driving a truck across the screen from left to right, as animated by Prog. 7–10.

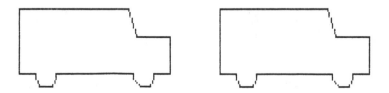

Program 7–11   Animation by scaling (sailboat).

```
10 'PROGRAM 7-11. SAILING INTO THE SUNSET.
20      'REPEATEDLY SCALES BOAT IN RELATION TO A FIXED POINT
30      '(-30,70). SCALING BOTH SHRINKS THE BOAT AND MOVES
40      'IT FROM RIGHT TO LEFT.
50   CLEARSCREEN
60   DIM X(10), Y(10), XN(10), YN(10)
70   YA = 5/6      'YA IS RESOLUTION ADJUSTMENT
80   GRAPHICS
90      '*************** CREATE BACKGROUND *********************
100  DRAWLINE 0,60 TO 319,60              'DRAW HORIZON
110      'DRAW HALF-CIRCLE FOR SETTING SUN
120  R = 25        'R IS SUN'S RADIUS
130  XS = 40       'CENTER SUN AROUND XS, YS
140  YS = 59
150  DA = 1 / R    'DA IS INCREMENT FOR ANGLE
160  C1 = 180 * 3.14159 / 180
170  C2 = 360 * 3.14159 / 180
180  FOR A = C1 TO C2 STEP DA
190      POINTPLOT XS + R * COS(A), YS + R * SIN(A) * YA
200  NEXT A
210      '************** READ BOAT POINTS AND DRAW **************
220  FOR K = 1 TO 9
230      READ X(K), Y(K)
240      Y(K) = Y(K) * YA
250      XN(K) = X(K)
260      YN(K) = Y(K)
270  NEXT K
280  GOSUB 510              'DRAW SAILBOAT
290      '******************** SAIL INTO SUNSET *******************
300  XF = -30                            'SCALE IN RELATION TO XF,YF
310  YF = 70
320  HS = .9               'SCALE BOAT TO 9/10 OF CURRENT SIZE
330  VS = .9
340      'CALCULATE CONSTANT PARTS OF SCALING EQUATIONS
350  XE = XF * (1 - HS)
360  YE = YF * (1 - VS)
370  FOR T = 1 TO 12
380      FOR K = 1 TO 9
390          XN(K) = X(K) * HS + XE + H
400          YN(K) = Y(K) * VS + YE + V
410      NEXT K
420      GOSUB 570        'ERASE OLD
430      GOSUB 510        'DRAW NEW POSITION
440      FOR K = 1 TO 9             'SAVE CURRENT POSITION IN X AND Y
450          X(K) = XN(K)
460          Y(K) = YN(K)
470      NEXT K
480  NEXT T
490  GOTO 650
500  '
510  '###################### DRAW SAILBOAT ########################
520  COLOR 1,0
530  FOR K = 1 TO 8
540      DRAWLINE XN(K),YN(K) TO XN(K+1),YN(K+1)
550  NEXT K
560  RETURN
570  '##################### ERASE SAILBOAT #######################
580  COLOR 0,0
590  FOR K = 1 TO 8
600      DRAWLINE X(K),Y(K) TO X(K+1),Y(K+1)
610  NEXT K
620  RETURN
630  '###########################################################
640  DATA 250,148,290,148,250,80,250,156,270,167
650  DATA 258,182,215,162,210,140,250,156
660  END
```

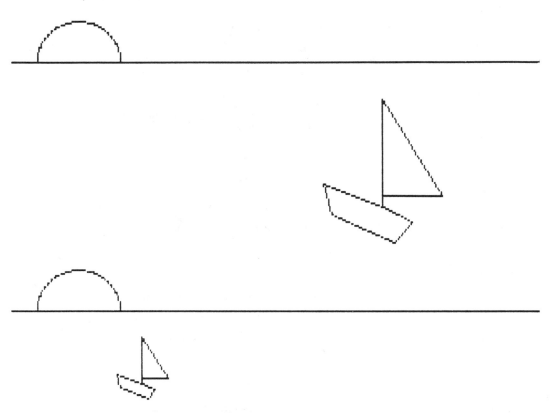

Figure 7–9 Sailing a boat into the sunset. Animation produced by Prog. 7–11 with scaling transformations.

7–3 COMPOUND MOTION

Pictures can be animated by moving different parts of the picture at the "same" time. We could have vehicles traveling in different directions, animals with legs moving, people with arms and legs moving, electrical or other networks with "flow" along several paths at once, or complex equipment with multiple moving parts. In animating the various parts of a display, it is important to coordinate the motions to provide as realistic a model of the action as possible.

Program 7–12 outputs the wagon shown in Fig. 7–10. The wheels of the wagon rotate alternately as the wagon is translated to the left. Spokes in each wheel are erased just before the rotated position is redrawn, so that blank areas are displayed for a minimum time. We also use a minimum number of spokes to reduce computation time. The more lines to be drawn in a picture, the more time the animation takes.

A walking robot is illustrated with Prog. 7–13. This example combines translation with moving feet. Figure 7–11 shows the output of this program for five positions of the motion, as the robot shuffles off to the right.

Program 7-12   Compound motion: moving wagon with turning wheels.

```
10 'PROGRAM 7-12. MOVING WAGON AND WHEELS.
20      'DRAWS WAGON AND THEN MOVES IT FROM RIGHT TO LEFT.
30      'WHEEL SPOKES ROTATE TWICE FOR EACH STEP OF WAGON
40      'MOVEMENT.
50   CLEARSCREEN
60   DIM X(20), Y(20), XN(20), YN(20)
70   YA = 5/6          'YA IS RESOLUTION ADJUSTMENT FOR Y VALUES
80   XA = 6/5          'XA IS RESOLUTION ADJUSTMENT FOR X VALUES
90   FOR K = 1 TO 18   'READ WAGON POINTS
100     READ X(K), Y(K)
110     Y(K) = Y(K) * YA
120     XN(K) = X(K)
130     YN(K) = Y(K)
140 NEXT K
150 H = -5                         'H IS HORIZONTAL TRANSLATION DISTANCE
160 A = 25 * 3.14159 / 180         'EXPRESS 15  IN RADIANS
170     'CALCULATE CONSTANT PARTS OF ROTATION EQUATIONS
180 CA = COS(A)
190 SX = SIN(A) * XA
200 SY = SIN(A) * YA
210 GRAPHICS
220 GOSUB 360               'DRAW WAGON
230     '*************** TRANSLATE, ERASE AND DRAW **************
240 GOSUB 480               'ROTATES SPOKES
250 IF XN(2) + H < O THEN 940          'IF MOVING LEFTMOST POINTS TAKES US
260 FOR K = 1 TO 18                    'OFF SCREEN, STOP. ELSE, CONTINUE.
270     X(K) = XN(K)               'STORE CURRENT POSITION IN X AND Y
280     Y(K) = YN(K)
290 NEXT K
300 FOR K = 1 TO 18
310     XN(K) = X(K) + H           'ADD TRANSLATION AMOUNT
320 NEXT K
330 GOSUB 770                      'ERASE CURRENT POSITION
340 GOSUB 360                      'DRAW NEW POSITION
350 GOTO 240
360 '######################### DRAW ROUTINE #########################
370 COLOR 1,0
380 FOR K = 1 TO 5
390     DRAWLINE XN(K),YN(K) TO XN(K+1),YN(K+1)
400 NEXT K
410 DRAWLINE XN(7),YN(7) TO XN(8),YN(8)
420 CIRCLEPLOT XN(9),YN(9),11       'WHEEL CENTERS ARE ARRAY ELEMENTS 9 AND 10
430 CIRCLEPLOT XN(10),YN(10),11
440 FOR K = 11 TO 17 STEP 2      'DRAW SPOKES
450     DRAWLINE XN(K),YN(K) TO XN(K+1),YN(K+1)
460 NEXT K
470 RETURN
480 '######################### ROTATE SPOKES ROUTINE #####################
490 YO = Y(9)                      'Y VALUE OF CENTER OF BOTH WHEELS
500 FOR S = 1 TO 2                 'ROTATE SPOKES TWICE
510     FOR K = 11 TO 18           'SAVE CURRENT POSITION OF SPOKES IN X AND Y
520         X(K) = XN(K)
530         Y(K) = YN(K)
540     NEXT K
550     XO = XN(9)                 'X VALUE OF CENTER OF FIRST WHEEL
560     FOR K = 11 TO 14
570         XS = XN(K)             'SAVE XN(K) FOR USE IN YN(K) CALCULATIONS
580         XN(K) = XO + (XN(K) - XO) * CA + (YN(K) - YO) * SX
590         YN(K) = YO + (YN(K) - YO) * CA - (XS - XO) * SY
600     NEXT K
610     XO = XN(10)                'X VALUE OF CENTER OF SECOND WHEEL
620     FOR K = 15 TO 18
630         XS = XN(K)             'SAVE XN(K) FOR USE IN YN(K) CALCULATIONS
```

Program 7-12 (cont.)

```
640          XN(K) = XO + (XN(K) - XO) * CA + (YN(K) - YO) * SX
650          YN(K) = YO + (YN(K) - YO) * CA - (XS - XO) * SY
660     NEXT K
670     COLOR 0,0
680     FOR K = 11 TO 17 STEP 2          'ERASE CURRENT POSITION
690          DRAWLINE X(K),Y(K) TO X(K+1),Y(K+1)
700     NEXT K
710     COLOR 1,0
720     FOR K = 11 TO 17 STEP 2          'DRAW NEW POSITION
730          DRAWLINE XN(K),YN(K) TO XN(K+1),YN(K+1)
740     NEXT K
750 NEXT S
760 RETURN
770 '######################### ERASE ROUTINE #########################
780 COLOR 0,0
790 FOR K = 1 TO 5
800     DRAWLINE X(K),Y(K) TO X(K+1),Y(K+1)
810 NEXT K
820 DRAWLINE X(7),Y(7) TO X(8),Y(8)
830 CIRCLEPLOT X(9),Y(9),11
840 CIRCLEPLOT X(10),Y(10),11
850 FOR K = 11 TO 17 STEP 2
860     DRAWLINE X(K),Y(K) TO X(K+1),Y(K+1)
870 NEXT K
880 RETURN
890 '################################################################
900 DATA 190,140,180,140,180,120,270,120,270,140,260,140,240,140,210,140
910 DATA 200,140,250,140
920 DATA 210,140,190,140,200,130,200,150
930 DATA 260,140,240,140,250,130,250,150
940 END
```

Figure 7–10 Compound motion. Animating a wagon with translation and rotating wheels (Prog. 7–12).

Program 7–13 Compound motion: walking robot.

```
10 'PROGRAM 7-13. WALKING ROBOT
20      'ROBOT MOVES FROM LEFT TO RIGHT ACROSS THE SCREEN.
30      'ROBOT BODY IS MOVED AN EQUAL DISTANCE EACH STEP.
40      'EACH LEG IS MOVED AN AMOUNT DETERMINED BY WHETHER
50      'WE'RE GOING TO DISPLAY WALKING POSITION #1 OR #2.
60      'IN POSITION #1, LEGS ARE CLOSE TOGETHER. IN
70      'POSITION #2, THEY'RE FAR APART.
80 '****************************************************************
90  CLEARSCREEN
100 DIM X(16), Y(16), XN(16), YN(16)
110 XM = 279           'XM IX MAXIMUM X VALUE FOR THIS SYSTEM
120 FOR K = 1 TO 16
130     READ XN(K),YN(K)
140 NEXT K
150 B = 15      'B IS AMOUNT TO MOVE BODY EACH TIME
160 P = 2       'P INDICATES WHICH WALKING POSITION WE WANT TO DISPLAY NEXT
170 GRAPHICS
180 GOSUB 510           'DRAW
190     '********************** TRANSLATE **********************
200     'SAVE CURRENT POINTS FOR LATER ERASING
```

Program 7-13 (cont.)

```
210 FOR K = 1 TO 16
220     X(K) = XN(K)
230     Y(K) = YN(K)
240 NEXT K
250 FOR K = 1 TO 8       'TRANSLATE BODY POINTS
260     XN(K) = X(K) + B
270 NEXT K
280 IF P = 2 THEN 340            'ARE WE GOING TO POSITION #2?
290     'OTHERWISE WE'RE GOING TO POSITION #1
300 FI = 10     'FI IS THE INCREMENT FOR FRONT FOOT
310 RI = 20     'RI IS INCREMENT FOR REAR FOOT
320 P = 2       'NEXT TIME WE'RE GOING TO POSITION #2
330 GOTO 380
340     'WE'RE GOING TO POSITION #2
350 FI = 20
360 RI = 10
370 P = 1       'NEXT TIME WE'RE GOING TO POSITION #1
380     'TRANSLATE REAR FOOT
390 FOR K = 9 TO 12
400     XN(K) = X(K) + RI
410 NEXT K
420     'TRANSLATE FRONT FOOT
430 FOR K = 13 TO 16
440     XN(K) = X(K) + FI
450 NEXT K
460 GOSUB 580               'ERASE CURRENT POSITION
470 GOSUB 510               'DRAW NEW POSITION
480 IF XN(1) + B > XM THEN 680          'IF MOVING RIGHTMOST POINT WE GO OFF
490 GOTO 190                            'SCREEN, STOP. ELSE CONTINUE.
500 '
510 '############################# DRAW ROUTINE ######################
520 COLOR 1,0
530 FOR K = 1 TO 15
540     DRAWLINE XN(K),YN(K) TO XN(K+1),YN(K+1)
550 NEXT K
560 DRAWLINE XN(16),YN(16) TO XN(1),YN(1)
570 RETURN
580 '########################### ERASE ROUTINE #####################
590 COLOR 0,0
600 FOR K = 1 TO 15
610     DRAWLINE X(K),Y(K) TO X(K+1),Y(K+1)
620 NEXT K
630 DRAWLINE X(16),Y(16) TO X(1),Y(1)
640 RETURN
650 '##############################################################
660 DATA 40,150,40,110,35,110,35,95,15,95,15,110,10,110,10,150
670 DATA 20,150,20,155,25,155,25,150,25,150,25,155,30,155,30,150
680 END
```

Figure 7-11 Compound motion. Robot walking across the screen, as produced by Prog. 7-13.

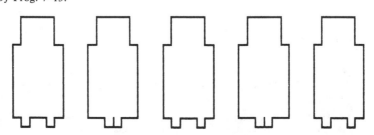

In Prog. 7–14, we display a running stick figure. Each "frame" of the motion was plotted on graph paper, then converted into screen coordinates to represent the running motion for the arms and legs. The two frames for each position of the runner are separately stored in arrays. This allows us to simply translate each frame, alternately, across the screen without recomputing relative positions of the figure parts. Figure 7–12 illustrates the resulting motion.

Program 7–14   Compound motion: running stick figure using "frames."

```
10 'PROGRAM 7-14. RUNNER.
20      'DISPLAYS A RUNNER ALTERNATING BETWEEN 2 POSITIONS (OR
30      'FRAMES) AT LOCATIONS ACROSS THE SCREEN. ARRAYS X1 AND
40      'Y1 HOLD ALL DATA POINTS FOR POSITION #1; X2 AND Y2
50      'HOLD POSITION #2.
60      '*************************************************************
70 CLEARSCREEN
80 DIM X1(15), Y1(15), X2(15), Y2(15)
90 XM = 320          'XM IS MAXIMUM X VALUE FOR THIS SYSTEM
100 FOR K = 1 TO 13    'READ POSITION #1
110     READ X1(K), Y1(K)
120 NEXT K
130 FOR K = 1 TO 12     'READ POSITION #2
140     READ X2(K), Y2(K)
150 NEXT K
160 XO = 0      'XO IS DISPLACEMENT ACROSS SCREEN
170 GRAPHICS
180 IF XO + X1(12) > XM THEN 800        'WOULD POSITION #1 STILL BE ON SCREEN?
190 GOSUB 270           'DRAW POSITION #1
200 GOSUB 390           'ERASE POSITION #1
210 XO = XO + 15        'MOVE OVER 15 UNITS
220 IF XO + X2(11) > XM THEN 800        'WOULD POSITION #2 STILL BE ON SCREEN?
230 GOSUB 510           'DRAW POSITION #2
240 GOSUB 630           'ERASE POSITION #2
250 XO = XO + 20        'MOVE OVER 20 UNITS
260 GOTO 190
270 '######################### DRAW POSITION #1 #########################
280 COLOR 1,0
290 FOR K = 1 TO 3                                      'DRAW ONE LEG AND BODY
300     DRAWLINE XO + X1(K), Y1(K) TO XO + X1(K+1), Y1(K+1)
310 NEXT K
320 DRAWLINE XO + X1(5), Y1(5) TO XO + X1(6), Y1(6)       'DRAW OTHER LEG
330 DRAWLINE XO + X1(6), Y1(6) TO XO + X1(7), Y1(7)
340 FOR K = 8 TO 11                                     'DRAW ARMS
350     DRAWLINE XO + X1(K), Y1(K) TO XO + X1(K+1), Y1(K+1)
360 NEXT K
370 CIRCLEPLOT XO + X1(13), Y1(13),10                    'DRAW HEAD
380 RETURN
390 '######################### ERASE POSITION #1 #########################
400 COLOR 0,0
410 FOR K = 1 TO 3
420     DRAWLINE XO + X1(K), Y1(K) TO XO + X1(K+1), Y1(K+1)
430 NEXT K
440 DRAWLINE XO + X1(5), Y1(5) TO XO + X1(6), Y1(6)
450 DRAWLINE XO + X1(6), Y1(6) TO XO + X1(7), Y1(7)
460 FOR K = 8 TO 11
470     DRAWLINE XO + X1(K), Y1(K) TO XO + X1(K+1), Y1(K+1)
480 NEXT K
490 CIRCLEPLOT XO + X1(13), Y1(13),10
500 RETURN
510 '######################### DRAW POSITION #2 #########################
520 COLOR 1,0
530 FOR K = 1 TO 2
```

Program 7-14 (cont.)

```
540      DRAWLINE XO + X2(K), Y2(K) TO XO + X2(K+1), Y2(K+1)
550 NEXT K
560 DRAWLINE XO + X2(4), Y2(4) TO XO + X2(5), Y2(5)
570 DRAWLINE XO + X2(5), Y2(5) TO XO + X2(6), Y2(6)
580 FOR K = 7 TO 10
590      DRAWLINE XO + X2(K), Y2(K) TO XO + X2(K+1), Y2(K+1)
600 NEXT K
610 CIRCLEPLOT XO + X2(12), Y2(12),10
620 RETURN
630 '####################### ERASE POSITION #2 #######################
640 COLOR 0,0
650 FOR K = 1 TO 2
660      DRAWLINE XO + X2(K), Y2(K) TO XO + X2(K+1), Y2(K+1)
670 NEXT K
680 DRAWLINE XO + X2(4), Y2(4) TO XO + X2(5), Y2(5)
690 DRAWLINE XO + X2(5), Y2(5) TO XO + X2(6), Y2(6)
700 FOR K = 7 TO 10
710      DRAWLINE XO + X2(K), Y2(K) TO XO + X2(K+1), Y2(K+1)
720 NEXT K
730 CIRCLEPLOT XO + X2(12), Y2(12),10
740 RETURN
750 '###############################################################
760 DATA 14,150,20,133,15,120,20,93,5,145,25,133,15,120
770 DATA 20,115,10,110,19,92,20,108,30,113,20,83
780 DATA 2,132,25,136,40,93,43,150,50,130,30,120
790 DATA 30,111,22,103,38,95,43,110,58,104,40,83
800 END
```

Figure 7–12 Compound motion, showing two frames used to produce a running stick figure in Prog. 7–14.

7–4 BACKGROUND MOTION

As the number of computations and lines to be drawn increases, the time required to animate a scene increases. For complex objects, the animation time can become so long that we lose the sense of motion we were trying to create on the screen. We can speed up the motion by animating only simple shapes that have fewer lines to be drawn, and we can limit the animation to simple types of motion. Another method is to move the background in a scene to give the appearance of motion.

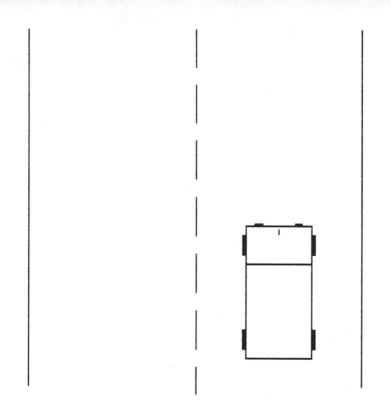

Figure 7–13 Simulation of the car movement up the screen can be produced by moving the center lines of the road down.

Figure 7–13 illustrates a simple form of background motion. If we move the centerline of the road down the screen, the car will appear to move up. Moving the telephone poles in Fig. 7–14 to the right can cause the truck to appear to move to the left. The telephone poles can be spaced and positioned so that they are never drawn on top of the truck. Otherwise, part of the truck will get erased. If we must move the background through an object, we can modify the background so that only part of the background or object is drawn at that point in the animation. But, again, these tests and modifications tend to slow the animation.

Figure 7–14 Simulating the truck movement to the left can be done by moving the telephone poles to the right.

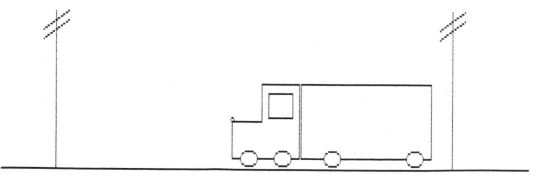

Many types of background motion are possible. Program 7–15 combines a background motion with simple object motion to simulate animation of a more complex object. The output is given in Fig. 7–15. A rotating bar connecting the wheels of a train and a series of constantly moving railroad tracks, made up of single pixels, are used to simulate the motion of a train. We can produce slower or faster motion of the background by taking smaller or larger displacements in the position of background objects. We can also slow the motion as much as we want with time delays between frames.

Program 7–15 Simulating movement with background motion: train with moving rod and moving tracks.

```
10  'PROGRAM 7-15. TRAIN WITH MOVING WHEEL ROD AND TRACKS.
20     'DRAWS A TRAIN AND ROTATES THE HORIZONTAL BAR CONNECTING
30     'THE TWO REAR WHEELS. ALSO MOVES POINTS ACROSS THE BOTTOM
40     'OF THE TRAIN, TO SIMULATE TRAIN TRACKS.
50     '*********************************************************
60  CLEARSCREEN
70  YA = 5/6     'YA IS RESOLUTION ADJUSTMENT
80  GRAPHICS
90     'DRAW TRAIN
100 READ X1,Y1
110 FOR K = 1 TO 25
120     READ X2,Y2
130     DRAWLINE X1,Y1 TO X2,Y2
140     X1 = X2
150     Y1 = Y2
160 NEXT K
170     'ADD WINDOW
180 READ XL, XR, YT, YB
190 FOR X = XL TO XR
200     DRAWLINE X,YT TO X,YB
210 NEXT X
220     'ADD DETAILS
230 FOR K = 1 TO 6
240     READ X1, Y1, X2, Y2
250     DRAWLINE X1,Y1 TO X2,Y2          'FINAL VALUES ARE THOSE FOR WHEEL BAR
260 NEXT K
270     'ADD WHEELS
280 FOR K = 1 TO 4
290     READ XC, YC, R
300     CIRCLEPLOT XC,YC,R        'FINAL XC AND YC VALUES ARE FOR REAR WHEEL
310 NEXT K
320     '
330     '**************** ROTATE WHEEL BAR, MOVE TRACKS ****************
340 Y = 152       'TRAIN TRACKS WILL BE AT A Y VALUE OF 152
350 R = 15        'R IS RADIUS OF WHEEL BAR'S ROTATION
360 RE = 360 * 3.14159 / 180     'CONVERT 360 AND 50 TO RADIANS
370 DA = 50  * 3.14159 / 180
380 FOR A = DA TO RE STEP DA
390     X1 = XC + R * SIN(A)
400     Y1 = YC + R * COS(A) * YA
410     COLOR 1,0
420     DRAWLINE X1,Y1 TO X1-90,Y1          'DRAW NEW BAR POSITION (90 UNITS LONG)
430     FOR X = XS TO 319 STEP 35           'PLOT TRACKS 35 UNITS APART
440         POINTPLOT X,Y
450     NEXT X
460     FOR X = XS TO 319 STEP 35           'ERASE TRACKS
470         POINTOFF X,Y
```

Program 7-15 (cont.)

```
480      NEXT X
490      XS = XS + 7      'NEXT SET OF POINTS WILL BE 7 PIXELS OVER
500      IF XS >= 30 THEN XS = 0          'XS = 0 SO POINTS KEEP COMING FROM LEFT
510      COLOR 0,0
520      DRAWLINE X1,Y1 TO X1-90,Y1       'ERASE CURRENT POSITION OF BAR
530 NEXT A
540 GOTO 380
550 '#####################################################################
560      'OUTLINE
570 DATA 270,130,290,130,290,50,300,50,300,30,220,30,220,70,200,70
580 DATA 200,50,170,50,170,70,90,70,90,50,100,40,60,40,70,50,70,70
590 DATA 60,70,50,80,50,110,60,120,40,120,20,150,50,150,50,130,90,130
600      'WINDOW
610 DATA 230,280,40,70
620      'DETAIL LINES
630 DATA 220,70,220,100,220,100,65,100
640 DATA 65,100,45,125,130,130,140,130
650 DATA 0,154,319,154,180,130,230,130
660      'WHEELS
670 DATA 65,140,10,110,130,20,160,130,20,250,130,20
680 END
```

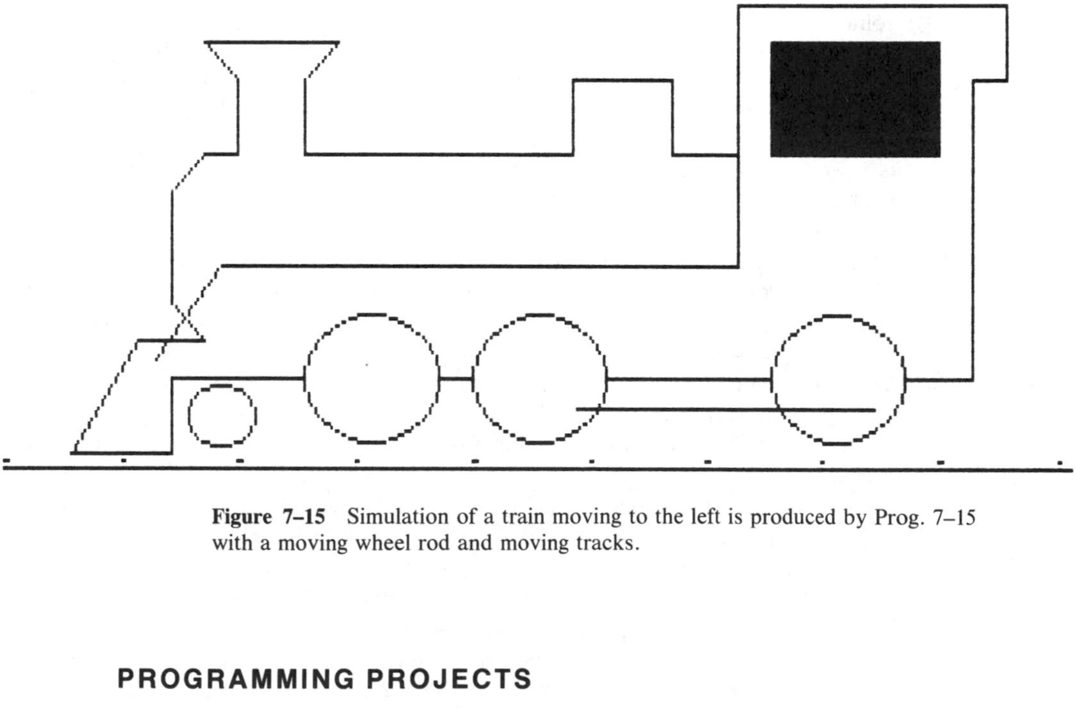

Figure 7-15 Simulation of a train moving to the left is produced by Prog. 7-15 with a moving wheel rod and moving tracks.

PROGRAMMING PROJECTS

7-1. Write a program to animate a pixel (or circle) between several vertical and horizontal boundaries. The position and length of each boundary can be randomly chosen. Move the point by 1-unit increments in both the horizontal and vertical directions, so that the animation path is along a diagonal line. Whenever the point encounters a vertical boundary or screen edge, reverse the X increment. When the point hits a horizontal wall or screen edge, reverse the Y increment. To determine when the point is about to hit one of the randomly positioned lines, use a function that tests for "pixel on" at the next path position before moving the point.

7–2. Modify the program in Prob. 7–1 to display the point (or ball) in various colors as it bounces around the screen. Other possible modifications include changing colors only when it rebounds, not erasing the point (so that a pattern of colors is displayed), or producing a sound whenever the point rebounds from a boundary.

7–3. Modify the program in Prob. 7–1 to move the point faster by setting the horizontal and vertical increments to some value greater than 1 (keeping both increments the same). Each pixel position along the path, from the current position to the possible final position, must now be tested to determine whether there is a wall along the line of motion.

7–4. Write a program to bounce a pixel (or circle) back and forth between any two specified points, (X1,Y1) and (X2,Y2). Increments for the motion (DX and DY) are chosen so that the ratio DY/DX is equal to the slope of the path. This is done by dividing the intervals X2–X1 and Y2–Y1 by 10, or some other convenient factor.

7–5. Write a program to create a maze inside the box of Prog. 7–3. Position a circle at some starting location and let interactive input (such as keyboard or paddles) determine the direction of motion. The motion can be limited to horizontal and vertical paths. Program the circle to move in unit steps with the direction of motion changed by the input or when the circle collides with a wall. Collisions can be determined by using a function that indicates whether or not a screen pixel position is on or off. Motion stops when the circle reaches the maze exit. To make this program into a competitive game, deduct points for wall collisions and print out the final score.

7–6. Modify Prog. 7–3 so that increments DX and DY may be assigned any initial values (DX <> DY). Also, accelerate the motion by increasing the increments by 5 after every third rebound from the left wall. The motion can be stopped when one increment exceeds 40.

7–7. Write a program to display a ball (or other object) that moves across the screen following the path of any specified curve. The curve could be a SIN function, fourth-degree polynomial, or any other equation that could simulate an up-and-down motion.

7–8. Write a program to display a point (or ball) that moves along a spiral path starting from the center of the screen. By alternating the color and not erasing the point, the screen can be filled with a color spiral. By reversing the motion when the point reaches the edge of the screen, the point can be made to repeatedly spiral in and out.

7–9. Write a program to animate a circle drawn at the center of the screen by scaling. Scale the circle up until it reaches the screen edges, then reverse the scaling. Continue to repeat the process with alternating colors as the circle increases and decreases in size.

7–10. Write a program that simulates motion of an object by moving the background. Examples are a train or ocean liner that emits smoke or the scenes from Fig. 7–13 or 7–14.

7–11. Write a program to display a clock face in the center of the screen. Draw the hands as arrows (for hours and minutes) and rotate the hands so that the smaller hand rotates through 30 degrees each time the larger hand makes one complete revolution (360 degrees). A second hand can be added that sweeps through 360 degrees for each 6 degrees of rotation of the minute hand.

7–12. Write a program to animate a straight line along each of the following curves by keeping the line tangent to the curve:

a. Ellipse
b. Third-degree polynomial
c. Sine curve

7–13. Write a program that will display an airplane or spacecraft flying loops around a circle.

Chapter 8

Windows
in the Display

Graphics displays can be manipulated in many ways. We have explored methods for changing display size and for moving the figures from one screen location or orientation to another. These transformations can be applied to a total display or to designated areas within a display. We can also select areas of a display for other types of modification. The areas could be "spotlighted" for special emphasis, they could be deleted from the display, or they could be retained and transformed while the rest of the display is deleted.

8–1 SPOTLIGHTING

We would often like to add special emphasis to some area of a display in order to focus attention there. The area to be spotlighted could be redrawn in a bright color or highlighted with added intensity. On some systems, a "high-intensity" option is available. This has the effect of making lines or text displayed with this option brighter than other parts of the screen. A similar effect can be produced by drawing the lines in the spotlight area with double thickness: drawing two lines 1 unit apart instead of a single line. Blinking a section of a display is another technique we can use to emphasize a screen area. We can also draw attention to a selected area by putting a circle or box around it, as shown in Fig. 8–1.

To superimpose a circle onto a display, we simply choose the center coordinates (XC,YC) and radius R for the circle. A circle–drawing routine or the CIRCLEPLOT command is then added to our program and referenced each time we wish to spotlight an area. We can write programs that allow us to experiment with different circle locations and sizes to achieve the exact spotlight effect desired, as in Prog. 8–1.

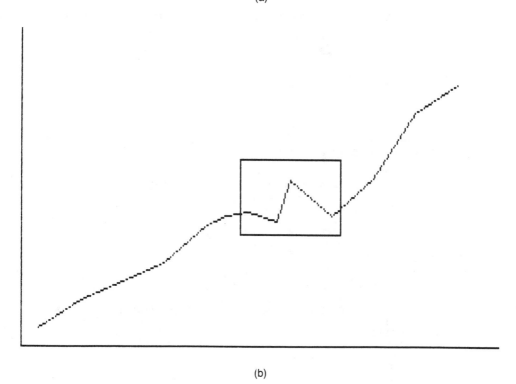

1. FRAME

2. SEAT

3. WHEELS

4. BRAKES

5. STEM

6. FORK

7. HANDLEBARS

(a)

(b)

Figure 8–1 Spotlighting displays with (a) a circle and (b) a box.

Program 8–1 Spotlighting with circles.

```
 10 'PROGRAM 8-1. CIRCLE SPOTLIGHTS.
 20  CLEARSCREEN
 30  DIM X(15), Y(15)
 40  XM = 299
 50  YM = 199
 60      '************** READ DATA POINTS FOR DISPLAY *********
 70      '
 80      '
 90      '
100      '
110      '
120 GOSUB 160             'DRAW DISPLAY
130 GOSUB 250             'CREATE CIRCLE SPOTLIGHT
140 GOTO 600
150 '
160 '######################### DRAW ROUTINE #########################
170 CLEARSCREEN
180 GRAPHICS
190      '
200      '
210      '
220      '
230 RETURN
240 '
250 '#################### ADD CIRCLE SPOTLIGHT ######################'
260 POSITION 2,1
270 PRINT "CIRCLE CENTER AND RADIUS";
280 INPUT XC, YC, R
290 IF XC+R<=XM AND XC-R>=0 AND YC+R<=YM AND YC-R>=0 THEN 340
300 POSITION 1,1
310 PRINT "CIRCLE OFF SCREEN"
320 PRINT "                              "
330 GOTO 260
340 CIRCLEPLOT XC,YC,R
350 POSITION 1,1
360 PRINT "                              "
370 POSITION 2,1
380 PRINT "                              "
390 POSITION 2,1
400 PRINT "TYPE E TO END, C TO CHANGE CIRCLE";
410 INPUT M$
420 POSITION 2,1
430 PRINT "                              "
440 IF M$ = "E" THEN 580
450     'ERASE CURRENT POSITION
460 COLOR 0,0
470 CIRCLEPLOT XC,YC,R
480 COLOR 1,0
490     'DID ERASING DESTROY DISPLAY?
500 POSITION 2,1
510 PRINT "DO YOU WANT TO RE-DRAW DISPLAY (Y/N)";
520 INPUT D$
530 POSITION 2,1
540 PRINT "                              "
550 IF D$ = "N" THEN 250
560 GOSUB 160
570 GOTO 250
580 RETURN
590 '##############################################################
600 END
```

For a box spotlight we could specify the four corners, or two diagonal corners, of the rectangle. We could also devise a routine that simply asks us where to put the center of the rectangle and how big it is to be (Fig. 8–2). This type of routine is illustrated in Prog. 8–2, which draws a box centered at coordinates (XB,YB) with a width W and a height H.

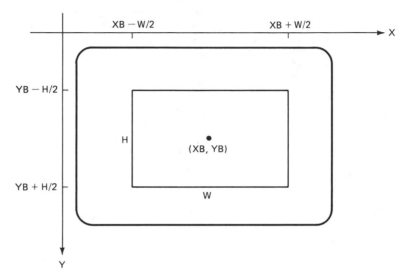

Figure 8–2 Coordinates for the corners of a rectangle can be determined from values for the width W, height H, and center position (XB,YB).

Program 8–2 Spotlighting with rectangles.

```
10 'PROGRAM 8-2. BOX SPOTLIGHTS.
20   CLEARSCREEN
30   DIM X(15), Y(15)
40   XM = 279
50   YM = 159
60       '************** READ DATA POINTS FOR DISPLAY *********
70       '
80       '
90       '
100      '
110      '
120 GOSUB 160          'DRAW DISPLAY
130 GOSUB 260          'CREATE CIRCLE SPOTLIGHT
140 GOTO 770
150 '
160 '####################### DRAW ROUTINE #######################
170 CLEARSCREEN
180 GRAPHICS
190      '
200      '
210      '
220      '
230      '
240 RETURN
250 '
```

Program 8-2 (cont.)

```
260 '#################### ADD BOX SPOTLIGHT #######################
270 POSITION 2,1
280 PRINT "BOX CENTER (X AND Y)";
290 INPUT XB, YB
300 POSITION 2,1
310 PRINT "                                    "
320 POSITION 2,1
330 PRINT "BOX WIDTH AND HEIGHT";
340 INPUT BW, BH
350     'DETERMINE BOX SIDES (LEFT, RIGHT, TOP AND BOTTOM)
360 L = XB - BW / 2
370 R = XB + BW / 2
380 T = YB - BH / 2
390 B = YB + BH / 2
400 IF L<R AND L>=0 AND R<=XM AND T<B AND T>=0 AND B<=YM THEN 450
410 POSITION 1,1
420 PRINT "BOX OFF SCREEN"
430 PRINT "                                    "
440 GOTO 270
450 DRAWLINE L,T TO L,B
460 DRAWLINE L,B TO R,B
470 DRAWLINE R,B TO R,T
480 DRAWLINE R,T TO L,T
490 POSITION 1,1
500 PRINT "                                    "
510 POSITION 2,1
520 PRINT "                                    "
530 POSITION 2,1
540 PRINT "TYPE E TO END, C TO CHANGE BOX";
550 INPUT M$
560 POSITION 2,1
570 PRINT "                                    "
580 IF M$ = "E" THEN 750
590     'ERASE CURRENT POSITION
600 COLOR 0,0
610 DRAWLINE L,T TO L,B
620 DRAWLINE L,B TO R,B
630 DRAWLINE R,B TO R,T
640 DRAWLINE R,T TO L,T
650 COLOR 1,0
660     'DID ERASING DESTROY DISPLAY?
670 POSITION 2,1
680 PRINT "DO YOU WANT TO RE-DRAW DISPLAY (Y/N)";
690 INPUT D$
700 POSITION 2,1
710 PRINT "                                    "
720 IF D$ = "N" THEN 260
730 GOSUB 160
740 GOTO 260
750 RETURN
760 '####################################################################
770 END
```

Spotlights with circles or boxes are useful for emphasizing parts of displays that accompany reports or presentations. A screen display with the spotlight in different locations can be output to a printer each time the spotlight location is changed. The printed displays can then be included in a report. We can make a moving spotlight to accompany a presentation, as well. The spotlight would change locations to coincide with the display area under discussion in the presentation. We could use some type of time delay to hold the spotlight in one position until we were ready to discuss the next area. The areas spotlighted in this way might be some type of list, parts of a graph, or the components of a diagram.

8–2 ERASING AND CLIPPING

Instead of emphasizing areas, we might want to eliminate parts of a developed display. We can use spotlight methods to identify areas for erasing or clipping. In the first case we delete the selected area; in the second we keep the area and delete the rest of the display.

ERASING

The box or circle method for spotlighting can be used to select areas for erasure. There are many reasons why we might decide to take out certain parts of a developed display. We may need to simplify a complicated display or to make room for additions to the display. We might be trying out various design layouts or experimenting with visual effects. Or we may need to provide space for enlarging or some other display manipulations.

The parts of a display to be eliminated could, of course, be taken out by changing the program to redraw the display without these parts. This might mean significantly altering the graphics display program. If we later wanted the parts back in, we would have to change the program again. If frequent display deletions are necessary, as in a design application, a general erasing program can be set up to erase everything within a designated area.

Identifying the area of a display to be deleted with a box provides a simple method for erasing characters, pixels, and line sections within the box. We just fill the rectangular area of the box with lines of the same color as the screen background. The program to accomplish this would need to have as input the screen background color and the size and location of the box. If no color option is available, we can use POINTOFF to erase each pixel within the box.

Erasing can also be done within a circular boundary. This would be a slower process than using a box since the program would have to calculate points along the circle boundary. These points would then be used as the endpoints for the lines painted into the circle interior. Some systems provide graphics options that allow the interior color of boxes or circles to be stated as a parameter. The interior of these figures is then automatically painted in the selected color when the figure is drawn.

CLIPPING

In some situations we would like to save an area in a display and erase everything else. This would be the case if we wanted to expand some small area in a picture or graph to the size of the screen, or if we wanted to have figures showing the parts of a display separately for a report or presentation. For this purpose, we can select the region to be saved within a rectangular area, or **window**. Erasing all parts of a display outside of this window is called **clipping**.

A program to perform general clipping must identify and save all text, unconnected pixels, and line sections of figures within the window area. Figure 8–3 illustrates a framed area or window selected on a diagram. Everything inside the window is to be saved; everything outside is to be clipped. The clipping program would check coordinate endpoints of the lines and text to determine what to save.

We first consider the design of a clipping program for points and lines. Our program will input the coordinates for the top left corner of the window as (XW,YW). The width and height of the window will be input as WW and HW. We will store display coordinates in arrays X and Y. Any coordinate information saved by the clipping program will be stored in new arrays.

An isolated point (one not part of a line) will be saved by the clipping program if it is inside the window. That is, its X coordinate value is between XW and XW + WW and its Y coordinate value is between YW and YW + HW. A line will be saved by the clipping program if both its endpoints are within the window area. It will be completely erased if all of the line lies outside the window. If parts of the line are outside the window, we will clip off the parts outside and save the segment that falls inside the window. Figure 8–4 illustrates the possible relationships between a line and a window. Intersection points with the vertical and horizontal boundaries of the window are calculated from the window coordinates and line equations (slope M and Y-intercept B), as shown in Fig. 8–5.

Figure 8–3   A window drawn around a section of a display identifies the text and figure parts to be saved by the clipping program.

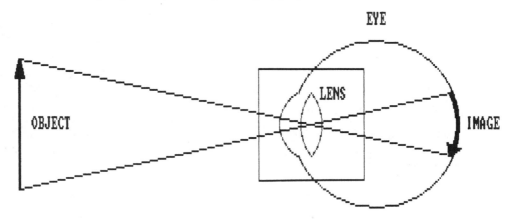

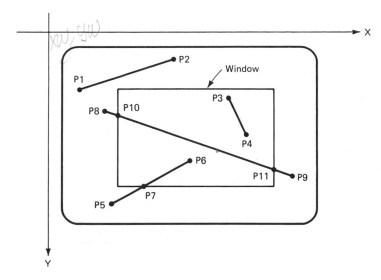

Figure 8–4 A line with endpoint positions P1 and P2, both outside a window, will be erased by the clipping program. A line with endpoints at P3 and P4, both inside the window, will be saved. The clipping routine will also save line segments from P7 to P6 and from P10 to P11.

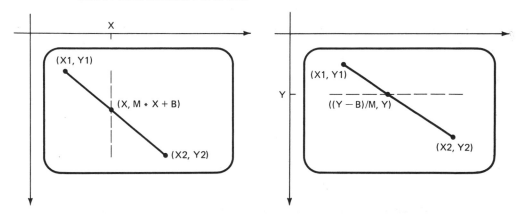

Figure 8–5 Line with slope M and Y-intercept B crossing vertical and horizontal boundaries: (a) intersection with the vertical boundary is at coordinates $(X, M * X + B)$; (b) intersection with the horizontal boundary is at coordinates $((Y - B) / M, Y)$.

In Prog. 8–3, we begin by testing coordinates against the left edge of the window. Points with an X coordinate greater than the X value of the left side of the window are stored in arrays X1 and Y1. Intersection points for the lines that cross the left window boundary are also stored in X1 and Y1. Next, the points stored in X1 and Y1 are clipped against the top edge of the window. All intersection points and any points with Y coordinate greater than this boundary are stored in arrays X2 and Y2. These remaining points are then clipped against the right edge. Arrays X1 and Y1 are reused to store intersections and points whose X coordinate is less than the X value of the right edge. Finally, we clip the points now held in arrays X1 and Y1 against the bottom border of the window. Arrays X2 and Y2 are used to store the final coordinates for all points and lines to be redrawn inside the window. Figure 8–6 shows a picture before and after clipping by Prog. 8–3.

TYPE G TO GO ON, C TO CHANGE WINDOW? ■

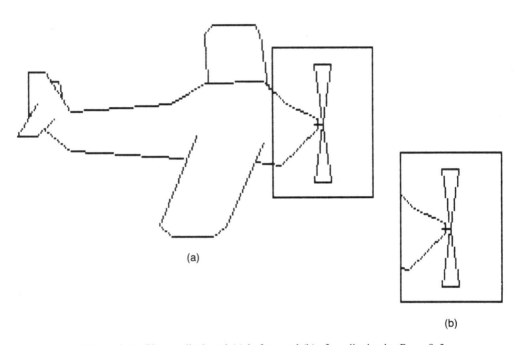

(a)

(b)

Figure 8–6 Picture displayed (a) before and (b) after clipping by Prog. 8–3.

Program 8–3 Point and line clipping (airplane).

```
10 'PROGRAM 8-3. CLIPPING OUTISDE A WINDOW.
20     'DRAWS A FIGURE FROM DATA POINTS STORED IN ARRAYS X AND Y.
30     'A WINDOW AREA IS SELECTED. LINES AND POINTS OUTSIDE OF
40     'THE WINDOW AREA ARE CLIPPED. CLIPPING OCCURS AGAINST EACH
50     'BOUNDARY IN THE ORDER LEFT, TOP, RIGHT, BOTTOM. DURING
60     'CLIPPING, POINTS STORED IN X AND Y ARE CLIPPED AGAINST THE
70     'LEFT EDGE; POINTS WITHIN THE WINDOW ARE STORED IN X1, Y1.
80     'THESE POINTS ARE THEN CLIPPED AGAINST THE TOP EDGE, WITH
90     'INCLUDED POINTS SAVED IN X2,Y2. POINTS IN X2,Y2 ARE THEN
100    'CLIPPED AGAINST THE RIGHT EDGE, AND X1,Y1 ARE RE-USED TO
110    'STORE POINTS STILL WITHIN THE WINDOW. THESE POINTS ARE
120    'FINALLY CLIPPED AGAINST THE BOTTOM EDGE, WITH INSIDE
130    'POINTS STORED IN X2,Y2. THE SCREEN IS CLEARED AND THE
140    'WINDOW AND THE PICTURE PART WITHIN THE WINDOW ARE DRAWN.
150    '*********************************************************
160 CLEARSCREEN
170 DIM X(8,20), Y(8,20), X1(8,20), Y1(8,20), X2(8,20), Y2(8,20)
```

```
180 XM = 319                   'XM, YM ARE MAXIMUM X AND Y VALUES FOR THIS SYSTEM
190 YM = 199
200     '******************* READ PICTURE PARTS *******************
210 READ N                     'N IS NUMBER OF PICTURE PARTS
220 FOR P = 1 TO N
230    READ NE(P)           'NUMBER OF ELEMENTS IN PART P
240      FOR E = 1 TO NE(P)
250         READ X(P,E), Y(P,E)
260      NEXT E
270 NEXT P
280 GRAPHICS
290 GOSUB 340                 'DRAW PICTURE
300 GOSUB 450                 'ESTABLISH WINDOW
310 GOSUB 850                 'CLIP OUTSIDE OF WINDOW
320 GOSUB 2480                'DRAW CLIPPED POINTS
330 GOTO 2740
340 '##################### DRAW ROUTINE #####################
350 CLEARSCREEN
360 FOR P = 1 TO N
370    IF NE(P) > 1 THEN 400            'MORE THAN ONE POINT
380    POINTPLOT X(P,1),Y(P,1)          'ONLY ONE POINT IN THIS PART
390    GOTO 430                         'GO ON TO NEXT PART
400    FOR E = 1 TO NE(P)-1
410       DRAWLINE X(P,E),Y(P,E) TO X(P,E+1),Y(P,E+1)
420    NEXT E
430 NEXT P
440 RETURN
450 '################# ESTABLISH WINDOW #####################
460 POSITION 1,1
470 PRINT "TOP LEFT CORNER OF WINDOW";
480 INPUT XW, YW
490 POSITION 1,1
500 PRINT "                              ";
510 POSITION 1,1
520 PRINT "WIDTH AND HEIGHT OF WINDOW";
530 INPUT WW, HW
540 POSITION 1,1
550 PRINT "                              ";
560 L = XW
570 R = XW + WW
580 T = YW
590 B = YW + HW
600 IF L<R AND L>=0 AND R<=XM AND T<B AND T>=0 AND B<=YM THEN 660
610 POSITION 1,1
620 PRINT "WINDOW OFF SCREEN. TRY AGAIN"
630 POSITION 1,1
640 PRINT "                              ";
650 GOTO 460
660 DRAWLINE L,T TO L,B
670 DRAWLINE L,B TO R,B
680 DRAWLINE R,B TO R,T
690 DRAWLINE R,T TO L,T
700 POSITION 1,1
710 PRINT "TYPE G TO GO ON, C TO CHANGE WINDOW";
720 INPUT M$
730 IF M$ = "G" THEN 840
740    'ERASE CURRENT POSITION
750 POSITION 1,1
760 PRINT "                              ";
770 COLOR 0,0
780 DRAWLINE L,T TO L,B
790 DRAWLINE L,B TO R,B
800 DRAWLINE R,B TO R,T
810 DRAWLINE R,T TO L,T
820 COLOR 1,0
```

```
830 GOTO 450
840 RETURN
850 '########################### CLIPPING ROUTINE ###########################
860    '
870    'CLIP POINTS IN X AND Y AGAINST LEFT EDGE. STORE IN X1 AND Y1.
880 P1 = 1
890 FOR P = 1 TO N
900    E1 = 0
910    FOR E = 1 TO NE(P) - 1
920       IF X(P,E) >= L THEN 940
930       IF X(P,E) <  L THEN 1020
940       'FIRST POINT OF LINE IS IN
950       E1 = E1 + 1
960       X1(P1,E1) = X(P,E)
970       Y1(P1,E1) = Y(P,E)
980       'WHAT ABOUT SECOND POINT?
990       IF X(P,E+1) < L THEN GOSUB 1190     'OUT, SO FIND INTERSECTION
1000       'ELSE IT'S IN, SO JUST CONTINUE
1010       GOTO 1070
1020          '-------------------------------------------------
1030       'FIRST POINT IS OUT
1040       'WHAT ABOUT SECOND POINT?
1050       IF X(P,E+1) >= L THEN GOSUB 1190    'IN, SO FIND INTERSECTION
1060       'ELSE IT'S OUT, SO JUST CONTINUE
1070    NEXT E
1080    'TAKE CARE OF FINAL POINT
1090    IF X(P,NE(P)) < L THEN 1130
1100    E1 = E1 + 1
1110    X1(P1,E1) = X(P,NE(P))
1120    Y1(P1,E1) = Y(P,NE(P))
1130    IF E1 = 0 THEN 1160              'NO ELEMENTS IN WINDOW
1140    ME(P1) = E1      'ELSE, SAVE NUMBER OF INCLUDED ELEMENTS
1150    P1 = P1 + 1     'GO ON TO NEXT PART
1160 NEXT P
1170 MN = P1 - 1          'MN IS NUMBER OF PARTS WITH POINTS INSIDE L
1180 GOTO 1260
1190            '^^^^^^^^ FIND INTERSECTION ROUTINE ^^^^^^^^^^
1200 E1 = E1 + 1
1210 M = (Y(P,E+1) - Y(P,E)) / (X(P,E+1) - X(P,E))
1220 Y1(P1,E1) = M * (L - X(P,E)) + Y(P,E)
1230 X1(P1,E1) = L
1240 RETURN
1250         '****************************
1260    'CLIP POINTS IN X1, Y1 AGAINST TOP. STORE INSIDE POINTS IN X2, Y2
1270 P1 = 1
1280 FOR P = 1 TO MN
1290    E1 = 0
1300    FOR E = 1 TO ME(P) - 1
1310       IF Y1(P,E) >= T THEN 1330
1320       IF Y1(P,E) <  T THEN 1420
1330       'FIRST POINT OF LINE IS IN
1340       E1 = E1 + 1
1350       Y2(P1,E1) = Y1(P,E)
1360       X2(P1,E1) = X1(P,E)
1370       'WHAT ABOUT SECOND POINT?
1380       IF Y1(P,E+1) < T THEN GOSUB 1580    'OUT, SO FIND INTERSECTION
1390       'ELSE IT'S IN, SO JUST CONTINUE
1400       GOTO 1460
1410          '-------------------------------------------------
1420       'FIRST POINT IS OUT
1430       'WHAT ABOUT SECOND POINT?
1440       IF Y1(P,E+1) >= T THEN GOSUB 1580   'IN, SO FIND INTERSECTION
1450       'ELSE IT'S OUT, SO JUST CONTINUE
1460    NEXT E
```

```
1470     'TAKE CARE OF FINAL POINT
1480     IF Y1(P,ME(P)) < T THEN 1520
1490     E1 = E1 + 1
1500     Y2(P1,E1) = Y1(P,ME(P))
1510     X2(P1,E1) = X1(P,ME(P))
1520     IF E1 = 0 THEN 1550             'NO ELEMENTS IN WINDOW
1530     ME(P1) = E1    'ELSE SAVE # OF INCLUDED ELEMENTS
1540     P1 = P1 + 1    'GO ON TO THE NEXT PART
1550 NEXT P
1560 MN = P1 - 1          'MN IS # OF PARTS WITH POINTS INSIDE L, T
1570 GOTO 1680            'GO ON TO CLIP AGAINST RIGHT BOUNDARY
1580     '       '^^^^^^^^^^^^ FIND INTERSECTION ROUTINE ^^^^^^^^^^^^^^
1590 E1 = E1 + 1
1600 IF X1(P,E+1) <> X1(P,E) THEN 1630
1610 X2(P1,E1) = X1(P,E)           'VERTICAL LINE
1620 GOTO 1650
1630 M = (Y1(P,E+1) - Y1(P,E)) / (X1(P,E+1) - X1(P,E))
1640 X2(P1,E1) = (T - Y1(P,E)) / M + X1(P,E)
1650 Y2(P1,E1) = T
1660 RETURN
1670                     '***************************
1680     'CLIP POINTS IN X2, Y2 AGAINST RIGHT. STORE INSIDE POINTS IN X1, Y1.
1690 P1 = 1
1700 FOR P = 1 TO MN
1710     E1 = 0
1720     FOR E = 1 TO ME(P) - 1
1730         IF X2(P,E) <= R THEN 1750
1740         IF X2(P,E) >  R THEN 1840
1750         'FIRST POINT IS IN
1760         E1 = E1 + 1
1770         X1(P1,E1) = X2(P,E)
1780         Y1(P1,E1) = Y2(P,E)
1790         'WHAT ABOUT SECOND POINT?
1800         IF X2(P,E+1) > R THEN GOSUB 2000    'OUT, SO FIND INTERSECTION
1810         ELSE IT'S IN, SO JUST CONTINUE
1820         GOTO 1880
1830             '----------------------------------------
1840         'FIRST POINT IS OUT
1850         'WHAT ABOUT SECOND POINT?
1860         IF X2(P,E+1) <= R THEN GOSUB 2000   'IN, SO FIND INTERSECTION
1870         'ELSE IT'S OUT, SO JUST CONTINUE
1880     NEXT E
1890     'TAKE CARE OF FINAL POINT
1900     IF X2(P,ME(P)) > R THEN 1940
1910     E1 = E1 + 1
1920     X1(P1,E1) = X2(P,ME(P))
1930     Y1(P1,E1) = Y2(P,ME(P))
1940     IF E1 = 0 THEN 1970           'NO ELEMENTS IN WINDOW
1950     ME(P1) = E1    'ELSE, SAVE # OF INCLUDED ELEMENTS
1960     P1 = P1 + 1    'GO ON TO NEXT PART
1970 NEXT P
1980 MN = P1 - 1         'MN IS # OF PARTS WITH POINTS INSIDE L, T, R
1990 GOTO 2070           'GO ON TO CLIP AGAINST BOTTOM BOUNDARY
2000         '^^^^^^^^^^^^ FIND INTERSECTION ROUTINE ^^^^^^^^^^
2010 E1 = E1 + 1
2020 M = (Y2(P,E+1) - Y2(P,E)) / (X2(P,E+1) - X2(P,E))
2030 Y1(P1,E1) = M * (R - X2(P,E)) + Y2(P,E)
2040 X1(P1,E1) = R
2050 RETURN
2060                     '***************************
2070     'CLIP POINTS IN X1, Y1 AGAINST BOTTOM. STORE INSIDE POINTS IN X2, Y2
2080 P1 = 1
2090 FOR P = 1 TO MN
2100     E1 = 0
```

```
2110      FOR E = 1 TO ME(P) - 1
2120          IF Y1(P,E) <= B THEN 2140
2130          IF Y1(P,E) >  B THEN 2230
2140          'FIRST POINT IS IN
2150          E1 = E1 + 1
2160          Y2(P1,E1) = Y1(P,E)
2170          X2(P1,E1) = X1(P,E)
2180          'WHAT ABOUT SECOND POINT?
2190          IF Y1(P,E+1) > B THEN GOSUB 2390    'OUT, SO FIND INTERSECTION
2200          'ELSE IT'S IN, SO JUST CONTINUE
2210          GOTO 2270
2220             '-------------------------------------------
2230          'FIRST POINT IS OUT
2240          'WHAT ABOUT SECOND POINT?
2250          IF Y1(P,E+1) <= B THEN GOSUB 2390   'IN, SO FIND INTERSECTION
2260          'ELSE IT'S OUT, SO JUST CONTINUE
2270      NEXT E
2280      'TAKE CARE OF FINAL POINT
2290      IF Y1(P,ME(P)) > B THEN 2330
2300      E1 = E1 + 1
2310      Y2(P1,E1) = Y1(P,ME(P))
2320      X2(P1,E1) = X1(P,ME(P))
2330      IF E1 = 0 THEN 2360               'NO ELEMENTS IN WINDOW
2340      ME(P1) = E1     'ELSE, SAVE # OF INCLUDED ELEMENTS
2350      P1 = P1 + 1    'GO ON TO NEXT PART
2360 NEXT P
2370 MN = P1 - 1          'MN IS # OF PARTS WITH POINTS INSIDE L, T, R, B
2380 RETURN               'END OF CLIPPING ROUTINE
2390         '^^^^^^^^^^^ FIND INTERSECTION ROUTINE ^^^^^^^^^^
2400 E1 = E1 + 1
2410 IF X1(P,E+1) <> X1(P,E) THEN 2440
2420 X2(P1,E1) = X1(P,E)          'VERTICAL LINE
2430 GOTO 2460
2440 M = (Y1(P,E+1) - Y1(P,E)) / (X1(P,E+1) - X1(P,E))
2450 X2(P1,E1) = (B - Y1(P,E)) / M + X1(P,E)
2460 Y2(P1,E1) = B
2470 RETURN
2480 '################## DRAW CLIPPED POINTS ##################
2490 CLEARSCREEN
2500 DRAWLINE L,T TO L,B
2510 DRAWLINE L,B TO R,B
2520 DRAWLINE R,B TO R,T
2530 DRAWLINE R,T TO L,T
2540 FOR P = 1 TO MN
2550     FOR E = 1 TO ME(P) - 1
2560         DRAWLINE X2(P,E),Y2(P,E) TO X2(P,E+1),Y2(P,E+1)
2570     NEXT E
2580 NEXT P
2590 RETURN
2600 '##############################################################
2610 DATA 7
2620     'OUTLINE
2630 DATA 12,195,127,210,130,232,105,232,100,213,90,200,75,165,77
2640 DATA 145,90,85,95,70,70,60,70,60,97
2650 DATA 3,69,106,85,120,152,125
2660     'WINGS
2670 DATA 6,160,110,138,168,145,175,170,175,178,168,200,115
2680 DATA 6,203,80,198,45,195,40,170,40,165,45,167,76
2690     'TAIL
2700 DATA 3,73,75,78,75,80,85
2710 DATA 4,65,90,53,110,65,110,75,100
2720     'PROPELLOR
2730 DATA 7,230,103,235,103,230,65,240,65,230,140,240,140,235,103
2740 END
```

Now let us expand Prog. 8–3 to clip any labels that might be in the display. We could treat labels like lines and save any part inside the window, but to simplify the program we will only save a character string label if it is entirely within the window boundaries. In Fig. 8–7, the only text information we would save for the window indicated is LABEL 3. Our test for saving a string will be to determine whether the string starts after the left window boundary and ends before the right window boundary. Also, the string must be on a print line that lies within the top and bottom window limits.

Our program will use the array T$ to store the text-character strings. Arrays XL and XR will be used to store the X locations for the beginning and ending positions of each string. Arrays YT and YB will be used to store Y coordinates for the top and bottom of the strings. Values for the string coordinates, XL, XR, YT, and YB, are obtained from the dimensions of the character pixel grid for a particular system (Section 3–2).

For our text-clipping program, we will assume that an 8 by 8 pixel grid corresponds to each character. We'll also assume that each character actually occupies a 6 by 7 pixel area of the grid. That leaves a two-pixel horizontal separation between characters and a one-pixel separation between the print lines (Fig. 8–8). Characters printed across a line begin at pixel locations 0, 8, 16, 24, . . . and end at pixel locations 5, 13, 21, and so forth. The tops of characters printed down the screen are at pixel locations 0, 8, 16, . . ., and the lower ends are at pixel locations 6, 14, 22, and so forth. To determine the beginning X coordinate for a character, we subtract 1 from the character print position and multiply by 8. To get the ending position, we add 5 to the beginning position. For a character printed at a location specified by POSITION 6,21, the beginning X coordinate is 160 and the ending X coordinate is 165. To determine the Y coordinate for the top of any character, we subtract 1 from the print line and multiply by 8. Adding 6 to the top value gives the Y coordinate for the bottom of the character. For the character location specified as POSITION 6,21, the Y coordinate of the top is 40 and the Y coordinate of the bottom is 46. These text-clipping modifications to Prog. 8–3 are included in Prog. 8–4. Output of this program is given in Fig. 8–9.

Figure 8–7 Clipping any text strings not completely inside the window will erase the strings "LABEL 1", "LABEL 2", and "LABEL 4".

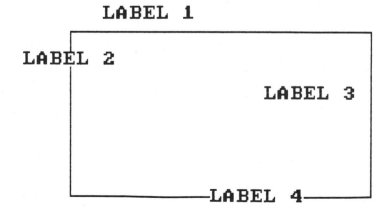

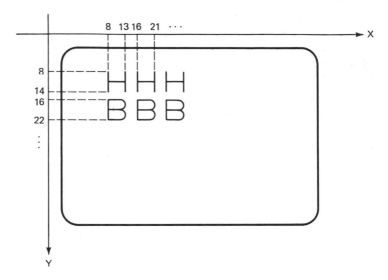

Figure 8–8 Coordinate positions for characters with an 8 by 8 pixel grid. Horizontally, characters start at pixel locations 0, 8, 16, . . . and end at pixel locations 5, 13, 21 and so on across the screen. Tops of the print lines are at pixel positions 0, 8, 16, . . ., and bottoms of the print lines are at pixel positions 6, 14, 22, and so on down the screen.

Program 8–4 Point, line, and text clipping (airplane).

```
10 ' PROGRAM 8-4. TEXT AND PICTURE CLIPPING (ADD TO PROG. 8-3)

171 DIM T$(10),RO(10),CO(10),TL(10),TR(10),TT(10),TB(10)

271     'READ IN TEXT ITEMS, ROW, AND COLUMN PLACEMENT
272 READ TN            'TN IS NUMBER OF TEXT ITEMS
273 FOR K = 1 TO TN
274     READ T$(K),RO(K),CO(K)      'RO & CO ARE ROW AND COLUMNS FOR TEXT
275     TL(K) = (CO(K) - 1) * 8              'CONVERT TO PIXEL POSITIONS
276     TR(K) = TL(K) - 1 + LEN(T$(K)) * 8
277     TT(K) = (RO(K) - 1) * 8
278     TB(K) = TT(K) + 7
279 NEXT K

315 GOSUB 2461  'CLIP TEXT

431     'PLACE TEXT ITEMS (PART OF DRAW ROUTINE)
432 FOR K = 1 TO TN
433     POSITION RO(K), CO(K)
434     PRINT T$(K);
435 NEXT K

2461 C1 = 0      'C1 IS COUNT OF TEXT ITEMS THAT ARE IN WINDOW
2462 FOR K = 1 TO TN
2463     IF TL(K)<L OR TR(K)>R OR TT(K)<T OR TB(K)>B THEN 2448
2464     C1 = C1 + 1
2465     T$(C1) = T$(K)
2466     RO(C1) = RO(K)
2467     CO(C1) = CO(K)
2468 NEXT K
2469 RETURN

2581     'ADD TEXT TIEMS
2582 FOR K = 1 TO C1
```

Program 8-4 (cont.)

```
2583    POSITION RO(K), CO(K)
2584    PRINT T$(K);
2585 NEXT K

2731    'TEXT ITEMS
2732 DATA 4
2733 DATA FUSELAGE,14,10
2734 DATA EMPENNAGE,7,4
2735 DATA WING,20,20
2736 DATA PROPELLOR,6,28
```

Figure 8–9 Picture with text displayed (a) before and (b) after clipping by Prog. 8–4.

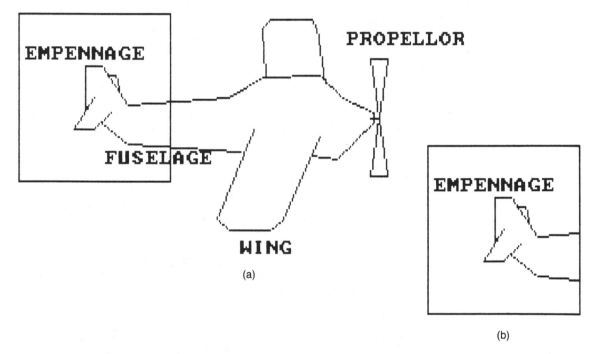

(a)

(b)

We can adapt Prog. 8–4 to other systems by using different dimensions for the character pixel grid. We could also modify the text clipping so that we save any part of a string that might be within the window. Improvements could be made in the line clipping to speed up the calculations, especially if very many lines are to be clipped. For instance, we could process each point in the picture once, instead of line by line. A code could be determined for each point, which gives the position of the point relative to the window boundary. This code can then be used to test the location of lines relative to the window. On some graphics systems, clipping is performed automatically once a window is specified.

After a picture is clipped, we could transform the window area in some way. We might display the window in another location, or we might scale or rotate the windowed part of the picture. We could also keep the original display and superimpose the window—perhaps enlarged—in one corner of the screen. The next section considers a method for transforming windows.

8–3 VIEWPORTS

Having established a window in a display, we can translate and scale the window to any size by moving it to a specified rectangular area on the screen. This area is called the **viewing area**, or **viewport**. We can establish both a window and a viewport on the screen by giving the coordinates for the top left corners and the size of each rectangular area, as shown in Fig. 8–10.

The window defines "what" we want to see in the display; the viewport establishes "where" we would like to see it on the screen. We can make the viewport larger or smaller than the window, or we can make it the same size. The viewport can be made to fill the screen or it can be set as a small insert in the display. We can make the window and viewport in separate screen areas, or we could make them overlap. If a viewport is used to enlarge an area of a picture, this enlargement can magnify details that are too small to be visible in the original display.

Figure 8–10   Window and viewport specifications. Upper left corner of the window is at position (XW,YW); upper left corner of the viewport is at position (XV,YV). Size of each area is specified by width and height (WW,HW and WV,HV). A point with coordinates (X,Y) in the window will be transformed to a new position (XN,YN) in the viewport.

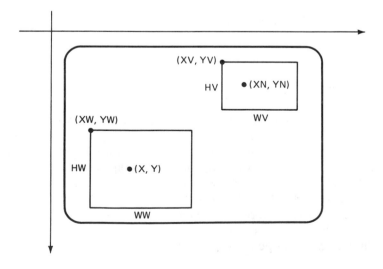

A program to transform a window area to a viewport area must transform the coordinates of each point in the window, such as (X,Y) in Fig. 8–10, to the corresponding new point (XN,YN) in the viewport. This transformation is accomplished in much the same way that we set up graphs on the screen within specified areas in Chapter 4. New coordinates in the viewport are related to the original coordinates of the point in the window by the relations

$$XN = (X - XW) * (WV / WW) + XV$$
$$YN = (Y - YW) * (HV / HW) + YV$$

(8–1)

The factors (WV/WW) and (HV/HW) in the equations of (8–1) represent the scaling transformation. We have a different size for the area in the viewport if these factors are not equal to 1. A value greater than 1 enlarges the window; a value smaller than 1 reduces the size. If the ratio WV/HV is not equal to the ratio WW/HW, we will distort the window area. This is equivalent to a different scaling for the X and Y directions, as discussed in Chapter 6. Terms XV and YV represent the translation. If these coordinates are different from XW and YW, the area has been moved.

A mapping from a window area to a specified viewport is accomplished by Prog. 8–5, an extension of Prog. 8–3. Figure 8–11 illustrates the output from this program. In this example, we demonstrate how viewports can be used to magnify details of a picture. The star on the airplane fuselage, seen as a cluster of points when displayed in relative scale, is clearly identified in the viewport display. Such viewport magnifications can be useful with maps or complex diagrams to show levels of detail.

Program 8–5 Displaying viewports (airplane).

```
2740 '########## PROGRAM 8-5. DISPLAY WINDOW AREA IN VIEWPORT ##########
2750     '                    ADD TO PROGRAM 8-3
2760        'ESTABLISHES A VIEWPORT ON THE SCREEN. TAKES THE PICTURE
2770        'PARTS FOUND TO BE INSIDE THE WINDOW AND MOVES THEM TO
2780        'THE CHOSEN VIEWPORT.
2790        '**************************************************
2800 DIM XN(8,20), YN(8,20)
2810 GOSUB 2850              'ESTABLISH VIEWPORT
2820 GOSUB 3070             'CONVERT WINDOW AREA TO VIEWPORT AREA
2830 GOSUB 3150             'DRAW PICTURE PART IN VIEWPORT
2840 GOTO 3280
2850 '################## ESTABLISH VIEWPORT ####################
2860 POSITION 1,1
2870 PRINT "TOP LEFT CORNER OF VIEWPORT";
2880 INPUT XV, YV
2890 POSITION 1,1
2900 PRINT "                              ";
2910 POSITION 1,1
2920 PRINT "WIDTH AND HEIGHT OF VIEWPORT";
2930 INPUT WV, HV
2940 POSITION 1,1
2950 PRINT "                              ";
2960 L = XV
2970 R = XV + WV
2980 T = YV
2990 B = YV + HV
```

```
3000 IF L<R AND L>=0 AND R<=XM AND T<B AND T>=0 AND B<=YM THEN 3060
3010 POSITION 1,1
3020 PRINT "VIEWPORT OFF SCREEN. TRY AGAIN"
3030 POSITION 1,1
3040 PRINT "                                      ";
3050 GOTO 2860
3060 RETURN
3070 '############ CONVERT WINDOW AREA TO VIEWPORT AREA #############
3080 FOR P = 1 TO MN
3090     FOR E = 1 TO ME(P)
3100         XN(P,E) = (X2(P,E) - XW) * (WV / WW) + XV
3110         YN(P,E) = (Y2(P,E) - YW) * (HV / HW) + YV
3120     NEXT E
3130 NEXT P
3140 RETURN
3150 '##################### DRAW CLIPPED POINTS ###################
3160 CLEARSCREEN
3170 DRAWLINE L,T TO L,B
3180 DRAWLINE L,B TO R,B
3190 DRAWLINE R,B TO R,T
3200 DRAWLINE R,T TO L,T
3210 FOR P = 1 TO MN
3220     FOR E = 1 TO ME(P) - 1
3230         DRAWLINE XN(P,E),YN(P,E) TO XN(P,E+1),YN(P,E+1)
3240     NEXT E
3250 NEXT P
3260 RETURN
3270 '####################################################################
3280 END
```

Figure 8–11 A window area of a picture (a) is magnified into a viewport area (b) by Prog. 8–5.

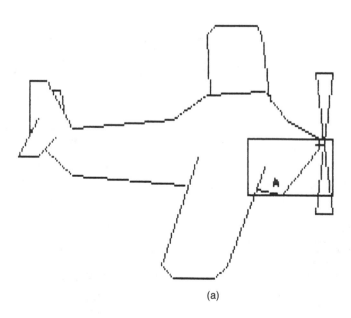

(a)

Figure 8-11 (cont.)

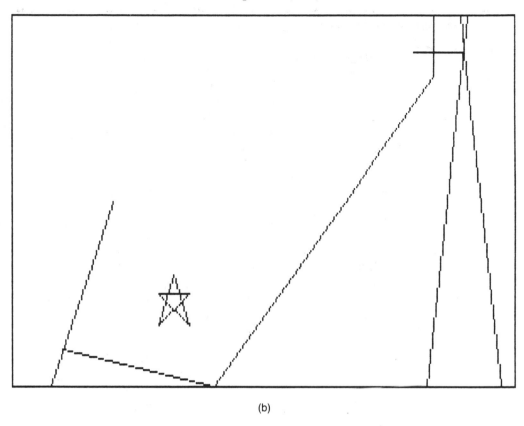

(b)

For some applications, we might want to display both the original scene and the viewport together on the screen. We could also window more than one area, producing more than one viewport. As a final transformation on a window, a viewport could be rotated to present the area in a different orientation.

PROGRAMMING PROJECTS

8–1. Write a spotlight program that will accent lines within the spotlight by drawing them in a brighter (or different) color, using either a rectangular or circular spotlight. As an additional feature, change the background color of the display area within the spotlight.

8–2. Develop a program that will spotlight areas of a display using an ellipse of any specified dimensions. Provide a routine to erase the elliptical spotlight area, as an input option.

8–3. Write a routine to clip character strings against a rectangular boundary by erasing only that part of the string within the window.

8–4. Write a clipping program that will erase all parts of a display outside of a specified circular area.

8–5. Write a clipping program that uses a viewport to enlarge some area of a picture, then superimposes the enlarged portion onto the original picture in one corner of the screen. Instead of erasing the entire screen, erase only the area that is to contain the viewport.

8–6. Modify Prog. 8–3 so that each point of a picture is compared to the window boundary only once. The position of each point relative to the window can be specified in an array that states whether the point is "IN" or "OUT," "ABOVE" or "BELOW," and "LEFT" or "RIGHT." This information could be coded in a character string of length 3 (for example, "OBR" would state that a point is outside, below, and to the right). After processing all points to set the position string for each point, the lines in the picture can be clipped by examining the corresponding position string for the endpoints. A line is saved if both points are "IN." It is eliminated if both points are "LEFT" or both points are "ABOVE," and so forth. Intersection points are then found for the overlapping lines. The position string can be reduced to two characters by setting the first character in the string to be "X" (inside), "A" (above), or "B" (below), and by setting the second character to "L" (left) or "R" (right).

8–7. Write a program that will display any number of viewports of picture areas on the screen.

8–8. Write a program that will rotate a viewport to any specified orientation.

Part IV

ADVANCED GRAPHICS

(Three Dimensions)

Real objects are perceived in three dimensions. They have depth as well as breadth and height. When we represent objects on a flat (two-dimensional) screen, we can either ignore the depth or project the objects onto the screen in such a way that depth is represented. By including depth, we can add greatly to the realism of a picture or to the information content of a graph. We now consider some of the ways to include this third dimension in our displays.

Chapter 9

Three-Dimensional Displays

A three-dimensional figure such as a box can be displayed on a video screen as a rectangle, Fig. 9–1(a). We obtain the width and height information from this flat representation, and we infer that the rectangle also has depth but that we are only looking at one side. A more realistic projection of the box on the screen is shown in Fig. 9–1(b). Now we are able to see other sides of the box, and we have a better grasp of the structure and actual dimensions of the solid object. Similarly, displaying graphs and charts in three dimensions allows us to include additional relationships and information.

Figure 9–1 A three-dimensional box represented (a) as a flat rectangle and (b) with depth.

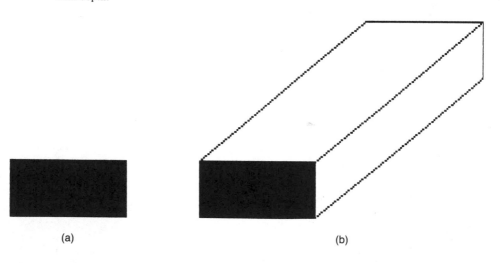

(a)   (b)

174

9–1 GRAPH PAPER LAYOUTS

The screen output of Fig. 9–1(b) was obtained from the graph paper layout in Fig. 9–2 by plotting the X and Y coordinates of points in the layout. We chose a view of the box that made three sides visible. But as originally drawn in Fig. 9–2, it is not clear which three sides are presented to us. We could be viewing the box from above and to the right or from below and to the left. To remove this ambiguity from the video display, we simply omitted the lines that were to be at the back of the box for the view we wanted to see. We drew the box without the lines connecting points 3 and 7, points 6 and 7, and points 7 and 8. This manual method can be used to display three-dimensional scenes: we draw all sides of an object or group of objects on graph paper, erase lines that are hidden for the view we want to display, and plot the remaining lines on the screen.

For some situations we would like to use a more general method for obtaining a three-dimensional view that would let the graphics display program distinguish the "front" and "back" of objects. A rotating figure that continuously brings different sides into view is constantly changing front faces into back faces. Various techniques can be used in display programs to distinguish the front from the back of three-dimensional objects, in order to give us depth information. One method is to erase all hidden parts of objects, as we did in the graph paper layouts. We can also project objects on the screen so that a perspective view provides depth information. A perspective view shows the parts of the display closer to us larger than the objects and surfaces farther away from us. Another technique is to

Figure 9–2 Graph paper layout for a three-dimensional box.

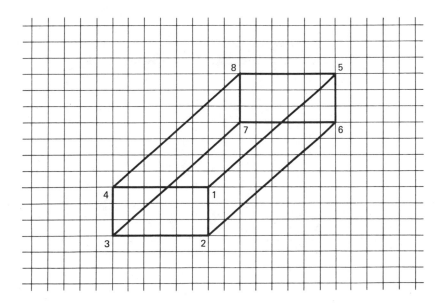

highlight nearer lines, so that front parts of objects are brighter than the back lines. More elaborate shading schemes can be used that produce gradual light to dark patterns across surfaces. Each of these methods requires that the depth of points in the picture be specified in the display program.

9–2 THREE-DIMENSIONAL COORDINATES

Figure 9–3 illustrates a coordinate representation for specifying the **depth**, or Z coordinate, in addition to specifying the X and Y coordinates. The upper left corner of the screen is chosen to be the coordinate origin for the three axes. As before, positive X values are measured from left to right across the screen, and positive Y values are measured from top to bottom. Coordinate Z values are measured from zero at the screen face, with positive values in back of the screen and negative values in front of the screen. Each point of a picture is then assigned three coordinate values, (X,Y,Z). Position on the screen is determined by the X and Y values, and Z denotes the depth of the point relative to the display screen. Points farther away have larger Z values; nearer points have smaller Z values. We use the Z coordinates to obtain different views of objects, to identify hidden lines or surfaces of objects, and to obtain perspective views.

Figure 9–3 Each point of a picture can be represented in terms of three coordinate values, (X,Y,Z). Positive Z values indicate distances in back of the display screen.

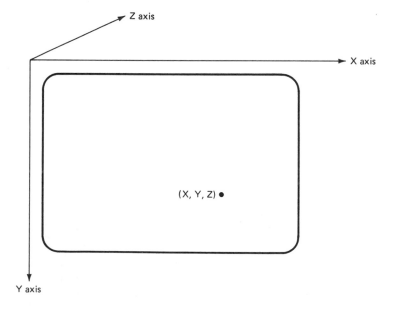

Different views of objects can be displayed by substituting the Z coordinate of each point for either the X or Y values when we plot screen positions. Thus, plotting (X,Z) for all points gives a top or bottom view and plotting (Z,Y) gives side views, as shown in Fig. 9–4. In the first case, we assume that Y values are positive in back of the screen. Otherwise, we have a bottom view. In the second case, we obtain a left-side view if X is assumed positive in back of the screen, and we obtain a right-side view if X is assumed positive in front of the screen. Such views are called **orthographic projections**. To obtain these top, bottom, or side views of an object, we input the (X,Y,Z) coordinates for each vertex and plot the appropriate coordinate pair, eliminating the ''back'' faces.

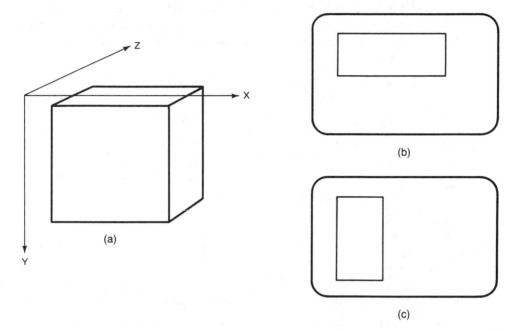

Figure 9–4 Orthographic projections. A three-dimensional object (a) can be viewed from the top or bottom by plotting (X,Z) values on the screen (b). Side views (c) are obtained by plotting (Z,Y) values.

9–3 ERASING HIDDEN LINES AND SURFACES

There are two general approaches to erasing hidden parts of objects. One approach is to think of an object in terms of its various surfaces. We can then identify and eliminate those surfaces that are in back of, or hidden by, other surfaces. The second method is to treat displays in terms of the component lines, identifying and erasing individual hidden lines instead of surfaces.

HIDDEN SURFACES

A technique for eliminating hidden surfaces in a display is to paint each surface onto the screen from back to front. Surfaces with larger Z values are painted first, so that closer surfaces obscure back surfaces if they overlap. Each surface can be painted in a different color, or they can all be painted with the background color—which erases hidden lines.

Program 9–1 illustrates this method of erasing hidden lines. Any number of rectangular faces may be input. Each plane face is assumed to be parallel to the display screen, so that only one Z value is specified for each plane. Interiors of the planes are filled with the background color after the faces are put in order, back faces first. Overlapping planes will then blank out the faces farther away (Fig. 9–5). Using different colors for different faces paints over the hidden lines instead of erasing.

Program 9–1   Erasing hidden lines by painting surfaces on the screen from back to front (rectangles).

```
10  'PROGRAM 9-1. BLANKING OUT BACKGROUND SURFACES.
20      'STORES X, Y, AND Z COORDINATES FOR TOP LEFT CORNER OF
30      'A NUMBER OF RECTANGULAR SURFACES, AS WELL AS WIDTH AND
40      'HEIGHT OF THE RECTANGLE. WILL SORT THE RECTANGLES IN
50      'ORDER OF DECREASING Z VALUES AND THEN DRAW. RECTANGLES
60      'ARE FILLED IN WITH BACKGROUND COLOR SO EACH RECTANGLE
70      'BLANKS OUT ANY THAT ARE BEHIND.
80      '*********************************************************
90  DIM X(10), Y(10), Z(10), W(10), H(10)
100 XM = 255
110 YM = 191       'XM AND YM ARE MAXIMUM VALUES FOR THIS SYSTEM
120     '*************** READ DATA FOR SURFACES ******************
130 READ N        'N IS NUMBER OF SURFACES
140 FOR K = 1 TO N
150     READ X(K), Y(K), Z(K), W(K), H(K)          'X,Y ARE TOP LEFT CORNER
160     IF X(K)<O OR Y(K)<O OR W(K)<O OR H(K)<O THEN 650    'W AND H ARE
170     IF X(K)+W>XM OR Y(K)+H(K)>YM THEN 650              'WIDTH AND
180 NEXT K                                                 'HEIGHT
190     '************* SORT FACES BY Z COORDINATES ***************
200 FOR P = 1 TO N - 1
210     B = P
220     FOR R = P + 1 TO N      'LOOK THROUGH THE REST OF THE Z VALUES
230         IF Z(B) > Z(R) THEN 250     'IF THEY ARE SMALLER, CONTINUE
240         B = R                       'ELSE, SET B TO ANY THAT ARE BIGGER
250     NEXT R
260     T = X(P)
270     X(P) = X(B)
280     X(B) = T
290     T = Y(P)
300     Y(P) = Y(B)
310     Y(B) = T
320     T = Z(P)
330     Z(P) = Z(B)
340     Z(B) = T
350     T = W(P)
360     W(P) = W(B)
370     W(B) = T
380     T = H(P)
```

Program 9-1 (cont.)

```
390      H(P) = H(B)
400      H(B) = T
410 NEXT P
420      '*********** DRAW SURFACES IN ORDER *********************
430 CLEARSCREEN
440 GRAPHICS
450 FOR K = 1 TO N
460      DRAWLINE X(K),Y(K) TO X(K)+W(K),Y(K)
470      DRAWLINE X(K)+W(K),Y(K) TO X(K)+W(K),Y(K)+H(K)
480      DRAWLINE X(K)+W(K),Y(K)+H(K) TO X(K),Y(K)+H(K)
490      DRAWLINE X(K),Y(K)+H(K) TO X(K),Y(K)
500      'FILL IN ENCLOSED AREA
510      COLOR 0,0
520      FOR YI = Y(K) + 1 TO Y(K) + H(K) - 1
530          DRAWLINE X(K)+1,YI TO X(K)+W(K)-1,YI
540      NEXT YI
550      COLOR 1,0
560 NEXT K
570      '***********************************************************
580 DATA 5
590 DATA 10,10,30,100,100
600 DATA 40,20,2,100,100
610 DATA 60,50,0,30,100
620 DATA 5,40,20,50,100
630 DATA 30,80,-5,120,100
640      '***********************************************************
650 END
```

Figure 9–5 Overlapping rectangular planes displayed by Prog. 9–1.

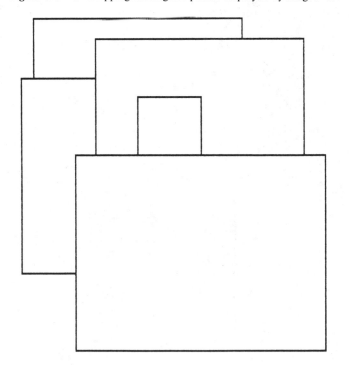

　　　Shapes other than rectangles could be used for the input faces. For example, we could input circles, triangles, or general polygons. The length of the interior "erase" line for each shape is determined by the boundary equations for that surface. We can also specify the Z coordinate of each point rather than just for each face. This allows a face to be tilted, with parts of the face farther from us than other parts. Sorting could then be accomplished according to the smallest Z value for each face. We might want to set up the faces so that they do not run into each other. Otherwise, two faces could alternately obscure one another, as shown in Fig. 9–6. We could allow for this possibility by finding the intersection line and dividing one or both planes into two parts, or we could use other geometric methods to determine which part of each face was visible. Finally, various curved surfaces, rather than planes, could be overlapped if we treated the curved surfaces as plane surfaces. We could blank out the interiors of the curved surfaces, then draw lines to indicate the curvature (Fig. 9–7).

　　　As an alternative to erasing the entire interior of all faces in a picture, we can employ methods to identify and eliminate only the surfaces that are actually hidden. For objects with symmetry, we can usually set up methods that decide visibility between two opposite faces. The box of Fig. 9–2 has three pairs of opposite faces. We can see only one face from each of these pairs at any one time. If we see the face with vertices 1, 2, 3, and 4, we cannot see face 5, 6, 7, 8. A program to eliminate hidden lines for this box need only display the side from each pair with the smaller Z value. This is accomplished with Prog. 9–2. This program displays all lines for a test box, then clears the screen and draws the visible sides only. If the box were rotating, Prog. 9–2 would recalculate the visible faces after each rotation. Similar methods can be used for other symmetrical objects.

Figure 9–6　Planes with variable depth may overlap and intersect so that part of each plane is obscured by the other.

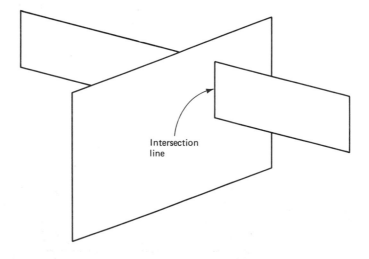

Intersection
line

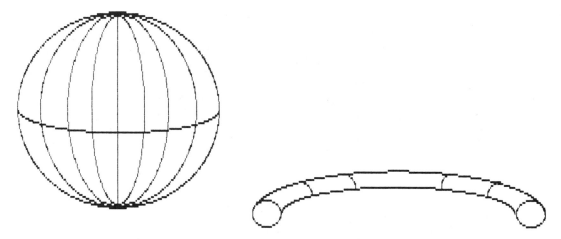

Figure 9–7 Representation of three-dimensional curved surfaces with lines drawn to indicate curvature.

Program 9–2 Eliminating hidden lines by displaying only the one visible surface from each pair of symmetrical faces of an object (box).

```
10 'PROGRAM 9-2. ERASING HIDDEN LINES BY SYMMETRY.
20      'READS AND STORES THE POINTS OF A 3-DIMENSIONAL BOX.
30      'COMPARES THE Z VALUES FOR EACH PAIR OF SYMMETRIC
40      'SURFACES AND DRAWS ONLY THE NEARER SURFACE.
50 CLEARSCREEN
60 DIM X(8), Y(8), Z(8)
70 XM = 39
80 YM = 39      'XM AND YM ARE MAXIMUM VALUES FOR THIS SYSTEM
90      '*************** READ VERTICES FOR CUBE *****************
100 FOR K = 1 TO 8
110     READ X(K), Y(K), Z(K)
120     IF X(K)<0 OR X(K)>XM OR Y(K)<0 OR Y(K)>YM THEN 650
130 NEXT K
140     '********************* DRAW ALL FACES ******************
150 GRAPHICS
160 FOR K = 1 TO 3
170     DRAWLINE X(K),Y(K) TO X(K+1),Y(K+1)
180     DRAWLINE X(K),Y(K) TO X(K+4),Y(K+4)
190 NEXT K
200 DRAWLINE X(4),Y(4) TO X(1),Y(1)
210 DRAWLINE X(4),Y(4) TO X(8),Y(8)
220 FOR K = 5 TO 7
230     DRAWLINE X(K),Y(K) TO X(K+1),Y(K+1)
240 NEXT K
250 DRAWLINE X(8),Y(8) TO X(5),Y(5)
260 FOR K = 1 TO 1000: NEXT K
270     '*************** DRAW ONLY VISIBLE FACES ***************
280 CLEARSCREEN
290 IF Z(1) = Z(5) THEN 400           'NEITHER SIDE IS VISIBLE
300 IF Z(1) > Z(5) THEN 360
310 FOR K = 1 TO 3                     'DRAW FACE CONTAINING POINT 1
320     DRAWLINE X(K),Y(K) TO X(K+1),Y(K+1)
330 NEXT K
340 DRAWLINE X(4),Y(4) TO X(1),Y(1)
```

Program 9-2 (cont.)

```
350 GOTO 410
360 FOR K = 5 TO 7                          'DRAW FACE CONTAINING POINT 5
370     DRAWLINE X(K),Y(K) TO X(K+1),Y(K+1)
380 NEXT K
390 DRAWLINE X(8),Y(8) TO X(5),Y(5)
400 IF Z(1) = Z(4) THEN 510                 'NEITHER SIDE IS VISIBLE
410 IF Z(1) > Z(4) THEN 470
420 DRAWLINE X(1),Y(1) TO X(2),Y(2)         'DRAW FACE CONTAINING POINT 1
430 DRAWLINE X(2),Y(2) TO X(6),Y(6)
440 DRAWLINE X(6),Y(6) TO X(5),Y(5)
450 DRAWLINE X(5),Y(5) TO X(1),Y(1)
460 GOTO 520
470 DRAWLINE X(4),Y(4) TO X(3),Y(3)         'DRAW FACE CONTAINING POINT 4
480 DRAWLINE X(3),Y(3) TO X(7),Y(7)
490 DRAWLINE X(7),Y(7) TO X(8),Y(8)
500 DRAWLINE X(8),Y(8) TO X(4),Y(4)
510 IF Z(1) = Z(2) THEN 650                 'NEITHER SIDE IS VISIBLE
520 IF Z(1) > Z(2) THEN 580
530 DRAWLINE X(1),Y(1) TO X(4),Y(4)         'DRAW FACE CONTAINING POINT 1
540 DRAWLINE X(4),Y(4) TO X(8),Y(8)
550 DRAWLINE X(8),Y(8) TO X(5),Y(5)
560 DRAWLINE X(5),Y(5) TO X(1),Y(1)
570 GOTO 650
580 DRAWLINE X(2),Y(2) TO X(3),Y(3)         'DRAW FACE CONTAINING POINT 2
590 DRAWLINE X(3),Y(3) TO X(7),Y(7)
600 DRAWLINE X(7),Y(7) TO X(6),Y(6)
610 DRAWLINE X(6),Y(6) TO X(2),Y(2)
620     '***********************************************************
630 DATA 19,22,0,19,28,10,11,28,60,11,22,50
640 DATA 29,10,100,29,16,110,21,16,160,21,10,150
650 END
```

A method for eliminating hidden surfaces that does not depend on object symmetry is given in Prog. 9–3. A rectangular bounding area is established for each face of the input object. Each vertex point of each face is tested against all other faces to determine whether that point is within the rectangular boundary of the face. If the point is within the boundary and has greater depth, the visibility flag for the face containing that point is set to "OFF." After all faces have been tested, the object is redrawn with visible faces only. Figure 9–8 shows the two views of an object output by this program.

Program 9–3 Erasing hidden surfaces by locating hidden vertices.

```
10 'PROGRAM 9-3. ERASING HIDDEN LINES BY RECTANGULAR BOUNDARIES.
20      'ALL FACES ARE INITIALLY SET TO "ON" AND ARE DRAWN.
30      'SMALLEST & LARGEST X AND Y AND Z VALUES ARE FOUND
40      'FOR EACH FACE AND STORED. THESE X AND Y VALUES ARE
50      'CONSIDERED TO BE THE "BOUNDING RECTANGLE" OF THE FACE.
60      'TAKING EACH FACE, ALL OTHER FACES ARE TESTED AGAINST
70      'IT. IF ANY VERTEX OF THE TEST FACE FALLS WITHIN THE
80      'BOUNDING RECTANGLE, Z VALUES ARE COMPARED. IF THE
90      'Z VALUE OF THE TEST FACE VERTEX IS GREATER THAN THE
100     'LARGEST Z VALUE FOR THE FACE, THEN THE TEST FACE IS
110     'TURNED OFF. WHEN ALL FACES HAVE BEEN TESTED AGAINST
120     'ALL OTHER FACES, WE RE-DRAW THE FIGURE, USING ONLY
```

Program 9-3 (cont.)

```
130      'THOSE FACES THAT ARE STILL "ON".
140      '*********************************************************************
150 DIM X(9,6), Y(9,6), Z(9,6), C$(9)
160 DIM XS(9), YS(9), ZS(9), XL(9), YL(9), ZL(9)
170 XM = 279
180 YM = 159     'XM AND YM ARE MAXIMUM X AND Y VALUES FOR THIS SYSTEM
190      '
200      '*********************** READ POINTS *************************
210 READ N        'N IS NUMBER OF SURFACES
220 FOR S = 1 TO N
230      C$(S) = "ON"
240      READ NV(S)        'NV IS # OF VERTICES IN SURFACE
250      FOR V = 1 TO NV(S)
260          READ X(S,V), Y(S,V), Z(S,V)
270          IF X(S,V)<0 OR X(S,V)>XM OR Y(S,V)<0 OR Y(S,V)>YM THEN 880
280      NEXT V
290      X(S,NV(S)+1) = X(S,1)
300      Y(S,NV(S)+1) = Y(S,1)
310 NEXT S
320 GRAPHICS
330 GOSUB 680          'DRAW FACES THAT ARE ON
340      '
350      '************ FIND OUTER BOUNDARIES FOR EACH FACE ***************
360 FOR S = 1 TO N
370      XS(S) = X(S,1)            'XS & XL ARE SMALLEST & LARGEST X VALUES
380      YS(S) = Y(S,1)
390      ZS(S) = Z(S,1)
400      FOR V = 2 TO NV(S)
410          IF X(S,V) < XS(S) THEN XS(S) = X(S,V)
420          IF Y(S,V) < YS(S) THEN YS(S) = Y(S,V)
430          IF Z(S,V) < ZS(S) THEN ZS(S) = Z(S,V)
440          IF X(S,V) > XL(S) THEN XL(S) = X(S,V)
450          IF Y(S,V) > YL(S) THEN YL(S) = Y(S,V)
460          IF Z(S,V) > ZL(S) THEN ZL(S) = Z(S,V)
470      NEXT V
480 NEXT S
490      '
500      '***************** TURN OFF HIDDEN FACES *********************
510 FOR S = 1 TO N
520      IF C$(S) = "OFF" THEN 640        'FACE IS ALREADY OFF
530      FOR R = 1 TO N
540          IF C$(R) = "OFF" OR R = S THEN 630            'NO NEED TO COMPARE
550          FOR V = 1 TO NV(R)
560              IF X(R,V) <= XS(S) OR X(R,V) >= XL(S) OR
                    Y(R,V) <= YS(S) OR Y(R,V) >= YL(S) THEN 620
570              'OTHERWISE POINT (R,V) IS WITHIN THE BOUNDING RECTANGLE
580              'IS IT IN FRONT OR IN BACK?
590              IF Z(R,V) <= ZL(S) THEN 630      'FACE R IS NOT IN BACK OF S
600              C$(R) = "OFF"           'FACE R IS IN BACK OF FACE S
610              GOTO 630              'GO ON TO TEST THE NEXT FACE
620          NEXT V
630      NEXT R
640 NEXT S
650 GOSUB 680          'DRAW FACES THAT ARE "ON"
660 GOTO 880
670 '
680 '######################### DRAW ROUTINE #########################
690 CLEARSCREEN
700 FOR S = 1 TO N
```

Program 9-3 (cont.)

```
710      IF C$(S) = "OFF" THEN 750      'SKIP THIS ONE - DON'T DRAW
720      FOR V = 1 TO NV(S)
730          DRAWLINE X(S,V),Y(S,V) TO X(S,V+1),Y(S,V+1)
740      NEXT V
750 NEXT S
760 RETURN
770 '
780 '#################################################################
790 DATA 7
800 DATA 5,90,140,60,150,140,10,150,110,0,120,70,20,90,110,50
810 DATA 4,150,110,10,150,140,10,230,80,110,230,50,100
820 DATA 5,230,50,100,230,80,110,170,80,160,170,50,150,200,10,120
830 DATA 4,170,50,150,170,80,160,90,140,60,90,110,50
840 DATA 4,90,140,50,150,140,10,230,80,110,170,80,160
850 DATA 4,150,110,0,230,50,100,200,10,120,120,70,20
860 DATA 4,90,110,50,120,70,20,200,10,120,170,50,150
870 '#################################################################
880 END
```

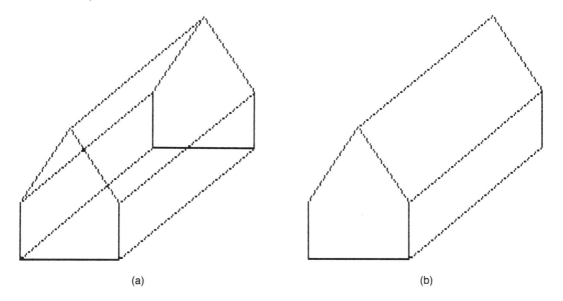

(a)   (b)

Figure 9-8 Three-dimensional object displayed (a) before and (b) after erasing
hidden surfaces by Prog. 9-3.

Objects with complex geometric shapes may be inaccurately drawn with the
techniques used in Prog. 9-3, since the visibility test is highly simplified. Each
face of the object is determined to be either completely visible or completely
hidden, so that partially hidden areas cannot be displayed. Also, the bounding
face area used to test for hidden points will become more inaccurate as the face
area differs from a rectangle. A long, thin, diagonal surface will have a large
rectangular boundary which could lead to an erroneous determination of visibility.

HIDDEN LINES

The preceding two programs tested object surfaces to determine visibility. Each surface tested was deemed either visible or invisible. We now consider a method for determining partial visibility by testing the visibility of individual lines instead of complete surfaces. Our program will test a line to determine if any part of the line is hidden by a surface.

A line and a surface can be related in several ways. In Fig. 9–9, the various relationships between a displayed line and a surface are illustrated. For this example, we assume that the surface is nearer to us than any of the lines. Then lines B and E are completely visible, line D is completely hidden, the top overlapping segment of line C is also hidden, and the middle overlapping section of line A is invisible. To simplify our hidden-line programs, we will assume that these are the only possible relationships. That is, a line can intersect a surface at no more than two points. This restricts surface shapes to be either circles, ellipses, or convex polygons [Fig. 9–10(a)], and eliminates from consideration all concave polygons [Fig. 9–10(b)] which could have more than two intersection points. We can treat objects with concave surfaces by redefining surface boundaries. Any concave surface can be reorganized into two or more convex polygons. But this technique will add additional lines to objects, which may be undesirable.

Figure 9–9   Possible line and surface relationships. Line A intersects the face boundary at two points; lines B and C intersect at one point; line D is completely hidden; and line E is completely visible. (All lines are assumed to have greater Z coordinates than the surface.)

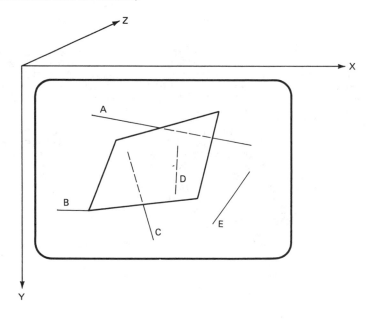

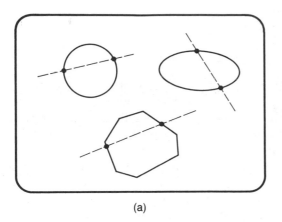
(a)

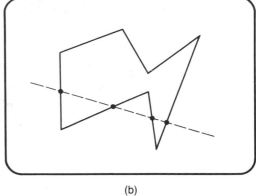
(b)

Figure 9–10 (a) Circles, ellipses, and convex polygons (interior angles less than 180 degrees) can have no more than two intersection points with a straight line. (b) Concave polygons (interior angles greater than 180 degrees) can have more than two intersection points with a straight line.

Program 9–4 demonstrates a method for detecting and erasing hidden segments of lines. Any number of surfaces may be input by specifying the coordinates for all vertices in each surface. For the demonstration example, we have 14 surfaces with four vertices each. The surfaces could all be part of one object, as in the example, or represent several different objects. Isolated straight lines can be input as surfaces with two vertices. After all surfaces have been defined, the program draws the input lines [Fig. 9–11(a)], then finds and erases each line segment hidden by a surface [Fig. 9–11(b)]. In order to avoid concave polygons, some surfaces of the object were reorganized to form two convex polygons.

Program 9–4 Erasing hidden line segments for partially visible lines and surfaces.

```
10  'PROGRAM 9-4. ERASING LINE SEGMENTS OF PARTIALLY VISIBLE SURFACES.
20      'ENDPOINTS OF LINES FOR EACH SURFACE, S (CANNOT BE CONCAVE) ARE
30      'STORED IN X1,Y1,Z1 AND X2,Y2,Z2. PROGRAM DRAWS FIGURE AND BEGINS
40      'TO ERASE HIDDEN LINES. EACH FACE IS TAKEN ONE AT A TIME. THE
50      'MINIMUM AND MAXIMUM X AND Y VALUES AND THE MINIMUM Z ARE FOUND
60      'TO ESTABLISH BOUNDARIES FOR THIS SURFACE. THE SLOPES AND Y
70      'INTERCEPTS OF EACH LINE OF THIS SURFACE ARE FOUND. THE PROGRAM
80      'THEN TAKES EVERY OTHER LINE OF EVERY OTHER FACE TO USE AS A
90      'TEST LINE AND TESTS IT AGAINST THE SURFACE (S). IF THE TEST LINE
100     'IS OUTSIDE THE BOUNDARIES OF THE SURFACE, THE LINE IS VISIBLE SO
110     'WE GO ON TO A NEW TEST LINE. OTHERWISE WE ATTEMPT TO FIND
120     'INTERSECTION POINTS OF THE TEST LINE AND THE VARIOUS LINES OF
130     'THE SURFACE (S). CHECKS MUST BE MADE TO DETERMINE IF THE
140     'CALCULATED INTERSECTION POINT IS ACTUALLY PART OF THE TWO LINES
150     '(PERHAPS THE TEST LINE AND/OR LINE OF THE SURFACE END BEFORE
160     'ACTUALLY INTERSECTING). Z VALUES ARE COMPUTED AND USED TO DETERMINE
170     'IF THE TEST LINE IS IN FRONT OR IN BACK OF THE SURFACE AT THE
180     'CALCULATED INTERSECTION POINT. IF WE FIND TWO INTERSECTION POINTS
190     'TO USE AS ENDPOINTS FOR A HIDDEN SEGMENT, WE ERASE THE SEGMENT.
200     'ONCE WE HAVE TESTED EVERY OTHER LINE OF THE FIGURE AGAINST
210     'THIS SURFACE AND ERASED HIDDEN SEGMENTS, WE GO ON TO THE
220     'NEXT SURFACE.
230     '*********************************************************************
```

```
240 CLEARSCREEN
250 DIM X1(14,4), X2(14,4), Y1(14,4), Y2(14,4), Z1(14,4), Z2(14,4)
260 DIM NV(14), M(4), B(4)
270 XM = 319
280 YM = 199
290     '************ READ DATA POINTS ******************
300 READ NS              'NS IS NUMBER OF SURFACES
310 FOR S = 1 TO NS
320 READ NV(S)           'NV(S) IS NUMBER OF VERTICES FOR THIS SURFACE
330     READ X1(S,1), Y1(S,1), Z1(S,1)
340     FOR V = 2 TO NV(S)
350         READ X1(S,V), Y1(S,V), Z1(S,V)
360         IF X1(S,V)<0 OR X1(S,V)>XM THEN 2300
370         IF Y1(S,V)<0 OR Y1(S,V)>YM THEN 2300
380         X2(S,V-1) = X1(S,V)
390         Y2(S,V-1) = Y1(S,V)
400         Z2(S,V-1) = Z1(S,V)
410     NEXT V
420     X2(S,NV(S)) = X1(S,1)
430     Y2(S,NV(S)) = Y1(S,1)
440     Z2(S,NV(S)) = Z1(S,1)
450 NEXT S
460     'DRAW POLYGON SURFACE
470 GRAPHICS
480 FOR S = 1 TO NS
490     FOR V = 1 TO NV(S)
500         DRAWLINE X1(S,V),Y1(S,V) TO X2(S,V),Y2(S,V)
510     NEXT V
520 NEXT S
530 COLOR 0,0
540 FOR S = 1 TO NS
550     GOSUB 650        'FIND BOUNDARIES & EQUATIONS FOR THIS SURFACE
560     FOR SR = 1 TO NS
570         IF S = SR THEN 610
580         FOR L = 1 TO NV(SR)
590             GOSUB 1000        'TEST FOR VISIBILITY. ERASE ANY HIDDEN PARTS
600         NEXT L
610     NEXT SR
620 NEXT S
630 GOTO 2300
640     '
650     '######## FIND BOUNDARY FOR SURFACE & EQUATIONS OF EACH LINE ##########
660     'FIND X, Y, AND Z BOUNDARIES FOR SURFACE
670 XL = X1(S,1)             'XL IS LOWEST X VALUE. WANT GREATEST X VALUE IN
680 XR = X1(S,1)             'XR, LOWEST Z VALUE IN ZF, LOWEST Y VALUE IN
690 YT = Y1(S,1)             'YT, AND GREATEST Y VALUE IN YB
700 YB = Y1(S,1)
710 ZF = Z1(S,1)
720 FOR K = 1 TO NV(S)
730     IF Z1(S,K) < ZF THEN ZF = Z1(S,K)
740     IF Z2(S,K) < ZF THEN ZF = Z2(S,K)
750     IF Y1(S,K) < YT THEN YT = Y1(S,K)
760     IF Y2(S,K) < YT THEN YT = Y2(S,K)
770     IF Y1(S,K) > YB THEN YB = Y1(S,K)
780     IF Y2(S,K) > YB THEN YB = Y2(S,K)
790     IF X1(S,K) > XR THEN XR = X1(S,K)
800     IF X2(S,K) > XR THEN XR = X2(S,K)
810     IF X1(S,K) < XL THEN XL = X1(S,K)
820     IF X2(S,K) < XL THEN XL = X1(S,K)
830 NEXT K
840     '************** DETERMINE LINE EQUATIONS ******************
```

Program 9-4 (cont.)

```
850      'FOR EACH LINE OF THE SURFACE, THE SLOPE AND Y INTERCEPT ARE
860      'FOUND AND STORED IN M AND B
870 FOR P = 1 TO NV(S)
880      IF Y1(S,P) = Y2(S,P) THEN 930        'HORIZONTAL LINE
890      IF X1(S,P) = X2(S,P) THEN 960        'VERTICAL LINE
900      M(P) = (Y2(S,P) - Y1(S,P)) / (X2(S,P) - X1(S,P))
910      B(P) = Y1(S,P) - M(P) * X1(S,P)
920      GOTO 970
930      M(P) = 0            'SLOPE OF HORIZONTAL LINE IS 0
940      B(P) = Y1(S,P)
950      GOTO 970
960      M(P) = 9999      'SLOPE OF VERTICAL LINE IS UNDEFINED
970 NEXT P
980 RETURN
990      '
1000     '##################### TEST LINE FOR VISIBILITY ####################
1010     'IF THE POINTS OF THE TEST LINE (SR,L) ARE OUTSIDE THE BOUNDARIES
1020     'OF THE SURFACE (S), THEN THE LINE IS VISIBLE IN RELATION TO THIS
1030     'SURFACE
1040 IF Z1(SR,L) <= ZF AND Z2(SR,L) <= ZF THEN 2130          'LINE IS VISIBLE
1050 IF Y1(SR,L) <= YT AND Y2(SR,L) <= YT THEN 2130          'LINE IS VISIBLE
1060 IF Y1(SR,L) >= YB AND Y2(SR,L) >= YB THEN 2130          'LINE IS VISIBLE
1070 IF X1(SR,L) <= XL AND X2(SR,L) <= XL THEN 2130          'LINE IS VISIBLE
1080 IF X1(SR,L) >= XR AND X2(SR,L) >= XR THEN 2130          'LINE IS VISIBLE
1090     'OTHERWISE AT LEAST ONE POINT IS WITHIN THE RECTANGLE THAT
1100     'BOUNDS THIS SURFACE
1110 'FIND SLOPE AND INTERCEPT OF TEST LINE. SAVE IN MT AND BT
1120 IF X1(SR,L) = X2(SR,L) THEN 1170              'VERTICAL LINE
1130 IF Y1(SR,L) = Y2(SR,L) THEN 1190              'HORIZONTAL LINE
1140 MT = (Y1(SR,L) - Y2(SR,L)) / (X1(SR,L) - X2(SR,L))
1150 BT = Y1(SR,L) - MT * X1(SR,L)
1160 GOTO 1210
1170 MT = 9999            'SLOPE OF VERTICAL LINE IS UNDEFINED
1180 GOTO 1210
1190 MT = 0               'SLOPE OF HORIZONTAL LINE IS 0
1200 BT = Y1(SR,L)
1210 C = 0                'C IS COUNT OF ENDPOINTS OF HIDDEN SEGMENT
1220     'TEST AGAINST ALL LINES OF THE SURFACE
1230 FOR K = 1 TO NV(S)
1240     'IF THIS IS A SHARED EDGE GO ON TO NEXT LINE OF SR
1250     IF X1(S,K)=X1(SR,L) AND Y1(S,K)=Y1(SR,L) AND X2(S,K)=X2(SR,L)
             AND Y2(S,K)=Y2(SR,L) THEN 2130
1260     IF X1(S,K)=X2(SR,L) AND Y1(S,K)=Y2(SR,L) AND X2(S,K)=X1(SR,L)
             AND Y2(S,K)=Y1(SR,L) THEN 2130
1270     IF M(K)=MT THEN 2090            'LINES ARE PARALLEL
1280     'OTHERWISE FIND INTERSECTION POINT XP,YP OF TEST LINE
1290     '(L OF SR) AND SURFACE LINE (K OF S)
1300     IF X1(S,K) <> X2(S,K) THEN 1340
1310     XP = X1(S,K)                            'FACE LINE IS VERTICAL
1320     YP = MT * XP + BT
1330     GOTO 1490
1340     IF X1(SR,L) <> X2(SR,L) THEN 1380
1350     XP = X1(SR,L)                           'TEST LINE IS VERTICAL
1360     YP = M(K) * XP + B(K)
1370     GOTO 1490
1380     IF Y1(S,K) <> Y2(S,K) THEN 1420
1390     YP = Y1(S,K)                            'FACE LINE IS HORIZONTAL
1400     XP = (YP - BT) / MT
1410     GOTO 1490
```

Program 9-4 (cont.)

```
1420    IF Y1(SR,L) <> Y2(SR,L) THEN 1460
1430    YP = Y1(SR,L)                               'TEST LINE IS HORIZONTAL
1440    XP = (YP - B(K)) / M(K)
1450    GOTO 1490
1460    XP = (BT - B(K)) / (M(K) - MT)
1470    YP = (MT * XP + BT)
1480    '
1490    'LINES INTERSECT AT XP,YP. IF XP,YP IS NOT BETWEEN THE ENDPOINTS
1500    'OF LINE K OF S, GO ON TO NEXT LINE (L OF SR)
1510    IF XP<X1(S,K) AND XP<X2(S,K) THEN 2090
1520    IF XP>X1(S,K) AND XP>X2(S,K) THEN 2090
1530    IF YP<Y1(S,K) AND YP<Y2(S,K) THEN 2090
1540    IF YP>Y1(S,K) AND YP>Y2(S,K) THEN 2090
1550    '
1560    'OTHERWISE FIND Z VALUE FOR XP,YP ON TEST LINE AND ON
1570    'SURFACE. IF Z VALUE FOR XP,YP ON TEST LINE (ZL) IS
1580    'LESS THAN Z VALUE FOR XP,YP ON SURFACE LINE (ZS) THEN
1590    'THE TEST LINE IS IN FRONT OF SURFACE, AND SO IS VISIBLE
1600    IF X1(SR,L) = X2(SR,L) THEN 1630
1610    ZL = (XP-X1(SR,L))/(X2(SR,L)-X1(SR,L))*(Z2(SR,L)-Z1(SR,L))+Z1(SR,L)
1620    GOTO 1640
1630    ZL = (YP-Y1(SR,L))/(Y2(SR,L)-Y1(SR,L))*(Z2(SR,L)-Z1(SR,L))+Z1(SR,L)
1640    'FIND Z VALUE OF INTERSECTION ON SURFACE LINE
1650    IF X1(S,K) = X2(S,K) THEN 1680
1660    ZS = (XP-X1(S,K))/(X2(S,K)-X1(S,K))*(Z2(S,K)-Z1(S,K))+Z1(S,K)
1670    GOTO 1690
1680    ZS = (YP-Y1(S,K))/(Y2(S,K)-Y1(S,K))*(Z2(S,K)-Z1(S,K))+Z1(S,K)
1690    IF ZL < ZS THEN 2090
1700    '
1710    'IF THE POINT XP,YP IS NOT BETWEEN THE ENDPOINTS OF LINE L OF
1720    'SR, THEN XP OR YP NEEDS TO BE ADJUSTED BY BEING SET EQUAL
1730    'TO THE APPROPRIATE ENDPOINT OF L OF SR
1740    IF XP < X1(SR,L) AND XP < X2(SR,L) THEN 1770
1750    IF XP > X1(SR,L) AND XP > X2(SR,L) THEN 1770
1760    GOTO 1840
1770    IF ABS(XP - X1(SR,L)) < ABS(XP - X2(SR,L)) THEN 1810
1780    XP = X2(SR,L)
1790    YP = Y2(SR,L)
1800    GOTO 1970
1810    XP = X1(SR,L)
1820    YP = Y1(SR,L)
1830    GOTO 1970
1840    IF YP < Y1(SR,L) AND YP < Y2(SR,L) THEN 1870
1850    IF YP > Y1(SR,L) AND YP > Y2(SR,L) THEN 1870
1860    GOTO 1970
1870    IF ABS(YP - Y1(SR,L)) < ABS(YP - Y2(SR,L)) THEN 1910
1880    YP = Y2(SR,L)
1890    XP = X2(SR,L)
1900    GOTO 1970
1910    YP = Y1(SR,L)
1920    XP = X1(SR,L)
1930    '
1940    'HAVE WE INADVERTENTLY GENERATED AN EDGE LINE? IF THE TEST
1950    'LINE HAS AN EQUAL SLOPE AND SHARES A POINT WITH ANY LINE
1960    'OF THIS SURFACE, THEN DON'T ERASE
1970    FOR J= 1 TO NV(S)
1980        IF MT = M(J) AND YP = M(J) * XP + B(J) THEN 2130
1990    NEXT J
2000    IF C <> 0 THEN 2050
```

Program 9-4 (cont.)

```
2010    XA = XP             'THIS IS THE FIRST POINT OF THE HIDDEN SEGMENT
2020    YA = YP             'STORE IN XA, YA
2030    C = C + 1
2040    GOTO 2090
2050    IF XP = XA AND YP = YA THEN 2090        'SAME POINT (VERTEX)
2060    XD = XP             'STORE SECOND POINT IN XD, YD
2070    YD = YP
2080    C = C + 1
2090 NEXT K
2100    '
2110 IF C < 2 THEN 2130
2120 DRAWLINE XA,YA TO XD,YD                    'ERASE HIDDEN LINE SEGMENT
2130 RETURN
2140 '############################################################################
2150 DATA 14
2160 DATA 4,30,130,67,30,170,71,230,170,21,230,130,17
2170 DATA 4,230,60,10,230,170,21,270,170,11,270,60,0
2180 DATA 4,270,60,0,270,170,11,300,140,61,300,30,50
2190 DATA 4,260,30,60,260,140,71,300,140,61,300,30,50
2200 DATA 4,130,100,99.5,130,140,103.5,260,140,71,260,100,67
2210 DATA 4,130,100,99.5,130,140,103.5,180,90,186.8,180,50,182.8
2220 DATA 4,110,50,200.3,110,90,204.3,180,90,186.8,180,50,182.8
2230 DATA 4,30,130,67,30,170,71,110,90,204.3,110,50,200.3
2240 DATA 4,230,60,10,230,130,17,260,100,67,260,30,60
2250 DATA 4,260,30,60,230,60,10,270,60,0,300,30,50
2260 DATA 4,110,50,200.3,60,100,117,130,100,99.5,180,50,182.8
2270 DATA 4,60,100,117,30,130,67,230,130,17,260,100,67
2280 DATA 4,110,90,204.3,60,140,121,130,140,103.5,180,90,186.8
2290 DATA 4,60,140,121,30,170,71,270,170,11,300,140,61
2300 END
```

Figure 9–11   A three-dimensional object (a) input to Prog. 9–4 is displayed (b) with hidden lines erased.

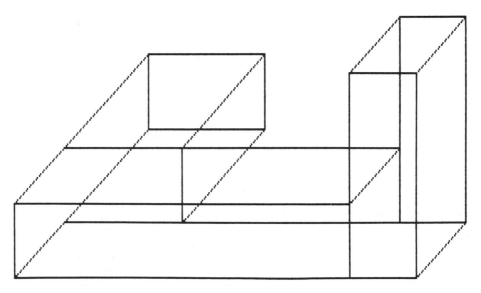

(a)

Figure 9-11 (cont.)

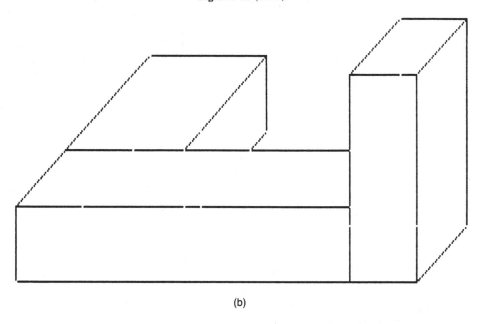

(b)

Each face input to Prog. 9–4 is selected in turn and all remaining lines in the display are tested for visibility with respect to the selected surface. If a line is outside the rectangular bounding area of the surface, it is visible. Otherwise, we have to test it against the actual polygon boundaries. This is done by calculating an intersection point for each boundary line of the surface. The test line and the boundary line intersect if this point is between the endpoints of both lines. In this case, we check to determine whether the Z value of the test line is greater than the Z value of the boundary line at that point. If so, the point is stored as one end of the hidden line segment. If the point is between the endpoints of the surface line and not between the endpoints of the test line, we store the nearest test line endpoint as one end of the hidden line segment. For all other cases, no point is stored. When two separate points on the test line have been found in this way, we erase the line segment between the two points. If two points cannot be found, the line is completely visible with respect to this surface.

This program could be expanded to allow concave surfaces and more complex intersection possibilities. A line intersecting a concave surface can have more than two intersection points. We could treat this situation by determining whether each line endpoint was inside or outside the polygon boundary and identifying the hidden segments from one end of the line. If one endpoint is inside, we erase the line segment from this endpoint to the first intersection point with the boundary along the line from that end. We also erase the segment from the second intersection point to the third, and so on. If an endpoint is outside, erasing is done between the first and second intersection points, between the third and fourth points, and so on. It is also possible for a line to be partially visible if it intersects a surface at an interior point. This can occur if either the line or the surface have varying values for Z coordinates, and one end of the line is in front of the plane and the other end behind the plane. We could locate the intersection point in this case by using the defining equations for three-dimensional lines and planes, but then more computation is required in the program. We have discussed a few of the many possible methods for erasing hidden lines and surfaces. Some methods work only for restricted shapes. Some methods require more memory or more computation time than others. As we allow more complicated shapes in our displays, we can expect the erasing techniques to become more complicated. Usually, we want to select a method that will erase hidden sections in the shortest time. This is especially important for applications involving animated displays.

9–4 PERSPECTIVE VIEWS

Erasing hidden lines in a three-dimensional scene provides depth information and adds realism to our flat representation. An additional means for achieving realism and depth in our displays is to project objects onto the screen in **perspective**. When we view natural objects, they appear smaller when they are farther away from us. A row of buildings, as in Fig. 9–12, appears as though the closer buildings are larger than the more distant buildings. In this perspective view, parallel lines appear nearer to each other in the distance than they do when closer.

To get a perspective view, we can lay out a scene like Fig. 9–12 on graph paper and project all parallel lines so that they meet at a distant point, called the

Figure 9–12 In a perspective view, parallel lines converge to a vanishing point so that distant objects appear smaller than nearer objects.

Vanishing point

vanishing point. The X and Y coordinates for the objects are then determined and plotted. In this way, we can display a perspective view of any scene drawn on graph paper. But each change in the scene and each different scene requires that we repeat the entire process from the graph paper layout.

Another way to achieve perspective is to use transformation equations for perspective in the display program. This provides us with greater flexibility. Animated scenes can then be projected in perspective, and we can put repeated patterns in perspective without having to manually determine the view for each occurrence of the pattern. The coordinates of the general house design in Fig. 9–12 can be defined once, then repeatedly plotted in relative size according to the depth position.

For any coordinate point (X,Y,Z) of a three-dimensional scene, the transformed position (XP,YP) on the screen to provide a perspective view is calculated as

$$XP = XV + (XV - X) * ZV / (Z - ZV)$$
$$YP = YV + (YV - Y) * ZV / (Z - ZV)$$

(9–1)

where the point (XV,YV,ZV) is our **viewing position** in front of the screen. The point (XV,YV) on the screen is the vanishing point for the perspective view. Figure 9–13 illustrates the relationship between these various coordinate values with a side view of the video screen. For points with Z = 0 there is no change in coordinates: (XP,YP) = (X,Y). For points in back of the screen (Z > 0), the projection onto the screen gets closer to the vanishing point as Z increases. The coordinate ZV must always be a negative number, since we are viewing from in front of the screen. Larger magnitudes of ZV will produce less perspective (less converging of parallel lines). As we move the viewing point closer to the screen, we increase the perspective view of the objects by displaying greater convergence of parallel lines.

Figure 9–13 A point with coordinates (X,Y,Z) is projected onto the screen at position (XP,YP) when our viewing position is at (XV,YV,ZV).

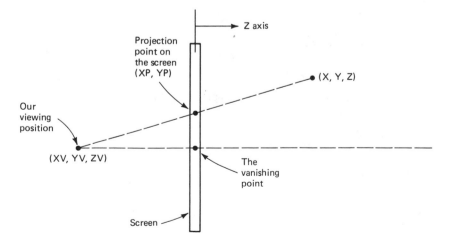

In Prog. 9–5, we calculate and display a perspective view of a road lined with telephone poles. The resulting output is shown in Fig. 9–14. This program illustrates the technique of repeatedly plotting a defined object (in this case, a telephone pole) by varying its depth and calculating the transformed positions from the perspective equations (9–1). We can vary the position of the vanishing point and the value of ZV, as long as objects are not projected off the screen.

Program 9–5   Drawing a three-dimensional scene with repeated perspective views of an object (road lined with telephone poles).

```
10 'PROGRAM 9-5. DRAWING TELEPHONE POLES IN PERSPECTIVE.
20       'TELEPHONE POLES ARE DEFINED ONCE IN DATA STATEMENTS.
30       'A VIEWING POINT (XV,YV, ZV) IS ESTABLISHED THROUGH INPUT.
40       'PERSPECTIVE EQUATIONS ARE USED TO CALCULATE NEW X AND Y
50       'COORDINATES FOR VARYING VALUES OF Z.
60  CLEARSCREEN
70  DIM X1(8), Y1(8), X2(8), Y2(8)
80  XM = 279
90  YM = 159       'XM AND  YM ARE MAXIMUM X AND  Y VALUES FOR THIS S YSTEM
100      'ESTABLISH VIEWING POINT
110 PRINT "ENTER X,Y,Z OF VIEWING POINT"
120 PRINT "X AND Y MUST BE ON SCREEN, Z MUST BE NEGATIVE"
130 INPUT XV, YV, ZV
140 IF XV<O OR XV>XM OR YV<O OR YV>YM THEN 110
150 IF ZV => O THEN 110
160 CLEARSCREEN
170 GRAPHICS
180 FOR K = 1 TO 6
190      READ X1, Y1, X2, Y2
200      FOR Z = 0 TO 5000 STEP 500
210          'CALCULATE CONSTANT PART OF EQUATION
220          P = -ZV / (Z - ZV)
230          'CALCULATE POINTS FOR LINE AT THIS Z VALUE
240          XA = XV + (X1 - XV) * P
250          YA = YV + (Y1 - YV) * P
260          XB = XV + (X2 - XV) * P
270          YB = YV + (Y2 - YV) * P
280          DRAWLINE XA,YA TO XB,YB
290      NEXT Z
300 NEXT K
310      'DRAW IN ROAD EDGES AND CENTER
320 FOR K = 1 TO 3
330      READ XA,YA
340      XB = XV + (XA - XV) * P
350      YB = YV + (YA - YV) * P
360      DRAWLINE XA,YA TO XB,YB
370 NEXT K
380      '********************************
390 DATA 50,45,50,155
400 DATA 40,60,60,60
410 DATA 40,50,60,50
420 DATA 260,45,260,155
430 DATA 250,60,270,60
440 DATA 250,50,270,50
450 DATA 70,155,160,155,240,155
460 END
```

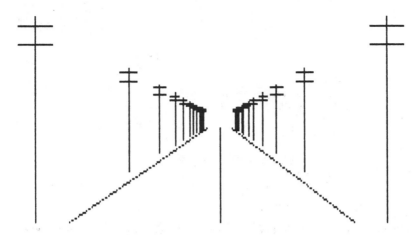

Figure 9–14 Output of Prog. 9–5, showing the perspective view of a road lined with telephone poles.

A perspective view of a single object is displayed by Prog. 9–6. The figure is defined as an orthographic projection in the center of the screen. By selecting various viewing positions, we can display different perspective views of the object (Fig. 9–15). This program illustrates a general method for defining a three-dimensional object in the screen coordinate system and projecting a particular view using the perspective transformation equations.

Program 9–6 Three-dimensional perspective views of a single object (box).

```
10 'PROGRAM 9-6. DEFINING AN OBJECT IN 3 DIMENSIONS USING PERSPECTIVE.
20      'DEFINES AN OBJECT IN 3 DIMENSIONS, ESTABLISHES A
30      'POINT FROM WHICH TO VIEW OBJECT, APPLIES PERSPECTIVE
40      'TO OBJECT'S POINTS AND DRAWS VISIBLE PORTIONS OF
50      'OBJECT. SYMMETRY OF OBJECT IS USED TO DETERMINE
60      'WHICH SIDES ARE VISIBLE.
70 CLEARSCREEN
80 DIM X(8), Y(8), Z(8), XP(8), YP(8), D(8)
90 XM = 255
100 YM = 191
110      '******************** READ DATA POINTS ********************
120 READ N
130 FOR K = 1 TO N
140    READ X(K), Y(K), Z(K)
150    IF X(K)<0 OR X(K)>XM OR Y(K)<0 OR Y(K)>YM THEN 880
160 NEXT K
170 GRAPHICS
180 FOR K = 1 TO N/2 - 1          'JUST DRAW FRONT FACE
190    DRAWLINE X(K),Y(K) TO X(K+1),Y(K+1)
200 NEXT K
210 DRAWLINE X(N/2),Y(N/2) TO X(1),Y(1)
220      '**************** ESTABLISH VIEWPOINT & DRAW ***************
230 POSITION 1,1
240 PRINT "ENTER COORDINATES OF VIEWING POSITION"
250 PRINT "Z COORDINATE MUST BE NEGATIVE"
260 PRINT "ENTER 0,0,0 TO QUIT"
270 INPUT XV, YV, ZV
280 IF XV = 0 AND YV = 0 AND ZV = 0 THEN 880
```

Program 9-6 (cont.)

```
290 IF ZV >= 0 THEN 240
300 IF XV = 0 AND YV = 0 AND ZV = 0 THEN 880
310     'PUT POINTS IN PERSPECTIVE
320 FOR K = 1 TO N
330     XP(K) = XV + (X(K) - XV) * -ZV / (Z(K) - ZV)
340     YP(K) = YV + (Y(K) - YV) * -ZV / (Z(K) - ZV)
350 NEXT K
360     'FIND DISTANCES OF POINTS FROM VIEWPOINT
370 FOR K = 1 TO N
380     D(K) = SQR((X(K)-XV)^2 + (Y(K)-YV)^2 + (Z(K)-ZV)^2)
390 NEXT K
400 GOSUB 420           'DRAW
410 GOTO 220
420 '########################### DRAW ROUTINE ###########################
430 CLEARSCREEN
440 IF D(1) = D(5) THEN 570
450 IF D(1) > D(5) THEN 520
460 IF Z(1) <= ZV THEN 570         'IS FACE SEEN FROM THIS VIEWING POINT?
470 FOR K = 1 TO 3                              'DRAW FACE CONTAINING POINT 1
480     DRAWLINE XP(K),YP(K) TO XP(K+1),YP(K+1)
490 NEXT K
500 DRAWLINE XP(4),YP(4) TO XP(1),YP(1)
510 GOTO 570
520 IF Z(5) >= ZV THEN 570         'IS FACE SEEN FROM THIS VIEWING POINT?
530 FOR K = 5 TO 7                              'DRAW FACE CONTAINING POINT 5
540     DRAWLINE XP(K),YP(K) TO XP(K+1),YP(K+1)
550 NEXT K
560 DRAWLINE XP(8),YP(8) TO XP(5),YP(5)
570 IF D(1) = D(4) THEN 700
580 IF D(1) > D(4) THEN 650
590 IF X(1) >= XV THEN 700         'IS FACE SEEN FROM THIS VIEWING POINT?
600 DRAWLINE XP(1),YP(1) TO XP(2),YP(2)         'DRAW FACE CONTAINING POINT 1
610 DRAWLINE XP(2),YP(2) TO XP(6),YP(6)
620 DRAWLINE XP(6),YP(6) TO XP(5),YP(5)
630 DRAWLINE XP(5),YP(5) TO XP(1),YP(1)
640 GOTO 700
650 IF X(4) <= XV THEN 700         'IS FACE SEEN FROM THIS VIEW POINT?
660 DRAWLINE XP(4),YP(4) TO XP(3),YP(3)         'DRAW FACE CONTAINING POINT 4
670 DRAWLINE XP(3),YP(3) TO XP(7),YP(7)
680 DRAWLINE XP(7),YP(7) TO XP(8),YP(8)
690 DRAWLINE XP(8),YP(8) TO XP(4),YP(4)
700 IF D(1) = D(2) THEN 830
710 IF D(1) > D(2) THEN 780
720 IF Y(1) <= YV THEN 830         'IS FACE SEEN FROM THIS VIEWING POINT?
730 DRAWLINE XP(1),YP(1) TO XP(4),YP(4)         'DRAW FACE CONTAINING POINT 1
740 DRAWLINE XP(4),YP(4) TO XP(8),YP(8)
750 DRAWLINE XP(8),YP(8) TO XP(5),YP(5)
760 DRAWLINE XP(5),YP(5) TO XP(1),YP(1)
770 GOTO 830
780 IF Y(2) >=YV THEN 830          'IS FACE SEEN FROM THIS VIEWING POINT?
790 DRAWLINE XP(2),YP(2) TO XP(3),YP(3)         'DRAW FACE CONTAINING POINT 2
800 DRAWLINE XP(3),YP(3) TO XP(7),YP(7)
810 DRAWLINE XP(7),YP(7) TO XP(6),YP(6)
820 DRAWLINE XP(6),YP(6) TO XP(2),YP(2)
830 RETURN
840     '************************************************************
850 DATA 8
860 DATA 150,40,0,150,80,0,100,80,0,100,40,0
870 DATA 150,40,30,150,80,30,100,80,30,100,40,30
880 END
```

```
ENTER COORDINATES OF VIEWING POSITION
Z COORDINATE MUST BE NEGATIVE
ENTER 0,0,0 TO QUIT
```

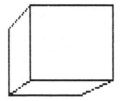

Figure 9–15 Perspective view of a three-dimensional object, displayed by Prog. 9–6 for a viewing position below and to the left of the object.

Hidden surfaces are identified in Prog. 9–6 by calculating distances from the viewing position. Since the box used for this example is symmetrical, we check the distances of symmetrically opposite faces. The face from each pair that is farther from the viewing position is not visible. Distance of a point (X,Y,Z) from (XV,YV,ZV) is computed as

$$D = SQR((X - XV)^2 + (Y - YV)^2 + (Z - ZV)^2) \qquad (9{-}2)$$

We next need to check the other face for visibility. It is possible that neither side is visible. For example, viewing the cube from directly in front hides all other sides. The sides, top, or bottom will be visible only if the viewing position is displaced from a direct front view. For nonsymmetrical objects, we can use the method of Prog. 9–4 and the distance D, calculated from (9–2), for depth checks.

9–5 SHADING AND HIGHLIGHTING

Depth information and realism can be enhanced in our three-dimensional scenes through the use of shading. Figure 9–16 illustrates a possible shading pattern for curved surfaces. Shading patterns can help to establish the contour or curvature of surfaces. Darker areas and shadows also help to identify the back parts of objects. To add shadows, we choose some position for the light source, such as to the left and in front of the screen, and apply the shading and shadows on the sides opposite from the light source. In general, subtle shading patterns and shadows are not effective unless the resolution of the graphics system is high. Simple shading of the sides opposite a selected light source position can be effective even with low resolution.

Some of the shading patterns discussed in Chapter 3 can be defined as routines to be used within a display program in much the same way that the interior areas of the rectangle of Prog. 9–1 were specified. The boundary of an area to be shaded is specified and the shading pattern applied to that area (instead of erasing, as in Prog. 9–1). Such routines are called shading masks and can be set up to shade various polygon, circular, or elliptic areas.

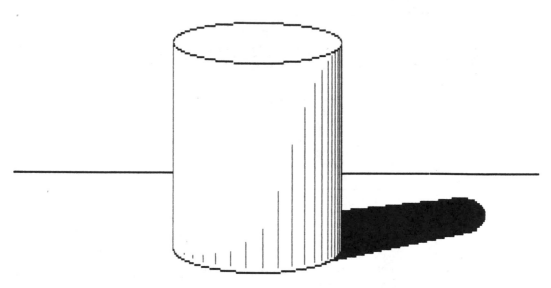

Figure 9–16 Shading patterns and shadows can help to add realism to three-dimensional scenes.

Highlighting can be used as an alternative to erasing hidden lines in a three-dimensional display. With this technique, we add depth information by simply identifying the front lines of objects. This can be accomplished by sorting the lines according to depth, and emphasizing closer lines with bright colors or with double-wide lines. Figure 9–17 shows an example of highlighting the front lines by making them bigger than the back, or hidden, lines. For objects drawn in outline form, highlighting can provide a quick method for identifying the front from the back of objects.

Figure 9–17 Highlighted lines of a three-dimensional object can be used to identify nearer sides.

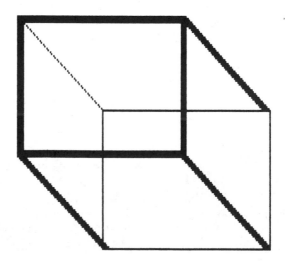

9–6 GRAPHS

Three-dimensional charts and graphs can be effective methods for presenting multiple relationships. The three-dimensional bar chart produced by Prog. 9–7 plots relationships between three variables: population figures for two cities over three decades. Figure 9–18 shows the output for the chosen data. This program uses the techniques discussed with Prog. 9–1. More distant surfaces are drawn first, so that the nearer surfaces overlap and erase the back surfaces. The height of the bars is scaled and plotted on the screen by the same methods discussed in Chapter 4. The spacing between bars is increased to display more clearly the height and position of all bars. Program 9–7 can be expanded to include additional variables. For example, we could plot each bar as total population, then subdivide each bar according to the percent of the population in various age ranges. The bar sections could then be color-coded to indicate age range. There are many possibilities for the labeling. We could devise identifying labels that are slanted to align with the directions of the bars, or we could simply code the bars with various colors or shading and use a key, as in Fig. 9–18.

Program 9–7   Three-dimensional bar graph.

```
10 'PROGRAM 9-7. THREE DIMENSIONAL BAR GRAPH
20  CLEARSCREEN
30  GRAPHICS
40      '**************** MAKE BACKGROUND ********************
50  X = 230
60  XI = 20
70  XR = 319
80  DRAWLINE X,0 TO X,120
90  DRAWLINE XL,30 TO XL,150
100 DRAWLINE XR,30 TO XR,150
110 A = 600              'A IS AMOUNT TO USE FOR LABEL
120 RO = 4
130 C$ = "E"            'C$ IS INDICATOR OF EVEN OR ODD NUMBERED ROW
140 FOR Y = 0 TO 120 STEP 120/6
150     DRAWLINE X,Y TO XL,Y+30
160     'ONLY PRINT LABEL AMOUNT ON EVEN NUMBERED ROWS
170     IF C$ = "O" THEN 240
180     POSITION RO,1
190     PRINT A
200     C$ = "O"
210     A = A - 200
220     RO = RO + 5
230     GOTO 250
240     C$ = "E"
250     DRAWLINE X,Y TO XR,Y+30
260 NEXT Y
270     'MAKE BASE
280 DRAWLINE 20,150 TO 109,180
290 DRAWLINE 109,180 TO 319,150
300 POSITION 23,17:PRINT "1950";
310 POSITION 22,26:PRINT "1960";
320 POSITION 21,35:PRINT "1970";
330 POSITION 25,1
340 PRINT " Buffalo              Atlanta";
350 ML = -30/210         'ML IS SLOPE OF LEFT GRID MARKINGS
```

Program 9-7 (cont.)

```
360 MR = 30/89            'MR IS SLOPE OF RIGHT GRID MARKINGS
370 H = 40                'H IS HORIZONTAL MEASUREMENT OF EACH BAR
380 C = 0                 'C IS COUNT OF HOW MANY CITIES HAVE BEEN GRAPHED
390 XL = 40               'LOWER LEFT POINT OF A BAR IS XL,YL
400 YL = 150
410 F = 3                 'F IS COLOR TO USE FOR FILLING IN BAR
420 O = 2                 'O IS COLOR TO USE FOR OUTLINE OF BAR
430 XS = 78
440       '
450       'MAKE CITY-COLOR CODE BLOCK
460 COLOR F,0             'USE FILL COLOR ON BLACK BACKGROUND
470 FOR X = XS TO XS+20
480     DRAWLINE X,191 TO X,199
490 NEXT X
500       '*************** MAKE BARS FOR CITIES ******************
510 FOR K = 1 TO 3
520     READ V
530     'SCALE POPULATION VALUE TO PIXEL RANGE
540     HT = (120 * V) / 600
550     GOSUB 700                 'FILL IN BOX AREA
560     GOSUB 970                 'MAKE BOX OUTLINE
570     XL = XL + 73              'MOVE OVER AND UP FOR NEXT BAR
580     YL = YL - 10
590 NEXT K
600 C = C + 1
610 IF C = 2 THEN 1080           'ARE WE DONE YET?
620     'RESET VARIABLES FOR NEXT CITY'S VALUES
630 XL = 91
640 YL = 165
650 F = 5                        'FILL COLOR FOR SECOND CITY
660 O = 4                        'OUTLINE COLOR FOR SECOND CITY
670 XS = 272
680 GOTO 450
690 '
700 '################## FILL IN BOX AREA ######################
710 BL = YL - HT - ML * XL       'BL IS Y INTERCEPT FOR UPPER LEFT EDGE OF BAR
720 BR = YL - MR * XL            'BR IS Y INTERCEPT FOR LOWER LEFT EDGE OF BAR
730 FOR X = XL TO XL+H/2
740     Y1 = ML * X + BL
750     Y2 = MR * X + BR
760     COLOR F,0
770     DRAWLINE X,Y1 TO X,Y2
780     COLOR O,0
790     POINTPLOT X,Y1
800     POINTPLOT X,Y2
810 NEXT X
820 YT = Y1               'YT AND YB AND TOP AND BOTTOM Y VALUES FOR THIS BAR
830 YB = Y2
840 BL = YB - ML * (XL + H/2)    'BL IS INTERCEPT FOR LOWER RIGHT EDGE OF BAR
850 BR = YT - MR * (XL + H/2)    'BR IS INTERCEPT FOR UPPER RIGHT EDGE OF BAR
860 FOR X = XL+H/2 TO XL+H
870     Y1 = MR * X + BR
880     Y2 = ML * X + BL
890     COLOR F,0
900     DRAWLINE X,Y1 TO X,Y2
910     COLOR O,0
920     POINTPLOT X,Y1
930     POINTPLOT X,Y2
```

Program 9-7 (cont.)

```
940 NEXT X
950 YR = Y2
960 RETURN
970 '###################### MAKE BOX OUTLINE ######################
980 COLOR 0,0            'GO TO OUTLINE COLOR
990 DRAWLINE XL,YL TO XL,YL-HT
1000 DRAWLINE XL+H/2,YB TO XL+H/2,YB-HT
1010 DRAWLINE XL+H,YR TO XL+H,YR-HT
1020 DRAWLINE XL,YL-HT TO XL+H/2,YB-HT
1030 DRAWLINE XL+H/2,YB-HT TO XL+H,YR-HT
1040 RETURN
1050 '###########################################################
1060 DATA 580,532,462
1070 DATA 331,487,498
1080 END
```

Figure 9–18 Three-dimensional bar chart showing population figures (in thousands) for two cities in the years 1950, 1960, 1970, produced by Prog. 9–7.

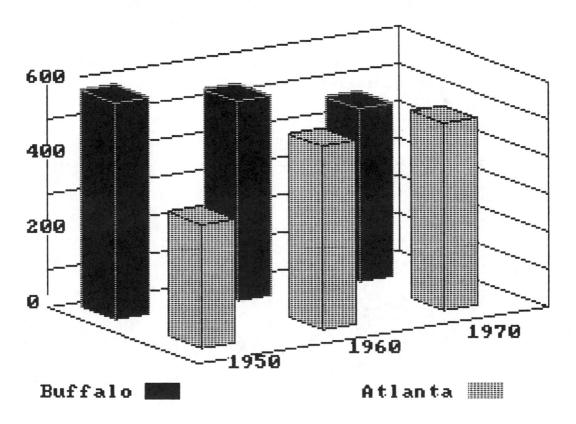

We can also plot curves in three dimensions to show relationships among several variables. As an illustration, Prog. 9–8 outputs a plot of the function $Y = YC + H * SIN(W * SQR(X * X + Z * Z))$ for a chosen range of X and Z coordinates and for selected constant values YC, H, and W. We have chosen the range of X values to be calculated according to the relationship $XR * SQR(1 - (Z * Z) / (ZR * ZR))$. This elliptic function causes the range of X values to change each time the Z-coordinate value changes. Thus, we begin by drawing a short curve (when Z is at the minimum value, $-ZR$), increase the length of the curves to a maximum (when $Z = 0$), and then decrease the length of the curves to the beginning size (when Z is at the maximum value, ZR). The resulting surface appearance is shown in Fig. 9–19. Any other functional relationship (such as a linear function or a constant) can be used to define the range of X values for each Z. The Z range and the constants XC, YC, H, W, XR, and ZR are chosen to fit the curve onto the screen. A screen size of 640 by 200 is assumed in Prog. 9–8. By plotting $X + Z$ and $Y + Z / 2$, instead of just X and Y, we shift each curve a little to the right and up the screen in order to spread the curves out and give a three-dimensional appearance.

Program 9–9 is a modification of Prog. 9–8 that eliminates overlapping lines, as shown in Fig. 9–20. This is accomplished by drawing the curves from "front" to "back" and by not drawing the hidden segments; that is, the curve segments

Program 9–8　Three-dimensional curve plotting.

```
 10 'PROGRAM 9-8. THREE-DIMENSIONAL PLOT.
 20     'PLOTS A SIN FUNCTION IN 3 DIMENSIONS. Z IS VARIED
 30     'FROM -ZR TO ZR. FOR EACH VALUE OF Z, A RANGE OF
 40     'X VALUES IS FOUND. VARYING X OVER THIS RANGE, A Y
 50     'VALUE IS CALCULATED, AND AN ADJUSTED X,Y IS PLOTTED.
 60     'XR AND ZR ARE CHOSEN SO THAT THE PLOT WILL FIT ON A
 70     '640 x 200 PIXEL SCREEN.
 80     '************************************************************
 90  CLEARSCREEN
100  GRAPHICS
110  XC = 320
120  YC = 115
130  XR = 175
140  ZR = 120              'Z WILL VARY FROM -ZR TO ZR
150  H = 40
160  W = .043
170  FOR Z = -ZR+1 TO ZR-1 STEP 10
180      XL = INT(XR * SQR(1 - (Z * Z) / (ZR * ZR)) + .5)
190      X = -XL
200      Y = H * SIN(W * SQR(X * X + Z * Z))
210      X1 = XC + X + Z
220      Y1 = 199 - (YC + Y + Z/2)
230      FOR X = -XL+1 TO XL-1 STEP 5
240          Y = H * SIN(W * SQR(X * X + Z * Z))
250          X2 = XC + X + Z
260          Y2 = 199 - (YC + Y + Z/2)
270          DRAWLINE X1,Y1 TO X2,Y2
280          X1 = X2
290          Y1 = Y2
300      NEXT X
310  NEXT Z
320  END
```

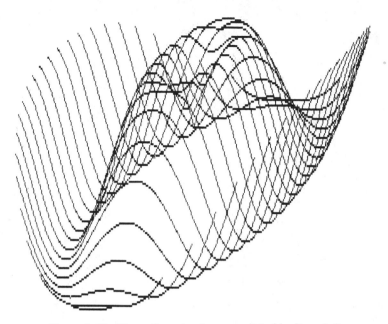

Figure 9–19 Three-dimensional curves plotted by Prog. 9–8.

that would overlap with previously drawn lines. For each value of X, an upper screen bound and lower screen bound of Y values is stored for the previously drawn curves. Any subsequently calculated curve sections that would fall within these bounds are not drawn. Subsequent curve sections that are outside the bounds are drawn and also cause the bounds to be reset. To conserve storage, the arrays UB and LB that store the bounds are dimensioned to the size of the maximum X range. This range can be calculated from the equations for X1 and X2 on lines 340 and 380 of the program. We can do this by analytical means, or we can write a short program to calculate plotted X values and print out the minimum and maximum values. For this example X1 has a range of 424. The parameter XA is set to the minimum X1 value minus 1 and is used as the offset to map the actual plotted X value into an array subscript.

Program 9–9 Three-dimensional curve plotting—displaying only visible line segments to give a surface appearance.

```
10  'PROGRAM 9-9. VISIBLE LINE PLOT OF A THREE-DIMENSIONAL GRAPH.
20     'PLOTS A SIN FUNCTION IN 3 DIMENSIONS. Z IS VARIED
30     'FROM -ZR TO ZR. FOR EACH VALUE OF Z, A RANGE OF
40     'X VALUES IS FOUND. VARYING X OVER THIS RANGE, A Y
50     'VALUE IS CALCULATED, AND AN ADJUSTED X,Y IS FOUND.
60     'FOR EACH POSSIBLE X, AN UPPER AND LOWER BOUND IS
70     'MAINTAINED, REFLECTING THE RANGE OF Y VALUES THAT
80     'HAVE ALREADY BEEN PLOTTED FOR THE X. EACH CALCULATED
90     'Y IS CHECKED AGAINST THESE BOUNDS - IF IT IS INSIDE
100    'THE BOUNDS IT IS SKIPPED, IF OUTSIDE THE BOUNDS WE
110    'DRAW THE POINT AND UPDATE THE BOUNDS.
120    'XR AND ZR ARE CHOSEN SO THAT THE PLOT WILL FIT ON A
130    '640 x 200 PIXEL SCREEN.
140    '************************************************************
150 CLEARSCREEN
160 DIM UB(424), LB(424)          'PLOT IS OVER 424 X VALUES
```

203

```
170 XC = 320
180 YC = 115
190 XR = 175
200 ZR = 120
210 H = 40
220 W = .043
230 XA = 107
240       'INITIALIZE ARRAYS
250 FOR S = 1 TO 424
260     UB(S) = 0
270     LB(S) = 1000
280 NEXT S
290 GRAPHICS
300 FOR Z = -ZR+1 TO ZR-1 STEP 5
310     XL = INT(XR * SQR(1 - (Z * Z) / (ZR * ZR)) + .5)
320     X = - XL
330     Y = H * SIN(W * SQR(X * X + Z * Z))
340     X1 = X + XC + Z
350     Y1 = INT(199 - (YC + Y + Z/2) + .5)
360     FOR X = -XL+1 TO XL-1
370         Y = H * SIN(W * SQR(X * X + Z * Z))
380         X2 = XC + X + Z
390         Y2 = INT(199 - (YC + Y + Z/2) + .5)
400         'IS THIS POINT WITHIN THE BOUNDS OF WHAT'S ALREADY DRAWN?
410         IF Y2 >= LB(X2-XA) THEN 450         'IN BOUNDS, SO DON'T DRAW
420         LB(X2-XA) = Y2                      'CHANGE BOUND
430         IF UB(X2-XA) = 0 THEN UB(X2-XA) = Y2     'SET UPPER BOUND TOO
440         GOTO 470
450         IF Y2 <= UB(X2-XA) THEN 480         'IN BOUNDS, SO DON'T DRAW
460         UB(X2-XA) = Y2                      'CHANGE BOUND
470         DRAWLINE X1,Y1 TO X2,Y2
480         X1 = X2                             'SAVE CURRENT POINT
490         Y1 = Y2
500     NEXT X
510 NEXT Z
520 END
```

Figure 9–20 Three-dimensional "surface" formed from the curves in Fig. 9–19 with hidden lines removed (Prog. 9–9).

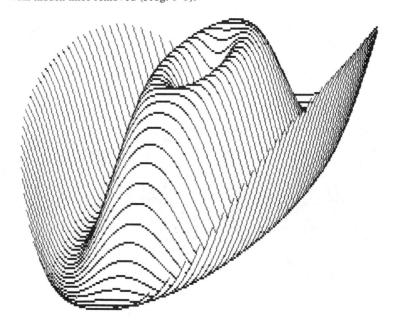

204

Three-dimensional curves can be plotted for any functional relationship involving the X, Y, and Z coordinates using techniques similar to those of Prog. 9–9. Coordinate points can be calculated from equations or supplied as data tables, such as topographic data on elevations or population density. Axes and labeling for the three coordinate directions can be added, as in the graph of Fig. 9–18.

PROGRAMMING PROJECTS

9–1. Lay out any three-dimensional object on graph paper, specifying (X,Y,Z) for each point in the object. Write a program to display any selected orthographic projection for this object.

9–2. Modify Prog. 9–1 to display any type of polygon. The screen may then be filled with combinations of triangles, rectangles, or other polygons. Boundary equations for each figure are straight lines, with slope and Y-intercept determined by line endpoints. Input to the program will be the set of vertices for each polygon.

9–3. Lay out any three-dimensional figure created with polygon faces on graph paper. Using the method of Prog. 9–1, display the figure with hidden surfaces removed by painting in the faces from back to front in various colors.

9–4. Modify Prog. 9–1 to display overlapping circles instead of rectangles. For each circle, input the center coordinates, radius, and depth. Sort the circles and paint them onto the screen, starting with the circle of greatest depth. The lower half of the circle has the boundary equation

$$Y = YC + SQR(R \char`\^ 2 - (X - XC) \char`\^ 2)$$

and the equation for the upper boundary is

$$Y = YC - SQR(R \char`\^ 2 - (X - XC) \char`\^ 2)$$

Vertical lines can be drawn between these two boundaries with X varying from XC − R to XC + R in steps of 1 unit.

9–5. Use the method of Prog. 9–2 to erase the hidden lines in any display of a solid bar whose ends are six-sided polygons (Fig. 9–21). Display all lines in the object, then determine which face from each of the four pairs of opposite faces is invisible and erase the hidden faces.

Figure 9–21 Hexagonal solid.

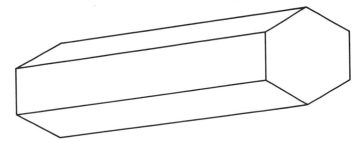

9–6. Using the method of Prog. 9–4, erase hidden lines behind circles. The program is to display any circle, then display a specified line and erase any part of the line hidden by the circle.

9–7. Lay out any three-dimensional object whose surfaces are convex polygons on graph paper. Write a program to display the object and use the method of Prog. 9–4 to erase any hidden lines. Finally, apply perspective equations (9–1) from any specified viewing position (XV,YV,ZV).

9–8. Modify Prog. 9–6 to display visible surfaces of a three-dimensional object using the method of Prog. 9–4 and equation (9–2).

9–9. Modify Prog. 9–4 to input concave polygon surfaces and straight lines. Find all intersection points (there may be more than two) of a line with a surface and erase the hidden segments.

9–10. Define a shading pattern to be used in a program displaying three-dimensional objects. For any displayed object, shade the faces opposite from a specified light source position.

9–11. Modify Prog. 9–7 to produce a three-dimensional bar chart with more than one section to each bar. Draw the different sections of each bar in a different color.

9–12. Using the technique of Prog. 9–8, plot a three-dimensional surface formed from the function

$$Y = A * SIN(X) + B * SIN(3 * X)$$

The parameters A and B are chosen so that the surface fits on the screen for the range of X and Z plotted.

Chapter 10

Three-Dimensional Transformations

We now extend two-dimensional transformation methods (translation, scaling, rotation) to include depth. These added transformation techniques will give us considerable flexibility in manipulating both three-dimensional and two-dimensional displays.

10–1 TRANSLATION

Equations for two-dimensional translation are extended to three dimensions by allowing for changes in Z coordinates. If we let H represent the amount of horizontal displacement of a point, V the amount of vertical displacement, and D the amount of depth displacement, then the translated position (XT,YT,ZT) of a point originally at position (X,Y,Z) is calculated as

$$
\begin{aligned}
XT &= X + H \\
YT &= Y + V \\
ZT &= Z + D
\end{aligned}
\tag{10–1}
$$

Positive values for H move a point to the right on the screen. Positive values for V move a point down the screen. Positive values for D move a point away from us, and negative values for D move a point closer to us. Values for the translation distances, H, V, and D, should not be chosen so large that we move points off the screen or so small that we simply replot the same points.

Pictures and graphs can be translated or animated in space by applying the same values for the translation distances, H, V, D, to all points in the display. We can use different values of H, V, or D for different points in the display, but then we distort the original shapes of the display.

An example of three-dimensional translation is given in Prog. 10–1. A block is translated and projected onto the screen. This program inputs the translation distances, calculates the new position, and applies the perspective equations discussed in Chapter 9 to display the translated object. For larger values of D, we diminish the size of the block and move it closer to the vanishing point. Figure 10–1 shows the original and translated positions for the values H = 60, V = 60, and D = 20.

Program 10–1   Three-dimensional translation and perspective views (block).

```
10  'PROGRAM 10-1. TRANSLATION IN 3 DIMENSIONS.
20       'DEFINES AN OBJECT IN THREE DIMENSIONS AND TRANSLATES
30       'IT TO VARIOUS LOCATIONS. OBJECT IS DISPLAYED IN
40       'RELATION TO A VIEWING POINT IN FRONT OF THE CENTER
50       'POINT OF THE SCREEN. SYMMETRY OF OBJECT IS USED
60       'TO DETERMINE WHICH SIDES ARE VISIBLE.
70  CLEARSCREEN
80  DIM X(8), Y(8), Z(8), XP(8), YP(8), D(8)
90  XM = 255
100 YM = 191
110      '******************** READ DATA POINTS ********************
120 READ N
130 FOR K = 1 TO N
140      READ X(K), Y(K), Z(K)
150      IF X(K)<0 OR X(K)>XM OR Y(K)<0 OR Y(K)>YM THEN 1020
160 NEXT K
170 GRAPHICS
180 FOR K = 1 TO N/2 - 1
190      DRAWLINE X(K),Y(K) TO X(K+1),Y(K+1)
200 NEXT K
210 DRAWLINE X(N/2),Y(N/2) TO X(1),Y(1)
220 XV = 128              'FIX VIEWING POINT AT SCREEN CENTER
230 YV = 96
240 ZV = -100
250      '******************** TRANSLATE OBJECT ****************************
260 PRINT "ENTER H, V, & D TRANSLATION AMOUNT"
270 PRINT "ENTER 1000,1000,1000 TO END"
280 INPUT H, V, D
290 IF H = 1000 AND V = 1000 AND D = 1000 THEN 1020
300      'CALCULATE NEW POINTS
310 FOR K = 1 TO N
320      XT(K) = X(K) + H
330      YT(K) = Y(K) + V
340      ZT(K) = Z(K) + D
350 NEXT K
360      'FIND DISTANCES AND PUT POINTS IN PERSPECTIVE
370 FOR K = 1 TO N
380      D(K) = SQR((XT(K)-XV)^2 + (YT(K)-YV)^2 + (ZT(K)-ZV)^2)
390      XP(K) = XV + (XT(K) - XV) * -ZV / (ZT(K) - ZV)
400      YP(K) = YV + (YT(K) - YV) * -ZV / (ZT(K) - ZV)
410      IF XP(K)>=0 AND XP(K)<=XM AND YP(K)>=0 AND YP(K)<=YM THEN 440
420      PRINT "COORDINATE OFF SCREEN. TRY AGAIN"
430      GOTO 260
```

Program 10-1 (cont.)

```
440 NEXT K
450 GOSUB 480              'DRAW
460 GOTO 260
470 '
480 '############################# DRAW ROUTINE #############################
490 CLEARSCREEN
500      '********* FRONT AND BACK FACES ************
510 IF D(1) = D(5) THEN 670                'NEITHER SIDE IS VISIBLE
520 IF D(1) > D(5) THEN 600
530 IF ZT(1) <= ZV THEN 670      'IS FACE SEEN FROM THIS VIEWING POINT?
540 FOR K = 1 TO 3                          'DRAW FACE CONTAINING POINT 1
550     DRAWLINE XP(K),YP(K) TO XP(K+1),YP(K+1)
560 NEXT K
570 DRAWLINE XP(4),YP(4) TO XP(1),YP(1)
580 GOTO 670
590       '
600 IF ZT(5) >= ZV THEN 670      'IS FACE SEEN FROM THIS VIEWING POINT?
610 FOR K = 5 TO 7                          'DRAW FACE CONTAINING POINT 5
620     DRAWLINE XP(K),YP(K) TO XP(K+1),YP(K+1)
630 NEXT K
640 DRAWLINE XP(8),YP(8) TO XP(5),YP(5)
650       '
660      '************* SIDE FACES ******************
670 IF D(1) = D(4) THEN 830                'NEITHER SIDE IS VISIBLE
680 IF D(1) > D(4) THEN 760
690 IF XT(1) >= XV THEN 830      'IS FACE SEEN FROM THIS VIEWING POINT?
700 DRAWLINE XP(1),YP(1) TO XP(2),YP(2)        'DRAW FACE CONTAINING POINT 1
710 DRAWLINE XP(2),YP(2) TO XP(6),YP(6)
720 DRAWLINE XP(6),YP(6) TO XP(5),YP(5)
730 DRAWLINE XP(5),YP(5) TO XP(1),YP(1)
740 GOTO 830
750       '
760 IF XT(4) <= XV THEN 830      'IS FACE SEEN FROM THIS VIEWING POINT?
770 DRAWLINE XP(4),YP(4) TO XP(3),YP(3)        'DRAW FACE CONTAINING POINT 4
780 DRAWLINE XP(3),YP(3) TO XP(7),YP(7)
790 DRAWLINE XP(7),YP(7) TO XP(8),YP(8)
800 DRAWLINE XP(8),YP(8) TO XP(4),YP(4)
810       '
820      '*********** TOP AND BOTTOM FACES **********
830 IF D(1) = D(2) THEN 970                'NEITHER SIDE IS VISIBLE
840 IF D(1) > D(2) THEN 920
850 IF YT(1) <= YV THEN 970      'IS FACE SEEN FROM THIS VIEWING POINT?
860 DRAWLINE XP(1),YP(1) TO XP(4),YP(4)        'DRAW FACE CONTAINING POINT 1
870 DRAWLINE XP(4),YP(4) TO XP(8),YP(8)
880 DRAWLINE XP(8),YP(8) TO XP(5),YP(5)
890 DRAWLINE XP(5),YP(5) TO XP(1),YP(1)
900 GOTO 970
910       '
920 IF YT(2) >= YV THEN 970
930 DRAWLINE XP(2),YP(2) TO XP(3),YP(3)        'DRAW FACE CONTAINING POINT 2
940 DRAWLINE XP(3),YP(3) TO XP(7),YP(7)
950 DRAWLINE XP(7),YP(7) TO XP(6),YP(6)
960 DRAWLINE XP(6),YP(6) TO XP(2),YP(2)
970 RETURN
980      '*********************************************************
990 DATA 8
1000 DATA 138,56,0,138,136,0,118,136,0,118,56,0
1010 DATA 138,56,40,138,136,40,118,136,40,118,56,40
1020 END
```

```
ENTER H, V, & D TRANSLATION AMOUNT
ENTER 1000,1000,1000 TO END
? ■
```

(a)

```
ENTER H, V, & D TRANSLATION AMOUNT
ENTER 1000,1000,1000 TO END
? ■
```

(b)

Figure 10–1 Output of Prog. 10–1, showing (a) the original and (b) translated
perspective views of an object from a viewing position of (128,96,–100).

10–2 SCALING

Generalizing the two-dimensional scaling equations to three dimensions is accomplished by allowing for a reduction or enlargement in the Z direction, as well as the X and Y directions. As with two-dimensional scaling, we choose a fixed position and calculate the new coordinate positions of each point of a display relative to this fixed position using specified scaling factors. Taking the fixed position at coordinates (XF,YF,ZF), we can calculate scaled coordinates (XS,YS,ZS) of a display point from the original coordinates (X,Y,Z) as

$$XS = X*HS + XF*(1-HS)$$
$$YS = Y*VS + YF*(1-VS) \qquad (10-2)$$
$$ZS = Z*DS + ZF*(1-DS)$$

where the scaling factors for each coordinate direction are denoted as HS, VS, and DS. Each of these scaling factors may be assigned any value greater than zero. Values greater than 1 produce an enlargement, while values smaller than 1 reduce the size of objects.

The scaling factors HS, VS, and DS are usually all assigned the same value. This uniformly enlarges or reduces the object by the same amount in all directions. If we want to stretch or shrink the object by different amounts in different directions, we could assign different values to the different coordinate scaling factors. Large values for the scaling factors can scale objects out of range of the screen size. Small values for the scaling factors can reduce objects to single points.

Scaling a picture using the calculations in (10–2) is illustrated by Prog. 10–2. This program scales a robot figure to any specified size relative to a fixed point on the robot. The robot is originally placed in the lower left corner of the screen, facing toward us. A viewing position, for perspective, is chosen to the right and above the robot. Visibility of the robot surfaces is determined relative to this point, and the scaled robot is drawn from the feet up, left to right. Figure 10–2 shows the output for both a size increase and decrease, in perspective, using the same scaling factor in all directions in order to produce uniform scaling. Input to the program can be set up to allow alternate picture definitions, variations of the fixed point and viewing point, and various scaling factors, HS, VS, and DS.

Program 10–2 Three-dimensional scaling and perspective views (robot).

```
10 'PROGRAM 10-2. SCALING IN 3 DIMENSIONS.
20     'DEFINES A ROBOT IN THREE DIMENSIONS AND SCALES
30     'IT IN RELATION TO XF,YF,ZF. A VIEWING POINT IS
40     'ESTABLSIHED AT XV,YV,ZV. PARTIAL SYMMETRY OF THE
50     'ROBOT IS USED TO DETERMINE WHICH SIDES ARE
60     'VISIBLE. THE INTERIOR OF EACH VISIBLE SIDE IS
70     'BLANKED OUT, ERASING ANY HIDDEN LINES.
```

Program 10-2 (cont.)

```
80   CLEARSCREEN
90   DIM X(10,4), Y(10,4), Z(10,4), XS(10,4), YS(10,4), ZS(10,4)
100  DIM XP(10,4), YP(10,4), D(10,4)
110  XM = 319
120  YM = 199       'XM AND YM ARE MAXIMUM X AND Y VALUES FOR THIS SYSTEM
130  XF = 80        'FIGURE IS SCALED IN RELATION TO XF,YF,ZF
140  YF = 110
150  ZF = 7
160  XV = 160       'XV,YV,ZV IS VIEWING POINT
170  YV = 10
180  ZV = -100
190      '******************** READ DATA POINTS **********************
200  READ NS      'NS IS NUMBER OF SURFACES
210  FOR S = 1 TO NS
220      READ NV(S)       'NV IS NUMBER OF VERTICES FOR THIS SURFACE
230      FOR P = 1 TO NV(S)
240          READ X(S,P), Y(S,P), Z(S,P)
250          IF X(S,P)<0 OR X(S,P)>XM OR Y(S,P)<0 OR Y(S,P)>YM THEN 1800
260      NEXT P
270  NEXT S
280  GRAPHICS
290  HS = 1                'USE SCALING VALUES OF 1 FOR INITIAL DISPLAY
300  VS = 1
310  DS = 1
320  GOTO 380
330      '********************** SCALE OBJECT ********************
340  PRINT "ENTER H, V, AND D SCALING FACTORS"
350  PRINT "ENTER 0,0,0 TO END"
360  INPUT HS, VS, DS
370  IF HS = 0 AND VS = 0 AND DS = 0 THEN 1800
380      '******************* CALCULATE NEW POINTS *****************
390  FOR S = 1 TO NS
400      FOR P = 1 TO NV(S)
410          XS(S,P) = X(S,P) * HS + XF * (1 - HS)
420          YS(S,P) = Y(S,P) * VS + YF * (1 - VS)
430          ZS(S,P) = Z(S,P) * DS + ZF * (1 - DS)
440          D(S,P) = SQR((XS(S,P)-XV)^2 + (YS(S,P)-YV)^2 + (ZS(S,P)-ZV)^2)
450          XP(S,P) = XV + (XS(S,P) - XV) * -ZV / (ZS(S,P) - ZV)
460          YP(S,P) = YV + (YS(S,P) - YV) * -ZV / (ZS(S,P) - ZV)
470          IF XP(S,P)>=0 AND XP(S,P)<=XM AND
                 YP(S,P)>=0 AND YP(S,P)<=YM THEN 500
480          PRINT "OFF SCREEN. TRY AGAIN"
490          GOTO 330
500      NEXT P
510  NEXT S
520  GOSUB 540          'DRAW FIGURE
530  GOTO 330
540  '########################## DRAW ROUTINE ########################
550  CLEARSCREEN
560  FOR S = 1 TO 8 STEP 2       'LOOK AT EACH PAIR OF SYMMETRIC SURFACES
570      '
580      '***************** FRONT AND BACK FACES ********************
590      IF D(S,1) = D(S+1,1) THEN 910          'NEITHER ONE IS VISIBLE
600      IF D(S,1) > D(S+1,1) THEN 800
610      IF ZS(S,1) <= ZV THEN 910        'IS FACE SEEN FROM THIS VIEWING POINT?
620      'BLANK OUT FRONT FACE INTERIOR
630      FOR X = XP(S,1) TO XP(S,4) STEP -1
640          DRAWLINE X,YP(S,1) TO X,YP(S,2)
```

```
650       NEXT X
660       'DRAW FRONT FACE OUTLINE (FACE WITH POINT (S,1))
670       FOR K = 1 TO 3
680           DRAWLINE XP(S,K),YP(S,K) TO XP(S,K+1),YP(S,K+1)
690       NEXT K
700       DRAWLINE XP(S,4),YP(S,4) TO XP(S,1),YP(S,1)
710       IF S <> 7 THEN 910              'ELSE DRAW IN EYES
720       FOR K = 1 TO 3
730           DRAWLINE XP(9,K),YP(9,K) TO XP(9,K+1),YP(9,K+1)
740           DRAWLINE XP(10,K),YP(10,K) TO XP(10,K+1),YP(10,K+1)
750       NEXT K
760       DRAWLINE XP(9,4),YP(9,4) TO XP(9,1),YP(9,1)
770       DRAWLINE XP(10,4),YP(10,4) TO XP(10,1),YP(10,1)
780       GOTO 910
790       '
800       IF ZS(S+1,1) >= ZV THEN 910      'IS FACE SEEN FROM THIS VIEWING POINT?
810       'BLANK OUT BACK FACE INTERIOR
820       FOR X = XP(S+1,1) TO XP(S+1,4) STEP -1
830           DRAWLINE X,YP(S+1,1) TO X,YP(S+1,2)
840       NEXT X
850       'DRAW BACK FACE OUTLINE (FACE WITH POINT (S+1,1))
860       FOR K = 1 TO 3
870           DRAWLINE XP(S+1,K),YP(S+1,K) TO XP(S+1,K+1),YP(S+1,K+1)
880       NEXT K
890       DRAWLINE XP(S+1,4),YP(S+1,4) TO XP(S+1,1),YP(S+1,1)
900       '
910       '*************************** SIDE FACES ***************************
920       IF D(S,1) = D(S,4) THEN 1290     'NEITHER ONE IS VISIBLE
930       IF D(S,1) > D(S,4) THEN 1120
940       IF XS(S,1) >= XV THEN 1290       'IS FACE SEEN FROM THIS VIEWING POINT?
950       'BLANK OUT RIGHT FACE INTERIOR
960       MT = (YP(S,1) - YP(S+1,1)) / (XP(S,1) - XP(S+1,1))
970       BT = YP(S,1) - (MT * XP(S,1))
980       MB = (YP(S,2) - YP(S+1,2)) / (XP(S,2) - XP(S+1,2))
990       BB = YP(S,2) - (MB * XP(S,2))
1000       FOR X = XP(S,1) TO XP(S+1,1)
1010           YT = MT * X + BT
1020           YB = MB * X + BB
1030           DRAWLINE X,YT TO X,YB
1040       NEXT X
1050      'DRAW RIGHT FACE OUTLINE (FACE WITH POINT (S,1))
1060      DRAWLINE XP(S,1),YP(S,1) TO XP(S,2),YP(S,2)
1070      DRAWLINE XP(S,2),YP(S,2) TO XP(S+1,2),YP(S+1,2)
1080      DRAWLINE XP(S+1,2),YP(S+1,2) TO XP(S+1,1),YP(S+1,1)
1090      DRAWLINE XP(S+1,1),YP(S+1,1) TO XP(S,1),YP(S,1)
1100      GOTO 1290
1110      '
1120      IF XS(S,4) <= XV THEN 1290       'IS FACE SEEN FROM THIS VIEWING POINT?
1130      'BLANK OUT LEFT FACE INTERIOR
1140      MT = (YP(S,4) - YP(S+1,4)) / (XP(S,4) - XP(S+1,4))
1150      BT = YP(S,4) - (MT * XP(S,4))
1160      MB = (YP(S,3) - YP(S+1,3)) / (XP(S,3) - XP(S+1,3))
1170      BB = YP(S,3) - (MB * XP(S,3))
1180      FOR X = XP(S,4) TO XP(S+1,4) STEP -1
1190          YT = MT * X + BT
1200          YB = MB * X + BB
1210          DRAWLINE X,YT TO X,YB
1220      NEXT X
```

Program 10-2 (cont.)

```
1230    'DRAW LEFT FACE OUTLINE (FACE WITH POINT (S,4))
1240    DRAWLINE XP(S,4),YP(S,4) TO XP(S,3),YP(S,3)
1250    DRAWLINE XP(S,3),YP(S,3) TO XP(S+1,3),YP(S+1,3)
1260    DRAWLINE XP(S+1,3),YP(S+1,3) TO XP(S+1,4),YP(S+1,4)
1270    DRAWLINE XP(S+1,4),YP(S+1,4) TO XP(S,4),YP(S,4)
1280    '
1290    '**************** TOP AND BOTTOM FACES *********************
1300    IF D(S,1) = D(S,2) THEN 1660    'NEITHER ONE IS VISIBLE
1310    IF D(S,1) > D(S,2) THEN 1500
1320    IF YS(S,1) <= YV THEN 1660      'IS FACE SEEN FROM THIS VIEWING POINT?
1330    'BLANK OUT TOP FACE INTERIOR
1340    ML = (YP(S+1,4) - YP(S,4)) / (XP(S+1,4) - XP(S,4))
1350    BL = YP(S,4) - ML * XP(S,4)
1360    MR = (YP(S+1,1) - YP(S,1)) / (XP(S+1,1) - XP(S,1))
1370    BR = YP(S,1) - MR * XP(S,1)
1380    FOR Y = YP(S+1,4) TO YP(S,4)
1390        XL = (Y - BL) / ML
1400        XR = (Y - BR) / MR
1410        DRAWLINE XL,Y TO XR,Y
1420    NEXT Y
1430    'DRAW TOP FACE OUTLINE (FACE WITH POINT (S,1))
1440    DRAWLINE XP(S,1),YP(S,1) TO XP(S,4),YP(S,4)
1450    DRAWLINE XP(S,4),YP(S,4) TO XP(S+1,4),YP(S+1,4)
1460    DRAWLINE XP(S+1,4),YP(S+1,4) TO XP(S+1,1),YP(S+1,1)
1470    DRAWLINE XP(S+1,1),YP(S+1,1) TO XP(S,1),YP(S,1)
1480    GOTO 1660
1490    '
1500    IF YS(S,2) >= YV THEN 1660      'IS FACE SEEN FROM THIS VIEWING POINT?
1510    'BLANK OUT BOTTOM FACE INTERIOR
1520    ML = (YP(S+1,3) - YP(S,3)) / (XP(S+1,3) - XP(S,3))
1530    BL = YP(S,3) - ML * XP(S,3)
1540    MR = (YP(S+1,2) - YP(S,2)) / (XP(S+1,2) - XP(S,2))
1550    BR = YP(S,2) - MR * XP(S,2)
1560    FOR Y = YP(S+1,3) TO YP(S,3) STEP -1
1570        XL = (Y - BL) / ML
1580        XR = (Y - BR) / MR
1590        DRAWLINE XL,Y TO XR,Y
1600    NEXT Y
1610    'DRAW BOTTOM FACE OUTLINE (FACE WITH POINT (S,2))
1620    DRAWLINE XP(S,2),YP(S,2) TO XP(S,3),YP(S,3)
1630    DRAWLINE XP(S,3),YP(S,3) TO XP(S+1,3),YP(S+1,3)
1640    DRAWLINE XP(S+1,3),YP(S+1,3) TO XP(S+1,2),YP(S+1,2)
1650    DRAWLINE XP(S+1,2),YP(S+1,2) TO XP(S,2),YP(S,2)
1660 NEXT S
1670 RETURN
1680    '*****************************************************************
1690 DATA 10
1700 DATA 4,60,140,0,60,150,0,55,150,0,55,140,0
1710 DATA 4,60,140,15,60,150,15,55,150,15,55,140,15
1720 DATA 4,75,140,0,75,150,0,70,150,0,70,140,0
1730 DATA 4,75,140,15,75,150,15,70,150,15,70,140,15
1740 DATA 4,80,90,0,80,140,0,50,140,0,50,90,0
1750 DATA 4,80,90,15,80,140,15,50,140,15,50,90,15
1760 DATA 4,75,70,0,75,90,0,55,90,0,55,70,0
1770 DATA 4,75,70,15,75,90,15,55,90,15,55,70,15
1780 DATA 4,70,75,0,72,77,0,70,80,0,68,77,0
1790 DATA 4,60,75,0,62,77,0,60,80,0,58,77,0
1800 END
```

```
ENTER H, V, AND D SCALING FACTORS
ENTER 0,0,0 TO END
?
```

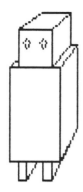

(a)

```
ENTER H, V, AND D SCALING FACTORS
ENTER 0,0,0 TO END
?
```

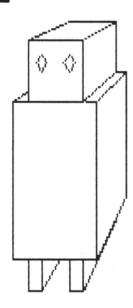

(b)

Figure 10–2 Scaling a figure in three dimensions. This output of Prog. 10–2 shows (a) the original, (b) enlarged, and (c) reduced perspective views. The viewing position is at coordinates (160,10,–100).

Figure 10-2 (cont.)

```
ENTER H, V, AND D SCALING FACTORS
ENTER 0,0,0 TO END
? ■
```

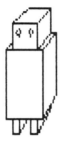

(c)

We can apply these same scaling techniques to graphs in three dimensions. But in many cases we can set up a graph showing three or more variable relationships with all screen coordinate positions specified in just two dimensions. For these situations, two-dimensional scaling methods are sufficient to handle reduction or enlargement requirements, as discussed in Chapter 6.

10–3 ROTATION

We have seen that an object can be rotated through an angle A about a specified point (XO,YO) in the X,Y plane by transforming all X and Y coordinates to rotated values (XR,YR) through the calculations

$$XR = XO + (X - XO) * COS(A) + (Y - YO) * SIN(A)$$
$$YR = YO + (Y - YO) * COS(A) - (X - XO) * SIN(A)$$

(10–3)

The angle A in these calculations must be specified in radians and is measured in a counterclockwise direction from position (X,Y) to position (XR,YR). Considering a three-dimensional object, such as the box in Fig. 10–3, we can visualize this rotation as occurring about a line through the point (XO,YO) that is parallel to the Z axis. All points of the object would be rotated about this line. This rotation would leave all Z coordinates unchanged.

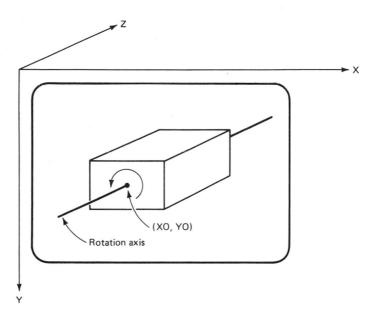

Figure 10–3 Rotating an object about an axis in the Z direction changes X and Y coordinates, but leaves Z coordinates unchanged.

In a similar way we can consider rotating three-dimensional objects about axes in other directions. Figure 10–4 shows a rotation axis that is parallel to the Y axis and through a point (XO,ZO). Rotation about this line would change each of the X and Z coordinates of the box to rotated values XR and ZR. We calculate XR and ZR from the equations

$$XR = XO + (X - XO) * COS(A) - (Z - ZO) * SIN(A)$$
$$ZR = ZO + (Z - ZO) * COS(A) + (X - XO) * SIN(A)$$

(10–4)

This rotation leaves Y values unchanged. Angle A in these calculations is measured in a counterclockwise direction as we look down on the "top" of the box. Another way to describe this direction of rotation is to imagine that we are standing at the origin of the coordinate system and looking along the positive Y axis. An object rotates counterclockwise for this viewing direction. If we want objects to rotate the other way, we use negative radian values for the angle A in calculations (10–4).

In Fig. 10–5, we take the rotation axis to be parallel to the X axis. If we rotate the box about this axis, each of the Y and Z coordinates of the box would be rotated to coordinates YR and ZR. These new coordinates are calculated from the relations

$$YR = YO + (Y - YO) * COS(A) + (Z - ZO) * SIN(A)$$
$$ZR = ZO + (Z - ZO) * COS(A) - (Y - YO) * SIN(A)$$

(10–5)

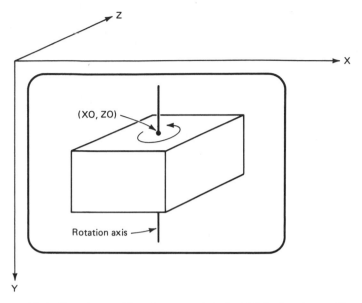

Figure 10–4   Rotating an object about an axis in the Y direction changes X and Z coordinates, but leaves Y coordinates unchanged.

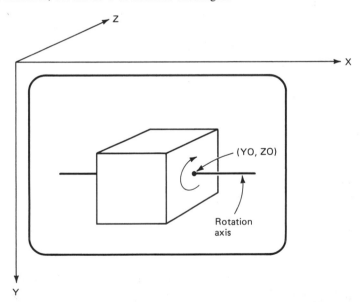

Figure 10–5   Rotating points of an object about an axis in the X direction changes Y and Z coordinates, while leaving X values unchanged.

The X values for this rotation are unchanged. Viewing the box on its "left" side (or standing at the origin and looking along the positive X axis), we have a counterclockwise direction of rotation for the angle A.

Many other rotation axes could be selected, but we can accomplish any other type of rotation with a combination of the three we have discussed. Rotating an object about an axis parallel to the Z axis (Fig. 10–3) simply "spins" the object, always presenting the same side to our view. Rotating an object about an axis parallel to the Y axis (Fig. 10–4) gives us side views of the object. Rotating about an axis parallel to the X axis (Fig. 10–5) gives us top and bottom views. To produce any combination of views, such as top and left side, we can transform an object through two or more rotations. The order in which rotations are applied is important, since we may get a different view by reversing the order of any two rotations.

Program 10–3 rotates a die in any combination of the three rotational transformations. Figure 10–6 shows the output of this program for rotation angles about each of the three axes we have discussed. In each case, an axis was chosen that passed through the center of the die. No perspective transformation was applied to the displayed view.

Program 10–3 Three-dimensional rotations (die).

```
10 'PROGRAM 10-3. ROTATION IN 3 DIMENSIONS
20      'DEFINES A SINGLE DIE IN THREE DIMENSIONS. POINTS FOR
30      'THE SIX FACES AND ALL SPOTS ARE STORED IN XR,YR,ZR.
40      'DIE CAN BE ROTATED ANY NUMBER OF DEGREES AROUND ANY
50      'AXIS. SYMMETRY OF THE SHAPE IS USED TO DETERMINE
60      'WHICH SIDES ARE VISIBLE.
70      '*************************************************************
80   CLEARSCREEN
90   DIM XR(29), YR(29), ZR(29)
100  XM = 319
110  YM = 199
120  READ XO, YO, ZO             'ROTATE AROUND THIS POINT
130  FOR K = 1 TO 29
140      READ XR(K), YR(K), ZR(K)
150      IF XR(K)<0 OR XR(K)>XM OR YR(K)<0 OR YR(K)>YM THEN 1150
160  NEXT K
170  GRAPHICS
180  GOSUB 510
190  POSITION 1,1
200  PRINT "ENTER Q TO QUIT"
210  PRINT "ROTATE AROUND WHAT AXIS";
220  INPUT R$
230  IF R$ = "Q" THEN 1150
240  PRINT "HOW MANY DEGREES";
250  INPUT A
260  A = A * 3.14159 / 180       'CONVERT A TO RADIANS
270      '*************** CALCULATE NEW POINTS ********************
280  IF R$ = "X" THEN 310
290  IF R$ = "Y" THEN 370
300  IF R$ = "Z" THEN 430
310  FOR K = 1 TO 29             'AROUND X AXIS
320      YS = YR(K)       'SAVE YR(K) FOR USE IN ZR CALCULATION
330      YR(K) = INT(YO + (YR(K) - YO) * COS(A) + (ZR(K) - ZO) * SIN(A)+.5)
340      ZR(K) = INT(ZO + (ZR(K) - ZO) * COS(A) - (YS - YO) * SIN(A)+.5)
350  NEXT K
360  GOTO 480
370  FOR K = 1 TO 29                   'AROUND Y AXIS
380      YS = YR(K)       'SAVE YR(K) FOR USE IN ZR CALCULATION
390      XR(K) = INT(XO + (XR(K) - XO) * COS(A) - (ZR(K) - ZO) * SIN(A)+.5)
```

Program 10-3 (cont.)

```
400     ZR(K) = INT(ZO + (ZR(K) - ZO) * COS(A) + (XS - XO) * SIN(A)+.5)
410 NEXT K
420 GOTO 480
430 FOR K = 1 TO 29               'AROUND Z AXIS
440     XS = XR(K)        'SAVE XR(K) FOR USE IN YR CALCULATION
450     XR(K) = INT(XO + (XR(K) - XO) * COS(A) + (YR(K) - YO) * SIN(A)+.5)
460     YR(K) = INT(YO + (YR(K) - YO) * COS(A) - (XS - XO) * SIN(A)+.5)
470 NEXT K
480 GOSUB 500
490 GOTO 190
500     '*************** DRAW ONLY VISIBLE FACES ****************
510 CLEARSCREEN
520 IF ZR(1) = ZR(5) THEN 680              'NEITHER SIDE IS VISIBLE
530 IF ZR(1) > ZR(5) THEN 610
540 FOR K = 1 TO 3                         'DRAW FACE CONTAINING 1 SPOT
550     DRAWLINE XR(K),YR(K) TO XR(K+1),YR(K+1)
560 NEXT K
570 DRAWLINE XR(4),YR(4) TO XR(1),YR(1)
580 CIRCLEPLOT XR(9),YR(9),1
590 GOTO 680
600     '
610 FOR K = 5 TO 7                         'DRAW FACE CONTAINING 6 SPOTS
620     DRAWLINE XR(K),YR(K) TO XR(K+1),YR(K+1)
630 NEXT K
640 DRAWLINE XR(8),YR(8) TO XR(5),YR(5)
650 FOR K = 24 TO 29
660     CIRCLEPLOT XR(K),YR(K),1
670 NEXT K
680 IF ZR(1) = ZR(4) THEN 860              'NEITHER SIDE IS VISIBLE
690 IF ZR(1) > ZR(4) THEN 790
700 DRAWLINE XR(1),YR(1) TO XR(2),YR(2)    'DRAW FACE CONTAINING 4 SPOTS
710 DRAWLINE XR(2),YR(2) TO XR(6),YR(6)
720 DRAWLINE XR(6),YR(6) TO XR(5),YR(5)
730 DRAWLINE XR(5),YR(5) TO XR(1),YR(1)
740 FOR K = 15 TO 18
750     CIRCLEPLOT XR(K),YR(K),1
760 NEXT K
770 GOTO 860
780     '
790 DRAWLINE XR(4),YR(4) TO XR(3),YR(3)    'DRAW FACE CONTAINING 3 SPOTS
800 DRAWLINE XR(3),YR(3) TO XR(7),YR(7)
810 DRAWLINE XR(7),YR(7) TO XR(8),YR(8)
820 DRAWLINE XR(8),YR(8) TO XR(4),YR(4)
830 FOR K = 12 TO 14
840     CIRCLEPLOT XR(K),YR(K),1
850 NEXT K
860 IF ZR(1) = ZR(2) THEN 1040             'NEITHER SIDE IS VISIBLE
870 IF ZR(1) > ZR(2) THEN 970
880 DRAWLINE XR(1),YR(1) TO XR(4),YR(4)    'DRAW FACE CONTAINING 2 SPOTS
890 DRAWLINE XR(4),YR(4) TO XR(8),YR(8)
900 DRAWLINE XR(8),YR(8) TO XR(5),YR(5)
910 DRAWLINE XR(5),YR(5) TO XR(1),YR(1)
920 FOR K = 10 TO 11
930     CIRCLEPLOT XR(K),YR(K),1
940 NEXT K
950 GOTO 1040
960     '
970 DRAWLINE XR(2),YR(2) TO XR(3),YR(3)    'DRAW FACE CONTAINING 5 SPOTS
980 DRAWLINE XR(3),YR(3) TO XR(7),YR(7)
990 DRAWLINE XR(7),YR(7) TO XR(6),YR(6)
1000 DRAWLINE XR(6),YR(6) TO XR(2),YR(2)
```

Program 10-3 (cont.)

```
1010 FOR K = 19 TO 23
1020     CIRCLEPLOT XR(K),YR(K),1
1030 NEXT K
1040 RETURN
1050     '************************************************************
1060 DATA 140,80,124
1070 DATA 164,56,100,164,104,100,116,104,100,116,56,100
1080 DATA 164,56,148,164,104,148,116,104,148,116,56,148
1090 DATA 140,80,100
1100 DATA 128,56,136,152,56,112
1110 DATA 116,68,136,116,80,124,116,92,112
1120 DATA 164,68,112,164,68,136,164,92,112,164,92,136
1130 DATA 128,104,112,128,104,136,140,104,124,152,104,112,152,104,136
1140 DATA 128,68,148,140,68,148,152,68,148,128,92,148,140,92,148,152,92,148
1150 END
```

Figure 10–6 Rotated views of a three-dimensional object (Prog. 10–3): (a) original view, (b) rotated 155 degrees about an X axis, (c) rotated 28 degrees about a Z axis, then (d) rotated 45 degrees about a Y axis.

(a)

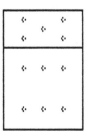

(b)

Figure 10-6 (cont.)

ENTER Q TO QUIT
ROTATE AROUND WHAT AXIS? ■

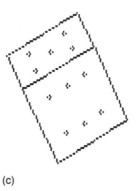

(c)

ENTER Q TO QUIT
ROTATE AROUND WHAT AXIS? ■

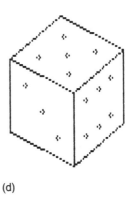

(d)

10–4 COMBINED TRANSFORMATIONS

We can collect the programs for the various transformations into one set of general routines. This general program could be organized so that an input figure is displayed and transformed through any combination of translation, scaling, rotation, and perspective views. We can use an interactive selection procedure for the transformations to be applied, with a termination signal to end the program. A hidden line (or surface) routine can be used to display only the visible sides of the object after a rotation or perspective transformation.

PROGRAMMING PROJECTS

10-1. Animate an object in three dimensions. The object can be translated back and forth across the screen with alternating positive and negative increments for the X and Z directions. Initially, move the object from left to right and increase the Z coordinate. When the object reaches the right side of the screen, reverse the X motion, leaving Y and Z coordinates constant. When the object returns to the left side of the screen, reverse the X direction and begin incrementing the Z coordinate in a negative direction. Repeating this motion, in perspective, moves the object along a figure 8 pattern in the X,Z plane.

10-2. Modify the program in Prob. 10-1 to animate an object along any three-dimensional curve.

10-3. Animate an object along a straight-line path in three dimensions that passes "behind" a rectangular wall drawn on the screen. Do not display the object when it is behind the wall. The program can be generalized to include several "wall" areas of various shapes.

10-4. Write a program to scale any two-dimensional or three-dimensional object by increasing its Z-coordinate position and applying the perspective equations.

10-5. Set up a program to scale a three-dimensional object in an arbitrary direction. This is accomplished by rotating the object to any specified position, then scaling in the X, Y, and Z directions.

10-6. Write a program that displays words written in large letters that decrease in size into the distance. This can be accomplished by rotating the word about a vertical line (parallel to the Y axis) through the left side of the word and applying the perspective equations. The word can then be translated (and scaled) to any screen position.

10-7. Write a program to display a globe formed with a rotated circle. Rotating a circle in three 30-degree steps about a diameter parallel to the Y axis produces a sphere shape with meridian lines. Taking smaller angular rotation steps, from the original position to 90 degrees, creates more meridian lines. The lines of latitude are drawn horizontally between the boundaries of the original circle position.

10-8. Repeat the method of Prob. 10-7 to form a cylinder by rotating a rectangle about a vertical axis, then about a horizontal axis to show the top or bottom. Erase hidden lines.

10-9. Write a program to display a "solid of revolution" formed from a straight line. Draw a diagonal line with different Z values for each endpoint. Then rotate the line about a vertical axis (parallel to the Y axis) through its midpoint. Rotating about a horizontal axis through the line midpoint then displays the ends of the hourglass figure. A hidden-line method can be applied to produce a realistic solid figure.

10-10. Set up a program to display a "solid of revolution" formed from a parabola. A displayed parabola can first be rotated about a vertical line (parallel to the Y axis) through its center in small angular steps from its original position to 180 degrees. Then, rotating it about a horizontal line (parallel to the X axis) that passes through the parabola will display the concave interior. Lines can be drawn joining the endpoints of the rotated parabola to give the figure a cup appearance.

10-11. Set up a three-dimensional bar chart at the screen center and apply rotations, translation, and perspective to position it at any other screen location and orientation.

10-12. Devise a general three-dimensional transformation program that combines the various transformations, the perspective equations, and a hidden-line (or surface) method, each written as a separate subroutine. For any object input to the program, a particular transformation is to be selected and the object is displayed in perspective with hidden lines removed. Transformations are to be repeatedly selected until a termination input (such as typing "STOP") is given.

10-13. Set up the program described in Prob. 10-12 so that a letter code is printed across the bottom (or top, or a side) of the screen. The letter code will select a particular option, including termination, when typed on the keyboard. As an alternative to keyboard selection, a light pen could be used to select options by touching the appropriate areas of the screen.

Part V

APPLICATIONS

(How Can We Use Graphics?)

In Part I, we started off with a survey of graphics applications areas. Now, after having explored the various methods that provide us with tools to create graphics displays, we can look at applications in greater detail. We will first consider efficient design methods for graphics programs, then discuss specific applications to business, education, and the home.

Chapter 11

Program Design

As we design programs for graphics applications, we may find our programs running out of storage, or taking too long to execute, or being too difficult to modify or debug. We can expect to encounter these problems more often as our programs become more complex unless we give some attention to the program design. By applying standard design practices before we jump into the coding, we can produce programs that have fewer problems and that can more easily be adapted to a variety of applications. In this chapter we will look over some of the techniques for good program design and their use in the organization of our graphics programs.

11–1 ORGANIZING GRAPHICS PROGRAMS

We will begin by examining the basic steps involved in development of programs. Then we will consider how to plan and organize our programs effectively at each step. In addition, efficiency considerations in terms of memory space or execution time may be important factors that influence our program design.

PROGRAM DEVELOPMENT PHASES

There are five phases to the design of any program (Fig. 11–1). We must (1) define and outline the major divisions, (2) decide on the sequence of statements (the algorithm) to use in the program, (3) write the actual program statements (the coding), (4) test the program, and (5) provide some explanation (documentation) in the program as to what the different parts of the program accomplish. We can save ourselves time and headaches by giving some thought to each of these steps as we develop our programs.

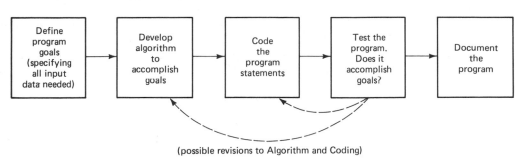

(possible revisions to Algorithm and Coding)

Figure 11–1 Program development phases.

Defining the major program divisions means that we decide exactly what we want the program to do and how we are going to provide data to produce the display. If we are going to create a picture, we define what we want in all parts of the picture. If we are producing a graph, we decide on the type of graph, its orientation, and its location on the screen. Data for producing the display could be defined in DATA statements, entered through INPUT statements, calculated from equations, or any combination of these. Input data can be entered once at the beginning of the program or the program can be set up to carry on an interactive dialogue with us. Specifying all input variables, the exact form of the data to be used, and the major types of processing needed (calculations, sorting, scaling the data to the screen size, etc.) will simplify our task of developing a detailed algorithm and the program statements. At this point we also want to keep in mind later transformations or modifications that we may want to make to our displays and provide for this in our program definition.

Once we have outlined our program goals and defined all data needed, we can develop the explicit steps needed to accomplish the processing for each part of the program. This is the algorithm development phase. Here we can set up the overall organization of our program according to standard structured programming methods. These methods enable us to organize our programs so that we can more easily test and debug the programs, and make later modifications, if necessary.

Basically, structured programming methods call for a modular program design that avoids a lot of program branches which can make it difficult to follow through the program logic. We set up each type of processing needed in the program (data input, data scaling, transformations, or plotting points) as a separate module. These modules could be subroutines or just separate blocks of coding. The idea behind creating the modules is that we do not mix different tasks of the program within one program division—each module performs only one task. Thus we have one module (or program part) that inputs data, another module that might sort the data, and so on. Later, it will be easy for us to determine what each part of the program does, if we are looking for an error or if we want to make changes. Also, each picture component or each graph part (axes, bars, curves) can be defined and displayed from a separate module. This allows us to delete, or add display parts easily. Finally, we arrange the modules in the order that we want to process them, from the beginning of the program to the end. We place modules, such as the plotting routines, that are to be used by other modules at the end of the program. Each module should be entered only at the beginning and exited only at the end of the module. This avoids multiple GOTO or RETURN statements that can complicate our program logic. We can list the order of the modules and show the individual processing steps using some form of flowcharting.

Coding the actual program statements in BASIC (or any other language) can now be done directly from our algorithm layout, module by module. To allow for possible later manipulations to our display, we should set up the coding so that all display points are stored in arrays. We can then easily add a transformation module to our program at some later time that could process the specified array points. Variable names should be chosen that are descriptive of the parameters they represent, and we should consistently use the same names from program to program. We could always use the name T for time quantities, A for angle, and X,Y for coordinates. This makes it easier to keep track of the processing steps in our programs, especially after we have written several different programs. An indentation scheme is very helpful in reading programs. We can indent all statements between the FOR and NEXT statements to more easily identify the body of each loop. We can also indent other sections of coding, like nested IF statements, to make the program more readable. Some systems automatically suppress any leading spaces on a statement line, which means that indentation is not a possible technique.

Testing of the program can be done one module at a time to simplify the debugging process. If this is not practical, we still want to determine that each module is performing the correct processing task. If our program is meant to display one particular picture or graph, it is a simple matter to decide if the program works right. The program is correct if we have the display we want. In this case, it is usually easy to determine what to fix if we do not have the right display. For programs with a more general purpose, as a program to graph any input curve, we should test the program for all possible logic paths. This includes testing for various curve types to be sure that the curve is always drawn in the correct area of the screen and that the axes and labeling are correctly positioned. If any part of the program is not functioning as it should, we can first check to be sure that the coding corresponds to the algorithm. We may only need to correct the program code, or we may need to start back at the algorithm development phase to correct the algorithm. Enough test data should be run so that we are satisfied that each module is correct.

Documenting the program is a continuous process through all phases of program development. The program definition, algorithm, and coding conventions are all part of documentation. We could set up a "documentation file" for our programs that would include the program definition and algorithm for our later reference. In addition, using descriptive variable names, indentation, a modular program design, and numerous REM statements can make our programs practically self-documenting.

EFFICIENCY CONSIDERATIONS

Other factors that may affect the organization of our graphics programs are memory limitations and time constraints. These considerations can directly conflict with our program design according to structured programming methods.

If memory limitations are a consideration, we may need to sacrifice some program readability and documentation to conserve space. We could, of course, divide the program so that our graphics display is created and manipulated in sections, using more than one program. We may also be able to shorten the program by eliminating repeated statements or parts of the program. This may mean combining modules or coding segments that destroy some of our modularity. Spacing on lines can be compressed, multiple statements can be included on each line, and REM statements can be deleted. All of these methods will conserve memory space, but they also make the program more difficult to understand, to debug, and to modify.

Time constraints can be accommodated with less effect on our structured design, and, in general, are not usually a major consideration unless we are animating a picture. To speed up our programs, we need simply to reduce calculations and processing. For animation, this means moving fewer parts and making each movement over a greater distance.

We can reduce calculations in several ways. Any redundant calculations should be eliminated. If we have done a calculation once, we want to make sure that we do not repeat it. This can sometimes happen in loops:

```
610   FOR I = 1 TO N
620       FOR J = 1 TO 1000
630           K = I + 3
  .
  .
  .
```

Here we are calculating $K = I + 3$ one thousand times for each of the N values of I. Statement 630 should come before statement 620 to avoid this type of redundancy. The trigonometric and exponential functions take considerable time to calculate. Often we can revise our algorithm to avoid these functions. In general, reducing all calculations to those involving only additions and subtractions with integers will speed up the execution.

We might also be able to reduce computation by including more IF statements to bypass unnecessary calculations. However, this will increase storage requirements. Eliminating or reducing the dimension of arrays can also save time. It takes longer to calculate the memory address of a two-dimensional array item than a one-dimensional array item. Also, one-dimensional arrays take longer to access than undimensioned variables. Another way to shorten execution time is by writing our programs in assembly language or a high-level compiler language rather than in an interpretive language.

Some microcomputer systems offer special graphics features that can be used to increase the speed of our programs. These features include special functions to perform animations, transformation operations, and windowing.

11–2 INTERACTIVE METHODS

An effective way of providing input to many graphics programs is through an interactive dialogue. Using this technique, the program can carry on a limited conversation with us at certain stages of the processing by asking what we would like to do next. Our choices can be presented as a menu of options, and we can select an option with one of several interactive input devices. There are a number of interactive input devices available. The most common devices are the keyboard, light pen, graphics tablet, and paddles.

MENU SELECTION

A list of processing options presented by a program is referred to as a menu. Many of our example programs have used menus as a means for selecting screen location, transformation method to be applied, or the picture component to be transformed. Anytime we set up a generalized graphics program that allows several processing options, we can use a menu scheme to select options. The form of the menu will depend on the type of interactive input device to be used.

Our programming examples have assumed that we are interacting with the graphics program only through the keyboard. For keyboard input, a numerical or alphabetical listing of options (Fig. 11–2) is a simple and effective menu selection method. Typing the number or letter of an option causes the program to branch to

Figure 11–2   A menu selection scheme with numbered options.

```
SELECT PICTURE TO BE DISPLAYED:

        1 - FIRE ENGINE

        2 - BOY AND DOG

        3 - CLOWN

        4 - AIRPLANE

        5 - ROBOT

        6 - SAILBOAT

        7 - FISH
```

the appropriate module that will accomplish that option (such as drawing the clown when we type in the number 3). We can use this selection scheme for listing many different types of program options. Figure 11–3 shows menu selection for shading patterns, and Fig. 11–4 lists a menu of possible calculations that might be carried out for a set of input data. Any character string or key on the keyboard could be used to make a menu selection, but numbering or lettering the items is a good choice for most applications.

A menu can fill the screen, or a menu can be placed to one side, the top, or the bottom. If we fill the screen with the menu, we need to erase the menu after the selection is made. Placing the menu in a smaller part of the screen allows us to include the picture together with the menu, as illustrated in Fig. 11–5. In this case, we can leave the menu on the screen after the selection has been made. This is helpful if the options are to be repeatedly offered for selection, since the display does not have to be redrawn after each menu selection. After all selections have been made, the menu can be erased. Presenting the menu and display together is also useful when we are using other types of interactive devices and when we want to list multiple menus. A drawback to displaying the menu and the picture or graph together is that our effective screen size is reduced by the amount of area the menu occupies.

Figure 11–3   A menu to select shading patterns.

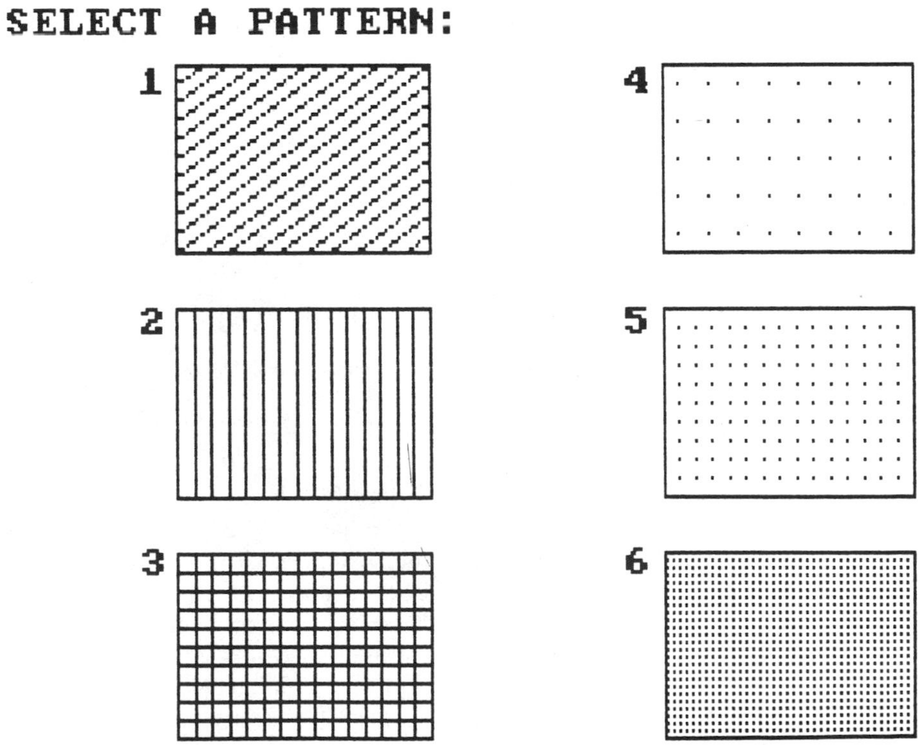

WHICH CALCULATION NEXT?

M: MEAN AND VARIANCE CALCULATION
L: LEAST SQUARES LINEAR CURVE FIT
Q: QUADRATIC CURVE FIT
C: CUBIC CURVE FIT
G: GOODNESS OF FIT TEST

Figure 11–4 A menu of processing options for a set of data.

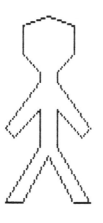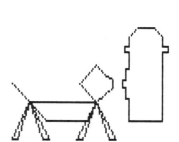

1-BOY 2-DOG 3-HYDRANT
PICTURE PART TO MOVE (0 TO END)? ■

Figure 11–5 Menu and picture displayed together.

LIGHT PENS

Figure 11–6 shows a light pen being used to select menu options. A light pen is a pencil-shaped device that can detect the light emitted from a particular point on a video screen. The emitted light comes from the glow of the phosphor coating on the screen as the electron beam sweeps across it. If an activated light pen is pointed toward a spot on the screen as the electron beam lights up that spot, the coordinates of the point are stored in memory. Since the electron beam sweeps across each point on the screen about 30 times every second, the detection of a lighted spot by the light pen is essentially instantaneous.

232

Figure 11-6 Menu selection using a light pen.

Activating a light pen is accomplished in different ways. Some pens have a push-tip that is activated by pressing the tip against the screen. Others have a button on the side of the pen that we must press to activate it. A third type is activated by touching a metal band near the tip of the pen. Commands are available on many microcomputer systems that can be incorporated into a BASIC program to test for an activated light pen. When a light pen is determined to be "on" by the program, the current screen coordinates of the pen can be used for menu selection, for plotting a point or drawing a line, or for positioning displayed objects.

Menu selection using a light pen is accomplished in a program by testing the coordinates returned by the pen to determine which item is being selected. The item selected is the one that contains the pen coordinates within its rectangular boundary. In Fig. 11–7, suppose that the coordinates of the pen lie within the rectangular boundary of the words FIRE TRUCK. By testing the Y value of these coordinates, we can determine that FIRE TRUCK has been selected. Items listed in a menu, such as in Fig. 11–7, should be widely separated so that coordinate positions can be clearly determined to be in only one area. Menu items can be listed as words, as color rectangles for color selection, or as shapes for object selection.

We can use a light pen in ways other than as a menu selection device. A BASIC program can be set up to plot a continuous stream of coordinates or a series of straight lines as an activated light pen is moved around the screen. This allows us to actually draw objects and pictures on the screen, although a steady hand is needed to display objects accurately. We can use this same program to

```
POINT THE LIGHT PEN
AT THE ITEM TO BE DRAWN:
```

```
AIRPLANE
```

```
FIRE TRUCK
```

```
SAILBOAT
```

Figure 11–7 An activated light pen pointed at the words FIRE TRUCK will cause a coordinate position within the rectangle to be stored in memory.

display a picture traced onto the screen with a light pen from a layout on any transparent paper. The program could then store coordinates for this picture in a display file that could later be transformed, say, and combined with other displays or text. We could also devise programs to display any predetermined shape (line, rectangle, polygon, circle) at any position selected by a light pen. Translation, scaling, or rotation of objects are other possible light-pen applications. We can translate an object by activating the pen at the new screen position. Scaling and rotation can be accomplished with menu selections.

Since the light pen must detect light from the screen in order to record coordinates, it cannot be used to select locations for positioning on a black background with most personal computers. For these systems, we need to use some background color other than black. On some systems, a little tracking cursor always sweeps across the screen emitting light, so that a pen can locate positions even on a black background.

GRAPHICS TABLETS

Like light pens, graphics tablets are devices for selecting coordinate positions on the video screen. But here, we locate positions from the tablet surface instead of directly from the screen. The coordinate reference of the tablet is the same as the screen, with the point (0, 0) in the upper left corner. A coordinate location will be stored in memory by the tablet whenever an activated hand cursor or stylus is placed at that coordinate position on the tablet. We activate a hand cursor or a stylus by pressing a button. Several buttons are often available to provide options, such as returning a single point or a continuous stream of points as we move about the tablet surface. Figure 11–8 shows one type of hand cursor tablet, and Fig. 11–9 shows a tablet with a stylus.

We select a position on the tablet by lining up cross hairs on the hand cursor over a point on the tablet. Many tablets measure coordinates using voltage differences on a grid of wires in the tablet surface. Each wire has a slightly different voltage, so that we have voltage differences in each direction across the tablet corresponding to coordinate differences. By activating the stylus or hand cursor, we cause the voltages at that position to be recorded. These voltages are converted to X,Y coordinates and stored in memory. Some tablets employ sound instead of voltages to determine coordinates. These sonic tablets contain small strip microphones along the edges of the tablet. When activated, the stylus tip generates a spark, creating sound which travels out to the edges of the tablet. The time that the sound takes to travel out to the microphones in the X and Y directions is converted to coordinate values. An assembly language program is

Figure 11–8 Graphics tablet with hand cursor.

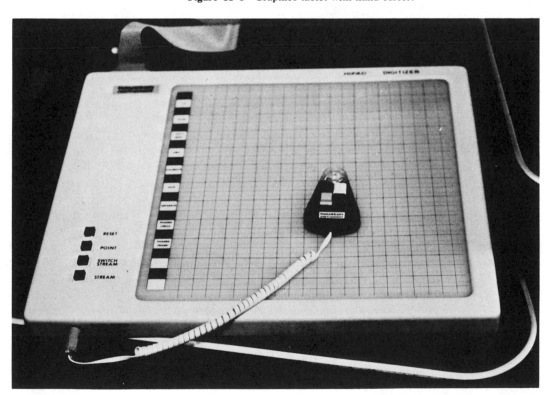

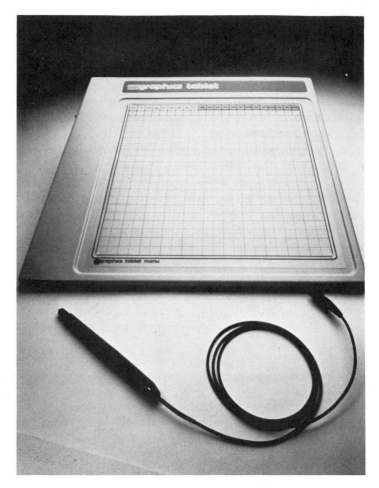

Figure 11–9 Graphics tablet with stylus. (Courtesy Apple Computer Inc.)

usually used to load coordinate data from the tablet into memory. This assembly program is then accessed from a BASIC program with a CALL statement. These programs will be different for different systems and for different types of tablets.

Interactive graphics uses of the tablet are similar to those of the light pen. The tablet can record coordinate positions much more accurately than the light pen, so that it is a good device for tracing graphs, charts, or pictures onto the screen. The coordinate positions of the display can then be stored for use later. Positioning of objects for translation is again accomplished by selecting a translated position on the tablet surface. We can also create figures on the screen by drawing lines, or we can use the tablet for menu selection. For menu selection, a transparent overlay can be used. The shapes of the menu items to be offered for selection are drawn on the overlay, and the overlay is placed on the tablet surface. Then selecting a coordinate position within the area of the tablet occupied by a particular shape selects that shape. We can similarly design overlays to go with programs that select colors or processing options.

PADDLES

There are a variety of paddle styles that can be attached to a microcomputer system. Typically, a paddle will contain a "joystick" that can be moved back and forth and up and down. Commands are available on most systems that can be put into a BASIC program to convert this stick movement into coordinate information. As the stick is moved in a particular direction, coordinates are generated for that direction. Thus we can move objects about the screen continuously as the paddle is moved. Paddle movement can also be converted into object scaling or rotation by our programs. Buttons or switches are available on some paddles so that they can be activated similarly to light pens and tablets. In this way we can use coordinates generated by paddle activation to make menu selections or to draw shapes.

11–3 PICTURE CONSTRUCTION

Interactive techniques can be used effectively in constructing pictures a piece at a time. We employed such techniques in an elementary way in Prog. 3–18, where we constructed a picture a line at a time. This method of stepwise picture construction can now be extended to include other shapes and transformations of these shapes. In this way, we can set up a number of basic "building blocks" and put together a picture using these predefined shapes. We can interactively move any of the shapes into a position within our picture with selected transformations. Program 11–1 outlines a method for constructing a picture with lines, triangles, rectangles, and circles. The program displays a menu of each shape at the the left of the screen. Another menu of transformation options is presented at the bottom of the screen. By blinking the word SELECT, the program indicates which menu we are to use next. Figure 11–10 shows the screen display of menus.

Program 11–1 Interactive picture design using basic shapes (line, triangle, box, circle) chosen from a menu.

```
10  'PROGRAM 11-1. BUILDING PICTURES FROM COMPONENT PARTS.
20      'DISPLAYS MENUS ON SCREEN LISTING CHOICES FOR
30      'SHAPES AND TRANSFORMATIONS.  EACH TIME A
40      'SHAPE IS SELECTED, ANY NUMBER AND COMBINATION
50      'OF TRANSFORMATIONS CAN BE APPLIED.
60      '*******************************************************************
70  CLEARSCREEN
80  YA = 5/12            'YA AND XA ARE RESOLUTION ADJUSTMENTS
90  XA = 12/5
100 XM = 639
110 YM = 199
120 GRAPHICS
130 GOSUB 830           'MAKE MENUS
140 AA = 0        'AA IS ACCUMULATED ANGLE THAT A CIRCLE HAS BEEN ROTATED
150      '*********************** INPUT CHOICES *********************
160 POSITION 1,1
170 PRINT "       ";       'BLINK SHAPE "SELECT"
```

Program 11-1 (cont.)

```
180 FOR K = 1 TO 300:NEXT K
190 POSITION 1,1
200 PRINT "SELECT:";
210 FOR K = 1 TO 300:NEXT K
220 A$ = INKEY$          'A$ IS CHOICE OF SHAPE
230 IF A$ = "" OR A$ < "1" OR A$ > "4" THEN 160
240 RO = VAL(A$) * 4
250 N = 0                'N INDICATES WHETHER CURRENT DISPLAY OF SHAPE
260 POSITION 23,1                      'SHOULD BE ERASED OR NOT
270 PRINT "SELECT:";     'BLINK SHAPE NUMBER AND TRANSFORMATION "SELECT"
280 POSITION RO,1
290 PRINT " ";
300 FOR K = 1 TO 300:NEXT K
310 POSITION 23,1
320 PRINT "          ";
330 POSITION RO,1
340 PRINT A$;
350 FOR K = 1 TO 300: NEXT K
360 B$ = INKEY$          'B$ IS CHOICE OF TRANSFORMATION
370 IF B$ = "" OR B$<>"T" AND B$<>"S" AND B$<>"R" AND B$<>"E" AND
        B$<>"N" AND B$<>"Q" THEN 260
380 IF B$ = "Q" THEN 3110
390 IF B$ <> "N" THEN 440
400 RESTORE              'GO BACK TO BEGINNING OF DATA
410 GOSUB 990
420      '******** ERASING? ********
430 GOTO 140
440 IF B$ <> "E" THEN 530
450 COLOR 0,0            'SET FOREGROUND COLOR TO BACKGROUND
460 IF B$ = "E" AND A$ = "1" THEN GOSUB 1070
470 IF B$ = "E" AND A$ = "2" THEN GOSUB 1100
480 IF B$ = "E" AND A$ = "3" THEN GOSUB 1160
490 IF B$ = "E" AND A$ = "4" THEN GOSUB 1430
500 RESTORE
510 GOSUB 990
520 GOTO 140
530 POSITION 23,1: PRINT "          ";
540 POSITION 24,1: PRINT "
                          ";
550      '****** TRANSLATING? ******
560 IF B$ <> "T" THEN 640
570 GOSUB 1850           'PRINT INSTRUCTIONS FOR TRANSLATION
580 COLOR 0,0            'SET FOREGROUND TO BACKGROUND TO ERASE
590 IF B$ = "T" AND A$ = "1" THEN GOSUB 1510
600 IF B$ = "T" AND A$ = "2" THEN GOSUB 1590
610 IF B$ = "T" AND A$ = "3" THEN GOSUB 1690
620 IF B$ = "T" AND A$ = "4" THEN GOSUB 1760
630      '******** SCALING? ********
640 IF B$ <> "S" THEN 720
650 GOSUB 2330           'PRINT INSTRUCTIONS FOR SCALING
660 COLOR 0,0
670 IF B$ = "S" AND A$ = "1" THEN GOSUB 1920
680 IF B$ = "S" AND A$ = "2" THEN GOSUB 2020
690 IF B$ = "S" AND A$ = "3" THEN GOSUB 2140
700 IF B$ = "S" AND A$ = "4" THEN GOSUB 2220
710      '****** ROTATING? ********
720 IF B$ <> "R" THEN 790
730 GOSUB 3000           'PRINT INSTRUCTIONS FOR ROTATING
740 COLOR 0,0
750 IF B$ = "R" AND A$ = "1" THEN GOSUB 2400
```

Program 11-1 (cont.)

```
760 IF B$ = "R" AND A$ = "2" THEN GOSUB 2540
770 IF B$ = "R" AND A$ = "3" THEN GOSUB 2740
780 IF B$ = "R" AND A$ = "4" THEN GOSUB 2830
790 N = 1                   'FROM NOW ON, ERASE OLD PICTURE OF SHAPE
800 GOSUB 960               'REDISPLAY TRANSFORMATION MENU
810 GOTO 260
820 '
830 '##################### DISPLAY MENUS #####################
840 POSITION 1,1: PRINT "SELECT:";
850 POSITION 4,1: PRINT "1.";
860 POSITION 8,1: PRINT "2.";
870 POSITION 12,1: PRINT "3.";
880 POSITION 16,1: PRINT "4.";
890 COLOR 1,0
900 GOSUB 990
910 GOSUB 1080
920 GOSUB 1100
930 AA = 0
940 GOSUB 1160
950 GOSUB 1430
960 POSITION 23,1: PRINT "SELECT:
  ";
970 POSITION 24,1: PRINT "T -TRANSLATE    S -SCALE    R -ROTATE    E -ERASE    N -
NEXT OBJECT    Q -QUIT";
980 RETURN
990       '*********** READ DATA POINTS ********************
1000 READ XP,YP,XQ,YQ
1010 READ XU,YU,XV,YV,XW,YW,XX,YX
1020 READ XC,YC,RX,RY
1030 READ XR,YR,XS,YS,XT,YT
1040 RETURN
1050 '
1060 '##################### DRAW ROUTINES #####################
1070      '*************** DRAW LINE ***********
1080 DRAWLINE XP,YP TO XQ,YQ
1090 RETURN
1100      '*************** DRAW BOX ***********
1110 DRAWLINE XU,YU TO XV,YV
1120 DRAWLINE XV,YV TO XW,YW
1130 DRAWLINE XW,YW TO XX,YX
1140 DRAWLINE XX,YX TO XU,YU
1150 RETURN
1160      '************ DRAW CIRCLE **********
1170 IF RX < RY THEN 1200
1180 R = RY
1190 GOTO 1210
1200 R = RX
1210 IF AA <> 0 THEN 1310     'SHAPE HAS BEEN ROTATED. USE ALTERNATE ROUTINE
1220 FOR A = 0 TO 1.5708 STEP 1/R      'PLOT 4 SYMMETRIC POINTS AT A TIME
1230     DX = RX * COS(A)
1240     DY = RY * SIN(A)
1250     POINTPLOT XC+DX,YC+DY*YA
1260     POINTPLOT XC+DX,YC-DY*YA
1270     POINTPLOT XC-DX,YC+DY*YA
1280     POINTPLOT XC-DX,YC-DY*YA
1290 NEXT A
1300 GOTO 1420
1310 CX = SIN(AA) * XA          'CALCULATE CONSTANT PART OF EQUATION
1320 CY = SIN(AA) * YA
1330 FOR A = 0 TO 3.14159 STEP 1/R
```

```
1340    X = RX * COS(A)                  'CIRCLE EQUATIONS
1350    Y = RY * SIN(A) * YA
1360    XH = X
1370    X = X * COS(AA) + Y * CX            'ROTATION EQUATIONS
1380    Y = Y * COS(AA) - XH * CY
1390    POINTPLOT XC+X,YC+Y        'PLOT 2 SYMMETRIC POINTS AT A TIME
1400    POINTPLOT XC-X,YC-Y
1410 NEXT A
1420 RETURN
1430    '********** DRAW TRIANGLE **********
1440 DRAWLINE XR,YR TO XS,YS
1450 DRAWLINE XS,YS TO XT,YT
1460 DRAWLINE XT,YT TO XR,YR
1470 RETURN
1480 '
1490 '########################### TRANSLATE ###############################
1500    '********** TRANSLATE LINE **********
1510 IF N = 0 THEN 1530        'IF N IS 0 SHAPE IS STILL IN MENU-DON'T ERASE
1520 GOSUB 1070                    'ERASE
1530 XP = XP + HT: YP = YP + VT
1540 XQ = XQ + HT: YQ = YQ + VT
1550 COLOR 1,0
1560 GOSUB 1070                    'DRAW
1570 RETURN
1580    '********** TRANSLATE BOX ***********
1590 IF N = 0 THEN 1610
1600 GOSUB 1100                    'ERASE
1610 XU = XU + HT: YU = YU + VT
1620 XV = XV + HT: YV = YV + VT
1630 XW = XW + HT: YW = YW + VT
1640 XX = XX + HT: YX = YX + VT
1650 COLOR 1,0
1660 GOSUB 1100                    'DRAW
1670 RETURN
1680    '********* TRANSLATE CIRCLE *********
1690 IF N = 0 THEN 1710
1700 GOSUB 1160                    'ERASE
1710 XC = XC + HT: YC = YC + VT
1720 COLOR 1,0
1730 GOSUB 1160                    'DRAW
1740 RETURN
1750    '********* TRANSLATE TRIANGLE *******
1760 IF N = 0 THEN 1780
1770 GOSUB 1430                    'ERASE
1780 XR = XR + HT: YR = YR + VT
1790 XS = XS + HT: YS = YS + VT
1800 XT = XT + HT: YT = YT + VT
1810 COLOR 1,0
1820 GOSUB 1430                    'DRAW
1830 RETURN
1840    '********** INSTRUCTIONS ***********
1850 POSITION 23,1: PRINT "        ";
1860 POSITION 23,1
1870 PRINT "HORIZONTAL AND VERTICAL DISTANCE TO TRANSLATE";
1880 INPUT HT, VT
1890 RETURN
1900 '
1910 '######################### SCALING ###############################
1920    '*********** SCALE LINE ***********
1930 IF N = 0 THEN 1950
```

Program 11-1 (cont.)

```
1940 GOSUB 1070              'ERASE
1950 XF = (XP + XQ) / 2
1960 YF = (YP + YQ) / 2
1970 XP = XP * HS + XF * (1 - HS): YP = YP * VS + YF * (1 - VS)
1980 XQ = XQ * HS + XF * (1 - HS): YQ = YQ * VS + YF * (1 - VS)
1990 COLOR 1,0
2000 GOSUB 1070             'DRAW
2010 RETURN
2020     '************** SCALE BOX ***********
2030 IF N = 0 THEN 2050
2040 GOSUB 1100             'ERASE
2050 XF = (XU + XV + XW + XX) / 4
2060 YF = (YU + YV + YW + YX) / 4
2070 XU = XU * HS + XF * (1 - HS): YU = YU * VS + YF * (1 - VS)
2080 XV = XV * HS + XF * (1 - HS): YV = YV * VS + YF * (1 - VS)
2090 XW = XW * HS + XF * (1 - HS): YW = YW * VS + YF * (1 - VS)
2100 XX = XX * HS + XF * (1 - HS): YX = YX * VS + YF * (1 - VS)
2110 COLOR 1,0
2120 GOSUB 1100             'DRAW
2130 RETURN
2140     '*********** SCALE CIRCLE **********
2150 IF N = 0 THEN 2170
2160 GOSUB 1160            'ERASE
2170 RX = RX * HS
2180 RY = RY * VS
2190 COLOR 1,0
2200 GOSUB 1160            'DRAW
2210 RETURN
2220     '*********** SCALE TRIANGLE *********
2230 IF N = 0 THEN 2250
2240 GOSUB 1430            'ERASE
2250 XF = (XR + XS + XT) / 3
2260 YF = (YR + YS + YT) / 3
2270 XR = XR * HS + XF * (1 - HS): YR = YR * VS + YF * (1 - VS)
2280 XS = XS * HS + XF * (1 - HS): YS = YS * VS + YF * (1 - VS)
2290 XT = XT * HS + XF * (1 - HS): YT = YT * VS + YF * (1 - VS)
2300 COLOR 1,0
2310 GOSUB 1430            'DRAW
2320 RETURN
2330     '*********** INSTRUCTIONS ***********
2340 POSITION 23,1
2350 PRINT "ENTER X AND Y SCALING FACTORS";
2360 INPUT HS, VS
2370 RETURN
2380 '
2390 '############################ ROTATION ############################
2400     '************ ROTATE LINE ***********
2410 IF N = 0 THEN 2430
2420 GOSUB 1070                    'ERASE
2430 XO = (XP + XQ) / 2       'FIND CENTER POINT OF LINE
2440 YO = (YP + YQ) / 2
2450 XH = XP                      'HOLD VALUE OF XP FOR USE IN Y CALCULATION
2460 XP = XO + (XP - XO) * COS(AR) + (YP - YO) * SIN(AR) * XA
2470 YP = YO + (YP - YO) * COS(AR) - (XH - XO) * SIN(AR) * YA
2480 XH = XP
2490 XQ = XO + (XQ - XO) * COS(AR) + (YQ - YO) * SIN(AR) * XA
2500 YQ = YO + (YQ - YO) * COS(AR) - (XH - XO) * SIN(AR) * YA
2510 COLOR 1,0
2520 GOSUB 1070                    'DRAW
2530 RETURN
```

Program 11-1 (cont.)

```
2540      '********** ROTATE BOX **************
2550 IF N = 0 THEN 2570
2560 GOSUB 1100                    'ERASE
2570 XO = (XU + XV + XW + XX) / 4      'FIND CENTER POINT OF BOX
2580 YO = (YU + YV + YW + YX) / 4
2590 XH = XU                      'HOLD CURRENT VALUE OF XU
2600 XU = XO + (XU - XO) * COS(AR) + (YU - YO) * SIN(AR) * XA
2610 YU = YO + (YU - YO) * COS(AR) - (XH - XO) * SIN(AR) * YA
2620 XH = XV
2630 XV = XO + (XV - XO) * COS(AR) + (YV - YO) * SIN(AR) * XA
2640 YV = YO + (YV - YO) * COS(AR) - (XH - XO) * SIN(AR) * YA
2650 XH = XW
2660 XW = XO + (XW - XO) * COS(AR) + (YW - YO) * SIN(AR) * XA
2670 YW = YO + (YW - YO) * COS(AR) - (XH - XO) * SIN(AR) * YA
2680 XH = XX
2690 XX = XO + (XX - XO) * COS(AR) + (YX - YO) * SIN(AR) * XA
2700 YX = YO + (YX - YO) * COS(AR) - (XH - XO) * SIN(AR) * YA
2710 COLOR 1,0
2720 GOSUB 1100                          'DRAW
2730 RETURN
2740      '************* ROTATE CIRCLE ******************
2750 IF N = 0 THEN 2780
2760 AA = AS
2770 GOSUB 1160                          'ERASE
2780 AA = AR + AS
2790 COLOR 1,0
2800 GOSUB 1160                          'DRAW
2810 AS = AA
2820 RETURN
2830      '********** ROTATE TRIANGLE **********
2840 IF N = 0 THEN 2860
2850 GOSUB 1430                          'ERASE
2860 XO = (XR + XS + XT) / 3      'FIND CENTER POINT OF TRIANGLE
2870 YO = (YR + YS + YT) / 3
2880 XH = XR
2890 XR = XO + (XR - XO) * COS(AR) + (YR - YO) * SIN(AR) * XA
2900 YR = YO + (YR - YO) * COS(AR) - (XH - XO) * SIN(AR) * YA
2910 XH = XS
2920 XS = XO + (XS - XO) * COS(AR) + (YS - YO) * SIN(AR) * XA
2930 YS = YO + (YS - YO) * COS(AR) - (XH - XO) * SIN(AR) * YA
2940 XH = XT
2950 XT = XO + (XT - XO) * COS(AR) + (YT - YO) * SIN(AR) * XA
2960 YT = YO + (YT - YO) * COS(AR) - (XH - XO) * SIN(AR) * YA
2970 COLOR 1,0
2980 GOSUB 1430                          'DRAW
2990 RETURN
3000      '********** INSTRUCTIONS ****************
3010 POSITION 23,1
3020 PRINT "NUMBER OF DEGREES TO ROTATE";
3030 INPUT AR
3040 AR = AR * 3.14159 /180          'CONVERT AR TO RADIANS
3050 RETURN
3060 '#########################################################################
3070 DATA 30,27,80,27
3080 DATA 80,45,80,70,30,70,30,45
3090 DATA 55,90,22,22
3100 DATA 30,130,80,130,55,110
3110 END
```

SELECT:

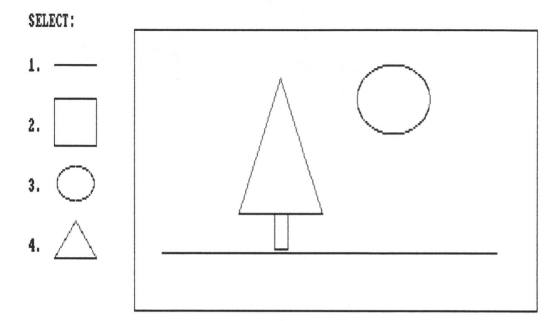

T -TRANSLATE   S -SCALE   R -ROTATE   E -ERASE   N -NEXT OBJECT   Q -QUIT

Figure 11–10 Display of menus and picture created by Prog. 11–1.

Program 11–1 is constructed of modules that perform each of the program tasks. Menu selection is made through the keyboard. We can adapt this program to light-pen input, say, by adding commands to test for pen activation. Then coordinate input would be tested to determine which menu item was selected. We could select translation distances, scaling factors, or rotation angles with a third menu. This menu can simply be a straight line (or series of lines) that is scaled to represent amount. For selection of rotation angle, the line could be scaled from 0 to 360. For translation distances, the line would be scaled from negative to positive values over the possible coordinate range.

Creating pictures in a stepwise manner, as in Prog. 11–1, provides a general approach for many applications areas. We could use this technique in design applications, graph plotting, art patterns, games, or for experimenting with shapes.

Chapter 12

Business Graphics

Business use of computer graphics represents one of the largest and most diversified applications areas. Computer-generated graphs, charts, and pictures are commonly used as aids to financial analysis, marketing studies, and in planning and decision making. These are typical functions in many different kinds of organizations. We can create graphs and charts to provide information on budgets, inventories, cash flow, net income, interest rates, return on investments, or portfolio analysis. We can plot graphs to show comparisons in pricing or product characteristics between competitors, to show regional buying habits, or to show sales trends plotted by region, salesperson, or year. Graphs of demographic data can be useful for locating potential customers or adjusting sales territories. Network graphs and time charts provide aids for project management. Pictorial layouts can help in planning for facility and equipment placement.

We can set up business graphs and charts so as to present data by geographic area or by division within an organization. We can also graphically correlate new data with old in order to provide quick comparison or for indicating future trends. Such graphs are used in internal reports, status reports to customers, or presentations. Figures N, O, and P of the color insert illustrate possible graph forms. In this chapter, we discuss some of the methods for producing various types of business graphs and charts.

12–1 GENERAL TECHNIQUES

Graph-plotting methods were introduced in Chapters 4 and 5. We now consider some extensions to these basic methods that are commonly used in business graphics.

Figure 12–1 Computer graphics can help reduce meeting times through faster presentation of concepts and data relationships. (Courtesy Chromatics, Inc.)

A common technique used with pie charts is to emphasize one or more sections by displacing the sections radially out from the center. An example of such an exploded pie chart is shown in Fig. 12–2. The technique used in Prog. 12–1 to produce this chart is based on the method we discussed in Section 5–4 for positioning labels on pie charts. We first determine the angular bounds of the section to be exploded. Then we calculate the angle of the radius line for the middle of this section. Finally, we locate a center point for the exploded section out from the chart center along this radius and draw the section from that point. Program 12–1 exploded sections by taking the displacement distance out from the center to be one-fifth of the radius of the chart.

Program 12–1 Exploded pie chart.

```
10  'PROGRAM 12-1. EXPLODED PIE CHART.
20      'MAKES LABELED PIE CHART WITH ANY SINGLE SECTION EXPLODED.
30  CLEARSCREEN
40  DIM N$(8), V(8)
50  PRINT "ENTER MAXIMUM HORIZONTAL AND VERTICAL"
60  PRINT "VALUES FOR THIS RESOLUTION MODE"
70  INPUT XM, YM
80  PRINT "ENTER NUMBER OF CHARACTERS THAT CAN BE"
90  PRINT "PRINTED ACROSS SCREEN IN THIS
100 PRINT "RESOLUTION MODE"
110 INPUT C1
120 PC = XM / C1         'PC IS PIXELS PER CHARACTER HORIZONTALLY
```

```
130 PRINT "ENTER NUMBER OF PRINT LINES AVAILABLE"
140 PRINT "IN THIS RESOLUTION MODE"
150 INPUT R1
160 PR = YM / R1          'PR IS PIXELS PER CHARACTER VERTICALLY
170 PRINT
180 PRINT "ENTER CENTER COORDINATES FOR PIE CHART"
190 INPUT XN, YN
200 PRINT "ENTER RADIUS"
210 INPUT R
220 IF XN+R > XM OR XN-R < 0 OR YN+R > YM OR YN-R < 0 THEN 1020
230 PRINT
240      '*********************** INPUT DATA *********************
250 PRINT "ENTER NUMBER OF DIVISIONS (UP TO 8)"
260 INPUT N
270 PRINT "ENTER NAME AND VALUE FOR EACH DIVISION"
280 T = 0
290      'INPUT DATA. FIND TOTAL (T) OF ALL VALUES.
300 FOR K = 1 TO N
310      INPUT N$(K), V(K)
320      T = T + V(K)
330 NEXT K
340 PRINT "EXPLODE WHICH DIVISION (1 -"; N; ")";
350 INPUT E
360 IF E < 1 OR E > N THEN 340
370      '*********************** MAKE PIE CHART ****************
380 CLEARSCREEN
390 GRAPHICS
400 YA = 5 / 6          'YA IS RESOLUTION ADJUSTMENT
410 B = 0               'B IS ANGLE THAT DETERMINED PRECEDING LINE
420 S = 0
430 RE = 360 * 3.14159 / 180     'RE IS RADIAN EQUAIVALENT OF 360
440 FOR K = 1 TO N
450      XC = XN         'XN,YN IS CENTER FOR NORMAL SECTION
460      YC = YN
470          'LINE TO PLOT IS BASED ON THE VALUE OF THIS
480          'DIVISION PLUS PRECEDING DIVISIONS (S)
490      S = S + V(K)
500          'ANGLE TO USE IS THE PERCENTAGE OF THE
510          'CIRCLE EQUAL TO S / T
520      A = RE * S / T
530      IF K <> E THEN 660       'IS THIS SECTION TO EXPLODE?
540      AC = B + (A - B) / 2     'AC IS ANGLE OF LINE THAT HALVES DIVISION
550      XE = XC + R/5 * COS(AC)           'YES, SO MAKE NEW CENTER (XE,YE) 1/5
560      YE = YC + R/5 * SIN(AC) * YA         'OUT FROM NORMAL CENTER. THEN
570      XP = XE + R * COS(B)                 'FIND ENDPOINTS AND DRAW IN
580      YP = YE + R * SIN(B) * YA            'SECTION.
590      DRAWLINE XE,YE TO XP,YP
600      XP = XC + R * COS(A)
610      YP = YC + R * SIN(A) * YA
620      DRAWLINE XC,YC TO XP,YP
630      XC = XE
640      YC = YE
650      '
660      FOR A1 = B TO A STEP 1/R
670          XP = XC + R * COS(A1)
680          YP = YC + R * SIN(A1) * YA
690          POINTPLOT XP,YP
700      NEXT A1
710      DRAWLINE XC,YC TO XP,YP
720      'PUT LABEL ON DIVISION
730          'FIND A POINT 4 UNITS OUTWARD FROM THE CENTER
```

Program 12-1 (cont.)

```
740          'POINT OF THE ARC BELONGING TO THE DIVISION
750     AC = B + (A - B) / 2     'AC IS ANGLE FROM HORIZONTAL OF THE LINE
760     XL = XC + (R + 4) * COS(AC)       'THAT WOULD HALVE THIS DIVISION
770     YL = YC + (R + 4) * SIN(AC) * YA
780        '(XL,YL) IS THE POINT USED TO ANCHOR LABEL
790        'USE THE POINT AS START OF LABEL IF IT'S ON RIGHT
800        'SIDE OF CIRCLE, AS END OF LABEL IF IT'S ON LEFT,
810        'AS MIDPOINT IF IT'S ON TOP OR BOTTOM OF CIRCLE
820      'POINT IS START OF LABEL
830     IF XL > XC + 10 THEN 930
840      'POINT IS END OF LABEL
850     IF XL < XC - 10 THEN 900
860      'OTHERWISE POINT IS MIDPOINT OF LABEL. ADJUST XL BY
870      'ONE-HALF THE NUMBER OF PIXELS NEEDED FOR LABEL
880     XL = XL - LEN(N$(K)) / 2 * PC
890     GOTO 930
900      'POINT IS END OF LABEL. MOVE BACK BY THE NUMBER
910      'OF PIXELS REQUIRED FOR LABEL
920     XL = XL - LEN(N$(K)) * PC
930        'CONVERT THE PIXEL LOCATION (XL,YL) TO THE CLOSEST
940        'CORRESPONDING PRINT POSITION
950     RO = INT(YL / PR)+1
960     CO = INT(XL / PC)+1
970     POSITION RO,CO
980     PRINT N$(K);
990      B = A
1000 NEXT K
1010 GOTO 1030
1020 PRINT "COORDINATE OUT OF RANGE"
1030 END
```

Figure 12–2   Exploded pie chart displayed by Prog. 12–1.

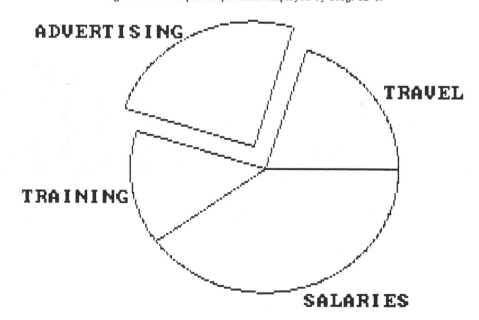

There are times when we would like to produce graphs showing negative quantities, such as financial losses. We can do this by plotting negative values below a horizontal axis, as shown in Fig. 12–3. These graphs are produced by simply extending the vertical axis below the horizontal axis and labeling both positive and negative values.

Plotting two types of graphs on the same axis is an effective means for condensing charts or comparing data. Program 12–2 gives an example of plotting a bar chart on one part of the horizontal axis and a curve on another part. Different scaling is used for each part of the horizontal axis, while one vertical axis serves both graphs. This allows us to plot portions of a data set, for example, in two different forms. Figure 12–4 shows the resulting output.

Presenting data in different graphical forms can aid in interpreting the data. Program 12–3 outlines a modular design that allows us to choose the graph or chart type, as well as the data to be plotted. This general design can be useful for producing different graph forms with the same data and to experiment with various parameter changes.

Figure 12–3 Graphs can show both positive and negative quantities.

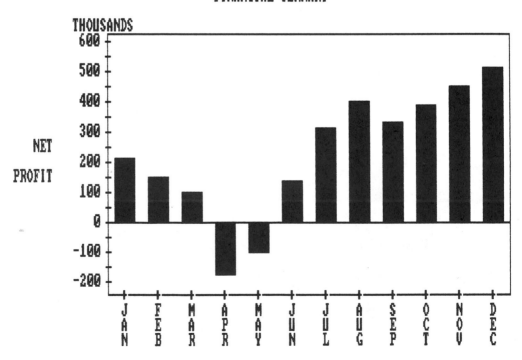

Program 12–2 Combination graphs: bar chart and line graph.

```
10  'PROGRAM 12-2. COMBINED BAR AND CURVE CHART ON X AXIS,
20      'WITH SAME SCALING ON Y AXIS.
30      'ASSUME A SCREEN SIZE OF 640 x 200 PIXELS, WITH 25 PRINT LINES
40      'OF 80 CHARACTERS EACH. DATA VALUES ARE SCALED TO PIXELS
50      '28 - 156.   MONTHS USE EVERY 40 PIXELS, STARTING AT 148.
60      '*************************************************************
70  DIM X(12), Y(12)
80  CLEARSCREEN
90  GRAPHICS
100 PRINT
110 PRINT TAB(34); "SALES FIGURES"
120 DRAWLINE 128,24 TO 128,162
130 DRAWLINE 128,162 TO 608,162
140 DRAWLINE 608,162 TO 608,24
150 DRAWLINE 608,24 TO 128,24
160     'MAKE NOTCHES FOR SALES MAGNITUDES
170 FOR Y = 28 TO 156 STEP 8
180     DRAWLINE 125,Y TO 131,Y
190 NEXT Y
200     'LABEL THE NOTCHES
210 RO = 20
220 FOR S = 0 TO 800 STEP 100
230     POSITION RO,13
240     PRINT USING "###"; S
250     RO = RO - 2
260 NEXT S
270     'MAKE NOTCHES FOR QUARTERS AND WEEKS
280 FOR CO = 24 TO 40 STEP 8
290     POSITION 21,CO
300     PRINT "+";
310 NEXT CO
320 FOR CO = 48 TO 73 STEP 5
330     POSITION 21,CO
340     PRINT "+";
350 NEXT CO
360 PRINT TAB(22);"FIRST    SECOND    THIRD    40   42   44   46   48   50"
370 PRINT TAB(22);"      QUARTERS                        WEEKS"
380 POSITION 11,3
390 PRINT "MONTHLY"
400 POSITION 13,3
410 PRINT " SALES"
420     'DRAW CHART BARS
430 T = (156 - 28) / 800
440 X1 = 163
450 FOR K = 1 TO 3
460     READ S
470     Y = INT ((800 - S) * T + 28.5)
480     FOR X = X1 TO X1+40
490         DRAWLINE X,Y TO X,156
500     NEXT X
510     X1 = X1 + 64
520 NEXT K
530 X = 384
540 FOR K = 1 TO 6
550     READ S
560     Y(K = INT((800-S) * T + 28.5)
570 NEXT K
580 FOR K = 1 TO 5
590     DRAWLINE X,Y(K) TO X+40,Y(K+1)
600     X = X + 40
610 NEXT K
620 DATA 310,420,599,598,623,592,670,740,695
630 END
```

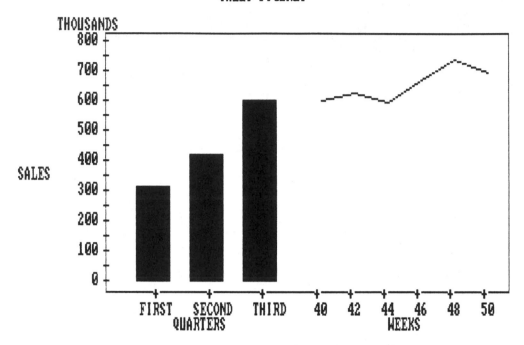

Figure 12–4 A combination bar chart and line graph produced by Prog. 12–2, showing one vertical scale and two different horizontal scales.

Program 12–3 General graphing program—allowing graph type to be chosen.

```
10  'PROGRAM 12-3. GENERALIZED GRAPHING PROGRAM.
20      'ALLOWS INTERACTIVE INPUT OF DATA AND CHOICE OF
30      'CHART FORMAT (LINE, BAR, OR PIE CHARTS).
40      'DESIGNED FOR 640 BY 200 PIXEL SCREEN.
50      '**********************************************************
60  PC = 8        'PC IS HORIZONTAL PIXELS PER CHARACTER
70  PR = 8        'PR IS VERTICAL PIXELS PER CHARACTER
80  YA = 5/12            'YA IS RESOLUTION ADJUSTMENT
90  CLEARSCREEN
100 PRINT "1 - LINE       2 - BAR       3 - PIE"
110 PRINT "WHAT KIND OF CHART";
120 INPUT C$
130 PRINT "TITLE OF CHART";
140 INPUT T$
150 GRAPHICS
160 IF C$ = "1" OR C$ = "2" THEN GOSUB 210
170 IF C$ = "1" THEN GOSUB 630
180 IF C$ = "2" THEN GOSUB 740
190 IF C$ = "3" THEN GOSUB 860
200 GOTO 1520
210 '####################### LINE OR BAR CHART #######################
220 PRINT "ENTER NUMBER OF DIVISIONS"
230 INPUT N
240 D = INT(568 / N)
250 PRINT "ENTER NAME AND VALUE OF EACH DIVISION"
260 FOR K = 1 TO N
270     INPUT L$(K),S(K)
```

Program 12-3 (cont.)

```
280     IF LEN(L$(K)) < D/8 THEN 320    'WILL THE LABEL FIT?
290     PRINT "LABEL TOO LONG. MAXIMUM LENGTH IS";D/8
300     PRINT "NEW LABEL";
310     INPUT L$(K)
320 NEXT K
330 PRINT "ENTER MINIMUM AND MAXIMUM VALUES FOR VERTICAL AXIS"
340 INPUT LO, HI
350 R = HI - LO                      'R IS RANGE OF VALUES
360 RS = (180 - 20) / R               'RS IS RATIO TO USE IN SCALING
370 CLEARSCREEN
380 DRAWLINE 71,20 TO 71,180
390 DRAWLINE 71,180 TO 639,180
400 DRAWLINE 639,180 TO 639,20
410 DRAWLINE 639,20 TO 71,20
420 POSITION 1,1        'PRINT TITLE
430 P = 40 - LEN(T$) / 2          'CENTER THE TITLE
440 PRINT TAB(P);T$
450 RO = 23
460 Y = 180
470 FOR K = 0 TO 5                'LABEL VERTICAL AXIS WITH SUCCESSIVE FIFTHS
480     POSITION RO,1             'OF THE SCALING RANGE
490     L = LO + R * K / 5
500     PRINT USING "###.###";L
510     DRAWLINE 70,Y TO 639,Y
520     RO = RO - 4
530     Y = Y - 32
540 NEXT K
550     'LABEL THE DIVISIONS
560 POSITION 25,1
570 FOR K = 1 TO N
580     P = INT((72 + (K-1) * D + D/2) / PC - LEN(L$(K))/2 + .5) + 1
590     PRINT TAB(P);L$(K);
600 NEXT K
610 RETURN
620 '
630 '############################### LINE CHART #########################
640 FOR K = 1 TO N
650     Y(K) = INT((HI - S(K)) * RS + 20.5)
660 NEXT K
670 X = 71 + D/2
680 FOR K = 1 TO N-1
690     DRAWLINE X,Y(K) TO X+D,Y(K+1)
700     X = X + D
710 NEXT K
720 RETURN
730 '
740 '############################### BAR CHART #########################
750 YO = INT(HI * RS + 20.5)              'FIND WHERE 0 IS
760 X1 = 71 + D/6
770 FOR K = 1 TO N
780     Y = INT((HI - S(K)) * RS + 20.5)
790     FOR X = X1 TO X1 + D * 2/3
800         DRAWLINE X,Y TO X,YO
810     NEXT X
820     X1 = X1 + D
830 NEXT K
840 RETURN
850 '
860 '############################### PIE CHART #########################
870 XC = 320
880 YC = 110
890 R = 160
900 PRINT "ENTER NUMBER OF DIVISIONS (UP TO 6)"
```

Program 12-3 (cont.)

```
910 INPUT N
920 PRINT "ENTER NAME AND VALUE FOR EACH DIVISION"
930 T = 0
940      'INPUT DATA. FIND TOTAL (T) OF ALL VALUES.
950 FOR K = 1 TO N
960      INPUT N$(K), V(K)
970      IF V(K) > 0 THEN 1010
980      PRINT "VALUE MUST BE POSITIVE. RE-ENTER VALUE"
990      INPUT V(K)
1000     GOTO 970
1010     T = T + V(K)
1020 NEXT K
1030 CLEARSCREEN
1040 GRAPHICS
1050 POSITION 1,1
1060 P = 40 - LEN(T$) / 2         'CENTER THE TITLE
1070 PRINT TAB(P);T$
1080 CIRCLEPLOT XC,YC,R
1090 B = 0               'B IS ANGLE THAT DETERMINED PRECEDING LINE
1100 S = 0
1110 RE = 360 * 3.14159 / 180     'RE IS RADIAN EQUIVALENT OF 360
1120 FOR K = 1 TO N
1130         'LINE TO PLOT IS BASED ON THE VALUE OF THIS
1140         'DIVISION PLUS PRECEDING DIVISIONS
1150     S = S + V(K)
1160         'ANGLE TO USE IS THE PERCENTAGE OF THE
1170         'CIRCLE EQUAL TO S / T
1180     A = RE * S / T
1190     XP = XC + R * COS(A)
1200     YP = YC + R * SIN(A) * YA
1210     DRAWLINE XC,YC TO XP,YP
1220     'PUT LABEL ON DIVISION
1230         'FIND A POINT 4 UNITS OUTWARD FROM THE CENTER
1240         'POINT OF THE ARC BELONGING TO THE DIVISION
1250     AC = B + (A - B) / 2    'AC IS ANGLE FROM HORIZONTAL OF THE LINE
1260     XL = XC + (R + 4) * COS(AC)      'THAT WOULD HALVE THIS DIVISION
1270     YL = YC + (R + 4) * SIN(AC) * YA
1280         '(XL,YL) IS THE POINT USED TO ANCHOR LABEL
1290         'USE THE POINT AS START OF LABEL IF IT'S ON RIGHT
1300         'SIDE OF CIRCLE, AS END OF LABEL IF IT'S ON LEFT,
1310         'AS MIDPOINT IF IT'S ON TOP OR BOTTOM OF CIRCLE
1320     'POINT IS START OF LABEL
1330     IF XL > XC + 10 THEN 1430
1340      'POINT IS END OF LABEL
1350     IF XL < XC - 10 THEN 1400
1360      'OTHERWISE POINT IS MIDPOINT OF LABEL. ADJUST XL BY
1370      'ONE-HALF THE NUMBER OF PIXELS NEEDED FOR LABEL
1380     XL = XL - LEN(N$(K)) / 2 * PC
1390     GOTO 1430
1400      'POINT IS END OF LABEL. MOVE BACK BY THE NUMBER
1410      'OF PIXELS REQUIRED FOR LABEL
1420     XL = XL - LEN(N$(K)) * PC
1430        'CONVERT THE PIXEL LOCATION (XL,YL) TO THE CLOSEST
1440        'CORRESPONDING PRINT POSITION
1450     RO = INT(YL / PR)+1
1460     CO = INT(XL / PC)+1
1470     POSITION RO,CO
1480     PRINT N$(K);
1490     B = A
1500 NEXT K
1510 RETURN
1520 END
```

12–2 COMPARATIVE GRAPHS

We can plot two or more sets of data within one graph in order to compare relationships between variables, such as sales of products in relation to district or in relation to salesperson. There are several ways we can set up such comparative graphs.

In a bar graph, we can compare two sets of data by overlapping the bars (Fig. 12–5). Programs to produce this type of comparative graph can plot each data set in a different color, as in Prog. 12–4. The bars for one data set are shifted slightly and painted over the bars of the other set.

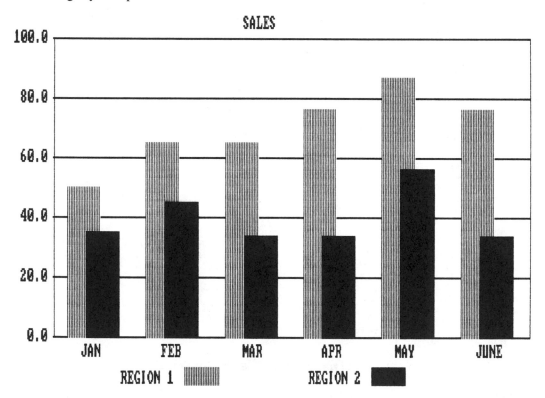

Figure 12–5 A comparative bar graph from Prog. 12–4, showing overlapping bars from two data sets plotted on the same axes.

Program 12–4 Comparative graph: overlaid bar charts.

```
10 'PROGRAM 12-4. TWO SETS OF DATA WITH OVERLAPPING VERTICAL BARS.
20      'PLOTS BARS FOR TWO SETS OF DATA SHARING THE SAME X AND Y AXIS.
30      'ASSUMES A SCREEN SIZE OF 640 x 200 PIXELS. DATA VALUES
40      'ARE SCALED TO PIXELS 12 - 172.
50      '****************************************************************
60 CLEARSCREEN
70 DIM L$(8), S1(8), S2(8)
80 PC = 8        'PC IS HORIZONTAL PIXELS PER CHARACTER
90      '******************** INPUT CHART LABELS AND DATA **************
```

Program 12-4 (cont.)

```
100   PRINT "TITLE OF CHART";
110    INPUT T$
120   PRINT "ENTER NAME OF FIRST SET OF DATA"
130  INPUT T1$
140  PRINT "ENTER NAME OF SECOND SET OF DATA"
150  INPUT T2$
160  PRINT "ENTER NUMBER OF DIVISIONS"
170  INPUT N
180  D = INT(568 / N)     'D IS AREA FOR EACH DIVISION
190  PRINT "ENTER LABEL AND TWO VALUES FOR EACH DIVISION"
200  FOR K = 1 TO N
210      INPUT L$(K),S1(K),S2(K)
220      IF LEN(L$(K)) < D/PC THEN 260     'WILL THE LABEL FIT?
230      PRINT "LABEL TOO LONG. MAXIMUM LENGTH IS";D/PC
240      PRINT "NEW LABEL";
250      INPUT L$(K)
260  NEXT K
270  PRINT "ENTER MINIMUM AND MAXIMUM VALUES FOR VERTICAL AXIS"
280  INPUT LO, HI
290  R = HI - LO                          'R IS RANGE OF VALUES
300  RS = (172 - 12) / R                  'RS IS RATIO TO USE IN SCALING
310      '*********************** DRAW GRID AND LABELS *******************
320  CLEARSCREEN
330  GRAPHICS
340  DRAWLINE 71,12 TO 71,172
350  DRAWLINE 71,172 TO 639,172
360  DRAWLINE 639,172 TO 639,12
370  DRAWLINE 639,12 TO 71,12
380  POSITION 1,1         'PRINT TITLE
390  P = 40 - LEN(T$) / 2          'CENTER THE TITLE
400  PRINT TAB(P);T$
410  RO = 22
420  Y = 172
430  FOR K = 0 TO 5                'LABEL VERTICAL AXIS WITH SUCCESSIVE FIFTHS
440      POSITION RO,3                   'OF THE SCALING RANGE
450      L = LO + R * K / 5
460      PRINT USING "####.#";L
470      DRAWLINE 70,Y TO 639,Y
480      RO = RO - 4
490      Y = Y - 32
500  NEXT K
510      'LABEL THE DIVISIONS
520  POSITION 23,1
530  FOR K = 1 TO N
540      P = INT((71+(K-1)*D+D/2)/PC - LEN(L$(K))/2 + .5) + 1
550      PRINT TAB(P);L$(K);
560  NEXT K
570      'MAKE CODE AREAS
580  POSITION 25,28-LEN(T1$)
590  PRINT T1$;
600  COLOR 7,0        'MAKE ORANGE BLOCK
610  FOR X = 228 TO 268
620      DRAWLINE X,190 TO X,199
630  NEXT X
640  POSITION 25,56-LEN(T2$)
650  PRINT T2$;
660  COLOR 2,0        'MAKE BLUE BLOCK
670  FOR X = 452 TO 492
680      DRAWLINE X,190 TO X,199
690  NEXT X
700      '*************************** MAKE BARS *************************
710  YO = INT(HI * RS + 12.5)          'FIND WHERE O IS
```

Program 12-4 (cont.)

```
720 X1 = 71 + D/6
730 FOR K = 1 TO N
740     Y = INT((HI - S1(K)) * RS + 12.5)
750     COLOR 7,0                    'MAKE ORANGE BARS
760     FOR X = X1 TO X1 + D * 5/12
770         DRAWLINE X,Y TO X,YO
780     NEXT X
790     X2 = X1 + D * 3/12
800     Y = INT((HI - S2(K)) * RS + 12.5)
810     COLOR 2,0                    'MAKE BLUE BARS
820     FOR X = X2 TO X2 + D * 5/12
830         DRAWLINE X,Y TO X,YO
840     NEXT X
850     X1 = X1 + D
860 NEXT K
870 END
```

Another type of comparative bar chart is shown in Fig. 12–6. This graph was produced by Prog. 12–5. In this example, the two data sets share the same X axis, but have different Y axes. This arrangement allows us to use a different vertical scaling for each data set.

Figure 12–6 Comparative graph displayed by Prog. 12–5, with bars drawn up for one data set and down for the other.

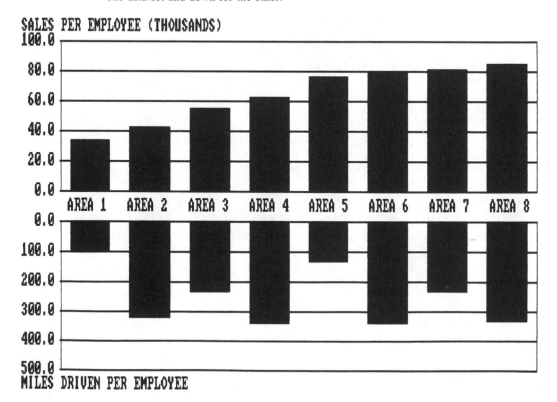

Program 12–5 Comparative graph of two bar charts: one up, one down.

```
10 'PROGRAM 12-5. COMPARATIVE BAR GRAPH WITH TWO Y SCALES.
20      'INPUTS TITLES AND TWO SETS OF DATA FOR ANY NUMBER
30      'OF DIVISIONS. DRAWS BARS FOR ONE SET OF DATA ON
40      'A VERTICAL AXIS IN THE TOP HALF OF THE SCREEN AND
50      'BARS FOR THE OTHER SET OF DATA ON A VERTICAL AXIS
60      'IN THE BOTTOM HALF OF THE SCREEN. DESIGNED FOR 640 BY 200
70      'PIXEL SCREEN.
80      '**********************************************************
90 CLEARSCREEN
100 DIM L$(15), T(15), B(15)
110 PC = 8        'PC IS HORIZONTAL PIXELS PER CHARACTER
120     '******************* INPUT DATA **********************
130 PRINT "ENTER NUMBER OF DIVISIONS"
140 INPUT N
150 D = INT(568 / N)              'D IS NUMBER OF PIXELS ALLOWED PER DIVISION
160 PRINT "ENTER NAME AND VALUES OF EACH DIVISION"
170 FOR K = 1 TO N
180     INPUT L$(K), T(K), B(K)
190     IF LEN(L$(K)) < D/PC THEN 230    'WILL THE LABEL FIT?
200     PRINT "LABEL TOO LONG. MAXIMUM LENGTH IS";D/PC
210     PRINT "NEW LABEL";
220     INPUT L$(K)
230 NEXT K
240 PRINT "ENTER LABEL FOR TOP VERTICAL AXIS"
250 INPUT T$
260 PRINT "ENTER MINIMUM AND MAXIMUM VALUES FOR TOP VERTICAL AXIS"
270 INPUT LT, HT
280 R1 = HT - LT
290 RT = (92 - 12) / R1            'RT IS RATIO TO USE IN SCALING TOP
300 PRINT "ENTER LABEL FOR BOTTOM VERTICAL AXIS"
310 INPUT B$
320 PRINT "ENTER MINIMUM AND MAXIMUM VALUES FOR BOTTOM VERTICAL AXIS"
330 INPUT LB, HB
340 R2 = HB - LB
350 RB = (188 - 108) / R2          'RB IS RATIO TO USE IN SCALING BOTTOM
360     '********************** DRAW BACKGROUND ********************
370 CLEARSCREEN
380 GRAPHICS
390 DRAWLINE 71,12 TO 71,92
400 DRAWLINE 71,92 TO 639,92
410 DRAWLINE 639,92 TO 639,12
420 DRAWLINE 639,12 TO 71,12
430 DRAWLINE 71,108 TO 71,188
440 DRAWLINE 71,188 TO 639,188
450 DRAWLINE 639,188 TO 639,108
460 DRAWLINE 639,108 TO 71,108
470 POSITION 1,4                  'PRINT TOP LABEL
480 PRINT T$
490 RO = 12
500 Y = 92
510 FOR K = 0 TO 5               'LABEL VERTICAL AXIS WITH SUCCESSIVE FIFTHS
520     POSITION RO,3            'OF THE SCALING RANGE
530     L = LT + R1 * K / 5
540     PRINT USING "####.#";L;
550     DRAWLINE 70,Y TO 639,Y
560     RO = RO - 2
570     Y = Y - 16
580 NEXT K
590 POSITION 25,4               'LABEL BOTTOM HALF
600 PRINT B$;
610 RO = 14
620 Y = 108
630 FOR K = 0 TO 5
640     POSITION RO,3
```

```
650     L = LB + R2 * K / 5
660     PRINT USING "####.#";L;
670     DRAWLINE 70,Y TO 639,Y
680     RO = RO + 2
690     Y = Y + 16
700 NEXT K
710     'LABEL THE DIVISIONS
720 POSITION 13,1
730 FOR K = 1 TO N
740     P = INT((72 + (K-1) * D+ D/2) / PC - LEN(L$(K))/2 + .5) + 1
750     PRINT TAB(P);L$(K);
760 NEXT K
770     '********************* MAKE BARS ********************
780 X1 = 71 + D/6
790 FOR K = 1 TO N
800     YT = INT((HT - T(K)) * RT + 12.5)
810     YB = INT(B(K) * RB + 108.5)
820     FOR X = X1 TO X1 + D * 2/3
830         DRAWLINE X,YT TO X,92
840         DRAWLINE X,YB TO X,108
850     NEXT X
860     X1 = X1 + D
870 NEXT K
880 END
```

Curves can be compared by simply plotting multiple sets of data points on the same graph. We can also construct a cumulative surface chart with methods demonstrated in Prog. 12–6. The resulting graph, shown in Fig. 12–7, plots the upper curve as the sum of the two data sets and uses shading to distinguish the areas. This type of graph can often lead to misinterpretations, since the upper line shows the sum of the two data sets and not actual data values.

Program 12–6 Cumulative surface chart, plotting two data sets.

```
10 'PROGRAM 12-6. SURFACE CHART WITH TWO SETS OF CUMULATIVE DATA.
20      'PLOTS LOWER CURVE FOR ONE SET OF DATA. PLOTS UPPER CURVE
30      'AS THE SUM OF FIRST AND SECOND SETS OF DATA. ASSUMES
40      'A SCREEN SIZE OF 640 BY 200 PIXELS.
50      '*********************************************************
60  CLEARSCREEN
70  DIM L$(20), S1(20), S2(20)
80  PC = 8        'PC IS HORIZONTAL PIXELS PER CHARACTER
90      '******************** INPUT CHART LABELS AND DATA ***************
100 PRINT "TITLE OF CHART";
110 INPUT T$
120 PRINT "ENTER NAME OF FIRST SET OF DATA"
130 INPUT T1$
140 PRINT "ENTER NAME OF SECOND SET OF DATA"
150 INPUT T2$
160 PRINT "ENTER NUMBER OF HORIZONTAL DIVISIONS"
170 INPUT N
180 D = INT(568 / N)
190 PRINT D
200 PRINT "ENTER LABEL AND TWO VALUES FOR EACH DIVISION"
210 M2 = 0      'M2 IS THE MAXIMUM VALUE IN ARRAY S2
220 FOR K = 1 TO N
230     INPUT L$(K),S1(K),S2(K)
240     S2(K) = S1(K) + S2(K)
250     IF S2(K) <= M2 THEN 270
260     M2 = S2(K)
270     IF LEN(L$(K)) < D/PC THEN 310      'WILL THE LABEL FIT?
```

```
280     PRINT "LABEL TOO LONG. MAXIMUM LENGTH IS";D/PC
290     PRINT "NEW LABEL";
300        INPUT L$(K)
310 NEXT K
320 PRINT "ENTER MINIMUM AND MAXIMUM VALUES FOR VERTICAL AXIS"
330 INPUT LO, HI
340 IF HI >= M2 THEN 380        'IS HI HIGH ENOUGH?
350 PRINT "MAXIMUM VALUE NOT ENOUGH. ENTER MAXIMUM AGAIN"
360 INPUT HI
370 GOTO 340
380 R = HI - LO                           'R IS RANGE OF VALUES
390 RS = (172 - 12) / R                  'RS IS RATIO TO USE IN SCALING
400     '*********************** DRAW GRID AND LABELS *******************
410 CLEARSCREEN
420 GRAPHICS
430 DRAWLINE 71,12 TO 71,172
440 DRAWLINE 71,172 TO 639,172
450 DRAWLINE 639,172 TO 639,12
460 DRAWLINE 639,12 TO 71,12
470 POSITION 1,1         'PRINT TITLE
480 P = 40 - LEN(T$) / 2         'CENTER THE TITLE
490 PRINT TAB(P);T$
500 RO = 22
510 Y = 172
520 FOR K = 0 TO 5                'LABEL VERTICAL AXIS WITH SUCCESSIVE FIFTHS
530     POSITION RO,3                  'OF THE SCALING RANGE
540     L = LO + R * K / 5
550     PRINT USING "####.#";L
560     DRAWLINE 70,Y TO 639,Y
570     RO = RO - 4
580     Y = Y - 32
590 NEXT K
600     'LABEL THE DIVISIONS
610 POSITION 23,1
620 FOR K = 1 TO N
630     P = INT((71+(K-1)*D+D/2)/PC - LEN(L$(K))/2 + .5) + 1
640     PRINT TAB(P);L$(K);
650 NEXT K
660     'MAKE CODE AREAS
670 POSITION 25,28-LEN(T1$)
680 COLOR 2,0            'FIRST DATA SET WILL BE IN BLUE
690 PRINT T1$;
700 FOR X = 228 TO 288
710     DRAWLINE X,190 TO X,199)
720 NEXT X
730 DRAWLINE 228,190 TO 288,190
740 DRAWLINE 228,199 TO 288,199
750 POSITION 25,56-LEN(T2$)
760 COLOR 5,0                    'SECOND (CUMULATIVE) DATA SET IS YELLOW
770 PRINT T2$;
780 FOR X = 452 TO 512
790     DRAWLINE X,190 TO X,199
800 NEXT X
810 DRAWLINE 452,190 TO 512,190
820 DRAWLINE 452,199 TO 512,199
830     '*************************** MAKE BARS **************************
840 YO = 171
850 X1 = 71 + D/2         'PUT FIRST POINT HALFWAY ACROSS THE FIRST DIVISION
860 Y1 = INT((HI - S2(1)) * RS + 12.5)
870 COLOR 5,0             'DRAW FROM TOP CURVE DOWN IN YELLOW
880 FOR K = 2 TO N
890     X2 = X1 + D
900     Y2 = INT((HI - S2(K)) * RS + 12.5)
910     M = (Y2-Y1) / (X2-X1)
```

258

```
 920        B = Y1 + 1 - M * X1
 930        FOR X = X1 TO X2
 940           Y = M * X + B
 950        NEXT X
 960        DRAWLINE X1,Y1 TO X2,Y2          'DRAW IN CURVE LINE
 970        X1 = X2                          'SAVE CURRENT POINT
 980        Y1 = Y2
 990 NEXT K
1000      'DO LOWER CURVE (FIRST SET OF DATA)
1010 X1 = 71 + D/2
1020 Y1 = INT((HI - S1(1)) * RS + 12.5)
1030 COLOR 2,0           'DRAW FROM LOWER CURVE DOWN IN BLUE
1040 FOR K = 2 TO N
1050      X2 = X1 + D
1060      Y2 = INT((HI - S1(K)) * RS + 12.5)
1070      M = (Y2 - Y1) / (X2 - X1)
1080      B = Y1 + 1 - M * X1
1090      FOR X = X1 TO X2
1100         Y = M * X + B
1110         DRAWLINE X,Y TO X,YO
1120      NEXT X
1130      DRAWLINE X1,Y1 TO X2,Y2          'DRAW IN CURVE
1140      X1 = X2
1150      Y1 = Y2
1160 NEXT K
1170 END
```

Figure 12–7 Cumulative surface chart produced by Prog. 12–6, with one data set
plotted as the lower line and the other data set added to the first to obtain the
upper line.

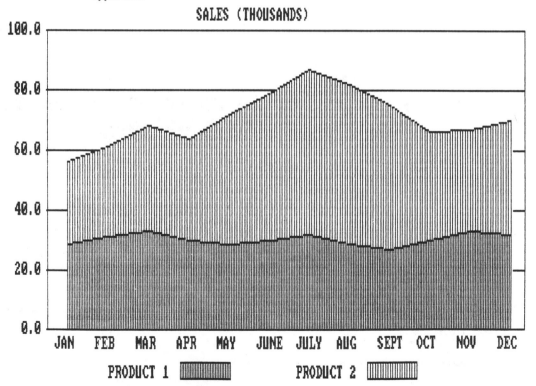

259

Shading patterns can be used to emphasize areas between curves, as shown in Fig. 12–8. This band chart was produced by Prog. 12–7. We can use this technique to help in estimating magnitude differences. Two different shading patterns are used in this example to identify profits from losses (that is, when one curve falls below the other).

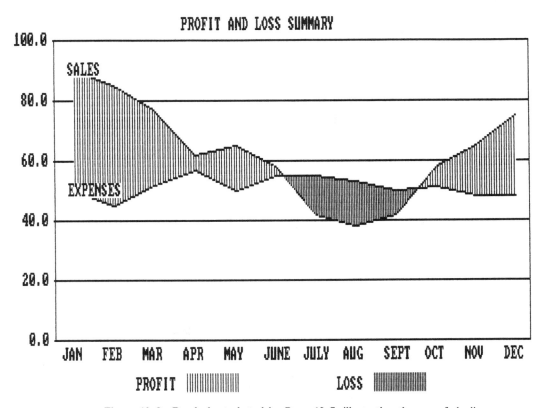

Figure 12–8 Band chart plotted by Prog. 12–7, illustrating the use of shading between data curves.

Program 12–7   Band chart, shading the area between two curves.

```
10 'PROGRAM 12-7. SHADED BAND CHART WITH TWO SETS OF DATA.
20      'PLOTS CURVES FOR TWO SETS OF DATA. SHADES IN AREAS WHERE
30      'CURVES CROSS. DESIGNED FOR SCREEN SIZE OF 640 x 200 PIXELS.
40      '*********************************************************
50 CLEARSCREEN
60 DIM L$(20), S1(20), S2(20)
70 PC = 8        'PC IS HORIZONTAL PIXELS PER CHARACTER
80      '******************** INPUT CHART LABELS AND DATA **************
90 PRINT "TITLE OF CHART";
100 INPUT T$
110 PRINT "ENTER NAME OF FIRST SET OF DATA"
120 INPUT T1$
130 PRINT "ENTER NAME OF SECOND SET OF DATA"
```

Program 12-7 (cont.)

```
140 INPUT T2$
150 PRINT "ENTER NAME OF AREA WHEN FIRST DATA IS GREATER THAN SECOND"
160 INPUT T3$
170 PRINT "ENTER NAME OF AREA WHEN SECOND DATA IS GREATER THAN FIRST"
180 INPUT T4$
190 PRINT "ENTER NUMBER OF HORIZONTAL DIVISIONS"
200 INPUT N
210 D = INT(568 / N)     'D IS NUMBER OF PIXELS PER DIVISION
220 IF D/2 <> INT(D/2) THEN D = INT(D/2+.5)*2    'MAKE D AN EVEN NUMBER
230 PRINT "ENTER LABEL AND TWO VALUES FOR EACH DIVISION"
240 FOR K = 1 TO N
250     INPUT L$(K),S1(K),S2(K)
260     IF LEN(L$(K)) < D/PC THEN 300    'WILL THE LABEL FIT?
270     PRINT "LABEL TOO LONG. MAXIMUM LENGTH IS";D/PC
280     PRINT "NEW LABEL";
290     INPUT L$(K)
300 NEXT K
310 PRINT "ENTER MINIMUM AND MAXIMUM VALUES FOR VERTICAL AXIS"
320 INPUT LO, HI
330 R = HI - LO                         'R IS RANGE OF VALUES
340 RS = (172 - 12) / R                 'RS IS RATIO TO USE IN SCALING
350     '*********************** DRAW GRID AND LABELS ******************
360 CLEARSCREEN
370 GRAPHICS
380 DRAWLINE 71,12 TO 71,172
390 DRAWLINE 71,172 TO 639,172
400 DRAWLINE 639,172 TO 639,12
410 DRAWLINE 639,12 TO 71,12
420 POSITION 1,1            'PRINT TITLE
430 P = 40 - LEN(T$) / 2         'CENTER THE TITLE
440 PRINT TAB(P);T$
450 RO = 22
460 Y = 172
470 FOR K = 0 TO 5                   'LABEL VERTICAL AXIS WITH SUCCESSIVE FIFTHS
480     POSITION RO,3                'OF THE SCALING RANGE
490     L = LO + R * K / 5
500     PRINT USING "####.#";L
510     DRAWLINE 70,Y TO 639,Y
520     RO = RO - 4
530     Y = Y - 32
540 NEXT K
550    'LABEL THE DIVISIONS
560 POSITION 23,1
570 FOR K = 1 TO N
580     P = INT((71 + (K-1) * D + D/2) / PC - LEN(L$(K))/2 + .5) + 1
590     PRINT TAB(P);L$(K);
600 NEXT K
610    'MAKE CODE AREAS
620 POSITION 25,28-LEN(T3$)
630 PRINT T3$;
640 FOR X = 228 TO 288 STEP 3
650     DRAWLINE X,190 TO X,199
660 NEXT X
670 POSITION 25,56-LEN(T4$)
680 PRINT T4$;
690 FOR X = 452 TO 512 STEP 2
700     DRAWLINE X,190 TO X,199
710 NEXT X
720     '*********************** PLOT CURVES *******************
730 YO = 171
```

Program 12-7 (cont.)

```
740 X1 = 71 + D/2          'PUT FIRST POINT HALFWAY ACROSS THE FIRST DIVISION
750 Y1 = INT((HI - S1(1)) * RS + 12.5)
760 R1 = INT(Y1/PC + .5)
770 C1 = INT(X1/PC + .5)                      'X1,Y1 AND X2,Y2 ARE FIRST CURVE.
780 X3 = X1                                   'X3,Y3 AND X4,Y4 ARE OTHER CURVE.
790 Y3 = INT((HI - S2(1)) * RS + 12.5)
800 R3 = INT(Y3/PC + .5)
810 C3 = INT(X3/PC + .5)
820 FOR K = 2 TO N
830     X2 = X1 + D
840     Y2 = INT((HI - S1(K)) * RS + 12.5)
850     M1 = (Y2-Y1) / (X2-X1)   'FIND SLOPE & INTERCEPT OF FIRST CURVE
860     B1 = Y1 - M1 * X1
870     X4 = X2
880     Y4 = INT((HI - S2(K)) * RS + 12.5)
890     M3 = (Y4-Y3) / (X4-X3)   'FIND SLOPE & INTERCEPT OF OTHER CURVE
900     B3 = Y3 - M3 * X3
910     'SHADING PATTERN (EVERY OTHER LINE OR EVERY THIRD LINE) IS
920     'DETERMINED BY WHICH CURVE IS ON TOP. DRAW EVERY SECOND LINE
930     'WHEN 3-4 CURVE IS ON TOP, EVERY THIRD LINE WHEN 1-2 IS TOP.
940     IF Y3 <= Y1 AND Y4 <= Y2 THEN 1050       '3-4 CURVE IS HIGHER THAN 1-2
950     IF Y3 > Y1 AND Y4 > Y2 THEN 1070         '1-2 CURVE IS HIGHER THAN 3-4
960     'OTHERWISE THE TWO CURVES CROSS
970     XP = INT((B1-B3) / (M3-M1) + .5)         'FIND X INTERSECTION OF CURVES
980     IF Y3 > Y1 THEN 1020
990     B = X3: E = XP: I = 2: GOSUB 1230        '3-4 CURVE IS ON TOP 'TIL XP
1000    B = XP: E = X4: I = 3: GOSUB 1230        'FROM XP ON, 1-2 CURVE IS TOP
1010    GOTO 1080
1020    B = X3: E = XP: I = 3: GOSUB 1230
1030    B = XP: E = X4: I = 2: GOSUB 1230
1040    GOTO 1080
1050    B = X3: E = X4: I = 2: GOSUB 1230
1060    GOTO 1080
1070    B = X3: E = X4: I = 3: GOSUB 1230
1080    DRAWLINE X1,Y1 TO X2,Y2          'DRAW IN BOTH CURVES
1090    DRAWLINE X3,Y3 TO X4,Y4
1100    X1 = X2
1110    Y1 = Y2
1120    X3 = X4
1130    Y3 = Y4
1140 NEXT K
1150 POSITION R1,C1                'LABEL THE START OF THE CURVES
1160 PRINT T1$;
1170 POSITION R3,C3
1180 PRINT T2$;
1190 GOTO 1330
1200 '
1210 '################## SHADE IN AREA #########################
1220 COLOR 0,0                      'BLANK OUT GRID LINES
1230 FOR X = B TO E
1240    YF = M1 * X + B1
1250    YS = M3 * X + B3
1260    DRAWLINE X,YF TO X,YS
1270    IF X/I <> INT(X/I) THEN 1300   'IS THIS LINE A MULTIPLE OF I?
1280    COLOR 1,0                'IF YES, CHANGE FOREGROUND AND DRAW
1290    DRAWLINE X,YF TO X,YS
1300 NEXT X
1310 RETURN
1320 '##############################################################
1330 END
```

12–3 MULTIPLE FORMATS

A useful technique for comparing two sets of data is to plot the data in several formats within the same graph. This allows us to display various types of relationships between data sets. The combination bar chart, line graph, and pie chart shown in Fig. 12–9 was output by Prog. 12–8. Relative magnitude between the two data sets is displayed with the bar chart. Cumulative totals are shown with the line graph. The pie chart shows total percentage for each data set. Color coding is used to identify the two sets of data.

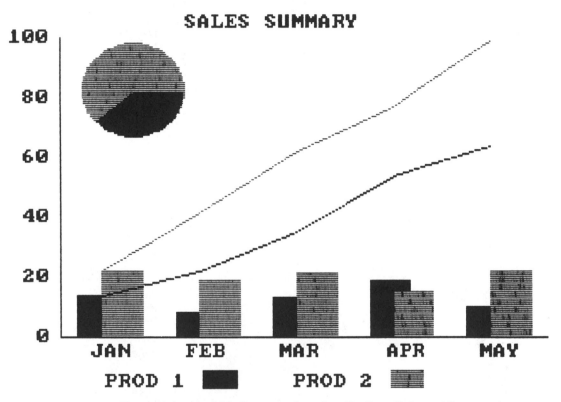

Figure 12–9   A multiple format graph produced by Prog. 12–8, providing several types of comparative information.

Program 12–8   Multiple formats: overlapping bar charts, cumulative line graphs, and pie chart.

```
10 'PROGRAM 12-8. TWO SETS OF DATA IN MULTIPLE FORMATS.
20      'INPUTS TWO SETS OF DATA. PLOTS DATA IN BAR GRAPH FORM, IN
30      'PIE CHART FORM TO SHOW PERCENTAGES OF TOTAL, AND IN CURVE
40      'FORM TO SHOW CUMULATIVE VALUES OVER TIME. ASSUMES SCREEN
50      'SIZE OF 320 BY 200 PIXELS.
60      '**************************************************************
70   CLEARSCREEN
```

```
80  DIM L$(5), S1(5), S2(5), C1(5), C2(5)
90  PC = 8            'PC IS HORIZONTAL PIXELS PER CHARACTER
100 XC = 73           'XC,YC IS CENTER OF PIE CHART
110 YC = 40
120 RA = 30           'RA IS RADIUS OF PIE CHART
130 YA = 5/6          'YA IS RESOLUTION ADJUSTMENT NEEDED FOR Y
140       '******************** INPUT CHART LABELS AND DATA **************
150 PRINT "TITLE OF CHART";
160 INPUT T$
170 PRINT "ENTER NAME OF FIRST SET OF DATA"
180 INPUT T1$
190 PRINT "ENTER NAME OF SECOND SET OF DATA"
200 INPUT T2$
210 PRINT "ENTER NUMBER OF DIVISIONS"
220 INPUT N
230 D = INT(290 / N)     'D IS NUMBER OF PIXELS PER DIVISION
240 T1 = 0               'T1 AND T2 ARE USED TO TOTAL DATA VALUES
250 T2 = 0
260 PRINT "ENTER LABEL AND TWO VALUES FOR EACH BAR"
270 FOR K = 1 TO N
280     INPUT L$(K),S1(K),S2(K)
290     T1 = T1 + S1(K)
300     C1(K) = T1
310     T2 = T2 + S2(K)
320     C2(K) = T2
330     IF LEN(L$(K)) < D/PC THEN 370      'WILL THE LABEL FIT?
340     PRINT "LABEL TOO LONG. MAXIMUM LENGTH IS";D/PC
350     PRINT "NEW LABEL";
360     INPUT L$(K)
370 NEXT K
380 PRINT "ENTER MINIMUM AND MAXIMUM VALUES FOR VERTICAL AXIS"
390 INPUT LO, HI
400 IF HI >= T1 AND HI >= T2 THEN 440
410 PRINT "MAXIMUM NOT LARGE ENOUGH. RE-ENTER MAXIMUM"
420 INPUT HI
430 GOTO 400
440 R = HI - LO                           'R IS RANGE OF VALUES
450 RS = (172 - 12) / R                   'RS IS RATIO TO USE IN SCALING
460       '************************* DRAW GRID AND LABELS *******************
470 CLEARSCREEN
480 GRAPHICS
490 DRAWLINE 30,12 TO 30,172
500 DRAWLINE 30,172 TO 319,172
510 POSITION 1,1          'PRINT TITLE
520 P = 20 - LEN(T$) / 2         'CENTER THE TITLE
530 PRINT TAB(P);T$
540 RO = 22
550 Y = 172
560 FOR K = 0 TO 5                  'LABEL VERTICAL AXIS WITH SUCCESSIVE FIFTHS
570     POSITION RO,1                   'OF THE SCALING RANGE
580     L = LO + R * K / 5
590     PRINT USING "###";L
600     RO = RO - 4
610     Y = Y - 32
620 NEXT K
630     'LABEL THE DIVISIONS
640 POSITION 23,1
650 FOR K = 1 TO N
660     P = INT((30+(K-1)*D+D/2)/PC - LEN(L$(K))/2 + .5) + 1
670     PRINT TAB(P);L$(K);
680 NEXT K
690     'MAKE CODE AREAS
700 POSITION 25,14-LEN(T1$)
710 COLOR 2,0               'MAKE FIRST DATA SET BLUE
```

264

```
720 PRINT T1$;
730 FOR X = 114 TO 134
740     DRAWLINE X,190 TO X,199
750 NEXT X
760 POSITION 25,28-LEN(T2$)
770 COLOR 4,0               'MAKE SECOND DATA SET GREEN
780 PRINT T2$;
790 FOR X = 226 TO 246
800     DRAWLINE X,190 TO X,199
810 NEXT X
820     '
830     '*************************** MAKE BARS ***************************
840 Y0 = 171
850 X1 = 30 + D/6
860 FOR K = 1 TO N
870     Y = INT((HI - S1(K)) * RS + 12.5)
880     COLOR 2,0
890     FOR X = X1 TO X1 + D * 5/12
900         DRAWLINE X,Y TO X,Y0
910     NEXT X
920     X2 = X1 + D * 3/12      'START SECOND BAR 3/12 OVER FROM FIRST
930     Y = INT((HI - S2(K)) * RS + 12.5)
940     COLOR 4,0
950     FOR X = X2 TO X2 + D * 5/12
960         DRAWLINE X,Y TO X,Y0
970     NEXT X
980     X1 = X1 + D
990 NEXT K
1000    '
1010    '*************************** MAKE LINES ***************************
1020 X = 30 + D * 5 / 12
1030 Y1 = INT((HI - C1(1)) * RS + 12.5)
1040 Y2 = INT((HI - C2(1)) * RS + 12.5)
1050 FOR K = 2 TO N
1060    Y3 = INT((HI - C1(K)) * RS + 12.5)
1070    Y4 = INT((HI - C2(K)) * RS + 12.5)
1080    COLOR 2,0
1090    DRAWLINE X,Y1 TO X+D,Y3
1100    COLOR 4,0
1110    DRAWLINE X,Y2 TO X+D,Y4
1120    X = X + D
1130    Y1 = Y3
1140    Y2 = Y4
1150 NEXT K
1160    '
1170    '*************************** MAKE PIE CHART ***************************
1180 CT = T1 + T2        'CT IS TOTAL OF BOTH DATA SETS
1190    'A1 IS PERCENTAGE OF CIRCLE (IN RADIANS) CORRESPONDING TO T1
1200 A1 = 360 * 3.14159 / 180 * T1 / CT
1210 DA = 1/RA/15        'STEP MUST BE VERY SMALL TO SOLIDLY FILL IN CIRCLE
1220 COLOR 2,0
1230 FOR A = DA TO A1 STEP DA
1240    X = XC + RA * COS(A)
1250    Y = YC + RA * SIN(A) * YA
1260    DRAWLINE XC,YC TO X,Y
1270 NEXT A
1280    'FILL REMAINDER OF CIRCLE WITH OTHER COLOR (FOR T2)
1290 COLOR 4,0
1300 FOR A = A1+DA TO 6.28318 STEP DA
1310    X = XC + RA * COS(A)
1320    Y = YC + RA * SIN(A) * YA
1330    DRAWLINE XC,YC TO X,Y
1340 NEXT A
1350 END
```

265

12–4 PROJECT MANAGEMENT GRAPHS

Graphs displaying a network of project tasks, as in Fig. 12–10, can be used as an aid in scheduling and monitoring the tasks. This type of graph is particularly useful with PERT-CPM project scheduling techniques. Tasks are represented in the network graph by lines and ordered from left to right, according to when they can be started. Circles are used to indicate the beginning and ending of tasks. The leftmost circle shows the start of the project, where tasks A, B, and C can be initiated simultaneously. Task D cannot be started until task A is completed, and task E must wait for tasks A, B, and D.

Project tasks can also be listed on a time chart to show actual starting and ending dates. The project time chart shown in Fig. 12–11 was produced by Prog. 12–9. This chart shows relative starting and ending weeks for each task in the project. Tasks are represented as horizontal bars, with the length of each bar proportional to the scheduled task time. Both network and time charts are useful for planning and managing projects.

Figure 12–10   A network graph showing the sequencing of the various tasks in a project.

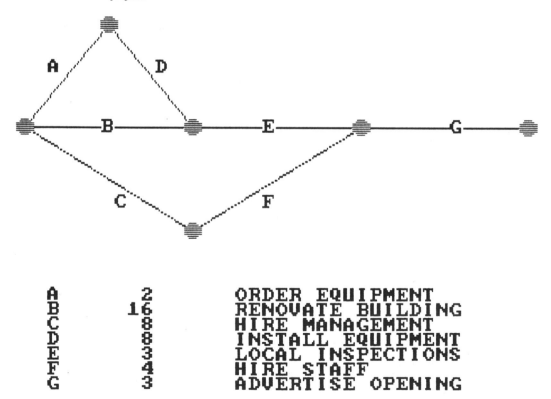

```
A          2        ORDER EQUIPMENT
B         16        RENOVATE BUILDING
C          8        HIRE MANAGEMENT
D          8        INSTALL EQUIPMENT
E          3        LOCAL INSPECTIONS
F          4        HIRE STAFF
G          3        ADVERTISE OPENING
```

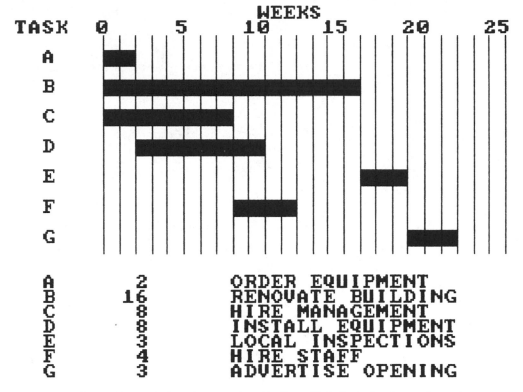

Figure 12–11   A time chart, produced by Prog. 12–9, displaying the starting and ending dates for scheduled project tasks.

Program 12–9   Time chart for scheduling tasks.

```
10  'PROGRAM 12-9. TIME DIAGRAM
20      'ASSUMES SCREEN SIZE OF 320 BY 200 PIXELS WITH
30      '40 CHARACTERS PER LINE.   TIME BARS ARE SCALED
40      'TO PIXELS 60 - 300.
50      '*******************************************************
60  CLEARSCREEN
70  GRAPHICS
80  READ TD$       'TIME DIVISION LABEL
90  READ ET,LT     'EARLIEST AND LATEST TIME DIVISION LABELS
100 RT = LT - ET              'RT IS THE RANGE OF TIME
110 RS = (300 - 60) / RT      'RS IS RATIO TO USE IN SCALING
120 POSITION 1,20
130 PRINT TD$;
140 POSITION 2,2
150 PRINT "TASK";
160 CO = 6
170 X = 60
180 FOR K = 0 TO 5         'LABEL COLUMNS IN SUCCESSIVE FIFTHS OF TIME RANGE
190     POSITION 2,CO
200     T = ET + RT * K/5
210     PRINT USING "###";T;
220     X = X + 48
230     CO = CO + 6
240 NEXT K
```

Program 12-9 (cont.)

```
250 I = 240 / 25          'MAKE 25 LINES ACROSS THE 240 PIXELS
260 X = 60
270 FOR L = 1 TO 26       '26 LINES IN ALL
280     DRAWLINE X,16 TO X,132
290     X = X + I
300 NEXT L
310 R1 = 19      'R1 IS ROW FOR PRINTING TABLE (BOTTOM OF SCREEN)
320 R2 = 4       'R2 IS ROW FOR PRINTING BAR'S LABEL (TOP OF SCREEN)
330 FOR K = 1 TO 7
340     READ C$,T$,S,D              'CODE, TASK NAME, START, DURATION
350     POSITION R1,4                     'MAKE TABLE AT BOTTOM
360     PRINT C$;
370     PRINT TAB(10); USING "##";D;
380     PRINT TAB(18);T$;
390     POSITION R2,4                     'MAKE BARS AT TOP
400     PRINT C$;
410     X1 = S * RS + 60          'FIND START POSITION OF BAR
420     X2 = (S + D) * RS + 60         'FIND FINISH POSITION
430     Y1 = (R2 - 1) * PR - 1         'Y VALUES ARE BASED ON ROW IN
440     Y2 = Y1 + 9                    'WHICH CODE LABEL WAS PRINTED.
450     FOR Y = Y1 TO Y2              'MAKE BARS 10 PIXELS HIGH.
460         DRAWLINE X1,Y TO X2,Y
470     NEXT Y
480     R1 = R1 + 1
490     R2 = R2 + 2
500 NEXT K
510     '**********************************************************************
520 DATA WEEKS,0,25
530 DATA A,ORDER EQUIPMENT,0,2
540 DATA B,RENOVATE BUILDING,0,16
550 DATA C,HIRE MANAGEMENT,0,8
560 DATA D,INSTALL EQUIPMENT,2,8
570 DATA E,LOCAL INSPECTIONS,16,3
580 DATA F,HIRE STAFF,8,4
590 DATA G,ADVERTISE OPENING,19,3
600 END
```

Chapter 13

Educational Graphics

The availability of low-cost microcomputer graphics systems provides a powerful educational resource at all levels, from grade schools to graduate schools. We can develop graphics programs for classroom demonstrations or for self-study projects in a lab. Such computer-assisted instruction (CAI) programs can be broadly classified as either drill and practice programs, tutorial and inquiry programs, or as simulations.

13-1 DRILL AND PRACTICE PROGRAMS

With drill and practice programs, we can repeatedly present practice problems on a video screen and ask for the answers. The problems could be questions about sentence structure, foreign languages, historical personalities, art forms, or geological eras. Answers could be chosen from a menu or typed in. We can design a drill and practice program to respond to an answer by displaying a simple message, such as "THAT'S RIGHT" or "THAT'S WRONG. TRY AGAIN." Usually it is better to have the program be a bit more helpful by furnishing additional information when a wrong answer is given. A chemistry drill on the periodic table might ask for the atomic number of a randomly selected element and respond to a wrong answer by citing which element, if any, has the stated atomic number. More elaborate programs could respond to a wrong answer with a series of "leading" questions or by displaying pictures and text to help in getting a right answer.

Graphics displays can aid in the statement of many drill and practice problems. A spelling drill could draw a picture of the object to be spelled (car, boat, tree, house), and questions for an economics class could use graphs and charts. Simply to make a more entertaining display, we can add pictures to accompany the statement of a problem or as part of the response to an answer. Program 13–1, an addition drill, uses pictures both for entertainment and as visual aids in the statement of the problem presented. Figure 13–1 shows the possible program outputs for the question 4 + 5 = ?. To provide some variety in the program responses, we could randomly choose different face designs and text phrases (GOOD, SWELL, NO, TOO BAD). We could also select a different shaped object for the problem statement each time.

Program 13–1 Arithmetic practice, presenting addition problems with prompts and pictures.

```
10  'PROGRAM 13-1. ARITHMETIC PRACTICE.
20       'USING RANDOM NUMBER FUNCTION, GENERATES ADDITION
30       'PROBLEMS AND PRESENTS THEM IN TEXT FORM (3 + 4 = ?).
40       'PRESENTS THE PROBLEM AS CIRCLES TO COUNT IF TWO
50       'INCORRECT RESPONSES ARE GIVEN. IF AN INCORRECT
60       'RESPONSE IS STILL GIVEN (TWICE MORE), WE GO ON TO
70       'ANOTHER PROBLEM. A COUNT (R) IS KEPT OF THE NUMBER OF
80       'PROBLEMS ANSWERED CORRECTLY ON THE FIRST TRY (WHEN
90       'C = 1). AFTER 5 PROBLEMS, A SMILEY FACE AND MESSAGE ARE
100      'DISPLAYED IF R IS GREATER THAN 3 (4 OR 5 RIGHT OUT OF 5).
110      'AFTER TEN PROBLEMS, A SECOND DISPLAY AND MESSAGE OCCURS
120      'IF R IS GREATER THAN 8.
130  '*******************************************************************
140  CLEARSCREEN
150  GRAPHICS
160  PRINT "HI!  WHAT'S YOUR NAME";
170  INPUT N$
180  PRINT "OKAY, "; N$; ", HERE WE GO!"
190  PRINT "SEE HOW MANY PROBLEMS YOU CAN GET RIGHT!"
200  FOR K = 1 TO 1000:NEXT K
210      '****************** GENERATE 10 PROBLEMS ******************
220  FOR P = 1 TO 10
230      C = 0    'C IS COUNT OF HOW MANY ANSWERS GIVEN TO THIS PROBLEM
240      J = INT(RND(1) * 9 + .5)
250      K = INT(RND(1) * 9 + .5)
260      CLEARSCREEN
270      POSITION 16,8
280      PRINT J;"+";K;"= ";
290      INPUT A
300      C = C + 1
310      IF A = J + K THEN 490            'RIGHT?
320      IF C <> 1 THEN 380
330      POSITION 18,5            'HAS ANSWERED ONCE. DO OVER
340      PRINT "THAT'S NOT RIGHT, ";N$
350      PRINT "    TRY AGAIN   "
360      FOR F = 1 TO 1000:NEXT F
370      GOTO 260
380      IF C <> 2 THEN 410
390      GOSUB 610                'HAS ANSWERED TWICE. GO TO DRAWING CIRCLES
400      GOTO 270
410      IF C <> 3 THEN 460       'HAS ANSWERED THREE TIMES. ONE MORE TRY
420      GOSUB 610
430      POSITION 4,1
440      PRINT "TRY ONE MORE TIME";
450      GOTO 270
460      POSITION 20,1            'GO ON TO NEXT PROBLEM
470      PRINT "LET'S TRY ANOTHER";
```

Program 13-1 (cont.)

```
480      FOR F = 1 TO 1000:NEXT F
490      IF C = 1 THEN R = R + 1              'RIGHT ON FIRST TRY
500      IF P = 5 AND R > 3 THEN GOSUB 790        'GO TO SMILEY FACE
510      IF P = 10 AND R > 8 THEN GOSUB 960       ' GO TO BALLOONS
520 NEXT P
530      '
540 CLEARSCREEN
550 POSITION 10,19
560 PRINT "BYE,"
570 POSITION 12,20-LEN(N$)/2
580 PRINT N$
590 GOTO 1260
600 '
610 '################### DRAW CIRCLES TO HELP GET ANSWER ##################
620 CLEARSCREEN
630 Y = 76
640 X = 8
650 FOR W = 1 TO J
660     CIRCLEPLOT X,Y,5
670     X = X + 16
680 NEXT W
690 POSITION 10,X/8+1
700 PRINT "+";
710 X = X + 20
720 FOR W = 1 TO K
730     CIRCLEPLOT X,Y,5
740     X = X + 16
750 NEXT W
760 RETURN
770 '
780 '############################ SMILEY FACE ##########################
790 CLEARSCREEN
800 POSITION 25,4
810 PRINT "SO FAR, SO GOOD, "; N$
820 CIRCLEPLOT 160,100,80
830 CIRCLEPLOT 130,80,5
840 CIRCLEPLOT 190,80,5
850 CIRCLEPLOT 160,100,3
860 FOR A = .79 TO 2.36 STEP 1/60         'MAKE MOUTH FROM 45 TO 135 DEGREES
870     XP = 160 + 60 * COS(A)
880     YP = 80 + 60 * SIN(A)
890     POINTPLOT XP,YP
900 NEXT A
910 FOR F = 1 TO 1500: NEXT F
920 COLOR 0,0
930 RETURN
940 '
950 '########################### BALLOONS ###########################
960 CLEARSCREEN
970 POSITION 4,17
980 PRINT N$
990 POSITION 6,18
1000 PRINT "THE"
1010 POSITION 8,17
1020 PRINT "GREAT!";
1030 CIRCLEPLOT 60,50,40
1040 CIRCLEPLOT 60,88,5
1050 DRAWLINE 60,91 TO 60,170           'PUT STRING ON BALLOON
1060 CIRCLEPLOT 280,50,30
1070 CIRCLEPLOT 280,78,3
1080 DRAWLINE 280,79 TO 280,180
```

```
1090 CIRCLEPLOT 140,130,35
1100 CIRCLEPLOT 140,163,3
1110 DRAWLINE 140,164 TO 140,199
1120 FOR Y = 2 TO 199 STEP 5              'MAKE CONFETTI
1130     X = RND(1) * 319
1140     CIRCLEPLOT X,Y,1
1150     FOR F = 1 TO 50:NEXT F
1160 NEXT Y
1170 X = 240: Y = 20: A = 0: R = 20: DA = 1/R/.5
1180 FOR Y = 20 TO 199                    'MAKE SPIRAL
1190     XP = X + R * COS(A)
1200     YP = Y + R * SIN(A)
1210     POINTPLOT XP,YP
1220     A = A + DA
1230 NEXT Y
1240 RETURN
1250 '############################################################################
1260 END
```

Figure 13-1 An arithmetic drill output from Prog. 13-1, displaying (a) prompts when a wrong answer is given, (b) a happy face for a series of right answers, and (c) balloons and streamers for a good final score.

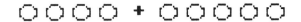

$$4 + 5 = ? \quad \blacksquare$$

(a)

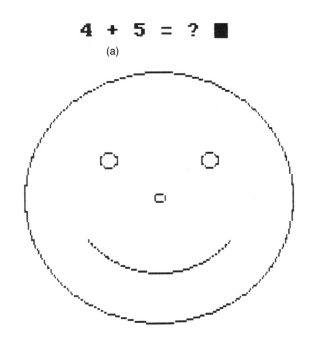

SO FAR, SO GOOD, PEGGY

(b)

272

Figure 13-1 (cont.)

(c)

13–2 TUTORIAL AND INQUIRY PROGRAMS

In tutorial and inquiry programs, we employ more extensive conversational methods. Tutorials can provide instructions to read and study certain materials (books, articles, films) for a self-paced course, then give a test over that material. Inquiry programs can carry on a conversation by both answering and asking questions. For example, an inquiry program can help train medical interns by responding to questions as if the program were a patient. The program's answers could then be used to make a medical diagnosis. Exams and questions provided by inquiry and tutorial programs can use graphics in much the same way as drill and practice programs.

For a self-study type of program we might produce a diagram of plant parts and a menu of terms, as in Fig. 13–2. The program could produce several such displays, evaluate the responses, and output a grade for the total performance. We can use this type of display as part of an examination program or for review and study in a tutorial or inquiry program.

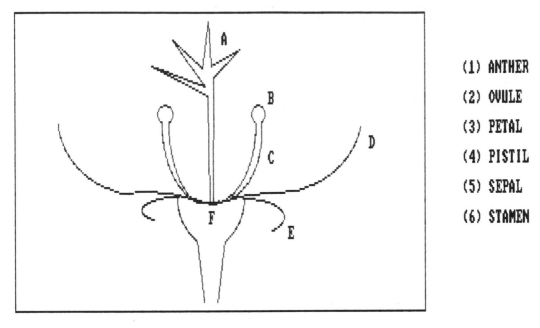

TYPE THE NUMBER OF PART B FROM THE LIST AT RIGHT:

Figure 13–2 Picture displayed as part of a self-study program.

13–3 SIMULATION PROGRAMS

We use simulation programs to demonstrate the behavior of various types of systems. An actual physical or biological model (or a hypothetical system) can be displayed in a lecture demonstration or as part of an individual study program. Simulation programs are particularly effective for studying systems with many parameters or systems that we cannot actually observe. Models of geopolitical systems, atomic and molecular structures, or relativistic motion of objects are examples of such systems. We can vary the parameters involved in these systems and watch the changes occur on the screen.

In many graphics simulations, we want to demonstrate complex motions, as in Prog. 13–2. Here, we produce an animated model of the solar system. Figure 13–3 shows several positions along the paths of motion of the moon and earth as they rotate about the sun. The actual output of Prog. 13–2 presents only one position at a time, erasing previous positions. Circular paths are used, and the objects are not drawn to scale.

Simulation programs can be designed as educational games. A gunnery game that plots the trajectory to a target, based on choices for projection angle, can be an effective learning program. This program can help in grasping the geometrical meaning of angular values, as well as demonstrating the relation between trajectory and angle of projection.

Program 13–2 Simulation: modeling the solar system with rotating moon and earth.

```
10  'PROGRAM 13-2. SOLAR SYSTEM.
20      'ILLUSTRATES MOTION OF SOLAR SYSTEM. MOON REVOLVES AROUND
30      'EARTH 12 TIMES FOR EVERY ONE REVOLUTION OF THE EARTH
40      'AROUND THE SUN. THE MOON'S ORBIT (RM) IS CHOSEN TO BE ONLY
50      'ONE-SIXTH AS LARGE AS THE EARTH'S (RE) -- SO THE MOON'S
60      'ANGULAR INCREMENT (1 DIVIDED BY THE RADIUS) IS SIX TIMES
70      'AS LARGE. USING STEP 1/RE AND 1/RM, THE MOON WOULD TRAVEL
80      'THROUGH ITS ORBIT SIX TIMES AS FAST AS THE EARTH. WE PLOT
90      'A NEW POSITION FOR THE MOON TWICE FOR EVERY POSITION OF THE
100     'EARTH, SO THE MOON TRAVELS TWELVE TIMES AS FAST.
110     '************************************************************
120 CLEARSCREEN
130 XS = 128        'PUT SUN AT CENTER OF A 256 x 192 SCREEN
140 YS = 96
150 RE = 72         'RE IS RADIUS OF EARTH'S ORBIT
160 RM = 12         'RM IS RADIUS OF MOON'S ORBIT
170 S = 15          'S IS RADIUS OF SUN
180 E = 5           'E IS RADIUS OF EARTH
190 M = 3           'M IS RADIUS OF MOON
200 GRAPHICS
210 CIRCLEPLOT XS,YS,S            'DRAW SUN
220 MO = 1/RM                     'ANGULAR INCREMENT FOR MOON IS 1/RM
230 FOR EO = 1/RE TO 6.28318 STEP 1/RE          'FOR EARTH IS 1/RE
240     COLOR 0,0
250     CIRCLEPLOT XE,YE,E                'ERASE EARTH
260     XE = XS + RE * COS(EO)
270     YE = YS + RE * SIN(EO)
280     COLOR 1,0
290     CIRCLEPLOT XE,YE,E                'DRAW EARTH
300     COLOR 0,0
310     CIRCLEPLOT XM,YM,M                'ERASE MOON
320     XM = XE + RM * COS(MO)
330     YM = YE + RM * SIN(MO)
340     COLOR 1,0
350     CIRCLEPLOT XM,YM,M                'DRAW MOON
360     MO = MO + 1/RM
370     COLOR 0,0
380     CIRCLEPLOT XM,YM,M                'ERASE MOON
390     XM = XE + RM * COS(MO)
400     YM = YE + RM * SIN(MO)
410     COLOR 1,0
420     CIRCLEPLOT XM,YM,M                'DRAW MOON
430     MO = MO + 1/RM
440 NEXT EO
450 GOTO 220
460 END
```

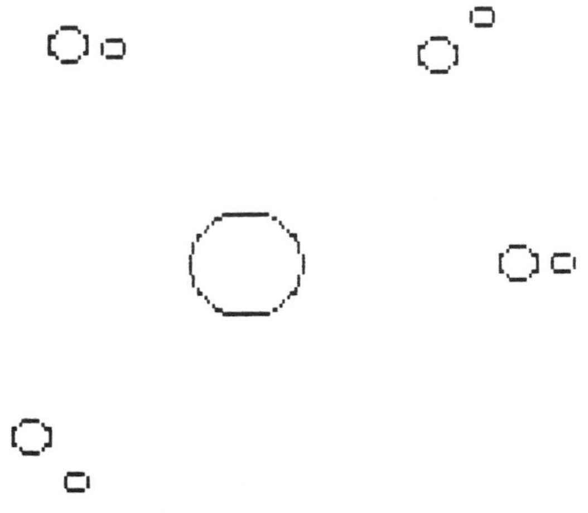

Figure 13–3 Simulation of the motion of the earth and moon about the sun, showing several positions from the output of Prog. 13–2.

13–4 COMPUTER-MANAGED INSTRUCTION

Graphics programs can be used as aids in record keeping and grading. Computer-managed instruction (CMI) programs can be designed to maintain records of grades, calculate grades, and provide statistics. We can use CMI programs to output graphs of grading distributions for a single exam, for a single course, for a particular course over several years, or for all courses taught during any time interval.

Chapter 14

Personal Graphics

For our final look at applications, we will discuss a few ways that we can put graphics to work for us personally. We can create personal graphics programs for recreation, education, or profit.

14–1 HOUSEHOLD GRAPHICS

There are many kinds of financial applications of graphics that can be useful for our home use. We can plot our various expenses or interest payments, analyze returns on investments, or graph potential savings due to energy conservation improvements to the home. Program 14–1 is an example of a monthly budget program to compare expenses. We have included only four categories of expenses in this example (Fig. 14–1). The bars are drawn for this graph to show percentage of expenditures in each category for one month. Many other types of expense graphs could be plotted. We could also accumulate weekly and monthly expenses in a data file. Then a budget program could be used to compare expenses over several months or years.

Program 14–1 Household budget bar chart.

```
10 'PROGRAM 14-1. HOUSEHOLD BUDGET SUMMARY
20      'PLOTS A BAR GRAPH OF MONTHLY HOUSEHOLD EXPENSES.
30      'BARS PLOTTED ARE THE PERCENTAGE OF THE TOTAL
40      'EXPENSES FOR THE MONTH. ALSO PRINTS THE ACTUAL
50      'EXPENSES IN EACH CATEGORY -- FOOD, CLOTHING,
60      'HOUSING, AND RECREATION. SCREEN SIZE IS 320 BY 200 PIXELS.
70      '*********************** INPUT DATA ***********************
80   CLEARSCREEN
90   D = INT(290 / 4)     'FOUR CATEGORIES OF EXPENSES
```

Program 14-1 (cont.)

```
100 RS = (172 - 12)          'RS IS RANGE OF PIXELS FOR BARS
110 T = 0                    'T IS TOTAL OF ALL EXPENSES
120 PRINT "ENTER MONTH NAME"
130 INPUT M$
140 PRINT
150 PRINT "F -FOOD        H -HOUSING & UTILITIES     C -CLOTHING    R -RECREATION"
160 PRINT
170 PRINT "ENTER EXPENSE AND CATEGORY CODE.        ENTER 0,Q TO QUIT"
180 INPUT E, C$
190 IF E = 0 AND C$ = "Q" THEN 300
200 IF C$ = "F" OR C$ = "H" OR C$ = "C" OR C$ = "R" THEN 230
210 PRINT "INCORRECT EXPENSE CODE"
220 GOTO 180
230 T = T + E
240     'ADD UP EXPENSES FOR EACH CATEGORY
250 IF C$ = "F" THEN FT = FT + E
260 IF C$ = "H" THEN HT = HT + E
270 IF C$ = "C" THEN CT = CT + E
280 IF C$ = "R" THEN RT = RT + E
290 GOTO 180
300     '*********************** DRAW GRID AND LABELS ******************
310 CLEARSCREEN
320 GRAPHICS
330 DRAWLINE 25,12 TO 25,172
340 DRAWLINE 25,172 TO 315,172
350 POSITION 1,1          'PRINT MONTH
360 P = 20 - LEN(M$) / 2          'CENTER THE MONTH
370 PRINT TAB(P);M$
380 RO = 22
390 Y = 172
400 FOR K = 0 TO 4                'LABEL VERTICAL AXIS WITH SUCCESSIVE FIFTHS
410     POSITION RO,1             'OF THE SCALING RANGE
420     L = LO + 100 * K / 5
430     PRINT USING "###";L
440     RO = RO - 4
450     Y = Y - 32
460 NEXT K
470 POSITION 2,1
480 PRINT "PERCENT";
490     'LABEL THE DIVISIONS
500 POSITION 23,1
510 PRINT "      FOOD      HOUSE     CLOTHES   LEISURE";
520     '*************************** MAKE BARS ************************
530 YO = 171
540 X1 = 25 + D/4          'START FIRST BAR 1/4 OVER IN FIRST DIVISION
550 Y = INT((1 - FT/T) * RS + 12.5)        'EACH EXPENSE CATEGORY IS WHAT % OF
560 GOSUB 700                              'THE TOTAL? SUBTRACT FROM 1 (SO BARS
570 Y = INT((1 - HT/T) * RS + 12.5)        'WILL GO UP SCREEN) AND MULTIPLY BY
580 GOSUB 700                              'THE RANGE OF PIXELS USED FOR BARS
590 Y = INT((1 - CT/T) * RS + 12.5)
600 GOSUB 700
610 Y = INT((1 - RT/T) * RS + 12.5)
620 GOSUB 700
630 POSITION 24,1
640 PRINT USING " $####.##    ####.##    ####.##    ####.##";FT;HT;CT;RT;
650 POSITION 3,24
660 PRINT "TOTAL EXPENSES";
670 POSITION 4,30
```

Program 14-1 (cont.)

```
680 PRINT USING "$####.##";T
690 GOTO 770
700 '########################## MAKE BAR ##############################
710 FOR X = X1 TO X1 + D / 2
720     DRAWLINE X,Y TO X,YO
730 NEXT X
740 X1 = X1 + D
750 RETURN
760 '#####################################################################
770 END
```

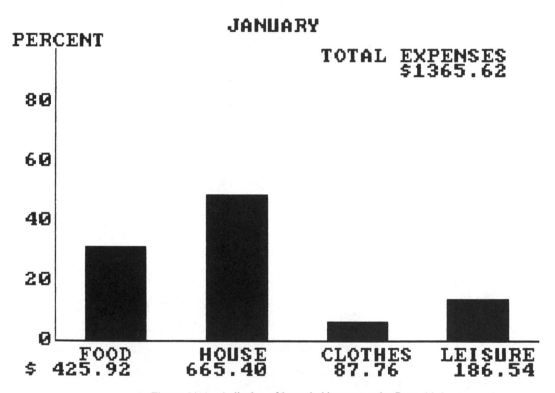

Figure 14–1   A display of household expenses by Prog. 14–1.

We can use graphs and charts for various nonfinancial home uses. A daily nutrition chart is shown in Fig. 14–2. This chart is the output of Prog. 14–2, which calculates the daily caloric intake and plots the percentages of calories from protein, carbohydrate, and fat sources in our diet. We could store this daily information in a data file and modify Prog. 14–2 to plot long-term comparisons. A more complete file of food types and food components could also be set up for such a program.

Program 14-2 Nutrition graph, plotting calories and nutrients in two bar charts
and a pie chart.

```
10 'PROGRAM 14-2. NUTRITION ANALYSIS.
20      'READS FOOD NAMES & RELATED QUANTITIES FROM DATA STATEMENTS
30      'INTO ARRAYS. READS THE NUMBER OF GRAMS OF FAT,
40      'CARBOHYDRATES, PROTEIN, POTASSIUM, AND SODIUM FOR
50      'AN AVERAGE SIZE SERVING. WE ENTER THE FOOD NAMES WE'VE
60      'EATEN FOR THE DAY. GRAMS OF FAT, PROTEIN, ETC. ARE ADDED
70      'FOR ALL THE DIFFERENT FOODS. GRAMS OF PROTEIN, FAT, AND
80      'CARBOHYDRATE ARE CONVERTED TO TOTAL NUMBER OF CALORIES
90      'CONSUMED. A PIE CHART SHOWING PERCENT OF TOTAL CALORIES
100     'FROM CARBOHYDRATE, FAT, AND PROTEIN SOURCES IS DISPLAYED.
110     'ALSO DRAWS TWO BAR CHARTS -- ONE SHOWING NUMBER GRAMS OF
120     'FAT, CARBOHYDRATE, AND PROTEIN; SECOND SHOWS NUMBER OF
130     'GRAMS OF POTASSIUM AND SODIUM CONSUMED. ASSUMES A SCREEN
140     'SIZE OF 320 BY 200 PIXELS. BARS ARE SCALED TO 12 - 172.
150     '*******************************************************
160 CLEARSCREEN
170 DIM F$(10),FA(10),CA(10),PR(10),PO(10),SO(10)
180 YA = 5/6
190 FOR K = 1 TO 10
200      READ F$(K),FA(K),CA(K),PR(K),PO(K),SO(K)
210 NEXT K
220     '***************** INPUT CHART LABELS AND DATA ***************
230 PRINT "ENTER EACH FOOD ITEM NAME. ENTER DONE TO QUIT"
240 INPUT F1$
250 IF F1$ = "DONE" THEN 370
260 FOR K = 1 TO 10        'FIND FOOD NAME IN ARRAY
270      IF F1$ = F$(K) THEN 310
280 NEXT K
290 PRINT "NOT FOUND. RE-ENTER OR ENTER NEXT FOOD NAME"
300 GOTO 240
310 FAT = FAT + FA(K)              'SUM UP FOOD COMPONENTS
320 CAT = CAT + CA(K)
330 PRT = PRT + PR(K)
340 POT = POT + PO(K)
350 SOT = SOT + SO(K)
360 GOTO 240
370     '******************** DRAW GRID AND LABELS ****************
380 CLEARSCREEN
390 GRAPHICS
400 H1 = PRT                  'FIND HIGHEST VALUE FOR FIRST BAR CHART
410 IF FAT > H1 THEN H1 = FAT
420 IF CAT > H1 THEN H1 = CAT
430 R1 = (172 - 12) / H1        'R1 IS SCALING RATIO TO USE FOR FIRST CHART
440 H2 = POT                  'FIND HIGHEST VALUE FOR SECOND BAR CHART
450 IF SOT > H2 THEN H2 = SOT
460 R2 = (172 - 12) / H2        'R2 IS SCALING RATIO TO USE FOR SECOND CHART
470 DRAWLINE 256,12 TO 256,172
480 DRAWLINE 256,172 TO 319,172
490 DRAWLINE 144,12 TO 144,172
500 DRAWLINE 144,172 TO 214,172
510 RO = 22
520 Y = 172
530 FOR K = 0 TO 5              'LABEL VERTICAL AXIS WITH SUCCESSIVE FIFTHS
540      POSITION RO,17            'OF THE SCALING RANGE
550      L = H1 * K / 5
560      PRINT USING "###";L;
570      POSITION RO,31
580      L = H2 * K / 5
590      PRINT USING "#.##";L;
600      RO = RO - 4
610      Y = Y - 32
620 NEXT K
630 POSITION 1,18
```

280

```
640 PRINT "GRAMS          GRAMS";
650    'LABEL THE DIVISIONS
660 POSITION 23,21
670 PRINT "F C P          P S";
680 POSITION 24,21
690 PRINT "A A P          O O";
700 POSITION 25,21
710 PRINT "T R O          T D";
720 '
730    '************************* MAKE BARS *************************
740 YO = 171
750 X1 = 160
760 Y = INT((H1 - FAT) * R1 + 12.5)
770 COLOR 2,0              'BLUE
780 GOSUB 910              'GO MAKE BAR
790 Y = INT((H1 - CAT) * R1 + 12.5)
800 COLOR 5,0              'YELLOW
810 GOSUB 910              'GO MAKE BAR
820 Y = INT((H1 - PRT) * R1 + 12.5)
830 COLOR 4,0              'GREEN
840 GOSUB 910              'GO MAKE BAR
850 X1 = 280              'MOVE OVER FOR SECOND BAR CHART
860 Y = INT((H2 - SOT) * R2 + 12.5)
870 GOSUB 910                  'GO MAKE BAR
880 Y = INT((H2 - POT) * R2 + 12.5)
890 GOSUB 910                  'GO MAKE BAR
900 GOTO 980
910    'MAKE BAR
920 FOR X = X1 TO X1 + 8
930    DRAWLINE X,Y TO X,YO
940 NEXT X
950 X1 = X1 + 16          'MOVE OVER FOR NEXT BAR
960 RETURN
970 '
980 '############################ MAKE PIECHART #######################
990 XC = 45
1000 YC = 78
1010 R = 40
1020 FAC = FAT * 9          'CONVERT GRAMS TO CALORIES
1030 CAC = CAT * 4
1040 PRC = PRT * 4
1050 CAL = FAC + CAC + PRC        'FIND TOTAL CALORIES
1060 POSITION 3,1
1070 PRINT "CALORIES - ";
1080 POSITION 4,3
1090 PRINT USING "####";CAL;
1100 POSITION 17,1
1110 PRINT "% OF TOTAL";
1120 POSITION 18,1
1130 PRINT "  FROM -";
1140 S = 0
1150 B = 0
1160 S = S + FAC
1170 COLOR 2,0            'BLUE
1180 GOSUB 1320          'MAKE PIE SECTION FOR FAT CALORIES
1190 S = S + CAC
1200 COLOR 5,0            'YELLOW
1210 GOSUB 1320          'MAKE PIE SECTION FOR CARBOHYDRATE CALORIES
1220 S = S + PRC
1230 COLOR 4,0            'GREEN
1240 GOSUB 1320          'MAKE PIE SECTION FOR PROTEIN CALORIES
1250 POSITION 20,1
1260 PRINT "FAT";TAB(10);USING"##";FAC/CAL*100;
1270 POSITION 21,1
```

```
1280 PRINT "CARBO";TAB(10);USING "##";CAC/CAL*100;
1290 POSITION 22,1
1300 PRINT "PROTEIN";TAB(10);USING "##";PRC/CAL*100;
1310 GOTO 1540
1320 '################ DRAW AND FILL IN PIECHART AREA ###############
1330 DA = 1/R/50          'NEED SMALL STEP TO FILL IN CIRCLE WITH SOLID COLOR
1340 A = 6.28318 * S / CAL                'A IS ANGLE OF END OF THIS SLICE
1350 FOR A1 = B TO A STEP DA              'B IS ANGLE OF END OF LAST SLICE
1360      XP = XC + R * COS(A1)
1370      YP = YC + R * SIN(A1) * YA
1380      DRAWLINE XP,YP TO XC,YC
1390 NEXT A1
1400 B = A
1410 RETURN
1420 '###########################################################
1430 DATA MILK,12,9,9,.122,.351
1440 DATA BACON,1,8,5,.163,.038
1450 DATA HADDOCK,5,6,20,.177,.348
1460 DATA TUNA,0,18,21,.688,.259
1470 DATA EGG,0,6,7,.066,.070
1480 DATA SPINACH,3,0,2,.040,.259
1490 DATA CORN,1.4,26.32,4.48,0,.231
1500 DATA DATES,.89,129,3.9,.002,1.15
1510 DATA LIVER,.6,.3,1.5,.022,3.04
1520 DATA CHILI,5.2,10.4,6.4,.001,.45
1530 '###########################################################
1540 END
```

Figure 14–2 Nutrition chart produced by Prog. 14–2.

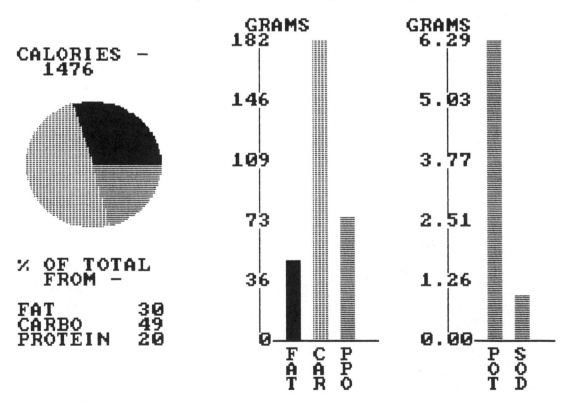

282

Program 14–3 produces a biorhythm graph, as shown in Fig. 14–3. This graph plots the theoretical ups and downs of our physical, emotional, and intellectual energy levels. The algorithm used for this graph assumes a 23-day cycle for the physical curve, a 28-day cycle for the emotional curve, and a 33-day cycle for the intellectual curve.

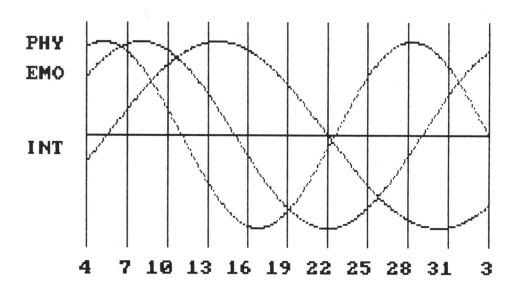

Figure 14–3 Biorhythm graph displayed by Prog. 14–3 for a birth date of August 4, 1963.

Program 14–3 Biorhythm graph.

```
10 'PROGRAM 14-3. BIORHYTHM
20     'GIVEN AN INDIVIDUAL'S BIRTHDATE AND A STARTING DATE,
30     'CONSTRUCTS BIORHYTHM CHART (WITH CURVES FOR EMOTIONAL
40     'PHYSICAL, AND INTELLECTUAL CYCLES) FOR THE NEXT 30 DAYS.
50     'CURVES ARE DRAWN WITH LABELS PLACED NEAR THE CURVES.
60     'LABELS ARE PLACED ON THE LEFT SIDE UNLESS ANY TWO
70     'OF THE CURVES START TOO CLOSE TOGETHER  -- THEN ONE OF
80     'THE LABELS IS MOVED TO THE RIGHT SIDE OF CHART. ASSUMES
90     'SCREEN SIZE OF 320 BY 200 PIXELS.
100    '*******************************************************************
110 CLEARSCREEN
120 DIM M$(12), DM(12), AD(13)
130 FOR K = 1 TO 12            'READ MONTH NAME, # OF DAYS IN MONTH, AND
140     READ M$(K), DM(K), AD(K)      'ACCUMULATED DAYS
150 NEXT K
```

Program 14-3 (cont.)

```
160 PR = 8        'PR IS NUMBER OF VERTICAL PIXELS PER CHARACTER
170 PI = 3.14159
180 H = 50                    'H IS HEIGHT OF THE CURVES
190 RR = (284 - 44) / 30          'RR IS SCALING RATIO - 30 X'S WILL USE 44-284
200     '
210     '*********************** INPUT DATE DATA *********************
220 PRINT "ENTER BIRTHDATE (MONTH,DAY,YEAR)"
230 INPUT MB,DB,YB
240 PRINT "ENTER START DATE FOR CHART (MONTH,DAY,YEAR)
250 INPUT MC,DC,YC
260     'FIND TIME BETWEEN CHART DATE AND BIRTH DATE
270 T = (YC-YB) * 365.25 + (AD(MC) - AD(MB)) + (DC - DB)
280     'FIND DISPLACEMENT FOR EACH CURVE
290 PD = 2 * PI * (T / 23 - INT(T / 23))
300 ED = 2 * PI * (T / 28 - INT(T / 28))
310 ID = 2 * PI * (T / 33 - INT(T / 33))
320     'FIND FREQUENCY FOR EACH CURVE
330 PW = 2 * PI / 23
340 EW = 2 * PI / 28
350 IW = 2 * PI / 33
360     '
370     '*********************** DRAW GRID *********************
380 CLEARSCREEN
390 GRAPHICS
400 POSITION 1,15
410 PRINT "BIORHYTHM"
420 POSITION 3,20-(13+LEN(M$(MC)))/2
430 PRINT "STARTING "; M$(MC); YC;
440 D = DC
450 X = 44
460 FOR CO = 5 TO 35 STEP 3
470     POSITION 22,CO
480     PRINT USING "##";D;
490     D = D + 3
500     IF D <= DM(MC) THEN 520          'STILL THE SAME MONTH?
510     D = D - DM(MC)                   'SET D TO START OF NEXT MONTH
520     DRAWLINE X,40 TO X,160
530     X = X + 24
540 NEXT CO
550 DRAWLINE 44,100 TO 284,100           'MAKE LINE AT GRAPH 0
560 POSITION 25,8
570 PRINT "BIRTHDATE:";DB;MB;YB
580     '*********************** DRAW CURVES *********************
590 FOR X = 0 TO 30 STEP .1
600     PY = INT(H * SIN(PW * X + PD) + .5)
610     XG = X * RR + 44          'SCALE THIS X TO AN X FOR THE GRAPH
620     POINTPLOT XG,PY+100
630     EY = INT(H * SIN(EW * X + ED) + .5)
640     POINTPLOT XG,EY+100
650     IY = INT(H * SIN(IW * X + ID) + .5)
660     POINTPLOT XG,IY+100
670     IF X = 0 THEN GOSUB 780          'GO DO LABELING
680 NEXT X
690 IF EL$ <> "YES" THEN 730     'NEED TO DO ANY LABELS ON RIGHT?
700 EP = INT((EY + 100) / PR + .5)
710 POSITION EP,38
720 PRINT "EMO";
730 IF IL$ <> "YES" THEN 770
740 IP = INT((IY + 100) / PR + .5)
```

Program 14-3 (cont.)

```
750 POSITION IP,38
760 PRINT "INT";
770 GOTO 970
780 '############### LABELING ON LEFT #######################
790 PP = INT((PY + 100) / PR + .5)   'PRINT POSITION FOR PHYSICAL
800 POSITION PP,2
810 PRINT "PHY";
820 EP = INT((EY + 100) / PR + .5)   'PRINT POSITION FOR EMOTIONAL
830 IF EP = PP THEN EL$ = "YES"            'WILL NEED LABEL ON RIGHT
840 IF EL$ = "YES" THEN 870
850 POSITION EP,2
860 PRINT "EMO";
870 IP = INT((IY + 100) / PR + .5)
880 IF IP = PP OR IP = EP THEN IL$ = "YES"  'WILL NEED LABEL ON RIGHT
890 IF IL$ = "YES" THEN 920
900 POSITION IP,2
910 PRINT "INT";
920 RETURN
930     '*****************************************************************
940 DATA JANUARY,31,0,FEBRUARY,28,31,MARCH,31,59,APRIL,30,90,MAY,31,120
950 DATA JUNE,30,151,JULY,31,181,AUGUST,31,212,SEPTEMBER,30,243
960 DATA OCTOBER,31,273,NOVEMBER,30,304,DECEMBER,31,334
970 END
```

Computer-generated pictures can be devised for many types of home use. We can create pictures for inclusion in graphs, in educational programs, as parts of games, or for decoration. A printed picture can be used as a wall decoration or on personally designed greeting cards. We could also create small pictures or designs for personalized stationery.

14–2 GAME PLAYING

Games can be both fun and educational. We can devise games that teach about numbers, arithmetic, letters, words, or spelling. Some games can help develop coordination.

With Prog. 14–4, we produce a ball and paddle game that requires some coordination to keep the ball in play. This program takes the box and bouncing ball of Chapter 7 and adds a paddle in place of the left wall. The ball starts at a random position within the box. Whenever the ball gets to the left side, we must bounce it back into the box. If we miss, the ball goes outside the box and stops. The number of consecutive times that we are able to bounce the ball off the paddle is our score. After every five paddle bounces, the ball speeds up a little. Figure 14–4 shows the display at the end of the game for one possible score. We could play this game alone and see how high we can score in a single game, or we could play in teams, adding the scores each time until one team reaches 100.

Program 14–4   Bouncing ball and paddle game.

```
10 'PROGRAM 14-4. BOUNCING BALL GAME.
20      'DRAWS THREE-SIDED BOX AND A PADDLE ON THE LEFT SIDE.
30      'BALL BOUNCES IN BOX (DX = DY = 5 AT GAME START) AND
40      'AGAINST PADDLE. PADDLE MUST BE POSITIONED, THROUGH
50      'KEYBOARD INPUT (HITTING "U" FOR UP AND "D" FOR DOWN).
60      'SPEED OF BALL INCREASES (BY INCREASING DX AND DY) WHEN-
70      'EVER BALL IS HIT BY PADDLE 5 TIMES AT THE SAME SPEED.
80      'SCORE IS UPDATED BY 1 FOR EVERY SUCCESSFUL BOUNCE OFF
90      'THE PADDLE. GAME CONTINUES UNTIL BALL IS MISSED BY PADDLE.
100     '*************************************************************
110 CLEARSCREEN
120 XL = 50      'XL,XR,YT,YB ARE BOUNDARIES OF BOX
130 XR = 300
140 YT = 20
150 YB = 160
160 YP = 160     'YP IS TOP POINT OF PADDLE
170 R = 3        'R IS RADIUS OF BALL
180 DX = 5       'BALL INITIALLY TRAVELS 5 UNITS IN EACH STEP
190 DY = 5
200 GRAPHICS
210     '*************************** DRAW BOX *************************
220 DRAWLINE XL,YT TO XR,YT
230 DRAWLINE XR,YT TO XR,YB
240 DRAWLINE XR,YB TO XL,YB
250 DRAWLINE XL,YP TO XL,YP+40   'DRAW PADDLE
260     '*************************** BOUNCE BALL *********************
270 XN = XL + INT((XR-XL) / 2)   'START BALL IN MIDDLE OF BOX
280 YN = YT + INT((YB-YT) / 2)
290 S = 0                        'S IS CURRENT SCORE
300 POSITION 1,36
310 PRINT USING "##";S
320 COLOR 0,0
330 CIRCLEPLOT X,Y,R             'ERASE CURRENT BALL POSITION
340 COLOR 1,0
350 CIRCLEPLOT XN,YN,R           'DRAW NEW POSITION
360     'MOVE PADDLE
370 A$ = INKEY$
380 IF A$ = "" THEN 450
390 COLOR 0,0
400 DRAWLINE XL,YP TO XL,YP+40            'ERASE CURRENT PADDLE POSITION
410 IF A$ = "D" THEN YP = YP + 15
420 IF A$ = "U" THEN YP = YP - 15
430 COLOR 1,0
440 DRAWLINE XL,YP TO XL,YP+40             'DRAW NEW PADDLE
450 X = XN                       'SAVE CURRENT POSITION IN X AND Y
460 Y = YN
470 BX = 0                       'BX AND BY ARE SWITCHES TO INDICATE
480 BY = 0                       'WHICH WALL WE'RE GOING TO HIT
490 M = DY / DX                  'M IS SLOPE OF BALL'S PATH
500     '
510     '*************************************************************
520     'WILL WE HIT A VERTICAL WALL?
530 IF DX > 0 THEN 600           'WE'RE GOING TO THE RIGHT
540     'OTHERWISE WE'RE GOING TO THE LEFT (DX IS NEGATIVE)
550 IF X + DX - R > XL THEN 650          'WE'RE STILL WITHIN THE BOX
560 BX = 1                       'GOING OUT OF BOX AT AN X WALL
570 XN = XL + R + 1              'NEW X IS JUST INSIDE LEFT WALL
580 GOTO 650
590     '^^^^^^^^^^^^^^^^^^^^^^^^^^^^^^^^^^^^^^^^^^^^^^^^^^^^^^^^^^^^^
600     'GOING RIGHT
610 IF X + DX + R < XR THEN 650         'WE'RE STILL WITHIN THE BOX
620 BX = 1                       'GOING OUT OF BOX AT AN X WALL
630 XN = XR - R - 1              'NEW X IS JUST INSIDE RIGHT WALL
```

```
640      '**********************************************************
650      'WILL WE HIT A HORIZONTAL WALL?
660 IF DY > O THEN 730              'WE'RE GOING DOWN
670      'OTHERWISE WE'RE GOING UP (DY IS NEGATIVE)
680 IF Y + DY - R > YT THEN 790         'WE'RE STILL WITHIN THE BOX
690 BY = 1                          'GOING OUT OF BOX AT A Y WALL
700 YN = YT + R + 1                 'NEW Y IS JUST INSIDE OF TOP
710 GOTO 790
720      '^^^^^^^^^^^^^^^^^^^^^^^^^^^^^^^^^^^^^^^^^^^^^^^^^^^^^^^^
730      'GOING DOWN
740 IF Y + DY + R < YB THEN 790         'WE'RE STILL WITHIN THE BOX
750 BY = 1                          'GOING OUT OF BOX AT A Y WALL
760 YN = YB - R - 1                 'NEW Y IS JUST INSIDE OF BOTTOM
770      '
780      '**********************************************************
790      'ARE WE BOUNCING OFF NO WALLS, AN X WALL, A Y WALL, OR BOTH WALLS?
800 IF BX = O AND BY = O THEN 850       'NOT BOUNCING
810 IF BX = O AND BY = 1 THEN 890        'BOUNCING OFF Y
820 IF BX = 1 AND BY = O THEN 930        'BOUNCING OFF X
830 IF BX = 1 AND BY = 1 THEN 1060        'BOUNCING OFF BOTH (IN A CORNER)
840 '
850 '##################### NOT BOUNCING #########################
860 XN = X + DX
870 YN = Y + DY
880 GOTO 330
890 '##################### BOUNCE OFF Y WALL ####################
900 XN = (YN - Y) / M + X
910 DY = - DY
920 GOTO 330
930 '##################### BOUNCE OFF X WALL ####################
940 YN = (XN - X) * M + Y
950 IF DX > O THEN 1040         'WE'RE GOING TO THE RIGHT
960     'GOING TOWARDS PADDLE. IS PADDLE IN GOOD POSITION?
970 IF YN < YP OR YN > YP+40 THEN 1140  'BALL IS MISSED BY PADDLE
980 S = S + 1                    'INCREASE SCORE
990 POSITION 1,36
1000 PRINT USING "##";S;
1010 IF S/5 <> INT(S/5) THEN 1040         'IF EQUAL, TIME TO SPEED UP BALL
1020 IF DX < O THEN DX = DX - 5
1030 IF DX > O THEN DX = DX + 5
1040 DX = -DX
1050 GOTO 330
1060 '##################### GOING INTO A CORNER ##################
1070     'WHICH WALL WOULD IT HIT FIRST?
1080 IF ABS(XN - X) < ABS(YN - Y) THEN 930         'BOUNCE OFF X
1090 IF ABS(YN - Y) < ABS(XN - X) THEN 890         'BOUNCE OFF Y
1100     'BALL IS EQUAL DISTANCE FROM X AND Y WALLS ON EACH SIDE OF CORNER
1110 DX = -DX
1120 DY = -DY
1130 GOTO 330
1140 '#################### MISSED THE BALL ######################
1150 XN = XL - R - 8       'DROP THE BALL DOWN TO THE GROUND ALONG
1160 YN = (XN - X) * M + Y                'LEFT SIDE OF BOX
1170 COLOR 0,0
1180 CIRCLEPLOT X,Y,R
1190 FOR YN = YN TO 190 STEP 5
1200     COLOR 0,0
1210     CIRCLEPLOT X,Y,R
1220     COLOR 1,0
1230     CIRCLEPLOT XN,YN,R
1240     FOR J = 1 TO 100: NEXT J
1250     Y = YN
1260     X = XN
```

Program 14-4 (cont.)

```
1270 NEXT YN
1280 '#################### PRINT THE SCORE ############################
1290 IF S < 24 THEN 1320
1300 Z$ = "INCREDIBLE"
1310 GOTO 1450
1320 IF S < 19 THEN 1350
1330 Z$ = "OUTSTANDING!"
1340 GOTO 1450
1350 IF S < 14 THEN 1380
1360 Z$ = "PRETTY GOOD"
1370 GOTO 1450
1380 IF S < 9 THEN 1410
1390 Z$ = "FAIR"
1400 GOTO 1450
1410 IF S < 4 THEN 1440
1420 Z$ = "IMPROVING"
1430 GOTO 1450
1440 Z$ = "AWFUL"
1450 POSITION 10,10
1460 PRINT "YOUR SCORE IS ";Z$
1470 POSITION 13,12
1480    '#################### PLAY AGAIN OR END? #################
1490 PRINT "LIKE TO PLAY AGAIN";
1500 INPUT C$
1510 IF C$ = "Y" THEN 180
1520 END
```

Figure 14–4 Two displays from the ball and paddle game of Prog. 14–4.

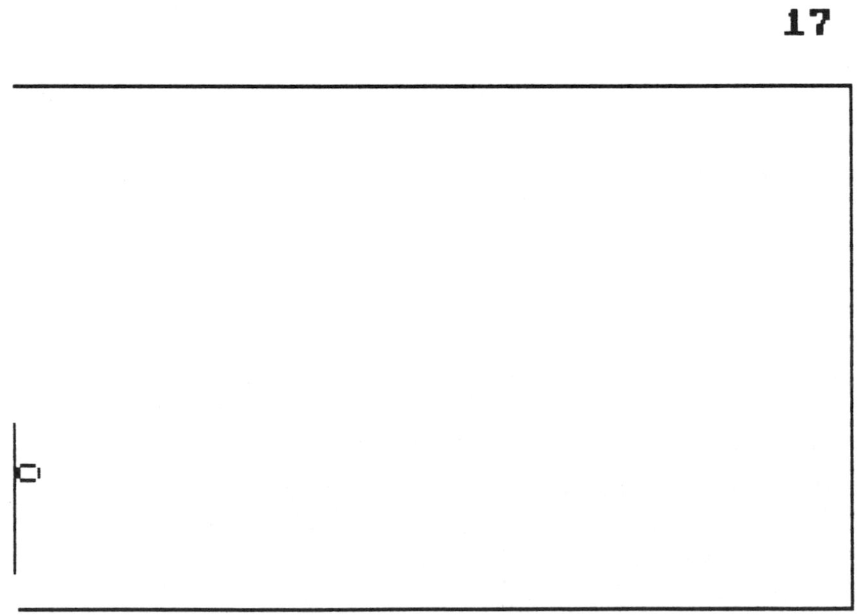

17

(a)

Figure 14-4 (cont.)

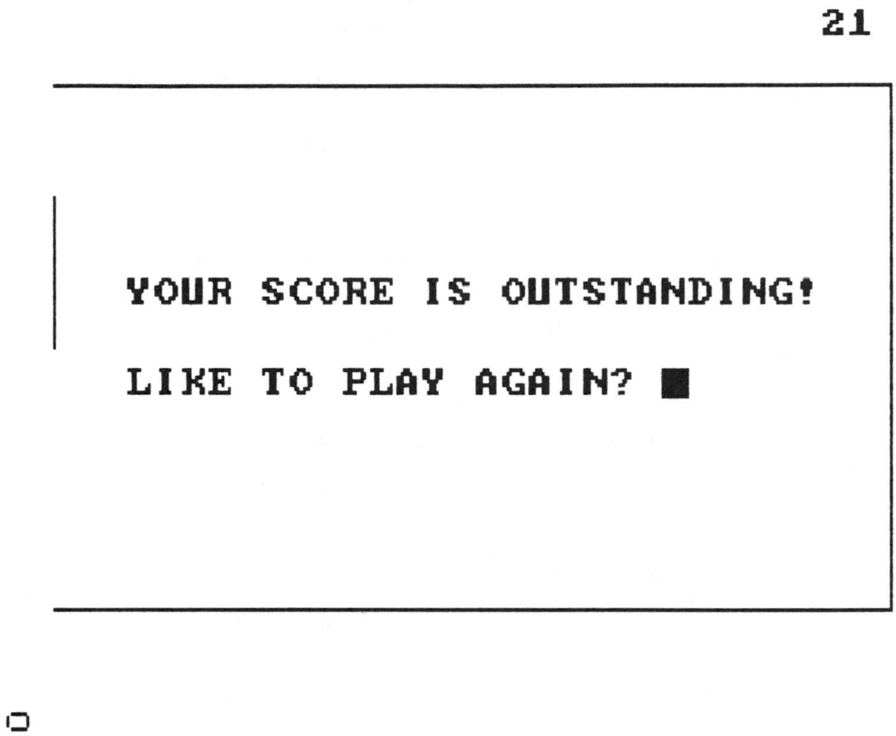

21

```
YOUR SCORE IS OUTSTANDING!

LIKE TO PLAY AGAIN? ■
```

(b)

Our final example is the archery game of Prog. 14–5. A box is placed at a random position on the right half of the screen, and we try to hit it with an arrow shot from the lower left corner. We choose an angle and an initial speed, and the arrow travels along a parabolic path, as discussed in Chapter 7. We have three shots from a quiver of arrows (Fig. 14–5) for each box. The program generates five boxes for each game, and displays the current box number and accumulated score. We count a hit on the first shot as 10 points, a hit on the second shot as 5 points, and a hit on the third shot as 2 points.

With many microcomputers, we can add sound output to programs. Sounds can be used with our games to coincide with the bounce of a ball or the landing of an arrow. We could even play a tune at the end of a game. Generating sounds can slow the processing unless the system has the capability to produce sound at the same time as the other processing is carried out.

Program 14–5 Arrow and target game.

```
10 'PROGRAM 14-5. ARROW AND TARGET GAME.
20      'REPEATEDLY DRAWS AND ERASES AN ARROW WHOSE TAIL
30      'IS A POINT ON A PARABOLA. REMAINDER OF THE ARROW
40      'IS FOUND USING THIS TAIL POINT, THE SLOPE OF THE
50      'LINE TANGENT TO THE CURVE AT THIS POINT, AND THE
60      'LENGTH OF THE ARROW
```

Program 14-5 (cont.)

```
70      '**********************************************************
80  XM = 319
90  YM = 199
100 XO = 15        'XO,YO IS STARTING POSITION OF ARROW
110 YO = 180
120 GRAPHICS
130 T = 1
140 SC = 0
150     '************* DRAW BOX TARGET AND PLAY *****************
160 CLEARSCREEN
170 GOSUB 1130          'DRAW QUIVER
180 J = 1        'J IS NUMBER OF ATTEMPTS AT THIS TARGET
190 POSITION 25,30
200 PRINT "SCORE";
210 POSITION 25,35
220 PRINT SC;
230 XL = 100 + RND(1) * 180      'RANDOMLY PLACE LEFT EDGE OF BOX
240 XR = XL + 35
250 YT = RND(1) * 165            'RANDOMLY PLACE TOP EDGE OF BOX
260 YB = YT + 35
270 DRAWLINE XL,YT TO XL,YB      'DRAW BOX
280 DRAWLINE XL,YB TO XR,YB
290 DRAWLINE XR,YB TO XR,YT
300 DRAWLINE XR,YT TO XL,YT
310     '************* CHOOSE ARROW ANGLE, SPEED ******************
320 POSITION 1,1
330 PRINT "                              ";
340 POSITION 1,1
350 PRINT "ANGLE (0-90)";
360 INPUT A
370 IF A >= 0 AND A <= 90 THEN 390
380 GOTO 350
390 A = A * 3.14159 / 180        'EXPRESS A AS RADIANS
400 POSITION 1,19
410 PRINT "SPEED";
420 INPUT S
430 G = 980                'G IS FORCE OF GRAVITY
440 LA = 40                'LA IS LENGTH OF ARROW
450 LT = 8                 'LT IS LENGTH OF TIP OF ARROW
460     'FIND RANGE AND HEIGHT OF ARROW'S FLIGHT
470 R = S * S * SIN(2 * A) / G        'R IS RANGE (ON X AXIS) OF ARROW FLIGHT
480     'DETERMINE COEFFICIENTS FOR PARABOLA'S EQUATION
490 C1 = G / (2 * (S * COS(A)) ^ 2)
500 C2 = - TAN(A)
510 GOSUB 1400             'REMOVE ARROW FROM QUIVER
520     '******************** MOVE ARROW ************************
530     'FIND ARROW TAIL POINTS ALONG THE PARABOLA AND DRAW ARROW
540 FOR X = R/10 TO R STEP R/8        'PLACE ARROW AT SUCCESSIVE TENTHS OF R
550     Y = C1 * X ^ 2 + C2 * X + YO
560     'X AND Y ARE THE TAILPOINTS ON THE PARABOLA
570     'FIND OTHER ENDPOINT OF ARROW
580     M = C1 * X * 2 + C2      'M IS SLOPE OF THE ARROW
590     A1 = ATN(M)              'INVERSE TANGENT OF M GIVES ANGLE A1
600     Y1 = Y + LA * SIN(A1)
610     X1 = X + LA * COS(A1)
620     IF X1 > XM OR Y1 > YM THEN 830        'IS OTHER ENDPOINT ON SCREEN?
630     IF X > R/10 THEN GOSUB 1620        'ERASE ARROW
640     'CALCULATE ARROW TIP
```

Program 14-5 (cont.)

```
650     M2 = M + .75                'SLOPE OF ONE TIP
660     A2 = ATN(M2)
670     X2 = X1 - LT * COS(A2)
680     Y2 = Y1 - LT * SIN(A2)
690     M3 = M - .75                'SLOPE OF SECOND TIP
700     A3 = ATN(M3)
710     X3 = X1 - LT * COS(A3)
720     Y3 = Y1 - LT * SIN(A3)
730     GOSUB 1560        'DRAW ARROW
740     IF X1 < XL OR X1 > XR THEN 780  'ARROW IS NOT IN BOX
750     IF Y1 < YT OR Y1 > YB THEN 780
760            'ARROW HAS HIT BOX
770     GOTO 930
780     XS = X            'SAVE CURRENT POSITION IN XS, YS, X1S, Y1S
790     YS = Y
800     X1S = X1
810     Y1S = Y1
820 NEXT X
830 J = J + 1
840 IF J > 3 THEN 870    'GO ON TO NEW TARGET OR STOP
850 GOSUB 1620
860 GOTO 310
870 IF T = 5 THEN 1710              'GAME OVER
880 T = T + 1                       'ELSE, GO ON TO NEXT TARGET
890 POSITION 25,1
900 PRINT "TOO BAD. TRY ANOTHER";
910 FOR J = 1 TO 600: NEXT J
920 GOTO 160
930     '************* ARROW HAS HIT BOX ************************
940     'INCREASE SCORE
950 IF J = 1 THEN SC = SC + 10
960 IF J = 2 THEN SC = SC + 5
970 IF J = 3 THEN SC = SC + 2
980 POSITION 25,35
990 PRINT SC;
1000 FOR TB = 1 TO 2                'BLINK "BULLSEYE"
1010     POSITION 25,1
1020     PRINT "BULLSEYE!";
1030     FOR M = 1 TO 300: NEXT M
1040     POSITION 25,1
1050     PRINT "           ";
1060     FOR M = 1 TO 300: NEXT M
1070 NEXT TB
1080 IF T <> 5 THEN 1100
1090 GOTO 1710
1100 T = T + 1
1110 GOTO 160                  'GO ON TO NEW TARGET
1120     '
1130 '#################### DRAW QUIVER ##########################
1140 POSITION 22,1
1150 PRINT T;
1160 XC = 10: YC = 150: RX = 10: RY = 3
1170 FOR AQ = 0 TO 6.28318 STEP 1/10
1180     XQ = XC + RX * COS(AQ)
1190     YQ = YC + RY * SIN(AQ)
1200     POINTPLOT XQ,YQ
1210 NEXT AQ
1220 YC = 185
```

Program 14-5 (cont.)

```
1230 FOR AQ = 0 TO 3.14159 STEP 1/10
1240    XQ = XC + RX * COS(AQ)
1250    YQ = YC + RY * SIN(AQ)
1260    POINTPLOT XQ,YQ
1270 NEXT AQ
1280 DRAWLINE 0,150 TO 0,185
1290 DRAWLINE 20,150 TO 20,185
1300 DRAWLINE 5,130 TO 5,152
1310 DRAWLINE 5,130 TO 2,133
1320 DRAWLINE 5,130 TO 8,133
1330 DRAWLINE 10,125 TO 12,153
1340 DRAWLINE 10,125 TO 7,128
1350 DRAWLINE 10,125 TO 13,128
1360 DRAWLINE 18,128 TO 15,152
1370 DRAWLINE 18,128 TO 15,131
1380 DRAWLINE 18,128 TO 21,131
1390 RETURN
1400 '################## REMOVE ARROW FROM QUIVER ##################
1410 COLOR 0,0
1420 IF J <> 1 THEN 1460
1430 DRAWLINE 10,125 TO 12,153            'REMOVE FIRST ARROW
1440 DRAWLINE 10,125 TO 7,128
1450 DRAWLINE 10,125 TO 13,128
1460 IF J <> 2 THEN 1500
1470 DRAWLINE 5,130 TO 5,152             'REMOVE SECOND ARROW
1480 DRAWLINE 5,130 TO 2,133
1490 DRAWLINE 5,130 TO 8,133
1500 IF J <> 3 THEN 1540
1510 DRAWLINE 18,128 TO 15,152           'REMOVE THIRD ARROW
1520 DRAWLINE 18,128 TO 15,131
1530 DRAWLINE 18,128 TO 21,131
1540 COLOR 1,0
1550 RETURN
1560 '######################### DRAW ARROW #########################
1570 COLOR 1,0
1580 DRAWLINE X,Y TO X1,Y1
1590 DRAWLINE X1,Y1 TO X2,Y2
1600 DRAWLINE X1,Y1 TO X3,Y3
1610 RETURN
1620 '######################### ERASE ARROW #########################
1630 COLOR 0,0
1640 DRAWLINE XS,YS TO X1S,Y1S
1650 DRAWLINE X1S,Y1S TO X2,Y2
1660 DRAWLINE X1S,Y1S TO X3,Y3
1670 COLOR 1,0
1680 RETURN
1690 '#############################################################
1700 '
1710 '**************** PLAY AGAIN OR STOP ************************
1720 CLEARSCREEN
1730 POSITION 12,30
1740 PRINT "FINAL SCORE -- "; SC
1750 PRINT
1760 PRINT TAB(10);"WANT TO PLAY AGAIN";
1770 INPUT C$
1780 IF C$ = "N" THEN 1800
1790 GOTO 130
1800 END
```

Figure 14–5 Initial and bullseye positions of the arrow for the archery game
(Prog. 14–5).

ANGLE (0-90)? 60   SPEED? 600

SCORE 0

ANGLE (0-90)? 60   SPEED? 600

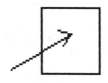

BULLSEYE!   **SCORE 35**

Appendix A

Graphics Command Conversion Table[a]

Hypothetical Command	Apple II Series Computers	TRS-80 Color Computer	IBM Personal Computer
CLEARSCREEN	HOME (or GR or HGR)	CLS[b] or PCLS[b]	CLS
POSITION R,C	VTAB R and HTAB C	PRINT @ N (0<=N<=511 specifies screen position)	LOCATE R,C[b]
GRAPHICS	GR or HGR	PMODE M[b] (0<=M<=4 sets resolution mode)	SCREEN M[b] (M=1,2: medium or high resolution)
COLOR F,B	COLOR = F or HCOLOR = F	COLOR F,B	COLOR F,B[b]
POINTPLOT X,Y	PLOT X,Y or HPLOT X,Y	PSET (X,Y)[b]	PSET (X,Y)[b]
POINTOFF X,Y	—	PRESET (X,Y)	PRESET (X,Y)[b]
DRAWLINE X1,Y1 TO X2,Y2	HPLOT X1,Y1 TO X2,Y2[b]	LINE (X1,Y1)-(X2,Y2)[b]	LINE (X1,Y1)-(X2,Y2)[b]
CIRCLEPLOT XC,YC,R	—	CIRCLE (XC,YC),R[b]	CIRCLE (XC,YC),R[b]

[a] Additional graphics commands are available on, or can be added to, some of the systems in this table.
[b] This command can be stated with additional or other parameter options.

294

Atari 400/800 Computers	Commodore Computers	Hewlett-Packard Series 80 Computers	Tektronix Computers (Plot 50 BASIC)	Intecolor 8000 Series Computers
PRINT CHR$(125) (or the GRAPHICS statement)	PRINT <clear key>	CLEAR or GCLEAR	PAGE	PLOT 12
POSITION C,R	PRINT and PRINT TAB	MOVE R,C	MOVE R,C	PLOT 3,C,R
GRAPHICS M (0<=M<=8 sets resolution mode)	PRINT CHR$ (to display special graphics characters)	GRAPH	—	PLOT 2
COLOR R (Selects color register R. Can be used with SETCOLOR statement.)	PRINT (with color keys)	—	—	PLOT 29:PLOT F and PLOT 30:PLOT B
PLOT X,Y	(Uses special graphics characters)	PLOT X,Y	MOVE X,Y and DRAW X,Y	PLOT 2,X,Y
—	—	PEN and PLOT X,Y	—	—
DRAWTO X,Y (from current position)	—	MOVE X1,Y1 and DRAW X2,Y2	MOVE X1,Y1 and DRAW X2,Y2	PLOT 2,X1,Y1 242,X2,Y2
—	—	—	—	(XC,YC,R,

Appendix B

Microcomputer and Graphics Periodicals

ACM Transactions on Graphics
P.O. Box 12105
Church Street Station
New York, NY 10249

BYTE
P.O. Box 590
Martinsville, NJ 08836

Compute!
P.O. Box 5406
Greensboro, NC 27403

Computer Decisions
Management Magazine of Computing
Hayden Publishing Co., Inc.
P.O. Box 13802
Philadelphia, PA 19101

Computer Graphics World
1714 Stockton
San Francisco, CA 94133

Computers and Programming
P.O. Box 1935
Marion, OH 43306

The Computing Teacher
c/o Computer Center
Eastern Oregon State College
La Grande, OR 97850

Computronics
H & E Computronics
50 North Pascack Road
Spring Valley, NY 10977

Creative Computing
P.O. Box 789–M
Morristown, NJ 07960

Dr. Dobb's Journal
People's Computer Co.
Dept. N1
1263 El Camino Real, Box E
Menlo Park, CA 94025

80 Microcomputer
Subscription Dept.
P.O. Box 981
Farmingdale, NY 11737

IEEE Computer Graphics & Applications
P.O. Box 24167
Los Angeles, CA 90024

INFOWORLD
375 Cochituate Road
Box 880
Framingham, MA 01701

Interface
The Computer Education Quarterly
116 Royal Oak
Santa Cruz, CA 95066

Interface Age
P.O. Box 1234
Cerritos, CA 90701

Microcomputing
Subscription Dept.
P.O. Box 997
Farmingdale, NY 11737

Nibble
Box 325
Lincoln, MA 01733

onComputing
P.O. Box 307
Martinsville, NJ 08836

PC Magazine
1528 Irving Street
San Francisco, CA 94122

Personal Computing
4 Disk Drive
Box 13916
Philadelphia, PA 19101

Popular Computing
Subscription Dept.
P.O. Box 307
Martinsville, NJ 08836

Softalk
Softalk Publishing Co.
11021 Magnolia Blvd.
North Hollywood, CA 91601

Index